DATE DUE

BRODART   Cat. No. 23-221

Jackson School Publications in International Studies

Senator Henry M. Jackson was convinced that the study of the history, cultures, political systems, and languages of the world's major regions was an essential prerequisite for wise decision making in international relations. In recognition of his deep commitment to higher education and advanced scholarship, this series of publications has been established through the generous support of the Henry M. Jackson Foundation, in cooperation with the Henry M. Jackson School of International Studies and the University of Washington Press.

THE FOUND GENERATION

Chinese Communists
in Europe during the Twenties

MARILYN A. LEVINE

University of Washington Press

Seattle & London

To my husband, Scott Thomas Kellogg

Library of Congress Cataloging-in-Publication Data
Levine, Marilyn Avra, 1953–
    The found generation : Chinese communists in Europe during the twenties / Marilyn A. Levine.
        p.   cm. — (Jackson School publications in international studies)
    Includes bibliographical references and index.
    ISBN 0–295–97240–8 (alk. paper)
    1. Chung-kuo kung ch' an tang—History.   2. Kung ch' ing t' uan (China)—History.   3. Chinese students—Europe—History.   4. Socialism and youth—China.   5. Chung-kuo kung ch' an tang.
    I. Title.   II. Series.
JQ1519.A5L38   1993   92–46157
324.251'075'09042—dc20   CIP

CONTENTS

ILLUSTRATIONS

ACKNOWLEDGMENTS

In several ways this book structurally reflects the concept of a voyage, so that the reader can gain some sensibility of the sojourn undertaken by the Found Generation. In a similar way, the research process for the book, which involved traveling to Asia and Europe, has also captured some of this wonder of discovery. One of the most pleasant facets has been to encounter so many interesting and knowledgeable people who have given generously of their time and encouragement. Thus, although I have a long list of acknowledgments, I want to mention that in the delights which were encountered during my research, the best memory I have is the graciousness of those around me, and I am profoundly grateful to all my colleagues.

In the United States, I would like to thank the following people for their assistance: Guy Alitto, Tsou Tang, David Roy, Susan Mann, George Chichih Chao, Cheng Yang Borchert, Akira Iriye, Li Yu-ning, Chun-tu Hsueh, Frank Shulman, Dilip Basu, Charles Hayford, John Israel, Peter Zarrow, Diane Scherer, Martin Rivlin, James Harrison, Bertram Gordon, Vera Schwarcz, Noel Riley Fitch, Robert Wohl, Peter Loewenberg, Herman Mast, Wang Chi, Mi Chu Wiens, Patrick Tseng, T. T. Hsia, and Julia Tung.

I have benefited from research conducted in Asia and Europe and would like to express my appreciation. I owe a very special thanks to my colleagues from Qinghua University, Department of Social Sciences, Liu Guisheng and Zhu Yuhe, who arranged numerous interviews and allowed me access to the archives at Qinghua. They also shared their own ideas, and we had lively discussions and debates that clarified several key issues. I would also like to thank other scholars and interviewees: Wang Rongyuan, Cai Bo, Sheng Cheng, Dr. Yang Kun, Yang Zaidao, the late Jiang Zemin, the late Zhang Shenfu, Zheng Chaolin, Li Xin, the late Li Zongyi, Ding Shouhe, Hou Junchu, Liao Yongwu, Feng Huaibi, the late Hu Hua, Wang Yongxiang, Zhang Hongxiang, Guo Sheng, and Shi Guang. In the Republic of China, I would like to thank Chen San-ching and Spencer Chin. In Hong Kong I have valued from a several-year exchange with Chan Kingtong.

My French colleagues have also provided inestimable assistance, and I sincerely appreciate their generosity. I would like to thank Yves Chevrier, Geneviéve Barman, the late Nicole Dulioust, Nora Wang, Ho Pu-yin, Christian Henriot, Danielle Li Chen Sheng, Jean-Louis Boully, François Fergani, Marianne Bastid, and Catherine Gipoulon. In Germany I would like to express my gratitude to Susanne Weigelin-Schwiedrzik.

I owe a boundless debt to Steven I. Levine, who gave me valuable guidance from the inception of this project and has patiently waded through several drafts of the manuscript. He has been both inspiration and mentor. Michael Hunt and Arif Dirlik gave me insightful commentary on the final drafts of the manuscript. I greatly appreciate their meticulous attention to detail and challenging questions. I am also grateful for the advice and enthusiasm of Don Cioeta and Pamela J. Bruton at the University of Washington Press.

My deepest debt goes to my husband, Scott T. Kellogg. Scott provided the project with material support, particularly in funding both research trips to Asia and Europe. Just as important was Scott's staunch belief in the book and his own example of engaged and creative scholarship.

All translations are my own except where the notes indicate I am quoting from a translated work. Although the book has greatly benefited from the suggestions of my colleagues, the responsibility for any errors in the book is mine.

ABBREVIATIONS

AAE	Archives du Ministère des affaires étrangères
AAFC	Association amicale franco-chinoise
AAUFC	Archives de l'Association universitaire franco-chinoise
AN	Archives nationales
AOM	Archives nationales, Section d'outre-mer
CCP	Chinese Communist Party
CFC	Comité franco-chinois de patronage des jeunes Chinois en France
CLC	Chinese Labor Corps
CYP	Chinese Youth Party
ECCO	European Branches of the Chinese Communist Organizations
ECCP	European Branch of the Chinese Communist Party
ECYC	European Branch of the Chinese Communist Youth Corps
EGMD	European Branch of the Chinese Nationalist Party (Guomindang)
FuFa	Qinghua University Faculty Research Unit on the History of the Communist Party, comp., *FuFa qingong jianxue yundong shiliao*
GMD	Chinese Nationalist Party (Guomindang)
PCF	Parti communiste français
PRC	People's Republic of China
ROC	Republic of China
SFEA	Sino-French Educational Association
SFI	Sino-French Institute (at Lyons University)
SLOTFOM	Service de liaison des originaires des territoires français d'outre-mer

PROLOGUE

May 9th—Sunday
In the morning I went to the park to read. It is now late spring. The
sunlight is mellow, very pretty . . . flowers are slowly opening, the
green leaves are already lush. Countless strollers sit beneath the trees,
in solemn contemplation, appreciating the natural beauty; or sitting
side by side chatting with several friends; or a couple in intimate tête-
à-têtes. . . . The small children follow the grown-ups, dancing and
singing; they are sublimely happy, taking the miseries of the world and
abandoning them to the clouds. . . . I sit on a stone bench, quietly
appreciating the beautiful scenery. Oh! Is this not heaven?
　　　　　　　　　—Wang Ruofei's St. Chamond Diary (1920)

Two years after writing this diary entry, Wang Ruofei was to be found in
another park, contemplating not the natural beauty of France but the future
of China. In quiet contrast to the spiritual malaise which permeated the
French youth of the same period,[1] Wang along with seventeen other
Chinese youth met in the Bois de Bolougne during the summer of 1922 to
form the European Branch of the Chinese Communist Youth Corps. For
three days the organizational goals, appropriate structures, and rules were
debated and elections held. Sitting on chairs rented from an old woman
who owned a tea concession in the park, some of the most important future
leaders of the Chinese Communist Party (CCP) were forging new traditions.
Unlike the majority of European youth, a portion of the Chinese youth
sojourning in Europe during the early twenties, although feeling the same
alienation of an exacerbated generational crisis as the Western youth,
found powerful and creative solutions.

　　The emergence of Chinese communism in Europe was a significant event
for Chinese revolutionary politics. The formation of the European Branch
of the Chinese Communist Youth Corps in a Parisian park was a far cry from
the secret formation of the CCP in a small room in Shanghai. It is a dramatic
comparison that of the fifty-seven founders of the CCP only two survived
purges, coups, and attrition within the CCP.[2] This strongly contrasts with
the low attrition rate of the European Branch of the Chinese Communist

---

1. I am thinking in particular of the scene in André Gide's *The Counterfeiters* where
Bernard Profitendieu, desiring to see his friend Olivier, has to posture with others, to "run
the gauntlet of several groups" of youth gathered in the Jardin du Luxembourg. The parks
were popular spots for political and artistic discussions. See André Gide, *The Counterfeiters*,
trans. Dorothy Bussy (New York: Vintage Books, 1951),51 (originally published in 1927).
　　2. Jacques Guillermaz, *A History of the Chinese Communist Party, 1921–1949*, trans.
Anne Destenay (London: Methuen, 1972), 54–60.

Youth Corps (ECYC) and the European Branch of the Chinese Communist Party (ECCP) (which I collectively call the ECCO, European Branches of the Chinese Communist Organizations). The majority of ECCO members remained Communists and survived the deadly vicissitudes of CCP politics.

Dozens of important Chinese Communist leaders were to emerge out of the ECCO. In addition to post-1949 Party luminaries such as Zhou Enlai, Zhu De, Deng Xiaoping, Chen Yi, Nie Rongzhen, and Li Fuchun, there were early CCP leaders such as Cai Hesen, Xiang Jingyu, Chen Yannian, Zhao Shiyan, and Liu Bojian.[3]

Representing a total of forty Chinese from France, Germany, and Belgium,[4] the eighteen youth in the Bois de Bolougne were led by the twenty-one-year-old Zhao Shiyan (1901–27), a Sichuanese youth leader since the May Fourth Movement who worked in factories in France and had connections with many groups in the rich organizational milieu of the Chinese community in France. Zhao Shiyan was a leader with insight and ability, one of the most brilliant early CCP leaders. He was the first general secretary of the ECYC, as well as of the French branch of the ECCP. After studying in Moscow for a year and a half, he returned to China in 1924 and was instrumental in the Northern CCP Bureau, edited the CCP journal *Zhengzhi shenghuo* (*Political Life*), and was elected to the CCP Central Committee in 1927. Zhao was also one of three leaders in the three Shanghai Uprisings, where he was betrayed and executed in the summer of 1927. Without Zhao Shiyan it is doubtful that the ECCO would have been formed.[5]

The first propaganda head of the ECYC was Zhou Enlai (1898–1976), another multitalented leader, whose northern accent was difficult for the others to understand but whose writings had been a main artery of communication within the Chinese community in France since 1921 and who rep-

3. Other notable leaders included Wang Ruofei, Li Lisan, Cai Chang, Li Weihan, Xiao San, Fu Zhong, Xu Teli, Zheng Chaolin, He Changgong, Mu Qing, Guo Longzhen, Luo Xuezan, Xiong Xiong, Xiong Rui, Chen Qiaonian, Zhang Bojian, Liu Qingyang, Zhang Shenfu, and Ren Zhuoxuan.

4. For the convenience of the reader, individual biographical descriptions of many of the important Chinese mentioned within this study are contained in Appendix 1, Biographies. More than 100 entries are listed in alphabetical order using the Pinyin spellings.

5. Zheng Chaolin interview, 29 October 1985 (Shanghai); Sheng Cheng interviews, 12 October, 18 October 1985 (Beijing). Impressions of Zhao Shiyan have remained vivid across a time span of over sixty years. The efflorescence of current CCP member biographies and memoirs in some part was motivated by the efforts of Zhao Shiyan's sister, Zhao Shilan, who in the sixties began to promote the collection of memoirs of Zhao Shiyan, of which several were later published in one of the most important books in current People's Republic of China (PRC) historiography, Zhongguo Shehui Kexueyuan Xiandaishi Yanjiushi [Research Unit on Contemporary History of the Chinese Academy of Social Sciences], *Yida qianhou* [Before and after the founding of the CCP], 2 vols. (Beijing: Renmin chubanshe, 1980).

resented the German branch of the ECCO. After Zhao Shiyan's departure for Moscow in 1923, Zhou became the general secretary and led the United Front with the European Branch of the Guomindang (EGMD), which not only predated the United Front in China but also exceeded it in terms of Communist influence. Noted for his flexibility, eloquence, and moderation, Zhou Enlai's contributions to the Chinese revolution were manifold and profound.

The third officer elected during the three-day meeting was Li Weihan (1897–1983), who represented the numerous Hunanese activists. Not as radical as some of his contemporaries, Li was the most important representative of the Hunanese community in the city of Montargis. Entrusted as the liaison with the CCP Central Committee in late 1922, on his return to China Li Weihan occupied the important post of head of the Hunan CCP Branch from 1922 until 1927. Li was one of the most influential of the ECCO returnees, as he was appointed to the CCP Central Committee in 1925. His later career did not reflect this early promise, but he did contribute to the CCP in the areas of the United Front and minority work.

The entire CCP political tapestry was reflected in the founding meeting of the ECCO, from Trotskyites such as Zheng Chaolin and Yin Kuan, to those who quit the CCP like Ren Zhuoxuan, to those who sacrificed themselves or were lost in early obscurity such as Yuan Qingyun and Li Weinong. Among the eighteen were the two sons of CCP cofounder Chen Duxiu—Chen Yannian and Chen Qiaonian—both of whom responded to skillful courting by Zhao Shiyan by changing their allegiance from anarchism to communism. After his return to China, Chen Yannian became the most important organizer in the south; he headed the Guangdong-Guangxi CCP Bureau. Both brothers were later executed by the Guomindang.

Zhang Guotao, who sat on the early CCP Central Committee, claimed that the returned members were a discernible and disciplined force within the Party. Zhang asserted that the returnees were dismayed "that laxity characterized everything the Party did. . . . they began stressing my proposal to bring about a unification of views and to introduce ideological training."[6] Zhang's observation raises several questions about the significance of ECCO leadership and issues such as Party discipline and ideology. Many of the ECCO leaders had important organizational experiences and theoretical training in Europe that shaped and sharpened their leadership style and abilities. The formation of the ECCO provided a strong focus for developing organizational skills, such as the use of propaganda, political

6. Chang Kuo-t'ao, *The Rise of the Chinese Communist Party: 1921–1938*, 2 vols. (Lawrence, Kans.: University of Kansas Press, 1971), 1:246.

agitation, and Party recruitment. These skills were honed in active political training and campaigns.

While in France, ECCO members encountered a sophisticated ideological and activist environment, and they had relative freedom in their political pursuits. The vision of Mao Zedong missing the Second Congress of the CCP in China because he had misplaced the secret address is in deep contrast to the second meeting of the ECCO in 1923, which was held in a police hall!

The ECCO returnees not only helped in directing the CCP at the central and regional levels by conducting major propaganda and strategic tasks. Many of them also provided leadership during all the important phases of CCP history. Li Lisan and Cai Hesen were leaders of the May Thirtieth Incident; Xiang Jingyu was the first head of the Women's Bureau; during the violence of 1927, three-fifths of the Central Committee of the August meeting were ECCO returnees; during the 1920s, the three major theoretical journals of the CCP were edited by ECCO returnees (Cai Hesen, Zhao Shiyan, and Zheng Chaolin); Zhou Enlai, Zhu De, Nie Rongzhen, Liu Bojian, Chen Yi, and others helped organize the Red Army; and Zhou Enlai, Zhu De, Chen Yi, Deng Xiaoping, Li Fuchun, Cai Chang, Xiao San, Nie Rongzhen, Li Weihan, and others were among the post-1949 leadership.

The formation and activities of the ECCO are critical areas of Chinese Communist Revolution historical scholarship. This study will focus on the formation of the ECCO and its significance in several different areas. First, there are important issues of ideology and organization. There were notable differences in the ECCO and the CCP in the fundamental areas of organization and ideology. One can discern a general pattern of organizational dynamics among revolutionary groups founded on the basis of New Culture values. Was there a different organizational impetus for the development of the ECCO because the ECCO politicization took place in activist Chinese communities in Europe? Because the ECCO met frequently and openly, with broader access to Marxist materials, did the manner of ECCO formation result in organizational values different from those of the CCP? In a related issue, the ECCO did not have direct Communist International supervision. Thus, did the different relationships that the CCP and the ECCO had with the Communist International have an impact on the perception of Party discipline and loyalty to the Comintern? After the Chinese Communist Parties were established, the concept of organizational discipline was valued over the purity of Marxist theoretical knowledge. Because of the greater freedom in Europe and the better access to propaganda, how substantive was the difference between ideology acquired in China and ideology acquired abroad, or was the shell of Chinese acculturation too strong to absorb new modes of thought and behavior? Since the three major CCP theoretical journals were to be edited by European returnees during the 1920s, it is important to ask, were the ECCO members able to acquire broader theoretical knowledge during their stay in Europe than was possible for their comrades who stayed at home?

Second, the ramifications of ECCO political leadership constitute a vital area of interpretation. Given the Chinese stress on personal relations based on region, school, and organizational linkages and the indisputable fact that ECCO members shared the experiences of radicalization, did this bind them together in a cohort after their return to China? Since the ECCO returnees made such significant contributions to revolutionary activity in China, it is critical to understand the qualitative nature of the leadership training they received in Europe. For example, how was political response to concrete situations, such as propaganda-agitation tasks, shaped by the European experience? The revolutionary situation in China differed from that in Europe, particularly in terms of the United Front with the Guomindang. In Europe the ECCO and the left-faction EGMD controlled the United Front. Did this sense of mastery and the free environment in the West create a false sense of security that hid from the ECCO returnees the violent potential within the radical milieu back in China?

Finally, viewing the total life cycles of these revolutionaries, one must also ask the fundamental question, why did they break with tradition? Why did they choose the uncertain hardship of revolutionary commitment over the honorable status of "returned student"? Unlike the circumlocutions and artistic posturings of their European counterparts, these eighteen men had turned from the deep-rooted Confucian intellectual heritage that was still prevalent among the majority of Chinese youth, which argued for measured reform. Rather than "walk to the revolution," as suggested by some of their contemporaries, these young Chinese desired a quicker tempo of change and pledged themselves to the discipline of a different set of ideals. Not knowing their varied fates, the blood and glory that would cover their future, eighteen Chinese sat and contemplated a revolution in the heat of a summer day, sheltered by sturdy trees, with sunlight dappling the leaves.

The following chapters discuss in detail the events leading up to the formation of the ECCO and its major transitions. Using the metaphor of a journey, our subject of inquiry is how order was generated from the chaos of the whirlpool of Chinese politics. The first chapter traces the context of radical Chinese politics, discusses the basic theme of generational conflict, and gives an introductory overview of the Work-Study Movement. After this broad overview of Chinese situational determinants and the broader generational context, the next two chapters explore the Work-Study Movement on three basic levels: the development of individual leaders, the youth groups of the New Culture Movement that led to the Work-Study Movement, and Work-Study Movement experiences themselves, such as the preparatory schools, the journey to France, working in French factories, and several other areas. The difficulties encountered by the Work-Study Movement and the activist response are described in chapter 4. Chapter 5 traces the formation of the ECCO, by first viewing the internal voyage, that ideological commitment process experienced by the political leaders, and then examining the actual ECCO founding process and subsequent activities, as well as important issues such as Comintern involvement. Chapter 6 discusses in greater depth the ECCO activities, such as polemics with the Anarchists and the Chinese Youth Party and, perhaps most important, the formation of the ECCO-EGMD United Front. Finally, the conclusion explores the political significance of the ECCO and of the Chinese who transformed themselves from youthful agitators to mature revolutionaries.

1
THE RISE OF THE
WORK-STUDY MOVEMENT

Those of the older generation over thirty, with their superficial knowledge of the New Learning, totally exert themselves on attaining power on their own behalf (like those returned students who studied in the East and West). Those of the older generation over fifty, with their corrupt old minds, are vehemently sworn to oppose world trends (like those who want to restore the legacy of the Qing dynasty). . . . Therefore our generation of youth has no option but to rise up and make our own plans, to break away from the concept of dependency.

—Zeng Qi, writing from France in 1922

The political chaos that characterized China in the twenties was matched by the frenetic experience of the Chinese youth, who were striving in a whirlpool of both ideas and organizational activities to seek the path to national salvation. This chapter explores the context for radical Chinese politics, the setting of generational conflict, and the overall dimensions of the movement to study abroad in France after the First World War. A cross-cultural comparison of the worldwide generational crisis that existed at the turn of the century suggests the overall thesis that Chinese youth in Europe formed a Found Generation, in contrast to the Lost Generation of Western youth.

THE HISTORICAL CONTEXT OF POLITICAL
RADICALIZATION IN EARLY REPUBLICAN CHINA

The revolutionary process in twentieth-century China has been rich in organizational and ideological diversity. The devolution of power during the later part of the Qing and the lack of political control by the Revolutionary Alliance (Tongmenghui) during the 1911 Revolution defused much of the revolutionary potential in the change from a monarchy to a republic. This was not clear at the time, and progressive as well as self-interested Chinese accepted the stability that went with the ascension of Yuan Shikai as the president of the Republic of China in 1912. During this initial period, the Revolutionary Alliance, led by Sun Yatsen, testified to its faith in the parliamentary system by becoming the Guomindang (Chinese Nationalist Party).[1]

Sworn to uphold the parliamentary system, Yuan Shikai tried to stop the flow of independent provincial power and used violent and arbitrary means to gather that power in his own hands. The assassination of Song Jiaoren, a popular Guomindang leader, and the 1913 Reorganization Loan alarmed many Chinese and resulted in an unsuccessful second revolution during 1913. At this point a government in opposition was established by Sun Yat-sen in Guangdong.

The chaos of warlord struggle exploded with dynamic force after the death of Yuan Shikai (1916) in both the provinces and the capital city of Beijing. For the decade between 1916 and 1927, cliques of warlords, often supported by foreign governments, frequently fought for control of the central government, which changed hands often. Serious problems of corruption and increasing foreign influence through loans and industrial investment resulted.

Patriotic Chinese began to reassess their values and options in light of the vanquished promise of the 1911 Revolution and the quest to ameliorate the conditions of warlord violence and instability as well as increasing foreign involvement in China. Thus, after 1915, the New Culture Movement emerged. The New Culture Movement was exemplified by its ostensible rejection of traditional values and the integration of new values with a new lifestyle, which was embraced particularly by Chinese youth. For the young Chinese the New Culture Movement meant a redefinition of their world, in which new concepts had to be reflected in actions. Thus, between 1915 and 1921, the introduction of new journals and new literature and a revolution in vernacular language were paralleled by the formation of youth groups, coeducational activities, and experimental lifestyles.

The sharpest expression and highest unity within the New Culture Movement arose during the May Fourth Movement (1919). The May Fourth Movement was a concerted protest that opposed the signing of the Versailles treaty by the Chinese government. This movement eventually became a national series of demonstrations, student and worker strikes, and consumer boycotts. Although China had contributed over 175,000 labor battalions to the Allied effort during the First World War, the Japanese demand for the Shandong Peninsula was agreed upon by the Western powers at the Versailles settlement. Clashing with the government and endur-

---

1. For a standard general history of the Republic era that highlights the warlord impact see James E. Sheridan, *China in Disintegration: The Republican Era in Chinese History, 1912–1949* (New York: Free Press, 1975).

ing violence and imprisonment, the demonstrators prevailed during the May Fourth Movement, and the government did not sign the Versailles treaty.

The series of social experiments making up the New Culture Movement suffered deep divisions after 1921. The debate, known as that of "Problems and Isms," wrenched apart the cohesion of the New Culture Movement. Basically, one side believed that a social revolution (that emphasized the education of the masses) must precede the political revolution. The other side believed that due to the intense suffering of the Chinese people, the political revolution must precede the social revolution. Thus, after 1921, a series of political parties arose, some with revolutionary intent, while those who believed in the social revolution often devoted themselves to education or governmental service.

The May Fourth Movement has often been cited as a turning point, a culmination of the New Culture Movement, but the rebellious youth of China were simultaneously exploring other avenues for social change. Among these were the Work-Study Mutual-Aid Corps (Gongdu huzhu tuan)[2] and the Diligent-Work Frugal-Study Movement (Qingong jianxue yundong; hereafter referred to as the Work-Study Movement). The Work-Study Movement was responsible for sending over 1,600 Chinese youth to France between 1919 and 1921. The goal was to promote national salvation by utilizing Western technology. This was to be accomplished through study at Western colleges financed with money obtained by working in French factories, which were experiencing a labor shortage after the First World War. The worker-students carried the activism of the New Culture Movement to France and participated in several demonstrations, which climaxed in Lyons in September 1921. Over one hundred Chinese youth were sent back to China for their action in occupying a dormitory at Lyons University. After this incident the organization of political activity changed from youth groups to full-fledged political parties. Chinese political parties formed in Europe ranged from the ECCO to the anti-Communist Qingniandang (Chinese Youth Party), and included as well the Guomindang, the Social Democrats, and the Anarchist Gongyushe (the Surplus Society). They were active from Paris to Lyons, from Berlin to Amsterdam.[3] The

2. A countrywide experiment from 1919 to 1920 whereby Chinese youth sought to inculcate the spirit of labor and mutual help. See Appendix 2, Organizations, for further information.

3. For a review of materials on the Work-Study Movement see Marilyn Levine, "ECCO Studies: Overview of an Emerging Field," *Republican China* 13 (April 1988): 4–23. Several other essays are in this special issue on the ECCO. However, here is a brief introductory note on Western and Chinese sources. There is very little written in Western languages in this area. A short essay was written during the sixties by Conrad Brandt ("The French-Returned Elite in the Chinese Communist Party," Institute of International Studies: Berke-

ECCO was a product of the New Culture Movement, and therefore the development of the ECCO reflects the chasms that had been carved by the political and social topography of modern Chinese history.

At first glance, the fervent political activity of Chinese youth after 1915 might appear to be a typical example of generational conflict. Indeed, the Chinese were part of a generational crisis that extended well beyond the usual range of intergenerational conflicts and transcended national and continental boundaries. The social and political conditions giving rise to these conflicts were essentially similar in many respects; however, their resolution took different forms. In the West, the effects of the First World War were severely disorienting to youth, who characterized themselves as the Lost Generation. It is argued here that the Chinese youth who went to France responded much more positively to their inner turmoil and attempted to resolve their generational and identity problems quite differently from their European contemporaries.

What were the bases of generational tension in the new industrial age? How was the age-old conflict between parent and child different from previous eras? What were the social and political consequences of these conflicts? A comparative analysis of the worldwide generational crisis during

---

ley Reprint no. 13 [Hong Kong: Hong Kong University Press, 1961]). Another essay was written by the French historian Annie Kriegel and included in her collection *Communismes au miroir français* (Paris: Gallimard, 1974). Three dissertations explore the Work-Study Movement and its politicizing effects: John Kong-Cheong Leung, "The Chinese Work-Study Movement: The Social and Political Experience of Chinese Students and Student-Workers in France" (Ph.D. dissertation, Brown University, 1982); Marilyn Avra Levine, "The Found Generation: Chinese Communism in Europe, 1919–1925" (Ph.D. dissertation, University of Chicago, 1985); and Nora Wang, "Paris/Shanghai, débats d'idées et pratique sociale, les intellectuels progressistes chinois, 1920–1925," 3 vols. (Thèses d'état, Université de Paris, 1986). A catalog of holdings now deposited at the Archives nationales, Paris, has been written by Geneviève Barman and Nicole Dulioust (*Etudiants-ouvriers chinois en France, 1920–1940* [Paris: Editions de l'Ecole des Hautes Etudes en Sciences Sociales, 1981]). The Chinese, both in the PRC and the Republic of China (ROC), have been more prolific in this area of study; several compendia and numerous books and articles have appeared. Among the most important are Qinghua University Faculty Research Unit on the History of the Communist Party, comp., *FuFa qingong jianxue yundong shiliao* [Documents on the travel to France Work-Study Movement], 3 vols. (Beijing: Beijing chubanshe, 1979–80) (hereafter cited as *FuFa*); Zhang Yunhou, Yan Xuyi, and Li Junchen, comps., *Liu Fa qingong jianxue yundong* [The travel to France Work-Study Movement], 2 vols. (Shanghai: Shanghai renmin chubanshe, 1980, 1986); and Chen Sanjing, *Qingong jianxue yundong* [The Work-Study Movement] (Taibei: Zhengzhong shuju, 1981). Two representative books on the ECCO and related studies are Wang Yongxiang, Kong Fanfeng, and Liu Pinqing, *Zhongguo gongchandang lü Ou zhibu shihua* [The history of the ECCO] (Beijing: Zhongguo qingnian chubanshe, 1985), and Guo Sheng, *Wusi shiqi de gongdu yundong he gongdu sichao* [The Work-Study Movement and Work-Study thought tide of the May Fourth period] (Beijing: Jiaoyu kexue chubanshe, 1986).

the twentieth century will deepen our understanding of the relation between these questions and the Work-Study Movement.

THE GENERATIONAL CRISIS

The emergence of modern society brought qualitative changes to the normal generational tensions in most societies around the world. The Industrial Revolution and its accompanying political and social changes brought
about massive changes in the communications and transportation infra-
structure and in the educational systems. From the end of the nineteenth
century onward, there was a transformation of traditional roles, in both the
family and society. The societal dislocations, which challenged traditional
relationships between parent and child, elicited responses that exceeded
the generational conflicts of the past.

Tracing the concept of "generationalism" in Europe at the turn of the
century, Robert Wohl suggests that generations are not determined by strict
chronological logic:

> What is essential to the formation of a generational consciousness is
> some common frame of reference that provides a sense of rupture with
> the past and that will later distinguish the members of the generation
> from those who follow them in time. This frame of reference is always
> derived from great historical events like wars, revolutions, plagues,
> famines, and economic crises.[4]

Nor can one assume that those who lived through a single great historical
event experienced it the same way. Actually, only a small number of persons register permanent change, even in an era of deep generational and
societal tension. Thus, Wilhelm Dilthey defined a generation as "constituted of a *restricted circle of individuals* who are bound together into a homogeneous whole by their dependence on the same great events and
transformations that appeared in their age of [maximum] receptivity, despite the variety of other subsequent factors" (emphasis mine).[5] There are
varying degrees of change and response to these cataclysmic events. Annie
Kriegel suggests a threefold classification: those who experience total
change (a small minority), those who retain the imprint (a larger

4. Robert Wohl, *The Generation of 1914* (Cambridge: Harvard University Press, 1979),
210.

5. Wilhelm Dilthey (1924), quoted in Carl E. Schorske, "Generational Tension and
Cultural Change: Reflections on the Case of Vienna," *Daedalus* 107 (Fall 1978): 121.

minority), and the unaffected (the majority).[6] The degree of change is an important factor in understanding the political conversions and ideals that transformed China in the 1920s.

The "Lost Generation of 1914," which emerged from the First World War, was not the first sign of generational conflict to issue from the process of modernization in the Western world. Wohl claims that on a broader scale one could see the generational conflict coalesce into a definitive "ideology of youth" before the war. Wohl, who compared the youth of Germany, France, England, Italy, and Spain, concluded:

> This ideology was a by-product of the century-long pursuit of social liberation. During the two decades before the Great War youth began to organize and to challenge collectively adult authority. . . . The Jugendbewegung in Germany and Austria, the nationalist revival in France, the revolt of young Socialists against the party leadership in Italy, and the mobilization of young intellectuals in Spain . . . were all manifestations of the desire of young people to broaden their personal feelings of generational uniqueness into social movements and to gain greater control over their fate.[7]

The traditional intergenerational conflicts had gained more momentum as the parent-child relationship was weakened by the development of broadened opportunities brought about by modernization. Parents could no longer guarantee their children a place in the social hierarchy of a mass society. "Once the father had ceased to be a bank of wisdom and traditional skills on which the son could draw for his future success, the father's stern demands for obedience, respect, discipline, and achievement in a fiercely competitive capitalist society were perceived by sons as expressions of an unbearable tyranny that justified every revolt."[8] Thus the young people of Europe were eager to change the world, and many welcomed the First World War. The results of the war were, however, traumatic. The ugliness of trench warfare and the colossal loss of life and economic destruction were followed by postwar inflation.[9]

6. Annie Kriegel, "Generational Difference: History of an Idea," *Daedalus* 107 (Fall 1978): 32–33.
7. Wohl, *The Generation of 1914*, 205. This insight into the changing concept of youth has been documented by other scholars. See, e.g., Fred Weinstein and Gerald M. Platt, *The Wish to Be Free: Society, Psyche, and Value Change* (Berkeley and Los Angeles: University of California Press, 1969); Phillippe Aries, *Centuries of Childhood: A Social History of Family Life*, trans. Robert Baldick (New York: Vintage Books, 1962).
8. Wohl, *The Generation of 1914*, 206.
9. According to Jean-Jacques Becker, the loss of men in France was the most dramatic,

Not only was the war itself different in its duration and intensity from other wars, but the peace negotiated at Versailles and the feelings of betrayal and disillusionment were all prominent factors in forming a sense of spiritual loss that often translated into an inability to act. Those that did act were often attracted to the extremes of fascism or communism because they had been alienated from liberal forms of democracy. Marc Bloch, a historian who fought in the First World War and was killed by the Gestapo for his underground activities during the Second World War, decried the apathy and detachment of the intellectuals during the interim between the wars. In a poignant passage of his book *Strange Defeat: A Statement of Evidence Written in 1940*, Bloch claims that his generation should have taken an active role in a reconciliation with Germany:

> We dared not stand up in the public and be the voice crying in the wilderness. It might have been just that, but at least we should have had the consolation of knowing that, whatever the outcome of its message, it had at least spoke aloud the faith that was in us. We preferred to lock ourselves into the fear-haunted tranquility of our studies. May the young men forgive us the blood that is red upon our hands![10]

The trend toward the more radical extremes was reflected in the development of Lenin's Third International. In their study of the development of the Communist International, Branko Lazitch and Milorad Drachkovitch claim that there was a generational rift within the Socialist movement. The Socialist youth were the largest section of support for Lenin's Comintern during 1920–21: "Nearly everywhere the 'old' and 'young' no longer spoke the same language."[11]

The First World War intensified the generational rift, one keenly felt by many Western youth. As F. Scott Fitzgerald's young protagonist Amory in the postwar novel *This Side of Paradise* claimed, "I'm not sure that the war itself had any great effect on either you or me—but it certainly ruined the

---

in comparison to the total population. For every 1,000 inhabitants, France mobilized 168 and lost 34; the United Kingdom mobilized 125 and lost 16; Germany mobilized 154 and lost 30 (Jean-Jacques Becker, *The Great War and the French People*, trans. Arnold Pomerans [New York: St. Martin's Press, 1986]). Antoine Prost (*Petite histoire de la France au siècle* [Paris: Librairie Armand Colin, 1979], 28–30) documents the destruction caused by the First World War as well as inflation in France, which trebled between 1914 and 1922 and doubled during the following six years.

10. Marc Bloch, *Strange Defeat: A Statement of Evidence Written in 1940*, trans. Gerard Hopkins (London: Oxford University Press, 1949), 172.

11. Branko Lazitch and Milorad M. Drachkovitch, *Lenin and the Comintern* (Stanford: Hoover Institution Press, 1972), 221.

old backgrounds, sort of killed individualism out of our generation."[12] From the American expatriate community in Paris to the literary circles of Hungarian youth such as Georg Lukács, the strain of the war exacerbated an already growing sense of generational isolation.[13] As Malcolm Cowley commented, this generation was lost because it "belonged to a period of transition from values already fixed to values that had to be created." They were lost not only in their future but in their past: "In Paris or Pamplona, writing, drinking, watching bullfights or making love, they continued to desire a Kentucky hill cabin, a farmhouse in Iowa or Wisconsin, the Michigan woods, the blue Juniata, a country they had 'lost, ah, lost,' as Thomas Wolfe kept saying; a home to which they couldn't go back."[14]

In his literary masterpiece *All Quiet on the Western Front*, Erich Remarque also uses the image of a lost heritage and an alienation of future energy:

> And even if these scenes of our youth were given back to us we would hardly know what to do. The tender, secret influence that passed from them into us could not rise again. . . . We could never again, as the same beings, take part in those scenes. . . . Today we pass through the scenes of our youth like travellers. We are burnt up by hard facts; like tradesmen we understand distinctions, and like butchers, necessities. We are no longer untroubled—we are indifferent. We long to be there; but could we live there? . . . We are forlorn like children, and experienced like old men, we are crude and sorrowful and superficial—I believe we are lost.[15]

The Chinese situation of intergenerational conflict reflected many elements of the Western arena. To be sure, the Chinese process of modernization was not as productive and enriching as that which occurred in the West. However, as in other Third World countries, the more universal processes of modernity united with particular historical circumstances to widen a gap

12. F. Scott Fitzgerald, *This Side of Paradise* (New York: Charles Scribner's Sons, 1920), 213.

13. There is a growing body of literature dealing with this theme of generational crisis and the notion of the Lost Generation. Malcolm Cowley, in *Exile's Return: A Literary Odyssey of the 1920s*, rev. ed. (New York: Viking Press, 1956), develops the theme of the Lost Generation very carefully and includes an appendix with the birth dates of 236 artists who he claims constituted this generational cohort. Also see Noel Riley Fitch, *Sylvia Beach and the Lost Generation: A History of Literary Paris in the Twenties and Thirties* (New York: W. W. Norton, 1983); Mary Gluck, *Georg Lukács and His Generation, 1900–1918* (Cambridge: Harvard University Press, 1985); Ernest Hemingway, *A Moveable Feast: Sketches of the Author's Life in Paris in the Twenties* (New York: Charles Scribner's Sons, 1964).

14. Cowley, *Exile's Return*, 9.

15. Erich Maria Remarque, *All Quiet on the Western Front* (Greenwich, Conn.: Crest, 1965), 76–77 (originally published in 1928).

between the young and old that was difficult to bridge. The steadily encroaching Western presence in China, the humiliating defeat in the Sino-Japanese War of 1895, the abolition of the traditional Confucian exams in 1905, the overthrow of the monarchy in 1911, and the ensuing warlordism were paralleled by a slow transition to a more modernistic society with mass communication and the Western, or New, Learning. The youth born between 1894 and 1904 felt morally and intellectually superior to their elders. Li Huang, writing sixty years later, recalls the disdain of youth for their elders, the rejection of the fathers by the sons:

> One could say that our elders during the end of the Qing, with few exceptions, were totally ignorant of the contents of the new knowledge and the influences of new trends. Because of this, the new and old generations were intellectually separated; the older generation did not have the knowledge or talents to lead the later generation; then the younger generation did not want to return to the former to be restrained and ardently spread [new knowledge] faster, with no serious competition from the lessons of the elders; the actions of the younger generation were therefore not very cautious![16]

Lai Jinghu also echoes this theme of relinquished leadership: "The older generation, because of intergenerational alienation, could not give the younger generation intellectual guidance. The youth therefore broke away from the family and from society and ran to outside sources to search for new knowledge, to our new road."[17]

Although later writings reflect a poignant regret at the hard-heartedness of youth, the writings of the time often highlighted this alienation. Zeng Qi (1892–1951), one of the founders of the Young China Study Association (Shaonian Zhongguo xuehui) and a major figure in founding the anti-Communist Chinese Youth Party, was not very sympathetic to the older generation. An article he wrote in 1922 claimed that the Young China Study Association was formed for the demands of the new age and because of disappointment in the older generation. Zeng contrasted the differences in values between the old generation and the new generation:[18]

16. Li Huang, "Xuedunshi huiyilu" [Memoirs from the Xue Dun study], Zhuanji wenxue 16 (March 1970): 12.

17. Lai Jinghu, "Minchu shidai de Hunan qingnian" [The youth of Hunan during the beginning of the Republic], Zhuanji wenxue 14 (March 1970): 40. Lai Jinghu, who passed away in August 1983, went to study in the United States and, after obtaining a doctorate, lived in New York.

18. Zeng Qi, "Xuehui wenti zatan" [A random discussion of the Study Society's problems], Shaonian Zhongguo 3 (March 1922): 76–80.

Old Generation	New Generation
Militarism	Peace
Capitalism	Socialism
Nationalism	Internationalism
Elitism	Universalism
Competition	Mutual aid
Familialism	Individualism
Stagnation	Creativity

In his study of the May Fourth era, Lin Yusheng claims that the youth responded to the increasing societal changes by totally rejecting traditional Chinese culture and values, a position he terms "totalistic iconoclasm." Lin argues that totalistic iconoclasm arose out of the interaction of historical forces and the immediate political events. Two factors were particularly prominent: the disintegration of traditional sociopolitical and cultural-moral orders and the demoralizing effect of the loss of universal kingship with the abolition of the monarchy. However, one must be cautious in using a term such as "totalistic iconoclasm." The new intellectuals of the May Fourth era may have wanted to reject the traditional order and values, but their behavior and frames of reference did not necessarily reject tradition-alism. Lin recognizes this himself when he adds a disclaimer: "I do not mean that among the Chinese all sense of traditional ideas or values was lost in the cultural and moral breakdown; rather, that the clusters of ideas and values fashioned in the integrated order of the past were either eroded or dislocated."[19]

Not all Chinese youth applauded this alienation of the generations. Writing in 1921, from the United States, Tingfu F. Tsiang decried his own generation of intellectuals as working against progress when they tended "to attribute all public and private ills to those of the old generation who refuse to accept the new."[20]

Several progressive members of the older generation recognized intergen-erational tensions. In an article in Xin qingnian (New Youth Magazine), Li Dazhao, who along with Chen Duxiu founded the CCP, addressed this increasing alienation by admonishing the youth that not every utterance of their elders was corrupt, that there needed to be orderly progress. To the elders he expostulated that they need not feel intimidated by the actions of

19. Lin Yusheng, The Crisis of Chinese Consciousness: Radical Anti-traditionalism in the May Fourth Era (Madison: University of Wisconsin Press, 1979), 17.
20. Tingfu F. Tsiang, "The Values of the New in China," Chinese Students' Monthly 16 (June 1921): 564.

the younger generation.[21] However, even among the most progressive of the elders, the intergenerational tensions still existed. There is some interesting evidence that Chen Duxiu's two sons, who went to Paris in 1919 as Anarchists, held their father in contempt. This was the same Chen Duxiu who energized the youth movement with his *New Youth Magazine* and was the first general secretary of the CCP![22]

Although the nature of intergenerational tension changed, it was a gradual process. This idea of gradual change is also prominent in the works of Schorske, Kriegel, and Wohl, who all claim that the preceding generations partially fashioned the fabric of changing values and acceptable behaviors. In the case of Asia, a foreign presence speeded this process. David Marr labels the Vietnamese intellectuals of the early 1900s as a "Generation of Lasts and Firsts."[23] This term seems applicable to the middle-aged Chinese promoters of the Work-Study Movement, such as Cai Yuanpei (1868–1940), Wu Zhihui (1864–1953), Li Shizeng (1881–1973), and Wu Yuzhang (1878–1966), all of whom received traditional Confucian educations, yet who also adapted Western ideas and modes of behavior into their activities. The best example was Cai Yuanpei, who "before the age of twenty-nine was totally versed in the old learning, at thirty he started to study science, at thirty-two he studied Japanese, at thirty-seven he started his study of German, taking his first trip to study philosophy and fine arts in Germany at the age of forty-one, . . . at the age of forty-seven he traveled to France to study French."[24] Cai vigorously used his new knowledge as president of Beijing University; the fostering of ideas of academic freedom was among his many accomplishments. He symbolized integrity and progressive ideals. Others, like Li Shizeng and Wu Zhihui, also assimilated the old and new, creating new educational and business ventures. They were the "Generation of Lasts and Firsts" in that they were the last to really build their careers in the Confucian system and among the first to seriously consider adopting Western knowledge. Yet, as we shall see, there were limita-

21. Li Dazhao, "Qingnian yu laoren" [Youth and elders], *Xin qingnian* 3 (April 1917): 1–3.

22. According to Zheng Chaolin the reasons for this alienation were differences in political philosophy as well as the fact that Chen Duxiu abandoned the mother of Chen Yannian and Chen Qiaonian for another woman (Zheng Chaolin interview, 29 October 1985 [Shanghai]). Also see Zheng Chaolin, "Huiyi Chen Yannian xiongdi" [Remembering Brother Chen Yannian], *Zhong bao* (Hong Kong) (December 1983): 54–56. For similar impressions see Zhang Shenfu in *Yida qianhou*, 2:549, and Chen Gongpei, ibid., 2:565.

23. David Marr, *Vietnamese Anticolonialism* (Berkeley and Los Angeles: University of California Press, 1971), chap. 4.

24. Wang Yunwu, "Cai Jiemin xiansheng de gongxian" [The contributions of Mr. Cai Jiemin], *Dongfang zazhi* 37 (16 April 1940): 4.

tions to their adaptability that later isolated them from many of their youthful following.

Thus, the twentieth century saw the blooming of a worldwide generational conflict, which the First World War elevated to an almost traumatic experience. The Chinese were certainly uprooted in their ideas, frenetically investigating all prominent, and not so prominent, ideas. Many Chinese youth who went to France, no matter what their later political persuasion, frequently used the phrase "searching for a path to national salvation." In the words of Li Weihan, which remind one of those of Marc Bloch in their poignancy, "What was the path toward national salvation? What was truth? Those of us at Montargis [France] had minds like blank sheets of paper."[25]

Given the universal aspect of the generational crisis, it is not surprising that the fundamental beliefs of Westerners and Chinese were not dissimilar. The credo of the Lost Generation as summarized by Cowley included the idea of salvation by the child, the idea of self-expression, the idea of paganism (the body is a temple), the idea of living for the moment, the idea of liberty, the idea of female equality, the idea of psychological adjustment, and the idea of changing place (they do things better in Europe).[26] As Cowley intimated, defining identity was linked with examination of a foreign city.

Post–World War I Europe, particularly the city of Paris, served as magnet and prism for this change. In his study on the impact of Paris on American literature, Jean Meral concluded that although the expatriates misunderstood many aspects of their environment, their "representation of Paris, with its peculiar distortions, does, however, tell us things about America and Americans." Meral continues:

> After 1917, a fresh wave of expatriates from widely differing social backgrounds gives a new image of America. The Parisian experience now becomes more acute, more fraught with personal implications. Arguments about America are echoed in crises of identity. . . . Paris, with its elemental and primordial nature, is a magic place in which a disorienting play of mirrors provokes anamorphoses. Paris is the city of la fête, of drunkenness and debauchery, steeped in an atmosphere of transgression, sexual liberation, and Freudian release.[27]

25. Li Weihan, "Huiyi Xinmin xuehui" [Memoirs of the New Citizens' Study Society], in Xu Rihui, ed., Wusi yundong zai Hunan huiyilu [Reminiscences of the May Fourth Movement in Hunan] (Hunan: Hunan renmin chubanshe, 1979), 36.

26. Cowley, Exile's Return, 60–61.

27. Jean Meral, Paris in American Literature, trans. Laurette Long (Chapel Hill: University of North Carolina Press, 1989), 243.

Most of these ideas were also prevalent in the New Culture Movement in China. The New Culture Movement emphasized the ideas of breaking away and liberation, the younger generation as the saviors of the country, female equality, the body as a shrine, going abroad to learn from more advanced countries, and the idea of self-expression. Chinese youth followed the values enunciated by Chen Duxiu in his call to youth:

1. Be independent, not servile.
2. Be progressive, not conservative.
3. Be aggressive, not retiring.
4. Be cosmopolitan, not isolationist.
5. Be utilitarian, not formalistic.
6. Be scientific, not imaginative.[28]

Although the ideas that informed the worldwide generational crisis mirrored each other in their calls for liberation and self-expression, displaying real areas of resonance, there were also important contrasts. First, the Chinese were not alienated by the technological-scientific revolution as were the Western youth, who had been living in a growing world of materialism. For those who participated in the Work-Study Movement, the technological aim of their search was explicit. They wanted the industrialization of China.

Second, the young Chinese intellectuals did not abandon the discipline of a scientific approach and were more keenly interested in elevating their intellects and their analytical capacities, rather than primarily concentrating on their senses, as the Western youth tended to do. Their cultural sensibilities were not alienated by an infusion of science and technology but rather were stimulated by their first glimpses of the modern world. One of the participants in the Work-Study Movement, the future Science and Technology minister of the PRC Nie Rongzhen, wrote in his memoirs about his first encounter with a train, over sixty years later, with a fresh sense of that initial awe and wonderment.

Third, in spite of their outward searching and vociferous adherence to the New Culture Movement in their behavior and many ideas, the Chinese youth had a tremendous confidence based on pride in Chinese culture and historical tradition. Calligraphy, poetry, hierarchical terms, and even traces of classical Chinese writing permeated the expressions and persona

28. Roger Pelissier, *The Awakening of China: 1793–1949*, trans. Martin Kieffer (London: Secker and Walbury, 1963), 268.

of the Chinese community in Europe. The Chinese were "obviously" more foreign than Americans traveling in Europe. However, one senses a greater sense of pride in their own culture, which made them more insular and confident at the same time. Thus, Chinese groups were able to maintain and transform themselves in a cohesive manner and even develop into political parties on a foreign soil.

Finally, the Chinese youth had not directly participated in the devastating fighting of the First World War, which was to permanently shadow the future actions of the Western youth. The young Chinese had a different experience of violence, a more immediate need of national salvation. Unlike the golden *Belle époque* of the French youth, the *Wanderwogel*-rich days of the German youth, the fishing ponds and green hills of the American youth, the Chinese had been born to the strident, harsh sounds of war and violence, and there was no specific sense of dislocation after 1918, because they had grown up surrounded by warlordism, local chaos, and dramatic changes. Thus, while the Western seekers of the new order had memories of a rosier age to shadow their solutions, the Chinese youth were not chained by youthful illusions and were freer in their search for solutions and new lifestyles and were more able to commit themselves and develop new ideas.

Thus, in contrast to the Western youth during this period who conceived of themselves as a Lost Generation, the contemporaneous group of Chinese youth became a Found Generation. This term refers to those Chinese who had been born in the decade after the Sino-Japanese War and who had tasted but not digested the old order. They were the last to be educated in Confucian classics, "as if it counted for a career," and the first to look to Western learning for the same reason. They were better able to assimilate and live with the accoutrements of modernity, such as the newspaper and railway, than their elders. Raised in an era of rocky transition, they were not dismayed by the disorder of the twenties and were more able to infuse their lives with exceptional freshness and vigorous purpose, a feat not attained by subsequent generations of Chinese or by their Western contemporaries.

AN OVERVIEW OF THE WORK-STUDY MOVEMENT

The Role of the Returned Student

The ideals enunciated in the New Culture Movement were nowhere better actualized than in the movement to work and study in France. The rationales and goals differed among individuals, but the path to national salvation was to be sought abroad.

TABLE I
Occupations of Chinese Returned Students (1917)

Occupation	Individuals	Percentage
Politics	1,024	61
Unemployed	399	24
Education	132	8
Military	56	3.3
Hospital	23	1.4
Business	20	1.2
Newspaper	16	1
Total	1,673	

SOURCE: "Qingnianhui yu liuxuesheng zhi guanxi: lü qingnian *Jinbu zazhi*" [The relationship between the youth organizations and the study abroad students: Excerpts from *Progressive Youth Magazine*], *Dongfang zazhi* 14 (September 1917): 196–98.

Going abroad to study had not been a popular practice in Chinese history. Even after the Western intrusion, it was not actively encouraged, for the most part, by the Qing dynasty. The traditional bond of the son with his family was particularly strong in Chinese culture. Confucian teachings admonished sons not to travel far when the parents were still living (*Fu mu zai, bu yuan you*). The aims as well as the popularity of study abroad changed in scope and dimension. Military technology had dominated the earlier pedagogy, but the turn of the century saw political orientations enter into the study-abroad endeavor.[29]

As this political aim was increasingly recognized, the "returned students" began to gain increasing valuation within China. As one article written in late 1917 proclaimed, "The returned students are national leaders-saviors of the nation."[30] Indeed, a 1917 survey of 1,673 returned students revealed that most went into politics, contrary to original intentions (see table 1). In the context of an increasing modernist thirst, the young Chinese who returned from study abroad possessed a special cachet because of their broader experiences and presumed better acquaintance with magical Western formulae.

29. Y. C. Wang, *Chinese Intellectuals and the West: 1872–1949* (Chapel Hill: University of North Carolina Press, 1966), 149–50.
30. "Qingnianhui yu liuxuesheng zhi guanxi: Lü qingnian *Jinbu zazhi*" [The relationship between the youth organizations and the study abroad students: Excerpts from *Progressive Youth Magazine*], *Dongfang zazhi* 14 (September 1917): 196–98.

The Development of the Work-Study Movement

The heightened patriotism and successes of the May Fourth Movement encouraged young Chinese to seek opportunities to study abroad during 1919. However, it was a long-standing commitment by several giants of modern Chinese education—Li Shizeng, Cai Yuanpei, and Wu Zhihui—that provided the original organizational impetus for the Work-Study Movement. Wang Jingwei, Chu Minyi, Zhang Ji, Wu Yuzhang, and several others also played important roles throughout the Work-Study Movement.

Cai Yuanpei was the most prominent promoter of the Work-Study Movement, and Wu Zhihui was perceived as the most artistic and elegant, but the most important figure in the movement was Li Shizeng. Li Shizeng's father, Li Hongzao, was a high official of the Qing; for that, his sons, after Hongzao's death, were awarded honorary offices. Li Shizeng used this opportunity to be posted as an attaché to Sun Baoqi in France in 1902.[31] A multifaceted individual, Li Shizeng obtained a degree in agriculture at the Ecole pratique du Chesnoy in Montargis, founded a soybean-processing factory and a publishing house, and helped create the Paris-based journal *Xin shiji* (*The New Century*), which advocated anarchism.

It was through Li Shizeng's French contacts, particularly in the city of Montargis, that the activities of the Frugal-Study Society prospered.[32] In February 1912, Li Shizeng, Cai Yuanpei, Wu Zhihui, and Wu Yuzhang formed the Frugal-Study Society (Jianxuehui), which encouraged sacrificing one's comfort and living thriftily and studying abroad in France. The objective was to promote a new set of ideals: people's virtue, people's knowledge, and people's will (*minde minzhi minli*).[33] Given the chaotic situation in China at the time, their accomplishments were considerable.

The Frugal-Study Society established a preparatory school in Beijing that taught French, Chinese, math, and practical studies such as hygiene. The first batch of sixty students left for France in mid-1912, using a land route through Siberia. The success of the school gained momentum for the move-

---

31. Howard L. Boorman and Richard C. Howard, eds., *Biographical Dictionary of Republican China*, 5 vols. (New York: Columbia University Press, 1967), 2:319; Li Shizeng, *Li Shizeng xiansheng wenji* [Collected writings of Mr. Li Shizeng], 2 vols. (Taibei: Zhongguo guomindang zhong yang weiyuan hui dangshi weiyuan hui, 1980).

32. The French in Montargis have been very proud of their association with Li Shizeng. In 1938, for example, in a college journal listing achievements of the Ecole pratique du Chesnoy, Li Shizeng is one of two students highlighted in the class of 1904 (*Le Chesnoysien* 5 [Mai 1938]: 5).

33. See, e.g., the conclusion of the influential *Lü Ou jiaoyu yundong* [The educational movement abroad in Europe] (Fall 1916), 121. This rare document, composed of several articles by Li Shizeng, Cai Yuanpei, Wu Zhihui, Wang Jingwei, and others, is quoted at length in Chen Sanjing, *Qingong jianxue yundong*.

ment, and schools were opened in Sichuan and Shanghai. Two more groups of students traveled to France before the program was abandoned a couple of years later. It is interesting to note that the original plan called for three thousand students to travel to France within five years.[34] The philosophy of frugal study was not restricted to France. For example, there were attempts to set up Frugal-Study societies to travel to England in 1913.[35]

Li Shizeng returned to Montargis in November 1912 and received the cooperation of the city government and local colleges in his projects. Official welcomes were accorded the incoming Chinese students, public meetings were held, and financial support was forthcoming. During a Montargis municipal council meeting, a part of the budget proposal included an increase for the "colony of Chinese students who have come to learn our language to follow through with specialized studies in Commerce, Industry, and Agriculture." The proposal echoed other public sentiments and favored the transplanting of French civilization and democracy in Chinese soil.[36]

Writing about the development of the Work-Study Movement in 1916, the *Lü Ou jiaoyu yundong* attributed the halt of the Frugal-Study Society activities in sending Chinese students to France to the Great War, which interrupted normal education in France.[37] Despite the war, however, the promoters of the Work-Study Movement continued their organizational activities. In March 1915, in Paris, the Qingong jianxuehui (Diligent-Work Frugal-Study Association) was formed upon the premise "to diligently approach work, to frugally seek study" (*qin yu gongzuo, jian yi qiuxue*). Many Chinese saw the worker shortage in France and the need for wartime factory labor as an opportunity for them to earn money and study in the West. The Diligent-Work Frugal-Study Association, however, specifically stated that it had no formal responsibilities or obligations. Its sole purpose was to encourage people to go abroad for study and to provide informal support.[38]

The organization with the most impact on the Work-Study Movement was the Sino-French Educational Association (Hua Fa jiaoyuhui). The pro-

34. Huang Liqun, *Liu Fa qingong jianxue jianshi* [A concise history of the travel to France Work-Study Movement] (Beijing: Jiaoyu kexue chubanshe, 1982), 5–7.

35. "Liu Ying jianxue yiqushu" [Interest in a Frugal-Study Association to travel to England], *Dongfang zazhi* 9 (February 1913), in Shu Xincheng, comp., *Zhongguo jindai jiaoyushi ziliao* [Chinese modern educational materials], 3 vols. (Beijing: Renmin jiaoyu chubanshe, 1961), 3:875–77. This three-volume compendium was originally published in 1927 in Shanghai.

36. "Séance du Conseil municipal du 10/11/1913" (Montargis), *Gatinais* (15 November 1913). This material was collected and kindly given to the author by François Fergani.

37. "Quzhong Falanxi jiaoyu zhi liyou" [The reasons for the tendency toward French education], *Lü Ou jiaoyu yundong*, in Chen Sanjing, *Qingong jianxue yundong*, 54.

38. Shu Xincheng, *Zhongguo jindai jiaoyushi ziliao*, 3:878–82; regulations are also listed in the *Lü Ou jiaoyu yundong*.

moters again included Li Shizeng, Cai Yuanpei, and Wu Zhihui. The initial organization included thirty-two French and thirty Chinese. The first Chinese president was Cai Yuanpei, who officiated at the first meeting on 29 March 1916, held in Paris.[39] The first French president of the Sino-French Educational Association (SFEA) was Alphonse Aulard (1849–1928), the famous historian of the French Revolution and a professor at the Sorbonne. Other French supporters included legislators, businessmen, and educators. There were two prominent representatives from the Rhône: Marius Moutet, the Socialist deputy from the Rhône, who served as one of the vice-presidents, and Edouard Herriot, the mayor of Lyons and senator from the Rhône, who later rose to prominence in the French Radical Party. Other French members included Li Shizeng's good friend Victor Falleau, a professor at the Agricultural College in Montargis and a notable sponsor of the 1912 efforts, who served as a secretary-adjoint in the initial SFEA.[40]

The aim of the SFEA was "the extension of relations between France and China and especially the moral, intellectual, and economic development of China by instruction in science and French ideas." Of the three stated sections of the SFEA, two were explicitly linked with the Work-Study Movement. The first section was to work on translating Chinese and French works. The second section was to establish scholarly exchanges. It urged that the number of Chinese students studying in France be increased and that facilities be provided for their stay in France. The third section, while having the general aim of promoting economic relations based on French traditions of equality, proposed that Chinese workers in France be organized.[41]

The SFEA had headquarters in Paris and Beijing, and it later established many branches. The association was the most active organization working on behalf of students who wanted to travel abroad. A Beijing preparatory school was founded in June 1917, and within eighteen months twenty schools were started. "Every place began to establish branches of the SFEA. The already-established Frugal-Study Society and Diligent-Work Frugal-Study Association also revived activities."[42] After one year of preparation in these schools, the students were processed under the auspices of the SFEA and then usually given fourth-class tickets to sail to France, a journey of forty to sixty days.

39. "Liu Ou Hua Fa jiaoyuhui yilan" [A glance at the European branch of the Sino-French Educational Association], *Jiaoyu gongbao* (September 1917), in *FuFa*, 1:197–209.

40. "Société franco-chinoise d'éducation statuts" (1916), AOM, SLOTFOM V, 43.

41. Ibid., article 2, 1. This emphasis on the work-study dimension is important because of Cai Yuanpei's later disclaimer on the intent of the organization.

42. Huang Liqun, *Liu Fa qingong jianxue jianshi*, 14–17.

Among the thousands of participants in the movement there were widely varying motivations for going to France. However, some commonly held themes can be identified. Almost everyone agreed that educational facilities in China were inadequate. In speaking at the opening of the Beijing Preparatory School for Travel Abroad to France in 1917, Cai Yuanpei explained the necessity of going outside China for education:

> If our country has schools already, why does this organization advise people to travel abroad? There are several reasons. First, the number of schools in our country is insufficient; there are graduates of elementary school who cannot obtain a middle school education; there are graduates of middle school who cannot obtain higher education. Second, the facilities of our schools are still incomplete, and the teaching personnel do not have the appropriate types of knowledge; our graduates cannot compete with graduates of the same level living in foreign countries. Last, regarding the facilities outside our schools like libraries, museums, botanical gardens and zoos, farm fields, and the number of factories, we just have not established enough to properly give our students practical experience or reference materials [can kao]. It is a case of doubling the amount of work with half the results [you shi bei gong ban zhi lu]. We must absolutely exhort our students to go abroad and study.[43]

Students incorporated these feelings of inferiority and national salvation in their speeches and writings too. One student reporting from France argued, "Unfortunately China is isolated from the rest of the world. She is not able to catch up with the science or industry of Western Europe. Unfortunately China is lacking in both great numbers of talented people and money; she cannot establish enough schools or factories. Unfortunately the schools China now has are not able to achieve enough to be of use to Chinese society."[44]

It was France, rather than Great Britain, Germany, or the United States, which was perceived as the best place for sojourning Chinese. This fact was reflected not only by the popularity of the Work-Study Movement but also by the great number of self-supporting Chinese students who went to France.[45] It should also be noted that thousands of Chinese laborers from

---

43. "Liu Fa jianxuehui jiangyanhui zhi yanshuo" [The speeches presented at the travel to France Frugal-Study Association meeting], Dongfang zazhi 14 (September 1917): 177–83. This quotation is on 177.

44. Zhuang Qi, "Liu Fa qingong jianxue" [The travel to France Work-Study Movement] Jiaoyu zazhi 12 (June 1920): 1.

45. According to Y. C. Wang there were over 6,000 Chinese students in France during the early twenties, more than any other country, including the United States (Chinese Intellectuals and the West, 110).

among the over 175,000-strong Chinese Labor Corps, which had aided the Allies during the First World War, elected to continue working in France in the early twenties.[46] The French were perceived as the most friendly of foreigners. "Frenchmen were fraternal and without boundaries toward foreigners, and that was the reason foreign students went to France in the greatest numbers."[47] The spirit of the French Revolution, of French fraternity, equality, and liberty, was a source of real inspiration for the Chinese.

There were several aspects of French society that were seen as resonating with the values and goals of the New Culture Movement. The concept of a popular education was highly attractive to the Chinese, who saw this trend exemplified in the French law of 1907 that separated the church and state in education. France was perceived as the most sophisticated Western country in terms of science, philosophy, and general intellectual trends. From the *philosophes* who prompted the French Revolution to Pasteur and the beginnings of microbiology, from Auguste Comte to Lamarck, the Chinese were excited to immerse themselves in a whole new world of advanced Western culture and knowledge. The more pragmatic goals of the Work-Study Movement were linked with gaining experience in factory work and pursuing technical educations in France. The Chinese hoped that the growth of Chinese technology and economic development would serve as a basis for raising the standard of living and education in China and promote the ultimate end of creating an informed and politically active citizenry. An important goal was to "interchange," that is, to communicate the highlights of Chinese culture to the French.[48] As Wu Yuzhang claimed in a speech, the object was not only to bring China into the major currents of world civilization but also to expound and propagate Chinese thought (*chanyang ruxian zheli*).[49]

The Role of Anarchism

Because its promoters were themselves prominent Anarchists, one of the most important dimensions of the Work-Study Movement was its reflection of the Anarchist trend of the early 1900s. Anarchism was perhaps the first

---

46. Chen Sanjing, *Huagong yu Ouzhan* [The Chinese Labor Corps in the First World War] (Taibei: Academia Sinica, 1986); Ta Chen, *Chinese Migrations, with Special Reference to Labor Conditions*, U.S. Department of Labor, Bureau of Labor Statistics (Washington: Government Printing Office, 1923), chap. 9.
47. *Lü Ou jiaoyu yundong*, in Chen Sanjing, *Qingong jianxue yundong*, 52.
48. Ibid., 51–53; also see the several speeches in "Liu Fa jianxuehui jiangyanhui zhi yanshuo," 177–83.
49. "Liu Fa jianxuehui jiangyanhui zhi yanshuo," 181.

important Western ideology to motivate Socialist and radical Chinese youth.[50] They followed the pattern of Western Europe in this regard, evolving from utopian-anarchism and utopian-socialism to Marxism and finally to Leninist forms of political action and party formation.[51]

There were two major Anarchist groups with an impact on Chinese youth that is often hard to assess. One group was in Tokyo and was led by Liu Shipei. The other group was located in Paris and included Li Shizeng, Wu Zhihui, Zhang Ji, and others of the *Xin shiji* circle. The influence of the Paris group was expressed in a multitude of publications,[52] a wide scope of enterprises in government and business spheres, and their general spirit of enthusiasm and sponsorship of overseas educational ventures.

Anarchism played an important role in the Work-Study Movement in several ways. First, it provided an ideology for mentors of the movement such as Li Shizeng and Wu Zhihui. Both Li Shizeng and Wu Zhihui stressed education as a primary means of revolutionary activity. "Revolution" could be attained only gradually and should be one of cooperation among groups:

> Li, who had a better scientific education than any other anarchist, or for that matter than nearly any Chinese intellectual of his day, . . . deprecated the understanding of evolution as a cruel process of the struggle for existence and natural selection where only the strong survive. . . . He saw two areas wherein revolution and evolution were working great changes: the world's various languages were evolving into a single, vastly improved language, and Chinese political and social thought was evolving toward anarchism.[53]

50. The transitional role of anarchism in modern China is explained in Peter Zarrow, *Anarchism and Chinese Political Culture* (New York: Columbia University Press, 1990); Arif Dirlik, *The Origins of Chinese Communism* (New York: Oxford University Press, 1989); Robert A. Scalapino and George T. Yu, *The Chinese Anarchist Movement* (Westport, Conn.: Greenwood Press, 1961); and Arif Dirlik, "The New Culture Movement Revisited: Anarchism and the Idea of Social Revolution in New Culture Thinking," *Modern China* 11 (July 1985): 251–300.

51. Although ignorant of the many specifics of the formation of the CCP, one of the numerous reports by the British intelligence service in the Far East clearly delineated the impact of anarchism on the development of bolshevism in China, noting the varying Anarchist cliques and leaders. The report claimed that the Bolshevists (meaning the Russians) did not control Chinese Anarchists: "There are however, certain interesting connections between the Bolsheviks and the Chinese Anarchists, particularly in the North of China" ("Bolshevism and Chinese Communism and Anarchism in the Far East," Sir B. Alston to Marquess of Curzon of Kedleston, November 1921, PRO, Foreign Office [FO] 371/6602 F4310/34/10).

52. Some of these are reproduced in Zhang Jun and Wang Renzhi, eds., *Xinhai geming qian shinian jianshi xuanji* [Collection of materials written during the ten years before the 1911 Revolution], 5 vols. (Beijing: Shenghuo, dushu, xinzhi sanlian, 1977).

53. Zarrow, *Anarchism and Chinese Political Culture*, 127–28.

In addition to a nonviolent, evolutionary approach to revolution by the Paris Chinese Anarchists, the ideology of anarchism gave these important leaders moral legitimacy, especially in their advocacy of cooperation. They had a firm moral purpose and this was in turn a source of respect and prestige in the eyes of the youth, who answered their call to study overseas. Anarchism was a form of moral power.

Second, anarchism encouraged the activist spirit and helped to stimulate the organizational propensity of Chinese youth along modern lines. They formed organizations, published newsletters, and were able to mobilize people for political education and action.[54] The Work-Study Movement was perhaps one of the most successful organizations developed by the Anarchists. The impetus of this Anarchist enterprise later was to serve as a bridge between youth group and political party.

Third, anarchism played a significant role in establishing important ideological concepts. Anarchists were among the first to promote ideas such as the importance of class divisions and of the Chinese workers. The Anarchist promoters of the Work-Study Movement heavily emphasized concepts such as group responsibility, the sacred nature of physical labor, and the need to break down class barriers between intellectuals and workers. The young Chinese were impressed by the moral arguments, which added ideological substance to the New Culture Movement. As Zhang Ruoming, a young Chinese feminist who traveled to France, wrote in 1921:

> The current dissemination of the New Culture Movement in China is a hodgepodge. . . . There are those who speak of "New Thought," those who say "Democracy," those who say "Marxism," those who introduce "Bolshevism." . . . [E]verything is different, but taken altogether it can be called no less than the secure life of "man." . . . We want to go one level further, not to seek the secure life for the intellectual class and not to seek the secure life for the laboring class; the higher goal is to combine the personality of the intellectual and laborer for everyone; there will be no so-called class, a person who is a laborer is [also] a laborer with knowledge.[55]

Another important Anarchist ideal that informed the Work-Study Movement was mutual aid (huzhu).[56] The concept of mutual aid, based on the Anarchist ideals of Kropotkin, held such sway over the worker-students

---

54. Dirlik, "The New Culture Movement Revisited," 262.
55. Zhang Ruoming, "Liu Fa jianxue sheng zhi konghuang yu Hua Fa jiaoyuhui" [The depression of the travel to France worker-students and the Sino-French Educational Association] (April 1921), in FuFa, 2:419–20
56. Guo Sheng interview, 6 December 1985 (Beijing).

that during the bleak winter of 1921, when the SFEA abrogated their economic support of impoverished worker-students, they began to form mutual aid groups in Paris.

Thus, the notion of revolution through evolution, the Anarchist organizational impetus, and the stress on the importance of labor were powerful forces for Chinese youth preoccupied by the concerns of the New Culture Movement:

> Anarchists' sensitivity to the social basis of individual liberation enabled them to inject social concerns into New Culture thinking, otherwise preoccupied with ideas and culture. It was in this regard that anarchists had a radicalizing impact on the New Culture Movement. While anarchists were also prominent among New Culture radicals as the only ones to take up questions of labor, and the need for intellectuals to be cognizant of the problems of the common people, their social message was to have the most profound effect on the consciousness and behavior of radical intellectuals. Before socialism had become a visible feature of the Chinese intellectual scene, anarchists had already introduced the issues of socialism.[57]

Although anarchism was an important source of moral, philosophical, and activist stimulation, and although the major promoters of the Work-Study Movement were Anarchists, the Work-Study Movement was by no means seen by the participants or most observers as an "Anarchist enterprise." The participants were under the sway of the broad value search of the New Culture Movement, and thus the great majority did not organize themselves, for example, into Anarchist youth groups or political parties. The Chinese youth paid homage to Anarchist leaders such as Li Shizeng, Wu Zhihui, and Cai Yuanpei. They believed in the Anarchist-inspired ideas of mutual aid and the sanctity of labor that lay at the philosophical heart of the Work-Study Movement. However, while embarking on the Work-Study enterprise, the youth did not conceive of themselves as Anarchists. The pervasive rationales for traveling to France of national salvation, cultural interchange, technological education, and so forth were not *self-consciously* linked with anarchism as a basis.[58]

Thus, although many of the Chinese youth who went to France shared the goal of national salvation through understanding Western technology

---

57. Dirlik, *Origins of Chinese Communism*, 76.

58. For a more detailed explication of this argument see Marilyn Levine, "The Diligent-Work, Frugal-Study Movement and the New Culture Movement," *Republican China* 12 (November 1986): 72–74.

and civilization, perhaps the most salient feature of their rationales for going to France was the incredible diversity and richness of motivations and philosophical underpinnings of these youth and their mentors. Many belonged to youth groups, which all displayed a tremendous thirst for theories and knowledge and sponsored frequent debates. Most youth were in a stage of exploration, their minds like skeins of multicolored yarn with strands linked to past ideas yet twisting to stretch for the new. The Found Generation was characterized by this openness and freshness.

A Profile of the Worker-Students

A 1920 survey of 1,230 worker-students by the SFEA revealed that most of the students were under twenty-five years old, with more than one-third under the age of twenty and only 10 participants over the age of thirty (see table 2).[59] The ratio of men to women was greater than the ratio that existed for Chinese students in the United States.[60] The Work-Study Movement included only about 40 women.[61]

The largest proportion of students came from the poorer provinces, such as Sichuan and Hunan, which were bearing the brunt of the civil war in China, unlike the students studying in North America, who were mostly from the richest provinces (see table 3). Wang found that about 44 percent of 1,862 Work-Study students came from Sichuan and Hunan, whereas 82 percent of the Chinese students in the United States came from the three richer provinces of Guangdong, Jiangsu, and Zhejiang. It seems likely that the increasing politicization of the students from Sichuan and Hunan was due in part to the poor economic conditions they endured. It has frequently been asserted that people from Hunan and Sichuan had a more activist character. It is certainly true that the political participation of the several hundred Guangdong students in France was relatively less. In general, the

59. Although the theft of over 1,200 dossiers has retarded a systematic collection of data on the Work-Study Movement, many fascinating records and statistics on the movement are still available.

60. Females studied in the United States in greater numbers. "By 1910 self-supporting female students abroad were competing on equal terms with males for government scholarships. In 1914, 94 out of 847 Chinese students in America were women; and in 1925 no less than 640 out of 1,637" (Wang, Chinese Intellectuals and the West, 73).

61. Geneviève Barman and Nicole Dulioust have written an article on the female Work-Study participants that includes short biographies; see "Un groupe oublie: Les étudiantes-ouvrieres chinoises en France," Etudes chinoises 6, no. 2 (1987): 9–46; also see Zhongguo geming bowuguan dangshi chenlie yanjiubu [The Research Section of the Museum of the Chinese Revolution and Party Exhibits], Zhongguo dangshi zhuyao shijian jianshi [A summary of important Chinese Party affairs] (Chengdu: Sichuan renmin chubanshe, 1982), 10.

TABLE 2
Age Distribution of Chinese Worker-Students in France

Age (years)	Individuals	Percentage
15	20	1.6
16–20	500	40.6
21–25	600	48.8
26–30	100	8.1
31+	10	0.8
Total	1,230 ($\bar{x} = 21.3 \pm 0.4$)	

SOURCE: Xiao Zizhang, "Liu Fa jianxue qingong liangnian lai zhi jingguo ji xianzhuang" [The past two years and current situation of the travel to France Work-Study Movement] (February 1920), in Qinghua University, FuFa qingong jianxue yundong shiliao, 1:86.

political involvement of Chinese students was greater in France than in other countries, as Wang has noted.[62]

In contrasting Chinese students who studied in France with those who studied in Germany, a survey of doctorates awarded in Europe between 1907 and 1962 indicates differences of orientation. Out of a total of 732 doctorates awarded to Chinese studying in Germany, 21 percent (154) were in the humanities and social sciences, and 79 percent (578) were awarded in the natural sciences. In contrast, the French situation was almost the reverse. Out of a total of 581 doctorates awarded to Chinese, 63 percent (367) were awarded in literature and law, and only 37 percent (214) were obtained in scientific and medical fields.[63]

Once the worker-students reached France they eagerly grasped both educational and labor opportunities. The SFEA survey of late 1920 showed that out of 1,414 worker-students, 1,077 were either going to school (498) or working in factories (579).[64] The majority of those who went to the factories worked for large companies like the Renault automobile factory or the Creusot-Schneider munitions works. The educational level of the students was generally not very high (see table 4). The vast majority of the students who went to school could do so only at a high school level. Given

62. Chinese Intellectuals and the West, 158–61, 111.
63. Yuan Tung-li, A Guide to Doctoral Dissertations by Chinese Students in Continental Europe, 1907–1962, Chinese Culture Quarterly reprint (1963), 151–53.
64. Société franco-chinois d'éducation, "Compte rendu au mois de novembre 1920," AAE, série E, Chine, vol. 48.

TABLE 3
Regional Origins of Chinese Worker-Students in France

Native Province	Individuals	Percentage
Sichuan	378	24.0
Hunan	346	22.0
Guangdong	251	16.0
Zhili	147	9.3
Fujian	89	5.7
Zhejiang	85	5.4
Jiangsu	69	4.4
Anhui	40	2.5
Hubei	40	2.5
Shaanxi	28	1.8
Jiangxi	28	1.8
Henan	25	1.6
Shandong	15	1.0
Guizhou	9	0.6
Guangxi	7	0.4
Shanxi	7	0.4
Yunnan	6	0.4
Fengtian	5	0.3
Total	1,575	

SOURCE: Zhou Enlai, "Qingong jianxue sheng zai Fa zuihou zhi yunming" [The final fate of the worker-students in France] (December 1921), in Qinghua University, *FuFa qingong jianxue yundong shiliao*, 1:42–43.

the instability of the times and the limitations of the Chinese educational system, it is surprising that a substantial majority of the students had completed the equivalent of a secondary education in China. Sympathetic educational institutions, like those in Montargis, set up special language courses in their colleges. Very few worker-students had professional backgrounds. For example, as of mid-1920, only fifty students had worked in a factory before coming to France (although practical experience was given in some preparatory schools).[65]

65. Xiao Zizhang, "Liu Fa jianxue qingong liangnian lai zhi jingguo ji xianzhuang" [The past two years and current situation of the travel to France Work-Study Movement] (February 1290), in *FuFa*, 1:87.

TABLE 4

Educational Background of Chinese Worker-Students in France

Type of School or Education	Individuals	Percentage
Middle school (high school)	470	41.3
Preparatory school[a] for going to France	300	26.3
Normal school (teaching college)	100	8.8
Technical school	100	8.8
University	90	8.0
Elementary school	30	2.6
Agricultural school	30	2.6
Schooling in Japan	30	2.6
Business school	20	1.8
Schooling in Southeast Asia	20	1.8
Mining school	10	0.9
Administrative school	10	0.9
Military school	10	0.9
Hospital	7	0.6
Hydraulic engineering school	5	0.4
Tea business	5	0.4
Total	1,137	

SOURCE: Xiao Zizhang, "Liu Fa jianxue qingong liangnian lai zhi jingguo ji xianzhuang" (February 1920), in Qinghua University, *FuFa qingong jianxue yundong shiliao*, 1:86–87. There were still 500–600 students yet to arrive. This was a mid-1920 survey.
[a]Attendees usually had elementary or high school backgrounds.

In sum, the typical Work-Study participant was male, in his early twenties, and very likely from Hunan or Sichuan. He had minimal educational background and little factory experience or skill preparation. After his arrival in France, he was exposed to both education and factory labor.

The worker-students were unified by a general desire for national salvation. Many belonged to regional or youth groups, but they all faced the tremendous challenge of a new culture, a new environment, new technologies, and a totally new world. Problems of adjustment were complicated by the growing unemployment situation in France and by poor organizational management by the SFEA. Thus, as seventeen different waves of Chinese youth left their native shores for France throughout 1920–21, the tension began to build, and the year 1921 saw three "struggles" that tended to unify and radicalize the worker-students.

The Three Struggles of 1921

The originators of the Work-Study scheme did not possess the complex organizational abilities needed to place thousands of students in jobs or schools in a foreign country, nor did they realistically assess the economic situation in France. The hundreds of new students who arrived each month between the end of 1919 and the beginning of 1921 faced increasingly dire living conditions. The promise of the Work-Study Movement went unfulfilled.

Zhou Enlai arrived in early 1921 and began to write a series of articles discussing the problems of the Work-Study Movement. Zhou felt that the SFEA was not exercising enough good sense in managing the student flow. Many of the students who came were too young, too unskilled, or too unhealthy to work. The SFEA also was not sufficiently familiar with the labor situation in France, and as a result 55 percent of the Work-Study Movement students were unemployed. Those who did secure employment found that the work was often physically exhausting and the wages were low. The basic premise that one could study Western knowledge after working in a factory for eight hours turned out to be untrue.[66] Zhou's articles constituted a good general critique of the movement. However, though severely disillusioned, he was not totally convinced that the Work-Study Movement was not practicable.

Li Huang, who was quite sympathetic to the SFEA administrator in Paris, Liu Hou (Liu Dabei), vividly describes the misery endured by many students who had no place to sleep but the floor of the Chinese Federation (Huaqiao xieshe) building (the Chinese Federation was a central gathering place that housed various Chinese organizations). At least 200 students slept in discarded tents on the lawn of the Chinese Federation. According to Li Huang, about 150 people were hospitalized or died.[67]

Two big problems were the lack of language proficiency and the fact that many students had never before had to endure hard physical labor. These difficulties were also exacerbated by the fact that there were real cultural differences and problems of adjustment.

Charges against the SFEA abounded. One article delineated three deficiencies of SFEA policy: (1) the jobs found were often underpaid or too difficult, and when a job change was requested, the SFEA was not flexible; (2) most of the students relied on the SFEA for life-saving loans, but these

---

66. Zhou Enlai, "Liu Fa qingong jianxue sheng zhi da bolan" [The giant wave of travel to France by the worker-students], *Yishi bao* (May 1921) (written in February and March), in *FuFa*, 1:11–12.

67. Li Huang, "Xuedunshi huiyilu," *Zhuanji wenxue* 17 (July 1970): 18.

were difficult to obtain and not timely; (3) the SFEA showed favoritism based on regional or personal affiliations.[68] In addition to these alleged faults, one of the more serious charges against the SFEA was that of corruption.

Of course, some of the leaders and administrators of the SFEA were aware of the problems and tried to solve them.[69] There can be no doubt that the SFEA had undertaken a difficult task. It had its defenders within the Work-Study Movement ranks, but the problems persisted and became even more pressing as the number of worker-students increased to 1,600 by early 1921. Finally, by the beginning of 1921, the Ministry of Education refused to allow more students to leave China, due to requests by Work-Study Movement promoters.

Another decisive step was Cai Yuanpei's trip to Europe to oversee the Work-Study Movement and to promote the establishment of special Chinese educational institutes at Lyons University and in Belgium. Many worker-students looked forward to Cai's arrival, hoping he would come up with a solution. However, Cai Yuanpei apparently spent little time on the Work-Study Movement investigation.[70] He published two announcements (12 January 1921 and 16 January 1921) that absolved the SFEA from all financial responsibility for the worker-students.[71] Cai recommended that the students form self-sufficient mutual aid groups. The rationale for his actions was that the SFEA was only one of three organizations that dealt with the Work-Study Movement. However, since the Diligent-Work Frugal-Study Association and the Frugal-Study Society were promoted by the same people as the SFEA, this seems a rather thin pretext.

Cai Yuanpei's treatment of the worker-students was rather shabby. His virtual abandonment of 1,600 Chinese students in France encouraged more militant questioning of their worldview. The worker-students were puzzled, hurt, and increasingly angry in response to the SFEA's relinquishment of

68. Bian Xiaoxuan, "Liu Fa qingong jianxue ziliao" [Travel to France Work-Study Movement materials], *Jindaishi ziliao* 2 (1955): 183–84.

69. For one spirited defense, which was also optimistic about the future of the Work-Study Movement, see Li Shizeng, "Li Shizeng jun liu Fa qingong jianxue wenda" [Mr. Li Shizeng answers questions regarding the travel to France Work-Study Movement], *Shishi xinbao* (28 February 1920), in *FuFa*, 2:336–41.

70. "Qingong jianxue de lishi" [The history of the Work-Study Movement] (1921), in Bian Xiaoxuan, "Liu Fa qingong jianxue ziliao," 185–86, asserts that Cai only met with Work-Study Movement participants for a couple of hours and did not read their appeals.

71. These announcements are given in full in Tian Yi, "Liu Fa qingong jianxue sheng shi guan qingyuan ji" [An account of the official petitions of the travel to France worker-students], *Jiaoyu zazhi* 13 (20 July 1921): 1–7.

responsibility. It may be that Cai's negative perception of the Work-Study students moved him toward such a severe stance.

The publication of Cai Yuanpei's announcements altered the forms of appropriate student action and induced changes in the alignment of political groupings during the turbulent year of 1921. The majority of students were appalled at Cai's announcements, but many still believed in the viability of the Work-Study Movement. A large group of students in Montargis, led by Cai Hesen, a leader of the New Citizens' Study Society and one of the earliest Marxists, believed in direct action. The Montargis faction believed that to support themselves via factory labor was to serve as slaves for the Capitalists, and they wanted the government to give them their educational and living fees. Accordingly, they went to petition the Chinese consulate and Foreign Minister Chen Lu for "the right to live, the right to study" (shengcun quan, qiuxue quan), asking for 400 francs each month for four years. Three to four hundred students gathered in front of the Chinese consulate on rue Babylon in Paris on 28 February 1921. Although Chen Lu tried to negotiate with them and spoke to the crowd, the police (who had been called in advance by the consulate) decided the situation was too tense and dispersed the crowd in a violent clash. The government offered only very limited support and free passage back to China.[72]

The Twenty-eighth Movement, so called because of the date of the demonstration, was important because although unsuccessful, it showed that some students were willing to take direct action. It also pointed to disunity among the Work-Study students. A faction led by Zhao Shiyan, Li Lisan, and Wang Ruofei despised the Montargis faction's refusal to work in the factories. Students did not need a handout from the government and could be "self-sufficient." But they were troubled by the obvious disunity and made serious efforts to establish relationships with the Montargis faction.

The summer of 1921 provided an ideal occasion for unification when what became known as the Loan Struggle burst upon the Chinese community in France. The Chinese government sent a representative in secret to negotiate with the French government for a large loan. However, this was discovered by the students and aroused their outrage because they knew it would be spent on more weapons in the continual civil war raging in China. What transpired was a series of giant protest meetings attended by people from many different organizations and factions. There was a flurry of denials by the Chinese legation and exposures by the Chinese community activists. Basically, Chen Lu deceived the Chinese community during July, and on 13 August the students beat up his representative at their meeting and

72. Ibid., 1–7; Li Weihan, "Huiyi Xinmin xuehui," 44–45.

coerced him into signing a statement that the government would refuse to sign any loan agreement.[73] The affair was complicated by the collapse of the Banque industrielle de Chine, where many Chinese had deposited and subsequently lost their hard-earned savings.[74] This collapse occurred shortly before the Loan Struggle. Thus, there was grave suspicion that there was governmental corruption that would support a loan to the Chinese warlord government but not support a faltering bank that could have helped the Chinese workers in France.

The anger aroused by the second struggle of 1921 over the proposed French loan to China outlasted its resolution. Even more militant actions ensued, the most important being the occupation by over a hundred students of a dormitory at Lyons University on 21 September 1921, in the third struggle of 1921. The student openings at the newly created Sino-French Institute at Lyons University had originally been promised by some SFEA promoters to the worker-students. The situation exploded when the students learned that Wu Zhihui was bringing more students from China (predominantly from Guangzhou) to become the first students at the institute. Lyons had been their last hope, especially as sources for loans and government support had totally dried up because of their loan protest. Starving and despairing, a vanguard of a hundred students went to Lyons University to make their demands known. It was asserted, even by more neutral sources, that Chen Lu had promised no legal repercussions and even gave them train money. However, the students were imprisoned in a military encampment and within a month they were deported back to their homeland.[75]

In the short run the affair at Lyons University seemed like a death knell for the Work-Study Movement. But in the long run this series of events had profound results, especially the radicalization of people like Zhao Shiyan and Wang Ruofei, who were involved in negotiations during the Lyons Incident. The Lyons Incident unified the two opposing factions of the Twenty-eighth Movement and also signaled the rise of new leaders, because several important leaders were deported, such as Cai Hesen, Li Lisan, and Luo Xuezan.

73. Zhou Enlai, "Lü Fa Huaren jujue jiekuan zhi yundong" [The movement of Chinese in France to refuse the loan], *Yishi bao* (August 1921), in *FuFa*, 2:459–66.

74. J. N. Jeanneney, "Finances, presse et politique: L'affaire de la Banque industrielle de Chine (1921–1923)," *Revue historique* 514 (April–June 1975): 377–416.

75. Yu Gong [Zeng Qi], "Qingong jianxue sheng jinzhan Lida zhi qianyin houguo" [The whole story of the occupation of Lyons University by the worker-students], *Xinwen bao* (November/December 1921), in *FuFa*, 2:571–82.

In the midst of an intensified generational crisis, over 1,600 Chinese youth traveled to France, seeking a path to national salvation. It was a time of transition for them in an epoch of tumultuous change. Yet in the face of an increasingly distressing situation, exacerbated by the struggles of 1921, many of these Chinese youth managed to define themselves and took the organizational initiative to commit themselves to active political roles. We have seen in broad strokes the whirlpool of rapid historical change and the richness of the New Culture Movement context as it mixed with the complexity of personal relationships, organizational ferment, and intellectual curiosity. Next, we will turn to the experiences of four key individuals in the Work-Study Movement to illuminate in more detail the evolution of the activist ideology.

2
FOUR VOYAGERS TO EUROPE

Edge of the mountain seacoast,
In a brief farewell with our young Chinese.
Brief farewell, long mutual remembrances,
Only ask on the manner of the plowing,
Not for the collection of the harvest.
Only we youth have this purity.

—Wang Guangqi, letter from the Indian Ocean (1920)

Wang Guangqi traveled to France to broaden his vision of the world and seek a way to save and enrich his homeland. Wang eschewed any ideological solution, but he was positive about the political actors—the youth of China. In a poem that he wrote while sailing in the Indian Ocean, Wang ended each stanza with a paean of praise for the power of youth: "Only we youth are able to rouse ourselves. . . . Only we youth are able to be self-supporting. . . . Only we youth have this purity. . . . Only we youth are bound together by our oath for good fortune or ill. . . . Only we youth, striving forth, striving forth!"[1]

Confidence in their own youthful idealism and in the sincerity of their intentions to save their country characterized the young Chinese who boarded ships to journey to France. Although these qualities were important means for facilitating their adaptation to a new world, perhaps the greatest advantage these youth possessed was that their childhood had occurred during a period of historical transition. The very traumas and tragedies that scarred the landscape of their earliest memories conditioned them to be an unusually flexible group. They were open to pondering new ideas in an era of cultural efflorescence. Traveling in the abysmal conditions of fourth-class accommodations aboard the ships to France, these determined and independent youth retained their emotional resilience and confidence.

Three of these lively voyagers, Cai Hesen, Zhao Shiyan, and Zhou Enlai, were destined to assume leadership roles in the ECCO. Because their leadership was important in forming and shaping the ECCO, it is useful to look at the individual processes of transformation. Cai Hesen (1895–1931), as the most active Marxist in the Chinese community in France, prepared the the-

1. Wang Guangqi, "Yinduyang zhong zhi benhui tongzhi shu" [Letter written in the middle of the Indian Ocean to this society's comrades] (1920), in idem, *Shaonian Zhongguo yundong* [The Chinese youth movement] (Shanghai: Zhonghua shuju, 1924), 192–93.

oretical groundwork for the ECCO. Zhao Shiyan (1901–27), with a magnetic personality and organizational ability, was instrumental in forming the ECCO and was elected its first general secretary. Zhou Enlai (1898–1976), who served as the second general secretary, developed the ECCO into a dynamic force within the Chinese community in Europe.

The fourth leader to be examined is Wang Guangqi, an apolitical intellectual. Outside the ECCO were youth who engaged in a wide range of political activities. Some followed the road of social democracy or fascism. Others took the more traditional routes of social reform, rejecting an explicit political path to salvation. Among the most poignant and enigmatic of the apolitical youth was Wang Guangqi (1892–1936), our exuberant youthful poet. A founder of the Shaonian Zhongguo xuehui (Young China Study Association) and the Gongdu huzhu tuan (Work-Study Mutual-Aid Corps), Wang was a key activist during the New Culture era. While writing prolifically on Chinese national salvation, Wang studied music in Germany, where he settled as an instructor at the University of Bonn. He died there in 1936.

Due to the dynamism and rich tapestry of the New Culture Movement, there are many Chinese leaders who deserve scholarly attention. Whereas this chapter examines the development of these four leaders, the next chapter will study a wide array of Chinese youth during their European sojourn. The historical development of ECCO formation can be understood in its full political and social significance by exploring the development of political leadership and organizational linkages during the New Culture era, followed by a broader survey of the social history of the Work-Study Movement.

This chapter focuses on two dimensions of political leadership: personality and organizational networks.[2] By looking at personality, including socioeconomic, regional, and educational background, insight into later political response can be gained. As Lewis Edinger suggests, "In politics, as in other interpersonal relationships, the degree to which an actor is inwardly or outwardly oriented is a function of personality. . . . His response to situational stimuli may be more or less automatic because his actions are narrowly circumscribed by the situational context or rigidly structured by his personality characteristics. But it may also result from a considered choice among the alternatives open to him in the light of available information."[3]

2. Personality and organization are two of the six explanatory variables that Glenn Paige has proposed in his study of political leadership. The other four variables are role, task, values, and setting. According to Paige, "They are posited as sources of explanation for the emergence, functioning, change and decline of whatever patterns of political leadership behavior are taken as the focus of analytical attention" (*The Scientific Study of Political Leadership* [New York: Free Press, 1977], 104).

3. Lewis J. Edinger, "Political Science and Political Biography," in Glenn D. Paige, ed., *Political Leadership: Readings for an Emerging Field* (New York: Free Press, 1972), 232.

All four leaders—Wang Guangqi, Cai Hesen, Zhao Shiyan, and Zhou Enlai—were principal actors in forming several of the most influential New Culture youth organizations: the Young China Study Association, the New Citizens' Study Society, the Self-Awakening Society, and the Work-Study Mutual-Aid Corps. These organizations represented a broad range of New Culture values and stretched from northern to southern China. The numerous organizations during the New Culture era played several crucial roles for the Chinese youth: as places of discussion and debate, as centers of radical action, and as places of refuge from family and educational pressures. Group affiliations, personal relationships, the ultimate expansion of regional outlooks, programs of action, and ideological dialogues contributed to the transformation of Chinese radical politics. Before the discipline of political party formation, organizational development was inextricably linked with the personalities of Chinese youth leaders.

Individual histories, including personal and organizational experiences, are more than facts for the curious. In Chinese political culture, personal ties and regional and organizational affiliations keenly influence behavior and are worthy of scholarly attention. Politics does not take place in a personal vacuum. As youthful revolutionaries, the Chinese who went to Europe were certainly more concerned with the future than the past. Yet they could neither break free from the influence of their own early training nor escape from their sense of immediacy. Thus, background factors such as personal ties and organizational affiliations are important in understanding how Wang Guangqi, Cai Hesen, Zhao Shiyan, and Zhou Enlai made their political commitments.

WANG GUANGQI AND THE YOUNG CHINA ETHIC

Wang Guangqi, perhaps the most ardent advocate of the Chinese youth renaissance, was born in Chengdu, Sichuan, in 1892.[4] Wang Guangqi's family was well known because his grandfather was a famous Sichuanese poet. Wang's

---

4. Li Wen and Bi Xing, eds., *Wang Guangqi nianpu* [A chronology of Wang Guangqi] (Beijing: Renmin yinyue chubanshe, 1987); Li Wen, Bi Xing, and Zhu Zhou, eds., *Wang Guangqi yanjiu lunwenji* [Collected essays of studies on Wang Guangqi] (Chengdu: Wang Guangqi yanjiu xueshu taolunhui, 1985); Guo Zhengzhao and Lin Ruiming, *Wang Guangqi de yisheng yu Shaonian Zhongguo xuehui: Wusi ren de beiju xingxiang ji qi fenxi* [An analysis of the life of Wang Guangqi and the Young China Study Association: A model of May Fourth tragedy] (Hong Kong: Baijie, 1978); Li Yipin, "Wang Guangqi," in Zong Zhiwen and Zhu Xinxian, eds., *Minguo renwu zhuan* [Biographies of the Republican period] (Beijing: Zhonghua shuju, 1981), 3:326–32. The biography by Zuo Shunsheng, written in 1936, claims Wang was born in 1891 (Zuo Shunsheng, "Wang Guangqi xiansheng shilue" [A narrative of Mr. Wang Guangqi], in Shen Yunlong, ed., *Wang Guangqi xiansheng jinian ce* [A commemoration of Mr. Wang Guangqi] [Shanghai: Wenhai, 1936], 188:1–14).

father died while he was an infant, and in 1914, his mother and brother died too.[5] Supported by his maternal uncle, Wang entered a private school at the age of nine. After the abolition of the examination system, Wang was sent to a Westernized elementary and high school in Chengdu, where he graduated in 1912 at the age of twenty. Other famous Sichuanese activists such as Li Jieren, Zhou Taixuan, and Zeng Qi attended the same school. According to Guo Zhengzhao and Lin Ruiming, Wang was married while still in Chengdu. His wife bore him two children, who died in infancy.[6]

In 1913 Wang went to study in Beijing, graduating in legal administration in 1918. While in Beijing, Wang worked as a journalist and as a secretary in the Office of Qing History to support himself.[7] Thus, in the pattern of his era, Wang began with a traditional education, but the largest part of his schooling was linked with Western learning. Deprived of his father and working his way as a journalist through college, Wang could identify firsthand with the New Culture Movement values of self-sufficiency and aggressiveness.

During his years in Beijing, Wang Guangqi immersed himself in the intellectual and organizational flow of the New Culture Movement. Although Wang was to become well known for his European essays, it was his support for the Young China Study Association that provided the most important orientation for his lifelong ideals. "The most worthwhile thing to recall about Mr. Wang Guangqi was that he founded and supported the Young China Study Association," exclaimed Wang's friend Zhou Taixuan at a memorial service for Wang in 1936.[8] This was a view shared by Wang's other friends.

The Young China Study Association, informally founded in 1918, was a vibrant part of the New Culture Movement. The major impetus behind the organization was a nucleus of Sichuanese intellectuals that included Wang Guangqi, Zeng Qi, Chen Yusheng, and Zhou Taixuan. However, the group was also supported by intellectuals from other regions, including prominent men like Li Dazhao (who was also a founder).[9]

---

5. Li Jieren, "Shiren zhisun" [Descendant of the poet], in Shen Yunlong, ed., *Wang Guangqi xiansheng jinian ce*, 18.

6. Guo Zhengzhao and Lin Ruiming, *Wang Guangqi de yisheng*, 10. The authors further assert that later Wang fell in love with another woman before leaving for Europe, but as a feminist he would not act upon his emotions since he was already married. I have seen scattered evidence and some allusions to this episode, and it seems as if Wang was depressed before his departure for Europe.

7. Ibid., 14–15; Li Yipin, "Wang Guangqi," 326.

8. Zhou Taixuan, "Mr. Wang Guangqi and the Young China Study Association," in Shen Yunlong, ed., *Wang Guangqi xiansheng jinian ce*, 19.

9. Zhou Taixuan, "Guanyu canjia faqi Shaonian Zhongguo xuehui de huiyi" [Remem-

In an article published in the second issue of *Shaonian Zhongguo* (August 1919), Wang Guangqi wrote about the goals and immediate tasks of the group. He conceptualized the Young China Study Association as the harbinger of a cultural revolution in Chinese society that had to precede any serious political revolution. He advocated a new lifestyle for the development of a "Young China." First, Young China must be creative, not just imitate the past or the West. Second, Young China must exercise its social responsibilities and not just base itself on the family system. Mutual systems of support should be developed within society, with a broadening of relationships (e.g., between intellectuals and workers). Third, Young China must adopt a scientific approach to all facets of reform. Wang divided the immediate tasks into two categories: (1) the tasks of inculcating revolutionary thought, which was to be brought about through increased education, publications, and newspaper development; and (2) the tasks of individual lifestyle reform that would correct unnatural lifestyles (those imposed by the family and the military system) and disorderly lifestyles (everyone must have articulated goals and time schedules). In his conclusion, Wang summed up the goal of the Young China Study Association in the motto "Our association dedicates itself to Social Services under the guidance of the Scientific Spirit, in order to realize our ideal of creating a Young China."[10] It is notable that the Young China Study Association stated goal of inculcating the scientific spirit contrasted with the revolt of Western youth against the materialist society engendered by science and technology.[11]

The Young China Study Association was organized more formally and expanded in a meeting on 1 July 1919.[12] Membership was obtained by an introduction from five members and approval by an advisory board. One had to not only live a virtuous and civic-minded life, believe in the values of struggle, practicality, firmness, and economy, but also participate in

---

brances of participating in the founding of the Young China Study Association], in Zhang Yunhou, Yan Xuyi, Hong Qingxiang, and Wang Yunkai, comps., *Wusi shiqi de shetuan* [The organizations of the May Fourth period], 4 vols. (Beijing: Sanlian, 1979), 1:536–49.

10. Wang Guangqi, "Shaonian Zhongguo zhi chuangzao" [The creation of the Young China Study Association], *Shaonian Zhongguo* 2 (19 August 1919): 1–7. As if to emphasize his seriousness, Wang's ending quote is totally in English.

11. Much of the zeal and many of the values and aspirations that young patriots like Wang Guangqi typified were similar to those of another era of American history and remind one of the writings of Benjamin Franklin.

12. Chow Tse-tsung, *The May Fourth Movement: Intellectual Revolution in Modern China* (Cambridge: Harvard University Press, 1960), 80; Chan Lau Kit-chang, *The Chinese Youth Party, 1923–1945*, Centre of Asian Studies Occasional Papers and Monographs, no. 9 (Hong Kong: University of Hong Kong, 1972), 3.

some area of study. There was a strong educational bias in the Young China Study Association.[13]

The association served as an important forum among intellectuals in their initial search for national salvation. The association had over one hundred members and published journals in Beijing, Nanjing, and Shanghai. The journals dealt with specific issues such as religious intrusion into Chinese education and the feminist movement and published important discussions of various social theories such as Marxism.

Li Huang's memoirs show us the informal nature of the Young China Study Association's meetings that he attended at Chen Yusheng's home: "Yusheng was a typical Sichuanese, fond of eating, fond of guests, indulging in high-flown talk [haochi haoke hao gaotan kuolun]. Thus, each week prepared food would be left to eat. After we discussed association business, we members would congregate and eat, casually talking, becoming very well acquainted with each other."[14] The association stimulated both serious discussions and close friendships.

It was through the vehicle of the Young China Study Association discussions and programs that individual differences began to emerge. This was in spite of the best intentions of Wang Guangqi, who did not want the association to espouse one particular doctrine but to unify different perspectives in order to bring about a new China. This could not be successful for long, and after 1921, when Li Dazhao, along with Chen Duxiu, began the formation of the CCP, the rift became increasingly wider, and the association became divided. The compromises at the yearly meetings were ineffectual and the group could not be revived after 1925.[15]

Wang's other important area of political involvement in Beijing was the promotion of the Work-Study Mutual-Aid Corps. Several branches of this Utopian-Anarchist ideal community were established in 1920 countrywide. The organizational plan was for students to live together, working six hours a day to provide for the common living expenses and going to school or studying for three hours. Wang Guangqi, as the main promoter of the Work-Study Mutual-Aid Corps scheme, demarcated the goals, which were to eradicate family dependence and free young Chinese from the "repression" of the family system. He asserted that students could overcome daily study problems, financial disparity, and hardships by mutual effort. Intel-

---

13. "Shaonian Zhongguo xuehui guiyue" [Regulations of the Young China Study Association], in Shaonian Zhongguo xuehui zhounian jinian ce [The Yearbook of the Young China Study Association] (1920), 33–39. I would like to thank Spencer Chin for giving me a photocopy of this document.

14. Li Huang, "Xuedunshi huiyilu," Zhuanji wenxue 16 (April 1970): 10.

15. Chan Lau Kit-chang, The Chinese Youth Party, 10.

lectuals would be nourishing healthy labor habits.[16] The combination of labor, education, and communal sharing was to forge a "new lifestyle."[17]

Established intellectuals such as Cai Yuanpei, Hu Shi, and Li Dazhao were very supportive of the new venture, contributing funds and ideas. Cai believed that mutual aid could help overcome educational inequality by giving an advanced education to those who otherwise could not afford one. He also thought that physical work (by scholars) was important to the development of equality and the evolution of a better society.[18]

Zhou Taixuan contended that the Work-Study Mutual-Aid Corps was "proof" to the critics that the whole concept of the Work-Study Movement was possible. The corps was a testing ground for those who could not afford to go overseas. The principle was the same: students could unify and overcome economic handicaps.[19]

Both male and female sections of the Work-Study Mutual-Aid Corps were established in several cities. Over 120 people participated.[20] Unfortunately, the experiments were disbanded after only a few months. Many reasons were given for the failure. A wide-ranging debate tended to either blame the inefficiency of the students[21] or the evils of a Capitalist system.[22]

Wang Guangqi's own analysis of the Work-Study Mutual-Aid Corps's failure stressed neither the impracticality of the scheme nor the overall economic context. He wrote, "It is a problem of people, not an economic

16. This value of mutual aid is a concrete example of the Anarchist influence on Chinese youth. According to Li Yipin, Wang was very attracted to the mutual aid writings of Kropotkin ("Wang Guangqi," 3:328–30).

17. Wang Guangqi, "Gongdu huzhu tuan," *Shaonian Zhongguo* (15 January 1920), in *FuFa,* 1:277–90. Wang includes the rationale, eighteen guidelines for the organization, and charts of projected expenses. For a general discussion of the Work-Study Mutual-Aid Corps see Guo Sheng, *Wusi shiqi de gongdu yundong he gongdu sichao,* 44–58, and Deng Ye, "Wusi shiqi de gongdu huzhu zhuyi ji qi shijian" [The ideology and practice of mutual aid during the May Fourth period], *Zhongguo xiandaishi fuyin baokan ziliao* 23 (1982): 9–15. Guo Sheng specifically states that Wang Guangqi was the major force behind the Work-Study Mutual-Aid Corps (49).

18. Cai Yuanpei, "Gongxue huzhu tuan de da xiwang" [The great hope of the Work-Study Mutual-Aid Corps], *Shaonian Zhongguo* (15 January 1920), in *FuFa,* 1:291–93; also cf. 294–96, where Cai Yuanpei discusses the relationship between the Work-Study Mutual-Aid Corps and the Work-Study Movement.

19. Zhou Taixuan, "Guonei zhi gongdu huzhu tuan" [The country's Work-Study Mutual-Aid Corps], *Lü Ou zhoukan* (20 March 1920), in *FuFa,* 1:302–4.

20. Guo Sheng, *Wusi shiqi de gongdu yundong he gongdu sichao,* 49.

21. E.g., see Hu Shi, "Gongdu zhuyi shixing de guancha" [An examination of the practice of work-study], *Xin qingnian* 7 (April 1920): 1–4.

22. See the essays of Yang Xianjiang, "Gongdu huzhu yu qingong jianxue" [The Work-Study Mutual-Aid Corps and the Work-Study Movement] (January 1923), in *FuFa,* 1:300–301; and [Shi] Cuntong, "Gongdu huzhu tuan de shiyan he jiaoxun" [The experiences and lessons of the Work-Study Mutual-Aid Corps], *Xingqi pinglun* (May 1920), in ibid., 1:324–43. Both Yang and Shi later joined the CCP.

problem." In Wang's estimation, future requirements for project implementation would have to include full understanding of the goals and necessities of the Work-Study Mutual-Aid Corps and the ability to practice these necessities (*ji neng liaojie, you neng shixing*). In response to the scorn critics had heaped on his hopes for a new lifestyle, Wang claimed that the corps had "by its very existence forged a new lifestyle . . . it had thus already taken place." Although Wang Guangqi affirmed his belief in the practicality of the Work-Study Mutual-Aid Corps, he held himself responsible for the debacle, apologizing fully for his lack of insight in recognizing the characteristics necessary for the organization.[23]

As a tangible manifestation of the social and political polemics of the New Culture Movement, the Work-Study Mutual-Aid Corps served to delineate for its members attitudes and, for some, commitments. Some scholars, such as Hu Shi, became more entrenched in their opposition to collectivist programs and ideologies. At the other pole, scholars such as Li Dazhao and Shi Cuntong became committed to a more activist policy, enlarging their vision of the scope of needed societal change and their own role in the drama. Between these two poles were others, like Zhao Shiyan, who were not disillusioned by the failure of the Work-Study Mutual-Aid Corps and participated in the Work-Study Movement.

Wang Guangqi was a key actor in the Young China Study Association and the Work-Study Mutual-Aid Corps, and he also became a proponent of work-study abroad and left for Germany in the spring of 1920. However, after 1920 Wang never repeated his role as a leading activist although he became a contributor to the ongoing dialogue on societal change. In his preface to *Shaonian Zhongguo yundong*, Wang claimed to have written over 300 articles from 1920 through 1924. In almost all of his writings he never cast off a special insularity, the label of "our generation" (*wubei*), of a "Young China." Wang never abandoned the ethos of the Young China Study Association. In a very real sense Wang Guangqi never emerged beyond the borders of the generational crisis and the ideology of youth.

CAI HESEN, THE THEORIST

Although he did not have the ebullient personality of Mao Zedong, his best friend in the Hunan First Normal Middle School, the names of Cai Hesen

---

23. Wang Guangqi, "Wei shenma bu neng shixing gongdu huzhu zhuyi" [Why the doctrine of work-study mutual-aid was not able to be practiced], *Xin qingnian* 7 (April 1920): 13–15. In an age when everyone was staunchly defensive, Wang's article is notable for its sincere apologetic tone. One should also note the Confucian stress on personal reformation as the key to organization.

and Mao Zedong were often linked. There was a common saying among the students of Hunan: "Hesen is the theorist; Runzhi [Mao] is the practitioner."[24] Cai's letters from France to his compatriots in China were full of his new Marxist-Leninist ideas, gleaned from the French newspapers.[25] Cai Hesen was on the CCP Central Committee as early as 1922, becoming the revolutionary agitator par excellence and editing the CCP journal Xiangdao (The Guide). He was instrumental in the strategic planning of the May Thirtieth Incident. (A series of strikes after Chinese workers were killed by foreign powers, the May Thirtieth Incident was the turning point of mass political participation in China.) In 1931, sternly obeying orders, Cai Hesen went to certain death in Hong Kong. During the transitional period of the early twenties, he served as a theoretical agitator, helping to stimulate ideological debate in France and promoting the development of the ECCO.

Cai's lineage included both scholars and merchants. On the maternal side there was a secretary to the famous suppressor of the Taiping Rebellion, Zeng Guofan. On the paternal side there was a family business that produced Yongfeng Chili Sauce. Cai's father, Cai Rongfeng, was ineffectual in the family business and through connections obtained a job in the Jiangnan Arsenal in Shanghai, where Cai was born in 1895, the fifth of six children.[26]

While Wang Guangqi's fatherless childhood was a result of premature death, Cai Hesen spent a fatherless childhood because his mother, Ge Jianhao, left her husband shortly after the birth of their sixth child, Cai Chang. Taking the baby and her youngest son, Cai Hesen, Ge Jianhao returned to Hunan. When Cai Rongfeng quit his job and followed, Ge refused to live with him.[27]

Cai's childhood was marked by extreme poverty, and he had to rebel against traditional patterns in several ways to obtain an education. His father's family apprenticed him for three years to the family business, which he detested, and he was ultimately supported by Ge Jianhao in his decision

24. Li Weihan, "Huiyi Xinmin xuehui," 54.

25. These letters are reproduced in Cai Hesen, Cai Hesen wenji [The collected works of Cai Hesen] (Beijing: Renmin chubanshe, 1980), and explored in some detail in Robert A. Scalapino, "The Evolution of a Young Revolutionary—Mao Zedong in 1919–1921," Journal of Asian Studies 1 (November 1982): 50–56; and Leung, "The Chinese Work-Study Movement," 334–49.

26. Luo Shaozhi, Li Peicheng, He Guozhi, and Yu Danyang, "Cai Hesen," in Hu Hua, ed., Zhonggong dangshi renwu zhuan [Biographies of personalities in Chinese Communist Party history] (Shaanxi: Shaanxi renmin chubanshe, 1980), 6:1–46; Huiyi Cai Hesen [Remembrances of Cai Hesen] (Beijing: Renmin chubanshe, 1980).

27. According to Cai Hesen's son, Cai Bo, who spent his earliest years with his grandmother Ge, the reason for this separation was that Ge could not tolerate Cai Rongfeng's having a "second wife" (Cai Bo interview, 4 October 1985 [Beijing]).

to go to school, refusing another apprenticeship term. Ge sold many of her own possessions so that Cai could study. At one point in Cai's studies, his younger sister, Cai Chang, was supporting their household, which also included an older sister and her child, as well as Ge Jianhao and Cai Hesen.[28]

Plagued by asthma and a poor family situation, Cai Hesen was self-taught when at the age of sixteen he managed to attend elementary school. Cai was three years older than Wang Guangqi when the latter began elementary school, and Wang had also taken private school (*sishu*) instruction. Although he was ridiculed as an older student, Cai Hesen excelled in his studies and by 1913 was enrolled in high school at the progressive Hunan First Normal Middle School. He subsequently attended a teaching college, where he graduated in 1917.[29] Cai was exposed to Western subjects, but he preferred Chinese traditional texts until after 1917, according to the diary of his good friend Zhang Kundi.[30]

During his formal education, Cai had developed several close relationships with other politically minded youth, such as Mao Zedong, Xiao Zisheng, Zhang Kundi, Luo Xuezan, Chen Chang, and Xiao Zizhang. They studied together, discussed the issues of the day, took trips around the province, and eventually formed the New Citizens' Study Society (Xinmin xuehui). It was in Cai Hesen's home that the New Citizens' Study Society was formed in April 1918. Dedicated to personal reformation, the society quickly evolved into a forum of political debate for the progressive youth in Hunan. The original group numbered fourteen. After the May Fourth Movement there were between sixty and seventy members.[31] Similar to the regulations of the Young China Study Association, if one wanted to join the New Citizens' Study Society one had to be introduced by five members and investigated by an advisory committee, and an announcement had to be made to the entire membership. The moral requirements were a mix-

28. Luo Shaozhi et al., "Cai Hesen," 6:3–5; Cai Bo interview, 4 October 1985 (Beijing). Cai Bo confirmed that his aunt Cai Chang had supported the household, but he claimed that Xiao Zisheng had not aided Cai Hesen, as Xiao claims in his book (Siao Yu [Xiao Zisheng], *Mao Tse-tung and I Were Beggars* [New York: Syracuse University Press, 1959], 47). It should be noted that in some ways Xiao Zisheng has the advantage: he knew Cai Hesen for several years, whereas Cai Bo had no opportunity to develop a relationship with his father because he was raised by relatives and because both his parents (his mother was Xiang Jingyu, the first head of the CCP Women's Bureau) were killed during his childhood.

29. Luo Shaozhi et al., "Cai Hesen," 6:2–3; Cai Hesen, *Cai Hesen wenji*, 833.

30. See Xu Deheng's memoir of Cai in *Huiyi Cai Hesen*, 34, where he quotes from Zhang Kundi's diary about Cai's intellectual preoccupations.

31. Li Weihan, "Huiyi Xinmin xuehui," 18–20, 25–27. Some of the most famous CCP leaders were New Citizens' Study Society members, such as Mao Zedong, Cai Hesen, Xiang Jingyu, Cai Chang, Li Fuchun, Li Weihan, Zhang Kundi, Luo Zhanglong, and Luo Xuezan.

ture of traditional values and the "new" concerns and behavioral norms of the day for youth. A member had to lead a pure life, be absolutely sincere, have a spirit of struggle, and serve the truth (later these last two changed to possession of a progressive attitude).[32] In addition there were prohibitions against arrogance, laziness, spendthrift ways, gambling, and visiting prostitutes.[33] Luo Zhanglong's account of the New Citizens' Study Society depicted three overall trends in the activities of the members. They participated in the "thought revolution" that was sweeping China; most of the members tried to improve their physical condition; and they gained revolutionary experience.[34] Revolutionary experience was gained by active participation in ongoing social movements and antigovernmental activities.

One facet of the New Citizens' Study Society that was not so evident in the Young China Study Association was an emphasis on female participation; a substantial number of women joined. Of forty new members who joined the society during the May Fourth Movement, Li Weihan tells us that almost half were women.[35]

Although most accounts of early CCP history tend to focus on the role of Cai Hesen and Mao Zedong, there was an equally prominent member of the New Citizens' Study Society who deserves attention. This was the society's first president and the most influential person in the Work-Study Movement: Xiao Zisheng.[36] Xiao was a teacher at Chuyi Elementary School and was known for his analytical and organizational abilities. In early 1919 he left for France and wrote a series of articles telling of his experiences and giving advice to those who would follow.[37]

---

32. "Xinmin xuehui huiwu baogao" [Report of the affairs of the New Citizens' Study Society] (Winter 1920), in FuFa, 2:3–7.

33. Li Weihan, "Huiyi Xinmin xuehui," 20.

34. Luo Zhanglong, "Huiyi Xinmin xuehui: You Hunan dao Beijing" [Reminiscences of the New Citizens' Study Society: From Hunan to Beijing], in Yida qianhou, 2:261–66.

35. Li Weihan, "Huiyi Xinmin xuehui," 25–27.

36. I find it particularly interesting that Xiao's younger brother Xiao Zizhang (Xiao San) does not even mention his brother's name in his account of the New Citizens' Study Society. Both Li and Luo mention Xiao Zisheng. E.g., see Xiao Zizhang, "Huiyi fu Fa qingong jianxue he lü Ou zhibu" [Remembering the travel to France Work-Study Movement and the ECCO], in Yida qianhou, 2:511–16.

37. Xiao Zisheng has several articles in Zhang Yunhou, Yan Xuyi, and Li Junchen, comps., Liu Fa qingong jianxue yundong; see the articles on 1:196–97, 221–31, among others. Xiao later worked in the Ministry of Education and was closely associated with Li Shizeng. After 1949 he went to Europe and then to Uruguay, where he tended an enormous library Li had transferred there. Xiao later wrote Mao Tse-tung and I Were Beggars (under the pseudonym Siao Yu), an account of their school days. He also wrote another autobiographical work (under the pseudonym Xiao Yu), Huiyi wode xiaoshi liaoliao [Memories of my

In addition to his position as president of the New Citizens' Study Society, Xiao became an SFEA secretary and favorite of Li Shizeng. A 1919 report in *Dagong bao* (Hunan) mentioned contacts who could help those who wanted to participate in the Work-Study Movement: "There is Mr. Xiao Xudong [Zisheng]. He is a Hunanese and has obtained the trust of Mr. Li [Shizeng], all public communication and pronouncements coming from his [Xiao's] pen."[38]

Although some Hunanese youth did participate in the Work-Study Mutual-Aid Corps, their basic effort went into promoting the New Culture Movement and the Work-Study Movement. The leaders of the New Citizens' Study Society were the most active youth in Hunan promoting the programs of both movements. Xiao Zisheng, Cai Hesen, and Mao Zedong were names known by most Hunanese youth who wanted to travel overseas.[39] Eventually, one-third of the membership (eighteen people) left for France.

Cai Hesen's efforts were important to both the New Citizens' Study Society and the Work-Study Movement. In June 1918, he went as an advance guard to Beijing to find out more about the Work-Study Movement for his fellow society members. Cai was intrigued with the sponsors of the movement and was pleasantly surprised by Cai Yuanpei and Li Shizeng, remarking that "Mr. Jiemin [Cai Yuanpei] is, as it is said, particularly trustworthy [*youzu xinshi*]."[40] Later that summer, over two dozen of his New Citizens'

---

youth] (Taiwan: Yiwen, 1969), which begins with his birth. A person of well-rounded capabilities, somehow Xiao never emerged as the leader his early career suggested.

38. "Guanyu Hunan liu Fa qingong jianxue xuesheng renshu ji Bali Hua Fa jiaoyuhui de jieshao" [The number of Hunanese students participating in the travel to France Work-Study Movement, and an introduction to the Sino-French Educational Association] (19 July 1919), in Hunan sheng zhexue shehui kexue yanjiusuo xiandaishi yanjiushi [Hunan Provincial Center for Philosophy and Social Sciences—the Modern History Research Unit], *Wusi shiqi Hunan renmin geming douzheng shiliao xuanbian* [Selected materials on the May Fourth period and the revolutionary struggles of the Hunanese] (Changsha: Hunan renmin chubanshe, 1979), 426–27. Xiao Zisheng was eager to help his friends, and they did rely on him for his connections. Two female members of the New Citizens' Study Society, Lao Junzhan (Qi Rong), who later married the famous activist Xu Deheng, and Wei Bi, were having difficulty dealing with the Shanghai Sino-French Educational Association and wrote to Run Zhi (Mao Zedong) and Ji Bo (Peng Huang) how Zisheng made them feel more secure. "Mr. Xiao Zisheng returned, so we were more reassured. Today we went to see Mr. Xiao Zisheng and spoke for three hours, informally discussing the situation in France. It really is extremely exciting" (Lao Junzhan and Wei Bi letter to Mao Zedong and Peng Huang, September 1920, in ibid., 43–44).

39. This is not an exaggeration. See Lai Jinghu, "Minchu shidai de Hunan qingnian," 37–41.

40. Cai Hesen letter to Xiao Xudong (Zisheng), July 1918, in *Cai Hesen wenji*, 3. This is an interesting remark given the events that would transpire a few years later, when Cai

Study Society comrades also came to Beijing to prepare themselves to participate in the Work-Study Movement. Cai was fired up with enthusiasm and before they arrived wrote of his aspirations to "create a free personality, a free position, and free enterprises."[41]

Cai became a Chinese tutor in one of the preparatory schools and roomed with Shen Yijia from October 1918 until February 1919. During this time Shen remembers that Cai was a believer in Mozi but began to seriously explore Marxist doctrine because of the success of the Russian Revolution.[42] Cai and Shen carried on animated debates that alienated Shen because he was very anti-Russian.[43] However, it should be noted that Cai was not a Marxist before he left the shores of China and that his ideological sophistication, like that of most other revolutionaries, took some time to develop.[44]

In December 1919, Cai Hesen left for France, accompanied by both his younger sister, Cai Chang, and his mother, Ge Jianhao, who was then in her midfifties. The Chinese press praised Ge Jianhao highly for her open-mindedness and spirit. On the trip to France, Cai fell in love with Xiang Jingyu (1895–1928), a fellow Hunanese and New Citizens' Study Society member, and they progressed both in their pursuit of a free relationship and in their burgeoning commitment to radical politics. As Liu Ang, a niece of Cai Hesen who wrote to the couple during this period recounts:

> On the long journey [to France], Comrade Jingyu and Comrade Hesen often discussed theories and political problems. They discussed ideals to their hearts' content. Their ambitions were the same, and there was mutual adoration. In the China of that period, a free romance was looked upon as an offense against public decency. But Comrade Jingyu did not concern herself with this and made their romance public. They wrote a poem, "The Progressive Alliance" [Xiangshang tongmeng], to express that they wanted to mutually progress forward on the road to

Hesen would feel abandoned and betrayed by Cai Yuanpei. Cai went on to say how he envied Cai Yuanpei his many talents.

41. Cai Hesen letter, 24 July 1918, in FuFa, 2:10.

42. The predisposition toward Mozi and the admiration of a Leninist party structure are not necessarily exclusive attitudes. Mozi was a philosopher during the chaos of the Zhou Dynasty Warring States Period and, in contrast to Confucius, deemphasized ritual. Mozi saw the responsibility of the individual to the group in terms of utilitarian, pragmatic group action. Mozi's utilitarian concern with social justice, tendency to a materialist view of society, and organizational emphasis are all traits of Marxism-Leninism.

43. Shen Yijia, "Wo suo zhidao de zaoqi zhi Cai Hesen" [The Cai Hesen I knew during his early period], in Huiyi Cai Hesen, 135–40.

44. E.g., see the essay by Zheng Xuejia, "Xinmin xuehui," in Chen Sanjing, comp., Qingong jianxue yundong, 612–28.

revolution. In June 1920, Comrade Jingyu and Comrade Hesen were married in Montargis, France. I can see in their wedding picture that they are sitting together, shoulder to shoulder, both holding open a copy of *Das Kapital*, which was one of Comrade Jingyu's favorite Marxist works. This picture means that their union was established on a mutual belief in Marxism.[45]

In contrast to Wang Guangqi, the European sojourn was the catalyst that galvanized Cai Hesen to develop into a political activist. Cai became the most important influence on the development of Marxism in the Chinese community in France, and his articles and letters to his compatriots in China were effective. While Wang argued for the permanent mission of the Young China Study Association, Cai precipitated the debates in the summer of 1920 that split the New Citizens' Study Society, eventually leading to its disintegration.

ZHAO SHIYAN, THE ORGANIZER

Although born several years later than Wang Guangqi, Cai Hesen, and Zhou Enlai, Zhao Shiyan died earlier. Yet his political maturation was swifter, and his political acuity placed him among the most advanced of revolutionary leaders in the twentieth century. A group picture of the ECCO in 1923 shows Zhao sitting in a Western suit, cross-legged on the ground in front of some trees. He looks assured, relaxed, and slightly mischievous. This assurance and poise never deserted Zhao, as the circumstances of his capture and death in 1927 indicate. Surrounded by the Guomindang and knowing his chances of escape were minimal, in his last free moments Zhao told his wife, Xia Zhixu, to warn others and gave her the address of Wang Ruofei. It was a coolly calculated instance of self-sacrifice.

Zhao Shiyan was born in Youyang, Sichuan, on 13 April 1901. He was the last of five sons, with three older sisters and one younger sister. His father was a landlord and businessman.[46] As the youngest son, Zhao Shiyan was somewhat spoiled by his mother and older sisters, but he also was influ-

---

45. Liu Ang, "Huiyi jingai de Xiang Jingyu tongzhi" [Remembering beloved comrade Xiang Jingyu], in *Jinian Xiang Jingyu tongzhi yingyong jiuyi wushi zhounian* [Remembering comrade Xiang Jingyu on the occasion of the fiftieth anniversary of her fearless martyrdom] (Beijing: Renmin chubanshe, 1978), 8–9.

46. For biographies of Zhao see Peng Chengfu, *Zhao Shiyan* (Chongqing: Chongqing chubanshe, 1983), and her essay in Hu Hua, ed., *Zhonggong dangshi renwu zhuan*, 7:1–48. No author's name is attached to the essay, "Zhao Shiyan shengping shiliao," *Wenshi ziliao xuanji* (Beijing) 58 (1979):36–163. Many of Zhao Shiyan's writings are in *Zhao Shiyan xuanji* [Selected writings of Zhao Shiyan] (Chengdu: Sichuan renmin chubanshe, 1984).

enced by the exploits of his older brothers, the oldest one a member of the Revolutionary Alliance (Tongmenghui). After private-school tutoring, Zhao went to a Western-style elementary school from 1912 to 1914. Graduating from elementary school in 1914, Zhao left home with his next-oldest brother, Zhao Shikun, and attended the secondary school attached to Beijing Normal College. Aided financially by brother number three, they lived frugally in a *tongxiang* (same-province) dormitory. Zhao was far more outgoing than his older brother. While Shikun concentrated on his studies, Shiyan seemed to blossom in the capital. He was involved in everything from athletic competitions and political activities to mediating the personal problems of others. One of his nicknames was the "diplomatic officer" (*waijiao dachen*). Zhao Shiyan formed many contacts outside school. At the age of sixteen, he drew the notice of older activists such as Wang Guangqi, Li Dazhao, Zhou Taixuan, and Zeng Qi. Zhou characterized Zhao as a person adept at organizing, a "key individual" (*hexin renwu*).[47]

Zhao excelled in his studies, particularly in English. He served as a translator when the school had an English-speaking visitor and tutored his fellow students who were having difficulties. Although Zhao's school performance was outstanding, he adopted a critical attitude to the curriculum and pedagogical practices at his high school. In several articles he argued for a quicker pace and more diversity in the texts.[48] His brother Shikun initially opposed all of the extracurricular activities, but Zhao Shiyan apparently gained his acquiescence.[49]

Even as a teenager, Zhao Shiyan was a person of boundless energy and advanced organizational capacity. He was one of the youngest members admitted into the Young China Study Association, introduced by Wang Guangqi and Li Dazhao in July 1919.[50] He had connections with other youth groups, led his high school contingent during the May Fourth demonstrations, and edited three newspapers at the same time.

Zhao's involvement in the various organizations was not superficial. For example, he was the moving spirit behind the Youth Study Society (Shaonian xuehui), which he helped organize at his school. The twenty members of the Youth Study Society were the more progressive students at Zhao's

47. "Zhao Shiyan shengping shiliao," 38–42.
48. Zhao Shiyan, "Xuexiao bu ji sishu hao" [(High) school is not up to the level of the private school], *Gongdu* (February 1920), in *Zhao Shiyan xuanji*, 33–38; and idem, "Xuexiao diaocha: Beijing gaodeng shifan fushu zhong xuexiao" [An investigation of Beijing normal high school], *Shaonian shijie* (March 1920), in *Zhao Shiyan xuanji*, 39–50.
49. "Zhao Shiyan shengping shiliao," 40.
50. I could not find the announcement of Zhao's entry into the Young China Study Association, but based on later relationships, I think it likely that Zeng Qi was also a mentor and introduced Zhao into the association.

high school. Zhao was the impetus behind several of their activities. In addition to editing a society newspaper, he arranged for speakers and gave speeches himself, and after graduation he still encouraged others, writing to them from France. Eventually four members followed Zhao Shiyan to France.[51]

In 1919 Zhao's family moved to the capital. His activities were immediately labeled as radical by his brother Zhao Shijue. But again Zhao withstood the family storm and managed to slip his sisters progressive literature. Actually the family had some reason for concern, as one of Zhao's newspapers was closed down by the government, and he was put in jail briefly.

Writing on the eve of his own graduation, during the week of the May Fourth Movement, Zhao spoke of the necessity for his generation to struggle toward reforming the currently evil society, "living in today's world, dealing with the intensely evil society [wan e shehui], if we do not struggle, how can we become men?"[52] Constantly using the term wubei (our generation), like his mentor Wang Guangqi, the sensible Zhao Shiyan recommended relying on family support at least until graduation so that one could have both the intellectual and the physical capacity to take advantage of the Work-Study Movement. However, for wubei, the ultimate need was to become self-sufficient, not to rely on the family, not to blindly follow a road set out by one's fathers and brothers, not to allow oneself to be married early. Zhao believed that the Work-Study Movement would allow his generation to fight the traditional Chinese family system and enter into the competitive twentieth century. Paraphrasing a Western quotation, Zhao proclaimed, "The lexicon of glorious youth does not contain the word 'defeat'!"[53]

Deeply involved in the generational crisis, Zhao epitomized the aggressive values of the New Culture Movement. Although he had impeccable credentials, he did not take university entrance exams but went to a Shanghai preparatory school for the trip to France. After reaching France in mid-1920, Zhao devoted himself exclusively to factory work and Chinese labor causes. He was to oppose Cai Hesen in the Twenty-eighth Movement, and yet before the end of 1921, Zhao would be working with Cai and others to form a Marxist party.

51. Zhang Yunhou et al., eds., Wusi shiqi de shetuan, 3:71–96, includes a general history of the Youth Study Society as well as a letter from Zhao Shiyan about factory work in France and a memoir piece by Xia Kangnong.
52. Zhao Shiyan, "Gongdu zhuyi yu jinri zhi zhongxue biye sheng" [The philosophy of work-study and today's high school graduates], Beijing gaodeng shifan xuexiao zhoukan 9 (5 May 1919), in Zhang Yunhou, Yan Xuyi, and Li Junchen, comps., Liu Fa qingong jianxue yundong, 1:343.
53. Ibid., 341–44.

ZHOU ENLAI, THE SYNCRETIST

Zhou Enlai's reputation as a world-class statesman and a moderating force among competitive factions was the result of a lengthy political transition. Zhou Enlai was born in Huaian, Jiangsu, on 5 March 1898. His family came from Shaoxing, Zhejiang. Like Wang Guangqi, Zhou's family belonged to the scholar class. However, Zhou's father was so shiftless that his uncles insisted on taking control of Zhou's upbringing. Zhou's mother died when he was nine years old, leaving him in the care of his aunts.[54]

Like Cai Hesen, Zhou moved several times during his early childhood. He was sent to one of the more advanced schools that offered Western training, spending two years (from age twelve to age fourteen) in Fengtian. Next, he attended a high school in Nankai that was founded by the famous educator Zhang Boling. Zhou's experiences during his school years in Nankai exerted a strong influence on his political socialization. He participated in the full range of school activities, from debates and patriotic societies to poetry writing and starring in school productions. By the age of sixteen Zhou had published articles skeptical of the Yuan Shikai warlord government, and by the spring of 1917, on the eve of his graduation, Zhou was inviting prominent educators like Cai Yuanpei and Wu Yuzhang to lecture at local political clubs.[55]

In the fall of 1917, Zhou Enlai left for Japan, where he stayed until April 1919. His sojourn in Japan was not a very productive or happy period, although he received some introduction to socialism. In March 1918, Zhou failed the entrance exams to a special Japanese program for the Chinese.[56]

---

54. Hsu Kai-yu, *Chou En-lai: China's Gray Eminence* (New York: Doubleday, 1968), 8. Next to Mao, Zhou Enlai is the most researched Chinese leader, in both Chinese and Western sources. In terms of the Western sources, an in-depth biography is still needed, but Hsu's is the most scholarly. Among others are Li Tien-min, *Chou En-lai* (Taibei: Institute of International Relations, 1970); John McCook Roots, *Chou: An Informal Biography of China's Legendary Chou En-lai* (New York: Doubleday, 1978); Dick Wilson, *Zhou Enlai: A Biography* (New York: Viking, 1984). There are several articles and biographies in Chinese: Nankai daxue Zhou Enlai yanjiushi [Nankai University Zhou Enlai Research Institute], "Zhou Enlai qingshaonian shidai jishi" [A chronicle of Zhou Enlai's youth], *Tianjin wenshi ziliao xuanji* 15 (May 1981): 1–85; Wang Yongxiang and Liu Pinqing, *Weile Zhonghua zhi jueqi: Zhou Enlai qingnian shiqi de shenghuo yu douzheng* [Rising up for China: The early period of the life and struggles of Zhou Enlai] (Tianjin: Tianjin chubanshe, 1980); Huai En, *Zhou zongli de qing shaonian shidai* [Premier Zhou's early period] (Chengdu: Sichuan chubanshe, 1979). Finally, for some very interesting ideas, the following graduate theses should be consulted: Rhoda Sussman Weidenbaum, "Chou En-lai, Creative Revolutionary" (Ph.D. dissertation, University of Connecticut, 1981), and Tan Guoying, "Zhou Enlai yu zhonggong zhengquan zhi jianli" [Zhou Enlai and the establishment of power by the Communists] (Master's thesis, National Zhengzhi University, 1978).

55. Nankai daxue Zhou Enlai yanjiushi, "Zhou Enlai qingshaonian shidai jishi," 1–12.

56. "Zhou Enlai zai Riben" [Zhou Enlai in Japan], in *Zhou Enlai de sheng ziliao xuanji*

He participated in patriotic associations in Tokyo and Kyoto, while waiting until he could retake the examinations after one year, but never attempted a second examination. In April 1919, Zhou returned home, where he became one of the key May Fourth Movement leaders in Tianjin.

The young Zhou Enlai applauded the New Culture values of study abroad but urged moderation, not wholesale adoption of Western values. In an essay written at the age of seventeen, he stated that experiences should be studied, not just book learning. In the same essay Zhou identified the serious danger to China from internal problems of ethics and spirit, as manifested in the warlord system, and from external problems, such as imperialism (especially that of the Japanese). Before he left for Japan, Zhou had written that the Chinese people should have a system based on the power of the people, such as in a republic. Students had a definite responsibility to society and should maintain a constructive attitude to problems. His fellow activists should be firm in promoting their objectives.[57]

Like Wang, Cai, and Zhao, Zhou Enlai also immersed himself in youth organizations. He was a member of the Tianjin gejie lianhehui (United Tianjin Student Association) and edited the *Xuesheng lianhehui bao* (*The United Student Association Newspaper*). The circulation for this paper was over 20,000 copies.[58] Divided into eight sections, the paper refused to print Japanese advertisements and discussed issues such as the overturn of the Anfu warlord clique, the Versailles Conference, and female equality.[59]

Zhou Enlai was active not only in publishing but also in organizing the Self-Awakening Society (Juewushe), one of the most progressive youth groups to emerge from the New Culture Movement. Chen Xiaocen, a founding member of the Self-Awakening Society, recounts the moment when the society was conceived, 2 September 1919, while eight Tianjin students were standing on a railway platform, returning from political activities in Beijing. The eight people included five women (Zhang Ruoming; Deng Yingchao, who later married Zhou Enlai; Guo Longzhen; Zhou Zhilian; and Li Zhi, who later married Chen) and three men (Zhou Enlai, Guan Yiwen, and Chen Xiaocen). Chen's account is very vivid in its recollections of personalities: Guo Longzhen, a rather taciturn, shy woman

---

[Selected materials on the life of Zhou Enlai] (Hong Kong: Xin zhong tu hua, 1977), 17–19, 21. Both of the full-length PRC books on Zhou's early period overlook his examination failures.

57. Nankai daxue Zhou Enlai yanjiushi, "Zhou Enlai qingshaonian shidai jishi," 10–11, 17–18.

58. Deng Yingchao, "Wusi yundong de huiyi" [Reminiscences of the May Fourth Movement], in *Zhou Enlai de sheng ziliao xuanji*, 21.

59. Nankai daxue Zhou Enlai yanjiushi, "Zhou Enlai qingshaonian shidai jishi," 28–32.

who spoke rarely but to the point; Deng Yingchao, the youngest member, lively and outspoken like her friends and fellow Self-Awakening Society members Li Zhi and Liu Qingyang; and of course Zhou Enlai, who was remembered as a prime organizer, with strong leadership ability and endurance for long hours of work and sacrifice.

They held their first meeting on 10 September 1919, in the French concession, with twenty people attending (ten women and ten men). Their first set of goals was to unify the Tianjin students and especially encourage organizational efforts by women. Although patriotism marked the Self-Awakening Society in its first phase, its second phase, according to Chen, was oriented toward societal and self reform.[60]

The Self-Awakening Society was smaller than the New Citizens' Study Society and the Young China Study Association. However, it was particularly successful in its original purpose: drawing together the patriotic movement and integrating the women into the movement. The women of the Self-Awakening Society were half the membership and were as aggressive as their male counterparts in pursuing their political activities. Guo Longzhen and Deng Yingchao organized a public-speaking group and campaigned on street corners to encourage the spreading of strikes and the boycott of Japanese goods. Li Zhi was stabbed by the police in a demonstration, and Zhou Zhilian was hospitalized for injuries to her foot and back.[61]

The strength of the women in the Self-Awakening Society was further demonstrated when two women, Guo Longzhen and Zhang Ruoming, were incarcerated with Zhou Enlai in January 1920 when they all went to protest the imprisonment of other Tianjin students. They were held from late January until July 1920.[62] Liu Qingyang, one of the original twenty members, took over from Zhou Enlai. She traveled to Nanjing and Shanghai, communicating and organizing demonstrations with student groups in these locations in order to protest the incarceration of twenty-six Tianjin students. These demonstrations involved thousands of participants.[63]

The most fiery of the Self-Awakening Society members was Ma Jun, a young Moslem from Guilin. He was such a powerful speaker that he single-

60. Chen Xiaocen, "Juewushe ji qi chengyuan" [The Self-Awakening Society and its founders], Tianjin wenshi ziliao xuanji 15 (May 1981): 156–94.

61. Ma Huiqing, "Wusi yundong zai Tianjin" [The May Fourth Movement in Tianjin], Jindaishi ziliao 2 (April 1958): 94, 104.

62. Ibid., 102–10. Both Guo Longzhen and Zhang Ruoming were to go to France, and along with Zhou Enlai and Liu Qingyang, joined the ECCO. Guo went back to China and was killed while performing CCP activities; Zhang quit the Party shortly after Zhou Enlai left France and graduated from the University of Lyons in 1930 with a dissertation on André Gide. Liu Qingyang also quit the CCP but kept alive her political involvement.

63. Ibid., 106–7.

handedly convinced the merchants in Tianjin to resume their strike. The merchants had sympathized with the demonstrations and closed their shops but were persuaded by the authorities to reopen. At a public meeting, Ma Jun let forth a stream of impassioned rhetoric, declaring that he would gladly sacrifice his life to get them to strike. He ended his speech by pounding himself against a pillar and shedding his own blood. The astounded merchants, after stopping Ma Jun from hurting himself further, were very moved and closed their businesses the next day.[64]

Regarding the second set of priorities of the Self-Awakening Society, which in general terms could be described as developing one's political consciousness, Deng Yingchao stated that the results were indefinite. All that the members knew about the revolutionary tide in Russia was that Lenin was a revolutionary leader and that he worked for the liberation of the workers and peasants. There was no deep understanding of Marxism or belief in it as a political credo. "However," Deng continued in her account, "in actuality we did have a kind of spontaneous intuitive knowledge; in order to save the country we had to break through the circle of students, to save the country one could not rely solely on the students but must 'call upon our comrades in arms.'"[65]

Zhou later claimed that his jail experience was one of the most important spurs to his ultimate conversion to Marxism. Along with the other interned students, he participated in activities that were designed to raise one's political consciousness, such as studying and discussing various theories, especially Marxism. The interned students also celebrated holidays such as May First, a commemoration of the May Fourth Movement, and personal holidays, such as Guo Longzhen's birthday.[66]

Several months after his release from jail, Zhou Enlai left for France. Although his jail experience may have predisposed him to Marxism, the evidence indicates that Zhou was not a committed Marxist when he left the shores of China. In addition, the jail experience could not have failed to have also had a dampening effect on Zhou's spirits. He agreed to serve as a correspondent for a Catholic-sponsored newspaper when he reached France, hardly the mark of an active Marxist radical. It would be the three struggles of 1921 that would put Zhou Enlai, along with Cai Hesen and Zhao Shiyan, on the road to the ECCO.

64. Ibid., 88–89; Ma Jun was one of the Self-Awakening Society members who later became a Communist.

65. Deng Yingchao, "Wusi yundong de huiyi," in *Zhou Enlai de sheng ziliao xuanji*, 21.

66. Nankai daxue Zhou Enlai yanjiushi, "Zhou Enlai qingshaonian shidai jishi," 40–47.

THE LOST LAND OF BLISS

In his analysis of the Vietnamese maturation process, David Forrest stresses the dramatic change that takes place in the life of a male child in a Confucian culture once he reaches seven years old. Indulged for the first few years of life, at the age of six or seven, he must make an abrupt ascent into a sterner world, where the father establishes his absolute authority. Forrest studied Vietnamese fairy tales and legends and claims that there is an analogy between lost childhood freedoms and the legend of the Land of Bliss, where a never-changing utopia is lost because the traveler who stumbled on this paradise must return to pay homage to his ancestors and subsequently never finds his way back.[67] The demarcations of childhood and poignant longings to recapture the carefree innocence of childhood exist to some degree in all cultures. Forrest is discussing the normal course of child rearing in Confucian culture, but one wonders about the effect of never experiencing a land of bliss during childhood. In a very real sense, a longing for childhood purity may be more pronounced in a generation that was never allowed the luxury of an untroubled childhood. This may help us understand why the generational crisis between 1915 and 1922 was so acute. The younger generation's search went beyond ideology into the roots of their own perceived lack.

Early family, educational, and organizational experiences influenced Wang Guangqi, Cai Hesen, Zhao Shiyan, and Zhou Enlai in several important ways. First, for the orphaned Wang Guangqi and Zhou Enlai, for Cai Hesen raised by an open-minded mother, and for Zhao Shiyan, the indulged youngest son who was away from parental authority during his early teens, there were real opportunities to stretch beyond the normal constraints of family relationships. For example, this could have fostered more sensibility to feminist issues, which played a key part in the New Culture Movement. Cai Hesen was strongly supported financially by his sister and mother, both of whom accompanied him to France. Zhao Shiyan was able to send radical literature to two of his sisters, both of whom became ardent Communists.[68] Although one could view the disruptions of their childhoods as factors in potential social alienation, they did allow more behavioral scope for the liberating values of the New Culture Movement.

67. David V. Forrest, "Vietnamese Maturation: The Lost Land of Bliss," *Psychiatry* 34 (May 1971): 111–39. The Chinese have identical utopian myths.
68. Zhao Shiyan's older sister Zhao Shilan became a historian after 1949 and compiled a whole series of memoirs on Zhao Shiyan. Zhao's younger sister, Zhao Juntao, worked as an underground member of the CCP. Her husband was killed in 1930, leaving her with two children. One of these children, Li Peng, became the premier of China in 1987.

Second, Wang Guangqi, Cai Hesen, Zhao Shiyan, and Zhou Enlai shared in a transitional epoch in education during their childhoods. They all experienced Confucian training, "as if it counted for a career," and matriculation in progressive, Western-style schools. This dual educational experience was unique to this generation. The abolition of examinations in 1905 and the Revolution of 1911 displaced the standard paths to personal careers. Perhaps this lack of career direction and their education in two systems broadened their intellectual horizons. However, although Wang, Cai, Zhao, and Zhou all attended progressive Western schools, only Wang Guangqi continued his Western studies at a university level after reaching Europe. Interestingly, only Wang Guangqi insisted on the necessity for the intellectual, apolitical leadership of a social revolution.[69]

Third, organizational affiliations were particularly important in the personal and political development of New Culture youth. For Wang Guangqi, the ethos of the Young China Study Association never lost its value and meaning. He constantly affirmed his belief in the need for a Chinese cultural renaissance. In contrast, the New Citizens' Study Society, the Self-Awakening Society, and the Youth Study Society served as important first phases of activism, but they did not outlast the unity of the May Fourth era as creative bases for Cai Hesen, Zhao Shiyan, and Zhou Enlai. However, for each person, these youth organizations were crucial in several ways. The youth organizations were crucibles of New Culture values such as progressive, especially Western, learning, virtuous and assertive behavior, and the promotion of feminism. Moreover, the widespread publication of journals and debates set up a basis for future interregional cooperation among political activists. For example, members of the Self-Awakening Society and the Young China Study Association, such as Liu Qingyang and Zeng Qi, were well known among other youth organizers when they reached France. This was to provide them with later opportunities for political linkages. Finally, the organizations promoted friendships. Personal relationships were often strengthened in the organizational context by shared pledges, serious debates, political activities, lifestyle experimentations, and above all a common sense of urgency.

Looking at the complex and rich texture of the childhood and youth of this particular generation gives valuable insight into the characteristics that distinguished them and their ideological odyssey. Perhaps we can look with some sadness at these children who never experienced the land of bliss, who

---

69. Perhaps a systematic analysis of Chinese students abroad during this period would show that the higher the educational degree, the lower the incidence of revolutionary involvement.

did not enjoy the childhood serenity of their parents and elder siblings. The swelling post-1895 national insecurity and tremendous social change that marked each facet of their growth increased the alienation within their families, saddled them with the new responsibilities of Western learning, and left them to strive for definition in a plethora of youth groups and new intellectual currents. These factors distinguished this generation from those born in the 1870s, as well as from those who constituted the generation of the Cultural Revolution more than half a century later. However, in another sense, because they could not lose something that they had never experienced, there were no phantoms of remembered pleasures to chase, and they were more open to the treading of fresh pathways. If they were not mourning the lost land of bliss, these Chinese youth were turning toward an unknown land with high hopes of personal transformation and national salvation. They were traveling to a new world.

3

A NEW WORLD

If you are lucky enough to have lived in Paris as a young man, then wherever you go for the rest of your life, it stays with you, for Paris is a moveable feast.

—Ernest Hemingway, *A Moveable Feast*

People say, "There is nothing unusual that Paris does not have." This is indeed the truth. Because after the First World War, Paris became the international capital and, especially, the center of world culture. Everything happened in Paris; the source of everything was in Paris.

—Sheng Cheng, *Bali Yiyu* (Memories of Paris)

After two years working in the factories of France, Chen Yi, the future foreign minister of China, was willing to admit that the reality of traveling to France and working in a factory differed from his expectations.[1] This was not an uncommon admission for the young Chinese, who had such high, and perhaps unrealistic, hopes of their Western journey.

The previous chapter explored individual preludes to the French sojourn and the formation of youth groups. This chapter will take the next step and look at the broader group experiences. Whereas in the last chapter we examined the Chinese youth in a familiar, if rapidly changing, Chinese environment, this chapter will examine the Chinese youth experience in Western Europe. We will discuss various situational determinants and common new experiences for the worker-students, such as the impact of the Chinese Labor Corps, the effect of travel to a foreign country, the parameters of adaptation to French culture and what that process entailed, from factory labor to educational institutions, and the important question of intercultural impressions of both the Chinese and the French. Ultimately questions of cultural adaptation would become obscured by political pressures within the Chinese community and the increasing deterioration of the Work-Study Movement. However, at the outset, the general mental orientation of the Chinese youth was one of open-mindedness and sensitivity to a "New World." Self-professed explorers, they were gathering impressions and experiences and seeking new knowledge with desperate energy and excitement.

1. Chen Yi, "Wo liangnian lai lü Fa de tongku" [My two years of misery in France], *Shishi xinbao* (31 October 1921), in *FuFa*, 3:56.

One of the first lessons for the worker-students was that the "pioneers" of intercultural experience had really been the Chinese Labor Corps, Chinese workers who aided the Allies during the First World War. Thus, before further examining the Work-Study Movement aspirants, we need to discuss the significance of the Chinese Labor Corps.

WORKERS AS SOLDIERS: THE CHINESE LABOR CORPS

A Chinese Labor Corps (CLC) song from the First World War cast corps tasks in high ethical tones: "Marchons, marchons toujours! Les hommes sont frères. Une armée nombreuse de travailleurs se levé pour le labeur et reconstruira, pour toi, humanité, l'édifice de la Paix!"[2]

In his meticulous study of the CLC, Chen Sanjing makes the salient point that a demand for Chinese labor existed well before the outbreak of war.[3] A lower European birthrate and the proverbial industriousness of the Chinese created the demand for Chinese workers. After the outbreak of war in 1914, the Chinese government remained neutral, but influential leaders, especially those with strong French ties like the financial wizard Liang Shiyi (Liang Yansun), advocated the policy of sending workers instead of soldiers (yi gong dai bing), in order to support the Allies without committing military troops. According to Liang's rationale, making a contribution to the war effort would certainly give China some leverage in postwar negotiations.[4] The negotiations for Chinese labor by the French, British, and American governments were rather protracted, and the battalions did not go into service until 1917. But their numbers eventually grew to enormous proportions, reaching between 175,000 and 200,000.[5]

These laborers had three- to five-year contracts negotiated by a Chinese syndicate and, later, the Chinese Emigration Bureau. The Chinese laborers under the British worked in industries and agriculture until August 1917, when China declared war on Germany. Afterward, large sections were transferred to work for the British army. The Americans also used the Chinese as physical laborers. The war-related tasks performed by the Chi-

---

2. *Le Temps*, September 1919, no. 30.

3. Chen Sanjing, *Huagong yu Ouzhan*, 6. I would like to thank Bernadette Li for her kindness in sending me this book. For background on Chinese laborers before the war, see Yen Ching-Hwang, *Coolies and Mandarins: China's Protection of Overseas Chinese during the Late Ch'ing Period, 1851–1911* (Singapore: University of Singapore Press, 1985).

4. Chen Sanjing, *Huagong yu Ouzhan*, 9–10.

5. Ibid., 34–35. I am giving the figure calculated by Chen Sanjing, whose very complete survey of the CLC utilizes extensive archival sources. According to Ta Chen, there were about 150,000 Chinese laborers (*Chinese Migrations*, 142–47). Ta Chen's 1923 monograph, of which chap. 9 deals with the CLC, is the best account of the CLC in English.

nese in France included employment in chemical laboratories, the manufacturing of guns, airplanes, and paper, construction work, and mining. The French also assigned the Chinese to rebury the dead in devastated districts.

The negotiated contracts provided for a salary of between one to two francs per day, with more money paid for hazardous or skilled labor. The British had a lower pay scale, and they put aside half of the wages to be remitted to the family of the worker in China. In general, the British tended to maintain the labor camps under military discipline, whereas the French treated the laborers as civilians.[6] Issues of medical compensation and liability for injuries and death were matters that were resolved slowly.[7]

Although the majority of the CLC worked in the north and northeast of France, it was the British who employed the most Chinese. According to Peter Scott, by the end of the war there were 195 companies of the CLC attached to the British Expeditionary Force, 57 companies of Indians, 42 companies of South Africans, and 16 companies of Egyptians. The Chinese were not only the least disturbed by the bombardments but also the most efficient. "By the end of the war, and for some considerable time thereafter, virtually all the cranes in Calais, Dieppe, Havre, Rouen and Zeneghem were operated by Chinese cranedrivers."[8]

The Chinese laborers in France were recipients of many social and educational benefits. In his comparative study, Ta Chen claimed:

> Never before in the history of Chinese labor abroad had the social welfare of the workers been so well looked after as was done in France. This work was done chiefly under the direction of the Y.M.C.A., many of whose workers among the Chinese were themselves Chinese. . . . The work done by the Y.M.C.A. among the Chinese was along social, recreational, and educational lines. Canteens were established. . . . Recreation in the form of moving pictures, concerts, theatricals, games, athletics, etc., was provided. . . . A Chinese weekly was issued. . . . Evening classes were formed in a variety of subjects. . . . When the Chinese first arrived in France, only about 20 percent were literate, but toward the end of 1921, when the educational work had been going on for over two years, this figure had risen to about 38 percent.[9]

6. Peter T. Scott, "Chinese in the Trenches," *War Monthly* 8, no. 76 (May 1980): 8–13 (I am grateful to the editor, Richard Lamb, for sending me this issue); Ta Chen, *Chinese Migrations*, 147–49.

7. Chen Sanjing, *Huagong yu Ouzhan*, 102–3.

8. Scott, "Chinese in the Trenches," 11–13.

9. Ta Chen, *Chinese Migrations*, 153–54.

According to Huang Liqun, the Chinese Labor School (Huagong xuexiao) was established in 1916. It was funded with 10,000 francs and began with twenty-four students. Prominent Chinese educators helped with the teaching. For example, Cai Yuanpei gave forty lectures covering a wide range of subjects at the school.[10] Available statistics for the years 1917–18 reveal an effort by the workers to improve themselves. *Huagong zazhi* (*The Chinese Labor Magazine*) was only circulated among 100 workers in May 1917, but it increased its readership by the middle of 1918 to 30,000. Students attending science, French, and Chinese classes numbered 20,000 by July 1918.[11]

Involvement in the education of the CLC was important in shaping the perspective of those who were to promote the Work-Study Movement, such as Cai Yuanpei and Li Shizeng. It enhanced their belief that the spheres of the intellectual and the laborer were not mutually exclusive. As we have seen, they were able to inspire thousands of Chinese youth with this vision. Furthermore, Cai, Li, and Wu were even more optimistic for their Work-Study Movement venture because the youth already had their basic education and could accomplish even more than the CLC.[12]

Not only was educating the CLC seen as a chance to extend education to the common people, but it was also a preemptive measure against the adoption of corrupt habits. As one student exhorted in the American-published *Chinese Students' Monthly*, "Shall we let these fellow-countrymen of ours be corrupted and return after the war a menace to the general welfare of our home communities, or shall we now extend to them a helping hand?"[13]

As might be expected there were also misunderstandings and problems of adaptation. According to Judith Blick, in their free time the laborers often gambled with their surplus wages, which prompted efforts to establish savings associations. A second large problem was alcoholism. Finally, there was the frequenting of prostitutes and the prevalence of venereal disease.[14] Judith Blick has characterized the attitude of the British and French toward

10. Huang Liqun, *Liu Fa qingong jianxue jianshi*, 13. For a list of the forty lectures see Chen Sanjing, *Huagong yu Ouzhan*, 126–27.
11. "Huagong jiaoyu wenti" [Problems of Chinese labor education], *Xin Zhongguo* (May 1919), in *FuFa*, 1:252–55.
12. Zhou Enlai, "Liu Fa qingong jianxuesheng zhi da bolan" [The giant wave of travel to France by the worker-students], *Yishi bao* (May 1921) (written in February and March), in *FuFa*, 1:3–4.
13. "Chinese Labor Battalions in France," *Chinese Students' Monthly* 13 (April 1918): 327.
14. Judith Blick, "The Chinese Labor Corps in World War I," East Asian Research Center Papers on China, no. 9 (Cambridge: Harvard University Press, 1955), 122. Blick's figure for venereal disease is 20 percent, which is accepted by Chen Sanjing, *Huagong yu Ouzhan*, 138.

the CLC participants as paternalistic: "They described their charges as being passive, goodnatured, playful, affectionate, but usually untrustworthy. Their feelings were heavily tinged with bewilderment, amusement and at the same time, real contempt for what they considered to be the childishness of the coolie."[15] The Chinese laborers often resented their treatment, especially by the British, and between 1916 and 1918 there were twenty-five strikes. Most of these resulted from simple misunderstandings due to differences in language and custom, but there were also strikes for contract violations.[16]

The overall impact of the French experience on the members of the CLC is difficult to assess. Ta Chen indicated that the sojourn of the Chinese laborers had deleterious effects on their lives. He quoted an excerpt from a letter of a YMCA worker:

> One would be more inclined to think that their stay abroad has done them more harm than good. They lived in abnormal conditions in France and had a comparatively easy life. On coming home they generally look for the kind of work that requires less exertion and yields greater profit. This, of course, is not easily found, and consequently they are a dissatisfied lot. True, their eyes were opened to newer things and their needs were enlarged, but their ability did not grow proportionately.[17]

A Returned Laborers' Union was formed in China. Although Blick concedes that this was one of the first modern unions organized in China, she claims it was out of touch with the labor issues of the time: "The direction that the Chinese labor movement took after the war varied considerably from that taken by the Returned Laborers' Union."[18] However, Chow Tse-tsung claims that this Returned Laborers' Union was quite important to the Chinese labor movement, becoming "the backbone of the new labor movement [in Shanghai]. . . . In Canton alone, twenty-six modern unions were organized by such returnees in 1919. These were considered the first Chinese labor unions in the modern Western sense. Unions of this kind in Canton increased to 130 in the following year."[19]

15. Blick, "The Chinese Labor Corps in World War I," 124.
16. Ta Chen, *Chinese Migrations*, 150–51; Blick, "The Chinese Labor Corps in World War I," 128–30.
17. Ta Chen, *Chinese Migrations*, 157–58.
18. Blick, "The Chinese Labor Corps in World War I," 132.
19. Chow Tse-tsung, *The May Fourth Movement*, 256.

The demobilization of the CLC was a prodigious task that took place over two to three years, as the Chinese often wanted to work until the end of their contracts.[20] In addition, between 10,000 and 30,000 laborers remained and renewed their contracts. According to one newspaper, in 1921 there were still 17,171 war workers in France.[21] Many of the laborers who stayed in France organized themselves into the Chinese Labor Union (Huagong hui) in January 1920. There were thirty-six sections with over 6,000 members. The major activities were to protect the rights of the Chinese laborers and extend education (over thirty schools were started). In the light of the spreading Work-Study Movement, many wanted to be released from their contracts in order to convert to "free labor." Another goal of the union was to encourage virtuous behavior with restrictions on prostitution, gambling, drinking, and opium.[22]

Another organization that undertook to protect the interests of Chinese labor was the Association générale des travailleurs chinois en France (Liu Fa canzhan Huagong zonghui). In 1925 it petitioned for compensation for injuries sustained during the war and for the erection of monuments and made other demands.[23] Thus, as political developments in the Chinese community quickened and sharpened during the early twenties, the Chinese laborers provided a rallying point for radical activity, especially in terms of trying to abolish the contracts made during the war. The CLC also provided a body of potential activists, which the ECCO, in particular, were able to mobilize effectively.

The services of the CLC were crucial to the war effort, but Chen Sanjing is correct in concluding that this contribution to the Allied effort had little diplomatic reward. The Allies paid very little attention to China's interests at Versailles in 1919, giving the Japanese the previously German-occupied territory of the Shandong Peninsula.[24] For example, when it was suggested in the British demobilization report that some Chinese officials receive decorations from the British, the eventual negative decision was influenced by opinions of an interdepartmental debate that included comments such as the "Chinese government were obstructive throughout the war. The coolie

20. E.g., see the report by G. S. Moss, "Demobilization of the Chinese Labour Corps," 31 October 1920, PRO, FO 371/6602 2509/33/10, 1–13.
21. An interesting last issue of a newspaper, which was probably called *The Awakened Lion* ([1 January 1921]: 8). Just this one issue of *Yishui xingshi* [The already sleeping awakened lion] is in AAE, série E, Chine, vol. 49.
22. "Bali Huagong hui" [The Parisian Chinese Labor Union], and "Lü Fa Huagong gonghui jianzhang" [Guidelines for the travel to France Chinese Labor Union], *Xin qingnian* 7 (1 May 1920): 1–7.
23. Chen Sanjing, *Huagong yu Ouzhan*, 156–57.
24. Ibid., 189–90.

scheme was put through despite their opposition. . . . the Chinese government deserves no recognition whatsoever."[25] In a very real sense, the establishment of the CLC was a misguided calculation from the perspective of advancing China's foreign policy objectives.

However, it is less easy to judge the consequences of the CLC as an intercultural enterprise. We have seen that many Chinese developed both technical and intellectual skills. There were political ramifications both for the China returnees and for the Chinese community in France. Finally, there were French who were responsive to the presence of the CLC phenomenon, both in a material sense, as aid in winning a war, and also in an educational sense, overcoming some cultural barriers. One example was Louis Grillet, one of the French officers who took over the direction of the CLC in China from Colonel Truptil.[26] He wrote a fascinating paper in 1918 in which he was excited about the cultural developments occurring in China, paying special attention to the influence of Cai Yuanpei, "who had a deep knowledge of economy and industry," and the SFEA. Grillet believed that China's economic potential was bound to be developed and suggested that the French should help foster this economic emergence through concrete economic plans and intercultural interchange, which was a restatement of the philosophy of the SFEA. In a confidential section he suggested a ten-step plan for this cooperation. Grillet was convinced that France held the greatest cultural affinities with China of any Western nation:

> The Chinese culture is essentially philosophical, moral, and social, and if during the [last] five centuries, from the Ming until 1905, the mode of recruitment of the scholars has stressed a literary education that is detrimental to the thought [process], this has been contrary to the aspirations of the Chinese and designed to serve the defense of the dynasties. By the same token, *the essence of French culture* is also completely philosophical, moral, and social; the differences are in the development of science, industry, and literature. (Emphasis mine)[27]

Grillet concluded that the French culture could inform the Chinese without threatening the integrity or independence of important Chinese values.

25. See the Minutes preceding Moss, "Demobilization of the Chinese Labour Corps."
26. "Recrutement de travailleurs Chinois pour l'agriculture et l'industrie pendant la guerre 1914–1918," AAE, série E, Chine, vols. 41, 145. Also see Chen Sanjing, *Huagong yu Ouzhan,* 29.
27. Louis Grillet, "Note du Chef de bataillon Louis Grillet sur un plan d'action pour le développement en Chine et de l'influence de la culture françaises," 20 November 1918, AAE, série E, Chine, vol. 47.

In conclusion, the CLC did not fulfill the expected foreign policy objectives during the First World War. It was, however, an important prelude to the Work-Study Movement, and it later provided key issues for agitation within the Chinese community in France during the early twenties. It also operated as a focus for the growth of intercultural relations.

TRAVEL AS A POLITICIZING EXPERIENCE

The phenomenon of travel as a politicizing experience deserves special consideration in and of itself. It wielded an important but almost tacit influence in several ways: by introducing the youth to new cultural and technological experiences, by promoting personal development, by widening their view of China and their sense of detachment, and by diversifying their skills. The linkage between travel and youth activism has been underscored by others. For example, C. T. Wang, writing in 1927 about the dramatic increase in the politicization and organization of Chinese youth, compared the Chinese youth movement to the German youth movement. Wang asserted that the increase in travel was an important factor in the mobilization of youth. He noted that before the First World War German youth had developed quite a few *Wandervogel* societies.[28]

For the majority of the worker-students the trip to France was physically uncomfortable. The students often traveled fourth class, in overcrowded and inadequate accommodations, with little lighting or fresh air. Although tempers sometimes were on edge, the "activist" spirit of the students asserted itself. Zhao Shiyan, writing of the voyage, discussed the growing chaotic situation and how the students began to pick leaders and organize ship duties, which were rotated from group to group.[29] Sometimes tensions were provoked between the sailors and the students. Xiao Zizhang recounted that a sailor struck a Chinese.[30]

One of the ways in which perspectives were broadened was by seeing firsthand racism, colonialism, and different cultures. Chen Yan, Chen Yi's older brother, was shocked at the treatment of the yellow and black races. He was very perturbed by what they saw in the colony of Indochina (the voyage entailed stopovers at Haiphong and Saigon). Chen Yan makes a striking point when he recognized the politicizing effect of travel: "This

28. C. T. Wang, *The Youth Movement in China* (New York: New Republic, 1927), 30. Wang's analysis of the youth movement is quite penetrating.

29. Zhao Shiyan, "Hanghai zhong zhi fu Fa xuesheng xiaoxi" [News of the students traveling to France aboard ship], *Chen bao* (21 May 1920), in *FuFa*, 2:125–28.

30. Xiao Zizhang, "Women yilu zenma yang daode Falanxi?" [How did we travel to France?] (August 1920), in *FuFa*, 2:133.

traveling was very significant to us; our patriotism increased more and more." Africa, the Indian subcontinent, Suez, the Mediterranean—the voyage was an eye-opener for Chen Yan: "The environment of different countries, . . . from the unfamiliar sights to the strange smells, often struck us speechless."[31]

Even within China, new knowledge garnered by travel galvanized youth. The trip from Sichuan to Shanghai was Nie Rongzheng's first venture out of his home province and was filled with "fresh sights." Nie particularly remembered waiting with breathless anticipation to see his first train. But he also noticed the poverty and misery in the big cities of China, and it filled him with determination to seek a path for national salvation.[32]

Writing a letter to his compatriots from the middle of the Indian Ocean, Wang Guangqi was aghast at the effects of colonialism and inequality: "In every place in Asia where a race has lost their country [wangguo minzu], their thought is far behind the white people, and then speaking of their physical capacity, they cannot deal [on the level] of the white people. That [all] makes their conquest easier." In the same article, written *before* he reached Europe, Wang admonished his Young China Study Association friends of their patriotic responsibility and then added that if they wanted to implement the spirit of the association, they absolutely must organize (buke bu zuzhi) national and international travel societies. They needed the travel experience to collect data about their country's condition. Travel abroad would facilitate a cultural interchange network and would serve as a conduit for Western knowledge and accurate information on Western educational institutions.[33]

For many young Chinese who left for the West, the new contacts with other cultures and the new sights inculcated a more sophisticated understanding of the world around them. The Work-Study travelers had an opportunity to see how Chinese lived in Southeast Asia and Hong Kong; they saw their first black person when they landed on the African coast; they tasted their first bite of Western food and sipped their first taste of French wine, wore their first tie. Most Work-Study wayfarers had their first sea voyage, experienced their first train ride, rode in their first taxi, heard their first phonograph and their first Western music, and snapped their first pictures.

31. Chen Yan, in Renmin de zhongcheng zhanshi: Mianhuai Chen Yi tongzhi [The peoples' loyal warrior: Our beloved comrade Chen Yi] (Shanghai: Renmin chubanshe, 1979), 49.
32. Nie Rongzhen, Nie Rongzhen huiyilu [The memoirs of Nie Rongzhen] (Beijing: Zhanshi chubanshe, 1983), 1:12–17.
33. Wang Guangqi, "Yinduyang zhong zhi benhui tongzhi shu," in idem, Shaonian Zhongguo yundong, 195–202.

The first contact with advanced technology was a very important milestone in the lives of these Chinese youth.

A related consequence of this travel experience for Chinese youth was that their self-confidence and adaptability grew. Many Chinese traveled in groups around Europe during their stay. They learned how to plan ahead and schedule, how to order a room for the night, how to find post offices and government agencies, and how to plan for their amusements, whether in the cafés or picnics in the park, *all in the context of a foreign country.*

Travel also created a greater detachment and objectivity, which affected their national perspective. For example, in addition to his penetrating analysis of the need for travel as a crucial tool in itself, Wang Guangqi continued to develop new insights after he reached Europe. From Frankfurt, Wang wrote even more strongly about the need for travel. "My first impression after arriving in Europe," wrote Wang, "is that my former conceptions [of the West] are in error."[34] In his postarrival reflections, rather than stressing travel as an educational experience, Wang emphasized that the crucial importance of travel was to remove young Chinese from the corrupt influence of Chinese society. The youth needed the distance of foreign shores to fathom not only Western knowledge but to understand their own failings and to prevent their actions from harming China. A national perspective could be gained only by viewing China from a foreign shore.

Wang's sense of detached objectivity in viewing Chinese affairs from abroad was a widely shared feeling. Not situated in the middle of the constant turmoil back in China, the Chinese abroad could often perceive the broader course of events. Thus, the young Chinese could not only view things Western but view the whole Chinese scene. How many of China's modern revolutionaries tried to foment revolt while abroad? Sun Yatsen, Liang Qichao, and Wang Jingwei are examples of revolutionaries who spent much time abroad. Travelers could remain in contact with friends at home and evaluate the situation at home from a detached perspective, while those left behind were certain to be involved. For example, while Mao Zedong was setting up Russian study societies in China, he was also concerned with questions of Hunan's autonomy and corrupt leadership much more directly than the Chinese activists in France, who responded to issues that involved the whole nation, such as the loan negotiations in 1921 and the foreign attempt to consolidate Chinese railways in 1923.

Zhao Shiyan provides us with a case of increasingly broader vision as a result of his distance from China. While in a Beijing high school, Zhao

---

34. Wang Guangqi, "Lü Ou zagan" [Random thoughts on traveling to Europe], *Shaonian Zhongguo* 2/5 (November 1920): 32.

belonged to a Sichuan *tongxiang* (same province) organization. Complain-
ing about the potential dangers they were encountering in the capital, Zhao
wrote about one Sichuanese who fell ill after working only one day in a
"Beijing factory" and was admitted to a "Beijing hospital," ate "Beijing
medicine," and *of course* died soon after.[35] In contrast, after two years of
mingling with Chinese from other provinces, he lost that regionalistic bias.
During 1922, he believed that his organizational efforts on behalf of the
ECYC were of paramount importance to the effort of creating revolution.
After the Lyons Incident, when Li Lisan and Chen Gongpei were urging
Zhao Shiyan to return to China and apparently outlining the despair in
Zhao's home province of Sichuan, Zhao emphatically wrote back, "I have
absolutely no relation with Sichuan; you must definitely stop importuning
me on this matter."[36]

Last, in certain ways travel contributed to flexibility and foresight, important leadership characteristics. Travel encourages adaptation to changing circumstances and teaches the value of planning ahead. Although their
linguistic abilities differed, the worker-students broadened their repertoire
of skills and gained new cultural insights.

Thus, the exposure to different cultures, customs, sights, and climates
certainly broadened one's perspective, developed personal abilities, and
could serve as a stimulus for political sensitivity and actions. As the Vietnamese proverb says, "When you travel one day, you learn a basketful of
wisdom" (*Di mot ngay dang; hoc mot sang khon*).

DISCOVERY OF A NEW WORLD

The participants in the Work-Study Movement were quite young. One of
the youngest Hunanese, Tang Duo, felt a sense of dislocation on his arrival
on foreign shores and recalled meeting with his older compatriots:

> Upon reaching France, we were sent to the small city of Montargis,
> south of Paris, to study. Cai Hesen, Cai Chang, Xiang Jingyu, Li Fu-
> chun, and others had arrived before, and there were other New Citi-
> zens' Study Society members; most were studying there. Here we were
> in this strange country, and the familiarity, warmth, and happy feel-
> ings were indescribable [upon meeting familiar people], especially as

35. Qin Sun [Zhao Shiyan], "Benhui de jingguo" [The experiences of this organization],
Gongdu (December 1919), in Zhang Yunhou, Yan Xuyi, and Li Junchen, comps., *Liu Fa
qingong jianxue yundong*, 1:376–78.
36. Zhao Shiyan letter to Chen Gongpei, 30 April 1922, in *FuFa*, 2:839.

they treated us younger people as small children, keeping us by their sides. It was as if we had a mountain to lean on.[37]

Traveling to a new country revealed the difference between the ideal and the reality and evoked different types of response, from excitement to alienation. Whatever their reactions to the new environment, the Chinese youth did not fulfill the common stereotype of the "quiescent Oriental."

The French Radical Environment

Imagine the difficulties involved in living in a foreign country that is recovering from a devastating wartime experience. Dislocations in the French economic, political, and social spheres abounded after the First World War. The Chinese had thought to take advantage of the loss of manpower due to the war, but the French economy experienced tremendous inflation and unemployment and subsequent labor unrest between 1919 and 1921:

> The index of wholesale prices, which had stood at 118 in 1914, reached 392 in 1918 and 412 in 1919, and then zoomed to 589 in 1920. In the first six months of 1919, alone, the franc lost half its value in relation to the dollar. . . . Not surprisingly, the workers grumbled at the growing gap between prices and wages, talked of profiteers who had grown rich on their blood, and threatened a reckoning. In 1918 there had been 499 strikes with 176,187 participants; in 1919 there were 2,206 strikes with 1,160,718 participants.[38]

Similar to the Chinese youth, the French workers and demobilized soldiers were dismayed at the Versailles settlement and the sense that their sacrifices had not gained a better world. Many French laborers, like workers throughout Europe, began to look at the promise of the Russian Revolution. For the first few years after the war it looked to many as though Ger-

37. Tang Duo, "Huiyi wode liangshi yiyou: Cai Hesen tongzhi" [Remembering my great teacher and good friend: Comrade Cai Hesen], in *Huiyi Cai Hesen*, 101–3. The Russian émigrés also had help in responding to the pressures of resettlement, and relied on "a network of waiting comrades, and a strong sense of purpose [to] help to mute these anxieties" (Martin A. Miller, *The Russian Revolutionary Emigres* [Baltimore: Johns Hopkins University Press, 1986], 8–9). Likewise, the American sojourners had a common meeting ground in Sylvia Beach's lending library, on the rue d'Odéon, where they could make contacts or just luxuriate in hearing the English language spoken (Fitch, *Sylvia Beach and the Lost Generation*).

38. Robert Wohl, *French Communism in the Making, 1919–24* (Stanford: Stanford University Press, 1966), 120.

many and perhaps France would follow the Bolshevik example. The Russians made prodigious efforts to attract Socialists to their banner and stimulated the founding of Communist parties by the formation of the Communist International (Comintern) in 1919. A dramatic Second Comintern Congress in the summer of 1920 allowed Lenin to split the Second International by the end of the year and attracted many Socialists of the major European countries into joining the Third International. However, the revolutionary sweep of Europe, anticipated by many, did not take place, although there were several revolts in Hungary, Germany, and Austria.[39]

The French Communist Party (Parti communiste français, PCF) was established at the Congress of Tours in December 1920. This effort to join the Third International was marked by internal divisiveness, highlighted by the Comintern's requirement that the aspiring Communist parties adhere to the Twenty-one Conditions to join the Third International. Covering areas such as Communist control of propaganda organs, working in the countryside, the need for a total rejection of reformist leaders, support for Soviet communism, the Conditions also called for a strict discipline imposed from the top: "Points 11–14 sought to tighten control of each party's operation. The central committee of each party must review parliamentary representatives and remove unreliable ones; it must also reassert complete control over the editorial policies of Communist newspapers. The party must apply the principle of 'democratic centralism' [emphasis in original] and it must be ruled by 'an iron discipline, almost a military discipline.'"[40]

The PCF was accepted for membership by the Soviet-controlled Third International only after they had conducted a series of purges of so-called centrist Socialists, such as the nephew of Karl Marx, Jean Longuet. This twenty-second condition seriously attenuated radical Communist politics. This began a process that Robert Wohl characterizes as Bolshevization, which meant a total subservience to the Soviet Communists. The divisiveness of the debates to join the Third International and the continuing series of purges, which were not for ideological reasons but were directed at obtaining total loyalty to the dictates of the Third International, alienated French workers, who were both "confused and disgusted by the constant feuding of the postwar years." According to Wohl:

> By 1921 the revolutionary onslaught had been stopped. . . . In France the prospects for a revolutionary party were not good. . . . The

39. Lazitch and Drachkovitch, *Lenin and the Comintern*.
40. James W. Hulse, *The Forming of the Communist International* (Stanford: Stanford University Press, 1964), 206.

French State was bankrupt. Its quest for security and reparations would inevitably cause it to fall out with its former allies. Such problems, however, could unite the nation as well as divide it. Most important of all, the French working-class movement was not what it had been in 1919–20. For one thing the balloon of mass syndicalism had burst. By the spring of 1921, the CGT [Confédération général du travail] had been reduced to its prewar strength of 600,000 members. For another, the combativeness of the working class had diminished. . . . It was not that the workers had given up their hostility to power and the State. They still felt oppressed and discriminated against. They continued to favor some kind of vague but total social transformation. Revolution, one might say, was in their blood, where working-class parents, propaganda, and experience had put it. . . . What they sought above all was peace and quiet and a secure job. . . . The appeals of agitators might win their sympathy, but they could not get them on the streets.[41]

The Chinese, as numerous publications reveal, were aware of these transformations. Like the French themselves, the young Chinese may not have understood all the ramifications, but they felt the swift cycle of tensions in the French radical milieu.

The Preparatory Schools

Before traveling to France most Chinese youth were uprooted in a first stage of dislocation by attending one of twenty preparatory schools. Later the preparatory schools would be criticized for their lack of rigorous training. Certainly there was inconsistency in training, depending on student aspirations as much as school curriculum. In general, the preparatory schools had two tasks. First, they were to prepare the Chinese youth in French language and some Western studies. Second, they were to include some technical training. Students would stay several months to a year before they left from Shanghai for France.

Since many students trained in locations other than their home provinces, the time spent at preparatory schools began a conditioning process for adaptation to different living conditions. Tang Duo, who was only thirteen years old when he attended a preparatory school in the north, recalled that Cai Hesen, who was an instructor in Chinese, severely chastised them for sneaking into town to eat more familiar southern food. Cai admonished

41. Wohl, *French Communism in the Making, 1919–1924*, 209.

them that if they could not survive unfamiliar Chinese food, how could they hope to eat Western food?[42]

Another example of the preparatory experience was that of He Chang-gong, who was from a poor farming family in Hunan. His ambition to go to France was supported most enthusiastically by his sister-in-law, who financed his efforts to attend a technical school. In the winter of 1917, He went with several people to Beijing and entered the Changxing dian preparatory school. In his memoirs he recounted the wonder of his first time in Beijing, laughing at the bright, colorful dress of the women, wondering at his first sight of a rickshaw—"everything was so fresh, we were curious about everything." He Changgong felt lucky to attend a preparatory school where one could obtain practical experience and education. Overall, the French instruction was not very good, and in He's opinion, hearing the French spoken on the ship was better than attending French classes at the preparatory school. In terms of factory skills, He Changgong learned how to use a file and hammer to shape steel. He and his compatriots were proud to be among the workers, and several stayed on to work in the school factory. Although the students lived very poorly, they had a cooperative spirit. Everyone shared in the tasks and shared their possessions, especially warm clothing in the cold Beijing winter. His special talent was "papering the windows." This preparation time was one of political maturation and personal excitement for He Changgong.[43]

He Guo, another Hunanese and a New Citizens' Study Society member, was also an early participant in the Beijing preparatory school experience. However, his diary (1918) shows a different view from that of He Chang-gong. He Guo was dismayed at the classwork, with two hours of regular studies and two hours of French in the morning and lectures in the afternoon. "The new vocabulary is just too much," He Guo complained. "Just going through two or three items wastes too much time; it is unspeakably difficult!"[44]

He Changgong's memoir was written several decades later, but He Guo's diary, written at the time, gives us a glimpse into the less than glorious aspects of the Work-Study experience. Not only were some participants lacking in self-confidence, but many were not excited to be in a new environment and missed their homes, especially at holiday times. In another entry, He Guo expressed his aching homesickness:

42. Tang Duo, "Huiyi wode liangshi yiyou: Cai Hesen tongzhi," 98.
43. He Changgong, *Qingong jianxue shenghuo huiyi* [Reminiscences of the Work-Study Movement] (Beijing: Renmin chubanshe, 1958), 2–3, 12–17.
44. He Guo, "He Guo riji" [The diary of He Guo] (1918), in *FuFa*, 2:28.

Last autumn I was in Changsha. I remember the brightness of the moon at night, meeting with friends, sailing in a boat, circling the area by water and land, not beginning our return until the dead of night. Today Zhang Zhifu [Kundi] and Mao Runzhi [Zedong] are probably in the same boat. Today I am a temporary resident in the northern capital. . . . If I look up at the moon, then I start to think of home; wandering around a strange city, I then start to feel a stranger's melancholy, 10,000 li from Yushan, an eldest, unskilled son, these thoughts are to no avail.[45]

Consistently miserable, He Guo did not lose track of his main motives, which were patriotic, and several entries outline his thoughts on ways to save the nation. He was impatient with endless intellectual discussion, and as a Work-Study participant he saw a distinct tie between thought and action: "One must abandon profitless thought. Thought and action must be consistent." He Guo further discussed the relation between violence and class conflict. He felt that a violent conflict brought on by the misery of the oppressed classes was unavoidable (*bumian you julie zhi baofa ye*).[46]

Thus, the preparatory school served as the first phase of the educational process in more ways than just disseminating knowledge, but it could never fully prepare students for the difficulties of adjusting to a different culture.

Dislocations and Adjustments

Once off the boat, many worker-students were quickly disabused of their notion of earning quick tuition for college. The money was not "easy" and the prices were higher than they had been led to believe. They had been told that one earned an average of 12 francs a day and could live comfortably on 5 francs a day.[47] However, the price inflation affected all sectors. According to a more realistic assessment of prices in *Dongfang zazhi*, coffee rose from 4 francs (1914) per kilo to 10 francs (1919) and in 1920 to 11 francs. A hat in 1914 cost 18 francs, the price more than doubled by 1919 to 40 francs, and in one year rose another 50 percent to 60 francs in 1920.[48]

Work-Study hopefuls at home were receiving many letters from those who arrived in France with helpful hints and more realistic portrayals of the economic hardship. For example, in July 1919, *Xiangjiang pinglun* (Hunan) published a letter from Yi Libin, who stated that "the Work-Study Move-

45. Ibid., 33.
46. Ibid., 36.
47. E.g., *Chen bao* (8 January 1921), in *FuFa*, 1:261–65.
48. "Bali zhi shenghuo" [Life in Paris], *Dongfang zazhi* 17 (25 May 1920): 40–41.

ment is practicable, no matter what person, no matter what place; you just have to be able to endure hardship." Yi gave two pieces of advice to help establish a proper attitude. First, one must learn not to waste money but to carefully consider every expenditure. Second, one must live simply. In Yi Libin's view, even though three meals eaten in France equaled little more than one Chinese repast, one could still survive.[49]

Other letters also expressed Chinese students' perceptions of their environment. Xie Ruiqi's ten-point epistle includes advice to his compatriots to bring more clothing and the warning that they should be prepared to spend ten years in France in order to accomplish their goals. But the most important thing, he suggested, was to subscribe to as many Chinese journals as they could, because "otherwise going to a foreign country, after several years one could completely become a foreigner and know nothing of the Chinese internal situation."[50]

In addition to the grueling economic problems, which placed many in physical distress, forcing them to live in tents or shabby rooms, with barely enough money to survive, there were other formidable barriers. One of the biggest problems was lack of language proficiency. He Changgong recommended fluency in French. The young Chinese often felt isolated and lonely without being able to communicate, and of course the French could not understand the Chinese.[51] Lack of linguistic fluency was a commonly recognized problem. The problem was exacerbated because frugal Chinese students often shared rooms and meals and, thus, commonly did not speak in French.

The language limitations not only had implications for survival but erected a barrier between the Chinese and French in terms of understanding the subtleties of the social and political environment. The American expatriates also experienced this language barrier. Because of this lack of fluency, Jean Meral makes the point that "the Americans are in a situation of political, economic, and cultural separateness. They only partly apprehend the social implications of Parisian life."[52]

The second great difficulty was the lack of technical expertise for factory work. The SFEA relied greatly on the generosity of French factories to arrange special apprenticeship programs for the Chinese. The young Chinese patriots, with their backgrounds in the Chinese intellectual milieu, even

49. Yi Libin, *Xiangjiang pinglun* (21 July 1919), in *FuFa*, 2:161–63.
50. Xie Ruiqi, *Dagong bao* (Hunan) (May 1920), in Zhang Yunhou, Yan Xuyi, and Li Junchen, comps., *Liu Fa qingong jianxue yundong*, 1:265–68.
51. He Changgong, *Qingong jianxue shenghuo huiyi*, 49. This was one of the reasons He Changgong moved to Belgium, to get away from a largely Chinese-speaking community.
52. Meral, *Paris in American Literature*, 242.

those accustomed to poverty in the countryside, were ill-adapted to the physical exigencies of the factory experience. They found the technical aspects and the physical demands difficult to endure.

Cultural differences also provided an imposing obstacle. Western food was often shunned in favor of cooking Chinese food. Li Huang recounted his embarrassment at the "provincial" nature of his compatriots and how he had to instruct them on the proper way to eat bread and drink wine and how to wear Western-style clothing instead of their cotton padded overcoats (*mianao*).[53]

Manifestations of racism, enhanced by the colonizer mentality of some French citizens, created negative feelings. Before he was expelled during the Lyons Incident, Chen Yi wrote:

> The worker-students [who were working in factories] do not have enough vigor, they are not acquainted with the skills, and their French is not fluent; naturally this is embarrassing. The factories have some ignorant people who constantly jeer at us; this really makes one disgusted. There is still another level [of Frenchmen] who look at a yellow face and consider that we are as stupid as black men. It is really hard to deal with their treatment of us.[54]

Perhaps equally detrimental to adaptation and intercultural understanding was the insularity and isolation of the Chinese within their own community, especially as their purported purpose was to learn from the West. Leaders such as Cai Yuanpei had wanted the students to go to France because they believed it was a truly egalitarian country. But the reality was that there was little genuine contact for many worker-students. This was due in part to the deficient linguistic and technical skills of the worker-students. But their pride in their own civilization and sophistication coupled with the intense organizational network of the Chinese community abroad also tended to create gulfs that made the transmission and internalization of new knowledge difficult or very selective.

Whatever their sense of dislocation or adjustment problems, however, most Chinese had to participate in either the factory or the educational environment.[55] Thus, even the most insular Chinese faced new experiences and acquired new knowledge at some level.

53. Li Huang, "Xuedunshi huiyilu," *Zhuanji wenxue* 16 (June 1970): 25.
54. Chen Yi, "Wo liangnian lai lü Fa de tongku," 3:56.
55. For hundreds of dossiers on factories and schools in which the Chinese worked, there is the material cataloged by Barman and Dulioust, *Etudiants-ouvriers chinois en France, 1920–1940*, deposited at the Archives nationales (AN, 47 AS 1–27).

In the Factories and Schools

Although there were different patterns of adjustment to a new environment, the worker-students were eager to fulfill their mission of national salvation, and most of them sought places in the French factories and schools. For many worker-students the involvement in physical labor in the factory and a sense of cultural dislocation produced profound alienation. In other cases, the New Culture ethos was evoked, and the Chinese youth were determined to benefit from the factory work experience.

In general, the Chinese intellectuals were not accustomed to physical labor. Shu Xincheng, the famous compiler, remarked: "The youth [during the May Fourth period] had spontaneously developed their patriotism and were disaffected with the status quo and thus intellectually had a demand for a 'path to follow.' However, because they lacked the confrontation experience alongside the workers and peasants, the so-called path to follow was dependent on a subjective foundation of thought."[56] Whether the Work-Study Movement laborers were happy or miserable in the factories, they would have agreed with Shu's statement that the actual work experience was unlike anything they had imagined. One of the more optimistic laborers, who wrote frequently throughout 1920–21, was Shu Guang. He wrote of labor conditions in the Creusot-Schneider factories and those of St. Etienne. At St. Etienne, Shu claimed the conditions were glorious. One had housing with heating, plumbing, and electricity and clothing provisions. The factory had old sections and new; work ranged from manufacturing cars and heavy machinery to making electrical parts. Originally the factory had employed seven to eight thousand workers, but during Shu's time there were only between two and three thousand. Shu was also pleased with the training program at Creusot-Schneider, and although the wages as a trainee were too low, he was happy to have the work experience and was satisfied with the accommodations. Shu claimed to have three hours a day to devote to studies.[57]

The happiest worker had to be Wang Ruofei, who enjoyed the rigors of the factory and the chance to observe the "real world." Wang thought the factory environment was a "natural sociology class." He liked being taught useful skills and took his work seriously. Wang also enjoyed Sundays in the park, delighting in the verdant trees and the sight of children playing. "I

---

56. Shu Xincheng, "Huiyi Wusi fandi douzheng de yimu" [Reminiscences of a chapter in the May Fourth anti-imperialist struggle], in Xu Rihui, ed., *Wusi yundong zai Hunan huiyilu*, 157.

57. Shu Guang wrote several articles in the winter of 1920 and beginning of 1921. See *FuFa*, 1:261–65, 2:256–71.

am currently seeking life studies," Wang exclaimed in his diary, "life knowledge, in contrast to emphasizing diplomas, just studying dead books." Wang
established the following daily schedule, which indicated his agreement
with Shu Guang that one could both work and study:

5:00 a.m.	Wake up
5:00–6:00	Study
6:30	Drink coffee
Go to factory	(15-minute walk)
7:00–11:30	Factory labor
11:30–12:30	Lunch
12:30–1:00 p.m.	Study
1:00–5:00	Factory labor
5:00–6:00	Dinner
6:00–9:00	Study
9:30 p.m.	Bedtime[58]

Wang did not feel disappointed at lacking the means to study at a university, because he believed that factory work was also a form of education and
a form of joy; he claimed, "Labor is a happy enterprise." However, he was
ambivalent because work could also be "shameful," especially as making
money for others did nothing for self-improvement. To further discipline
himself, Wang articulated four goals in his diary: to improve his labor habits, self-rectification (ba xing muo ding), to seek a method (to be of some
service to his country), and to realistically observe the condition of French
labor.[59] In these observations and goals one can see the attempt to involve
himself and learn from a new experience, and yet the traditional Confucian
value of "self-rectification" was still active, in addition to the preoccupation with finding some means to serve his country.

Not everything in the factory world was positive. Wang was appalled at
the unskilled types of labor that were given to Africans and their pitiful
wages of three to four francs even though their work required considerable
exertion. In contrast, the French workers were by and large lazy, in reality
working six hours rather than eight. Further, the personal habits of the
French worker did not hold much appeal for Wang Ruofei. He commented,
"Besides liking wine, the workers also like to smoke. Smoking and drinking—these two things are their whole life."[60]

58. Wang Ruofei, "Shengxia men qingong riji" [Diary of diligent labor at the Saint
Chamond factory], Shaonian shijie (1920), in FuFa, 2:238, 226.
59. Ibid., 212–38.
60. Ibid., 226–37.

Finally, Wang Ruofei had very little patience with complainers. He heartily advocated the New Culture value of self-sufficiency. Wang had some criticism for many who espoused the "sanctity of labor" and the glory and joy of factory work: "Indeed, when I look at their actual behavior, I have not seen them express any kind of happiness; quite the opposite, they pass their moments with melancholy demeanors."[61]

Many worker-students were disenchanted with their experiences. One disgruntled Work-Study participant, Zhu Xi, wrote a long article entitled "My Forty-one Months of Life in the Work-Study Movement" (spring 1923). Zhu Xi was from Zhejiang and went to France with several friends. Upon arriving in France, in May 1920, he decided to stay with his friends, who had no money. Apparently, they had no introduction from the SFEA, and the SFEA representative would not help them, so they tried to stay in the tents on the lawn in front of the Chinese Federation. However, there was no room, so they finally wangled some support from the association and were allowed temporarily to sleep on the floor of the building. After ten days a job opportunity was offered to them for performing physical labor and they accepted.[62]

Zhu Xi's first job was to cart around heavy loads. There was no set task, the labor was difficult, and when it became irregular, he quit. Life between jobs was squalid; Zhu moved to a tent, where the conditions were horrendous. Facilities were lacking and the deprivations were serious. Wind and rain penetrated the holes that riddled the tents. One of his colleagues died from an exclusively potato diet. Zhu appealed unsuccessfully to fellow Zhejiang workers to help him find work. Zhu's second job was in a rubber factory, where he helped transport pipes. Zhu worked for two months at this factory, receiving eighteen francs per day as his wages. He was dismissed because there was not enough work. He had saved five hundred francs but used it up in a month and sought help from the SFEA.

Although Zhu Xi participated in the Twenty-eighth Movement, he was not using his "unemployment" time to study. He just felt too cold and depressed to open a book. It was not until mid-March of 1921 that he found his third job at Creusot-Schneider, where he worked for a year before experiencing his third period of unemployment. After a waiting period in Paris, Zhu found another job in a car factory. In spite of personal setbacks, Zhu persisted and stayed in France for several years, eventually attending

61. Ibid., 229.
62. Zhu Xi, "Sishiyige yue de qingong jianxue shenghuo" [My forty-one months of life in the Work-Study Movement], Minguo ribao (March–May 1923), in FuFa, 2:295–331. The following account is based on this material.

universities both in Montpellier and Lyons and later becoming involved in the successful 1926 movement for the return of the Boxer Indemnity.[63]

Zhu Xi's story, which is full of anecdotal material about his work and living conditions, is typical in several ways: the constant changing of jobs, the difficulty of enduring hard physical labor, poor living conditions, several negative encounters with Westerners, and general depression.

There was a large group of laborers who translated these poor factory conditions into a political message that they were working under an oppressive Capitalist system. This was the opinion of Cai Hesen, Chen Yi, and He Guo. He Guo, writing under a pen name in 1920 in his usual gloomy vein, decried the factory work, where they were rushed, pressured, and then, the final insult, had to study French until 10:00 at night:

> Everyday we receive 14 francs, but in the end when one considers our time, our spirits, and our brains, are these worth only 14 francs? To help the production of the Capitalists, and not bearing any relationship to helping the common people—in fact there is a part of this work, creating explosives, that helps to kill people. Why do we carry on with this totally valueless work? Why must we suffer this way![64]

The many reactions and situations in the "factory experience" are unified in only one sense: no matter how terrible the situation, the students were furious at the thought that they might have to return to China prematurely. Zhu Xi, living in dreary misery, realized with a sense of humor that someone might ask him why he was living in a tent like a traveling bandit. "I could answer in one sentence," Zhu speculated. "Because we have no work and no money, it is not unnatural [bude buran]. There is definitely no one who likes living like this."[65] The key point is that Zhu never imagined someone saying, "Since you are suffering so much, why not return home?" Even the unhappy He Guo did not raise this question. Perhaps the possibility of failure was not something they could face after committing themselves to saving the nation. The insularity of the Chinese community reinforced this type of determination. The group identity often bolstered their self-confidence and acted as a constraint by imposing group norms.

Working in the factories gave many of these young Chinese a real connection with the working class; it certainly put them in the world of "reality" in

63. Zhu Xi dossier at Sino-French Institute, AAUFC; Jiang Tianwei, "Liu Fa qingong jianxue xiaoshi" [Small events of the travel to France Work-Study Movement], Wenshi ziliao 34 (1980): 30–40.

64. Pei Zhen [He Guo], "Wo zhi zuogong ganxiang" [My feelings about labor], Chen bao (24 December 1920), in FuFa, 2:249–52, quote on p. 250.

65. Zhu Xi, "Sishiyige yue de qingong jianxue shenghuo," 307.

terms of hard physical labor. When leaders such as Li Fuchun and Deng Xiao-ping later pursued modern industrial policies, their early European experience may have contributed to the human dimensions of their plans.

Education in France was almost as difficult to obtain as factory work. This was because the majority of the worker-students needed special classes set up for their language needs. It was fortunate that through decades of goodwill and the particularly solid connections of Li Shizeng, several programs were initi-ated with lycées and colleges in Paris, Grenoble, Fontainebleau, Melun, and Montargis. Most students spent from several weeks to months at these schools, awaiting the opportunities for work in the factories, where they could make money and then, they hoped, continue their education. In general, the formal educational experiences were brief, but they had two important functions: (1) they served as adjustment periods to French ways and as emotionally sta-bilizing experiences, because the Chinese youth were often with their compa-triots; and (2) the classes provided some language training.

Some students worked in the factories by day and went to school at night. By the end of 1921, the Alliance française had thirty-nine Chinese taking night courses.[66] Most of the students, however, found it too difficult to pur-sue both factory work and school at the same time. Instead the behavior pattern was to work for several months and then attend school for a few months. Most of the worker-students, and most Frugal-Study students, ended up working in the factories at some point in their stay in France.

Some writers, such as He Changgong and Li Huang, recounted their contacts with French families. But most of the Chinese worker-students did not have many contacts and stayed close within the Chinese community. The schools provided room and board, and for the most part, the Chinese preferred to room together. For example, at the College of Montargis, "the Chinese males had two floors out of a three-storied building for sleeping, eating (they cooked their own food), and classes. The women were in a different building. There were French students on one of the floors, but they never bothered with the Chinese students."[67] The students at these lycées were more fortunate than the two hundred Chinese sleeping in tents and on the floor of the Chinese Federation. Li Huang volunteered time as a French tutor for them but was dismayed by class sizes. He also felt that his students were not motivated.[68]

A different atmosphere prevailed at Charleroi University for Workers in Belgium, which several dozen Chinese attended, including Nie Rongzhen

66. AN, 47 AS 5/B-14.
67. Tang Duo, "Huiyi wode liangshi yiyou: Cai Hesen tongzhi," 102.
68. Li Huang, "Xuedunshi huiyilu," *Zhuanji wenxue* 16 (June 1970): 28.

Future Chinese leaders in Paris: Li Fuchun, Li Weihan, Deng Xiaoping, Zhou Enlai, Ren Zhuoxuan, and Nie Rongzhen

The S.S. *Porthos*, one of the ships that carried the worker-students to France, usually in fourth-class steerage. This picture is from a frequently sent postcard.

Founding members of the Self-Awakening Society in Tianjin. Half of the founding members were women. *Second row, third from left:* Ma Jun. *Second row, seventh from left:* Zhou Enlai.

The members of the Self-Awakening Society in Tianjin celebrating the release of several members from jail during the May Fourth Movement

Zhang Ruoming and Guo Longzhen (ca. 1920). They went to prison together for six months in 1920 and then traveled to France as Frugal-Study students. Both joined the ECCO, but Zhang Ruoming quit and pursued her studies, while Guo continued her revolutionary activities until her execution in 1931. (*Picture courtesy of Yang Zaidao*)

Zhao Shiyan (1901-27),
first general secretary
of the ECYC

Wang Guangqi
in Germany

Members of the New Citizens' Study Society gathered in a park in Montargis, after an important three-day meeting, 10 July 1920. The woman standing on the right is Xiang Jingyu. The woman in white in the back row is Cai Chang; next to her is her brother, Cai Hesen. In the back row, second from left is their mother, Ge Jianhao. The president of the society, Xiao Zisheng, is sitting in the front, facing to his right. Also present in the picture is the founder of the anti-Communist Chinese Youth Party, Zeng Qi, who is standing in front of Cai Chang.

The Zhang Shenfu ECCO nucleus group in Paris, March 1921. Liu Qingyang is in the front row, center. *Back row, from left*: no. 1, Zhang Shenfu; no. 3, Zhou Enlai; no. 4, Zhao Shiyan.

The second meeting of the ECYC in Paris, February 1923. *From left, front row:* no. 2, Zhao Shiyan; no. 6, Chen Qiaonian; no. 8, Chen Yannian; no. 11, Wang Ruofei. *Middle row:* no. 3, Liu Bojian; no. 4, Xiao San. *Back row:* no. 4, Fu Zhong; no. 9, Zhou Enlai.

and Jiang Zemin. According to Jiang Zemin the Belgians not only provided free facilities and less expensive tuition, but the feelings (*ganqing*) were more cohesive and the Belgian students were "particularly friendly to the Chinese [whereas] the French were not as warm as the Belgians."[69]

In general, the higher strata of the Chinese community received the greatest degree of educational cooperation. Those who advanced the most in their language abilities received the most encouragement and available funding. The development of cooperative ventures such as the Sino-French Institutes at Lyons University and Charleroi University for Workers in Belgium and the Chinese Institute of Higher Studies in Paris all cultivated high admission and performance standards for the Chinese students. This trend was ill-received by the majority of the worker-students, whose vehement opposition was to manifest itself in the Lyons Incident, which was to have dramatic consequences for the direction of Chinese politics.

Whether working in a factory, studying in school, or strolling in a park, the Chinese developed many impressions of their varying environments and often attempted through journals and letters to communicate these impressions to others. Subtle reflections or stereotypes, these impressions give us valuable insights into the reality of cultural interchange.

Cultural Impressions

Arbiters of high fashion and haute cuisine in their respective hemispheres, the Chinese and French sought to emphasize their areas of cultural similarities. Speaking at the first meeting of the Association amicale franco-chinoise in Paris on 24 May 1907, Minister to France Liu Sheshun elucidated the perceived commonalities between the two cultures:

> In China as in France, we have the cult of our glorious ancestors. In China as in France, we place all our pride of honor in our scholars, our philosophers, our poets, and our patriots. In China as in France, we have a profound love of productive peace and moralizing endeavors. We also practice solidarity and social foresight [*prévoyance sociales*] and the family virtues that are so honored in the West and particularly in France.[70]

In addition to the common cultural emphases noted by the Chinese minister and the larger societal trends of egalitarianism and anticlericalism artic-

69. Jiang Zemin interview, 25 October 1985 (Beijing).
70. "Discours de son Excellence M. le Ministre de Chine," *Bulletin de l'Association amicale franco-chinoise* 1 (July 1907): 18.

ulated by the promoters of the Work-Study Movement, there were other points of contact between the Chinese and the French. Both societies stressed elegant, often subtle, language, and many scholars in both cultures during the twentieth century zealously fought for the preservation of language forms. In a behavioral sense, the Chinese and the French are very dualistic societies, oscillating between the sensual and spontaneous on the one hand and ritualism and prescribed etiquette on the other. This is expressed in the art and philosophy of both cultures.[71]

As we shall see, the Chinese were thus very sensitive to many of the nuances of French culture. Their perceptions, however, were often tinged by the political pursuits that shadowed their observations, as well as by the cultural insularity and acculturation fears that have traditionally pervaded the Chinese abroad. This sensitivity to the concept of culture was not just an amusing pastime for the Chinese in the West. Some of the most radical moments of twentieth-century Chinese politics have emerged from the milieu of culture, such as the New Culture Movement and the Great Proletarian Cultural Revolution. The linkage between culture, ethics, and politics is not abstruse but is vitally alive for the Chinese.[72]

In an article on how the laborer ought to act on his return to China (1920), presumably written for repatriated CLC participants, Jun Yuan lists four objectives: to continue working, to spend spare time in seeking education, to practice the good points of Western civilization, and to transmit the good points of Western civilization.[73] But which elements were the "good points" of the West? Which elements should they absorb and emulate? According to Jun Yuan, an example of civilized behavior that he intended to implement on his return was the greater refinement of the West as exemplified by manners of the toilet—for example, closing the door when one is in the bathroom. Chinese habits were uncivilized (bu wenming)—they did not even have doors to their bathrooms!

Many Chinese were in fact overawed with the "refinement" of Western civilization and sought to absorb Western manners. As one Chinese student

71. In her article on Sino-Western cooperative educational enterprises, Ruth Hayhoe endorses the view that the affinity of the French and Chinese cultures aided the absorption of knowledge by the Chinese ("A Comparative Approach to the Cultural Dynamics of Sino-Western Educational Cooperation," China Quarterly 104 [December 1985]: 12–24).

72. It may be that we have to rethink the term "nationalism" when used with respect to China. The Chinese sense of unity may hinge more on common cultural identity. When we recognize the continuity of moral values in China during the last 150 years, it is clear how much modern ideology partakes of the traditional cultural ethos.

73. Jun Yuan, "Huagong guiguo hou yinggai zenma yang" [How Chinese laborers ought to behave after returning to the country], Huagong zazhi 43 (1920): 4.

in America who traveled to Europe related, there was an unconscious emulation of some characteristics of the host country:

> As one Chinese student [in Great Britain] said casually, "We never think of talking with the trades people." In Germany, Chinese students drink beer, use walking sticks and greet each other in stiff military fashion. In France they speak volubly and gesticulate expressively. This is all very natural. In America we yell and sing college songs and swap slang and jokes.[74]

Their immediate surroundings often inspired the Chinese to compare cultures. Reflecting in the middle of a Frankfurt graveyard, Wang Guangqi launched into a critique of the wastefulness of Chinese burial practices and in macabre tones discussed cremation, suicide, and the values of ancestor worship.[75] In the countryside of France, Li Sichun contended that the whole of civilization could be seen along a Montargis canal.[76] But like Wang Guangqi in the graveyard, Li Sichun used his surroundings to critique his own country. Thus, the tranquility of the canal at Montargis was troubled by his reflections on the different fishing techniques of the West and the East, with his conclusion that Eastern techniques symbolized sly and treacherous tendencies on the part of the Chinese.

Some Chinese perceived the West in ways that reflected the superiority of Chinese civilization. Writing on the depressing situation of German society, burdened by indemnities, the forfeiture of colonial possessions, the war losses in material and spiritual senses, Shen Yi concluded, "After I have gone abroad, I am absolutely certain that the Chinese are the most ethical people in the world."[77]

To be sure, the Chinese were also capable of understanding Europe on its own terms while taking courses and observing life in the streets. One of the more positive views of the French came from the multifaceted Sheng Cheng. Sheng Cheng, whose rapid progress in French allowed him considerable access to French society, attended the Congress of Tours in December 1920 and became a founder of the PCF. Sheng was the first Chinese to attend the College of Montpellier, and he was also a participant in the riotous antics of the Parisian artistic milieu during his visits to the capital. At

---

74. Y. Y. Tsu, "Chinese Students in Europe," *Chinese Students' Monthly* 19 (November 1923): 31–32.

75. Wang Guangqi, "Lü Ou zagan," 35–36.

76. Li Sichun, "Lü Fa de duanpian sixiang" [Short reflections on traveling to France], *Shaonian Zhongguo*, "Falanxi hao" [The French number], 2/4 (15 October 1920): 74–79.

77. Shen Yi, "Zhanhou Deguo zhi zhenxiang" [The real situation of postwar Germany], *Shaonian Zhongguo* 3/11 (June 1922): 34.

the age of eighty-six, his eyes lighting up with vivid memories, Sheng exclaimed at how full of creativity Paris in the twenties was, how alive: "Ah, I remember Dada!"[78] In his 1957 book, *Memories of Paris*, he described many aspects of Paris, from the architecture to the French character. Sheng Cheng was accepted into the café society of artists in Paris, and his 1929 book, *Ma mère*, one of the first literary attempts in French by a Chinese, was graced with a preface written by the famous poet Paul Valéry. Sheng's favorite *quartier* was Montparnasse, where the women threw themselves at the artists: "[One] just had to be an artist, and as for the women, [one could get] every size and shape, as a special prerogative of the artist."[79]

In addition to creative culture, some Chinese noted the psychic crisis that pervaded European youth after the war. They were aware of the different backgrounds of the Chinese youth crisis and the Western youth crisis. In a very perceptive and detailed article on German youth groups, Wang Guangqi traced the youth crisis there to the turn of the century and noted the impact of the *Wandervogel*, the reaction against materialism, the perceived need for simplicity, the rebellion against modernity and urbanization, among other characteristics. In France, during the war, Xie Hong remarked on the value transition in the French youth groups toward a steady emphasis on militarization.[80]

In postwar France, the dislocation caused by the unbalanced population demographics was evident to the Chinese. In the opinion of one Chinese student, "French women only like to have fun; they do not like to bear children; it can really cause worry about the population. Where we live . . . on the streets only the brightly dressed women walk back and forth; with the exception of the soldiers, the males are either very old or very young."[81]

In general, the Chinese were very impressed with the cohesiveness of the French family. In his article on living in a pension in Montargis, Hu Zhu applauded the balance of concern and independence in the French family.

78. Sheng Cheng interview, 12 October 1985 (Beijing). I could find no direct confirmation of Sheng's presence at the Congress of Tours, but police reports, letters, and articles all indicate the possibility. In addition, President Mitterand awarded Sheng Cheng the Legion of Honor for his activities during the 1920s.

79. *Bali Yiyu* [Memories of Paris] (Hong Kong: Yazhou, 1957), 4.

80. Wang Guangqi, "Deyizhi qingnian yundong" [The German youth group movement], *Shaonian Zhongguo* 4/5 (July 1923): 1–25; Xie Hong, "Faguo qingniantuan" [The youth groups of France], *Xin qingnian* 2 (October 1916): 1–3. Also see Liu Shuya, "Lü Ou zhanzheng yu qingnian zhi juewu" [The war in Europe and the awakening of youth], *Xin qingnian* 2 (October 1916):1–8.

81. Chen Chu, *Dagong bao* (Hunan) (May 1920), in Zhang Yunhou, Yan Xuyi, and Li Junchen, *Liu Fa qingong jianxue yundong*, 1:269.

He pointed out the wisdom of the small size, frugality, and regular routine of the French family.[82]

Analyses of Western arts and sciences were popular in the Chinese community. Almost every issue of the Young China Study Association's journal, *Shaonian Zhongguo*, had surveys, translations, and reportage from Europe, and the association also published several monographs. The October 1920 issue was a special "French number" and included surveys of French sociology, literature, fine arts, a tour of the Louvre (with photographs), an interview with an artist, a short biography of Jean Jaurès, an article on a French mathematician, translations of French poetry and literature, and several reflective essays on the nature of civilization and living in France.[83] In general, the survey articles sacrificed depth for breadth and often seemed to be more concerned with listing the names of French luminaries. However, the reflections on French civilization were very insightful. As the "oldest" civilization in Europe, French civilization was deemed to be the most advanced in Europe with respect to its intellectual, philosophical, and moral development. The elegance of the French language and the expressiveness of the French personality were also much admired.

The complex nature of cultural assimilation should not dissuade the historian from attempting to understand the flow of ideas between cultures. Motivated by national concerns, the Chinese were willing to explore Western ideas, notwithstanding their strong beliefs in the value of their own culture. The basic question is how deeply were they affected by these ideas? The mélange of impressions and the absorption of new values and ideas, some reaffirming or elaborating Chinese ideas, some totally Western in their worldview, cannot be considered separately from the complexities of the organizational milieu of the Chinese community abroad and the political struggles that occurred within that community. As we shall see in the following chapters, the meeting of East and West produced diverse political orientations.

MANDARINS IN OUR MIDST

During the postwar period, when the exclusion laws were still in effect in the United States, France was the destination for the refugees of the world. At the same time that over one hundred Chinese students were accepted into the scholastic community at Montargis, hundreds of Chinese were em-

82. Hu Zhu, "Wo zhude pension" [The pension where I live], *Shaonian Zhongguo*, "Falanxi hao" [The French number], 2/4 (15 October 1920): 79–85.
83. *Shaonian Zhongguo*, "Falanxi hao" [The French number], 2/4 (15 October 1920).

ployed at the nearby Langlee factory, as were some twelve hundred Russian refugees.[84] The French were very generous toward the Chinese who reached their shores. The government encouraged the placing of Chinese in educational institutions and factories and provided personnel and economic support.

Although the Chinese were well noted during this period for the profusion of their organizations, the French showed some of this same propensity. Most Western nations were eager to cultivate the Chinese, hoping to spread modern technology and create modern markets for their goods. Many of the Sino-French organizations formed in the 1900s desired to cultivate economic ties and develop Chinese science and technology, but there were also other objectives, based on political convictions and the desire for mutual understanding.

One such organization, the Association amicale franco-chinoise (AAFC), was formed in 1907 and headed by the former minister to China Georges Dubail. The organization was formed to promote the development of relations between the two countries and to aid travelers. The activities of the AAFC were mostly scholarly: publishing, building libraries, and holding educational lectures.[85] Although Dubail spoke of mutual comprehension, it was François Dujardin-Beaumetz, a civil engineer, who delivered a long and perceptive speech on "La mentalité chinoise." Dujardin-Beaumetz spoke on facets of Chinese civilization, comparing Confucius with Epicurus, listing the key concepts involved in political morality, and discussing values such as the importance of face and cultural aspects such as the Chinese written language: "It is an alphabet of human thoughts, a picturesque algebra of the sciences and arts." According to Dujardin-Beaumetz, nothing was more sacred than the government and the family in China.[86]

Among the French members of the AAFC were government dignitaries, businessmen, and educators, including Philippe Berthelot, Paul Labbé, Arnold Vissière, the Comte du Chaylard, Max Leclerc; on the Chinese side, most of the members were government officials. The AAFC later merged with the Comité franco-chinois de patronage des jeunes Chinois en France (CFC) in May 1923 to form the Association amicale et de patronage franco-chinoise.[87]

---

84. Paul Gache, *Les grandes heures de Montargis* (Roanne: Editions Horvath, 1980), 133–35.

85. "Statuts," in *Bulletin de l'Association amicale franco-chinoise* 1 (July 1907): 4–8.

86. One must remember that this speech was given in 1907, four years before the overthrow of the monarchy. F. Dujardin-Beaumetz, "La mentalité chinoise," ibid., 20–35.

87. See the notes and pamphlets in AAE, série E, Chine, vol. 498. Information can be found for the thirties in AN, 47 AS-1/A-3.

The accord between the Chinese and French continued during the war. Personal relationships between individuals facilitated the creation of the Chinese Labor Corps and spurred the formation of the SFEA, the recipient of considerable patronage and the organization responsible for the promotion of the Work-Study Movement. When the problems of the Work-Study Movement escalated, the CFC, formed in mid-1921, played a role in the political struggles of 1921 and assumed the burden of educational placement from the SFEA.[88]

The year 1920 was an especially fruitful year for French initiative in intercultural contact. Departing on a cultural mission, Paul Painlevé, the famous educator and aviator, spent three months traveling in China. Painlevé's journey gave rise to some interesting observations. He declared that although China had suffered from warlordism, the country was not in a state of stagnation, contrary to the conventional French view. The Chinese needed and wanted to cooperate with the Western democracies and to adopt Western technologies and systems:

> The thirst to learn and familiarize themselves with the occidental sciences is prodigious among the young generation of Chinese, and [in spite of] language differences, the mind of the Chinese is also susceptible to the rational culture of the European mind. . . . The Western nations must help China to first form a thousand scholars as rapidly as possible and then China can reclaim the place that she had formerly occupied and that she must occupy once more in the civilization of the world.[89]

A man who acted on his beliefs, Paul Painlevé promoted the foundation of the Institute of Chinese Higher Studies affiliated with the Institute of France, the Academy of Paris, and Beijing University. Founded in March 1920, the institute had as its aim "the developing of intellectual relations between France and China." The statutes went on to list objectives:

> 1. To give its cooperation to Chinese Advanced Studies, ancient and modern, in the French Universities and especially in the *University of Paris*. 2. To establish Chinese Libraries with a special staff of librarians and translators. 3. To create and maintain all French and Chinese organizations intended to enable the Chinese and French to acquire a *superior* French and Chinese instruction. 4. To encourage the founda-

---

88. The formation and activities of this committee will be covered more extensively in the following chapter.
89. *L'Asie française* 187 (December 1920): 428–29.

tion of a "Chinese Academy of Sciences," continuing and improving ancient Chinese Academies and intended to develop the study of Western Sciences in China. 5. To use all other means: bulletins, publications, records, prizes, and lectures; to assist and organize Committees. [Emphasis mine][90]

The establishment of the institute was a milestone in the promotion of Chinese studies in France. However, the objectives also highlight two important issues. First, implicit in the focus on Chinese cultural studies for the French and on "Western Sciences in China" is the common assumption that although both civilizations were equal in morality, the Chinese lack of technological progress was in need of redress. Second, why was no attention paid to the "work-study" scheme that was at that time being promoted by the Chinese founder of the institute, Cai Yuanpei? The institute was established *before* the problems of the Work-Study Movement emerged and *before* any alienation between Cai Yuanpei and the worker-students developed, and thus one must assume that the explicit elitist orientation of the institute was quite intentional. The argument that the Sino-French Institute at Lyons was also developed with the intention of being an advanced educational institution and was never intended to accommodate the needs of the worker-students gains in force.[91] The Sino-French Institute at the University of Lyons was established in 1921, with the first class matriculating in the fall of 1921.[92]

Not all reaction to the burgeoning growth of intercultural relations was positive. An article in *L'action française*, the organ of the radical right political group, decried the Institute of Chinese Higher Studies as a blind for Bolshevik action, as it was well known that Chinese congregated in secret societies. The perfidious influence of the Bolshevik Chinese as promoted by places like the institute would "overflow throughout the entire world!"[93]

While the educational elitism of some French organizations emphasized the technological disparity between the Chinese and French, other organi-

90. Institute of Chinese Higher Studies, pamphlet, AOM, SLOTFOM V, 43.

91. I am not suggesting that Cai Yuanpei could not have had a multifaceted view of Sino-French educational potentials. In fact, the objectives of the institute are fascinating for the foreshadowing of Cai's development of the Academia Sinica in later years.

92. For a brief introduction see, Chen Sanjing, "Minchu liu Ou jiaoyu de jiannan lishi: Liang Zhong Fa daxue chushen" [The difficult beginnings of study abroad in Europe: A preliminary examination of the Sino-French Institute at Lyons University], in *Zhongyang yanjiuyuan jindaishisuo minchu lishi yantaohui lunwenji* (Taibei: Academia Sinica, 1984): 991–1007. The Sino-French Institute will be explored in greater detail in the following chapter.

93. "Les dessous d'un institut," *L'action française*, 14 February 1921.

zations emphasized the moral mission of the French vis-à-vis inferior civilizations. One of these organizations was the Association France-Colonies, founded in 1923. Although it counted among its members well-known reactionaries like Maurice Barrès and Henri de Jouvenel, the association also enjoyed the patronage of Paul Appell, rector of the University of Paris, who had also sponsored the Institute of Chinese Higher Studies.[94] The Association France-Colonies wanted to foster better intercultural relations between France and her colonies, because the demographic vulnerability of France during the First World War demonstrated the need for a true union with the colonies if France was to be strong in manpower in the event of another war. The mission would have to address alleviating the physical misery of the colonial and learning about native cultures. This desire for solidarity with the natives not only would promote better mutual understanding but had the explicit aim of "contributing to make the native a normal man [homme normal], capable therefore of the most amount of useful labor."[95]

The attitudes of moral superiority and racism were not restricted to those who promoted the colonialist interests of France. Edouard Herriot, mayor of Lyons and senator from the Rhône, who helped sponsor the SFEA and the Sino-French Institute, sometimes succumbed to racial biases. As a friend of China, he published a pamphlet discussing the Manchurian question (1933), but he failed to catch his own racism when after denouncing the Japanese for trying to subject China to its rule, he continued with the thought that Japan would continue its expansion and if they triumphed it would be a victory "of the yellow race over the white race. And the white race, what is it doing? It is speechifying!"[96]

Romain Rolland, one of the most prominent internationalists of the twentieth century, winner of the Nobel Prize for literature, and sponsor of several anticolonialist forums and organizations, was also capable of racist remarks. He chastised the Europeans during the First World War for exposing European civilization to the foreign labor battalions. He wrote in his published journal that "the aspect of a great European nation being held at bay by these savage hordes is something I cannot contemplate without revulsion."[97]

One can discern different attitudes and beliefs and different objectives. There were those who promoted intercultural relations with economic

---

94. "Un oeuvre de salut public," Association France-Colonies, pamphlet, 1923, AOM, SLOTFOM III, 129.

95. "Statuts," article 3, in ibid., 9.

96. Edouard Herriot, "In the Far East" (1933), Pamphlets on the Sino-Japanese Question 5/5, U.S. Library of Congress.

97. Becker, The Great War and the French People, 87.

views in mind and those who were genuinely interested in sharing knowledge. There were colonialist and anticolonialist mentalities. Racial bias existed. However, there were some underlying attitudes that were shared to some degree by most French intellectuals. First, the Chinese were perceived as having a superior civilization in the East and were known to have had an influence on the *philosophes* such as Voltaire, but they were perceived by most French intellectuals as existing in a state of slow transition, their progress impeded by outmoded attitudes and a lack of technological background. Second, in general, the French had a basic desire to share with "less-developed" peoples the culture and enlightened values that had evolved in France during the seventeenth and eighteenth centuries. Although this desire was partially due to cultural arrogance, there was also a strong altruistic sentiment and, more than other colonialist powers, a sincere intent to learn about other cultures as well. Finally, whatever the rationale for promoting intercultural contact, the societal and political tensions that existed in China were far more intense than those in France. Therefore, the Chinese had greater motivation to study French culture and society than the reverse.

For the average Chinese youth traveling to France between 1919 and 1921, the reasons for the voyage were often seen in terms of the broader issue of national salvation. However, the voyage also became one of self-discovery. The preparatory schools, the SFEA, and the regional linkages provided some degree of training and support for each youth. Nevertheless, whether they could meet the challenge of adapting to a new diet, new vistas of culture and politics, new labor and educational experiences, new relationships, and group transformations depended on the strength of each individual. The new world of the West was complicated for the Chinese not only by the difference between the ideal and the reality but also by differences in personal strengths and backgrounds, a tendency toward cultural myopia, and differing goals of cultural interchange.

One is struck by the real diversity within the Work-Study Movement in France. Some youth were too anchored by Chinese culture to genuinely adopt any Western values, while some looked down upon their uncouth compatriots who could not distinguish between varieties of wine. Some youth approached the factories as a learning experience, while others looked upon the experience as dreaded physical misery. There were those worker-students who agitated for the remaining Chinese Labor Corps personnel, who were working under unfair contracts, and there were those worker-students who preferred to reduce their factory time to a minimum and concentrate on the educational objectives of the Work-Study scheme. Some youth assiduously studied the French language and were determined to cultivate Western friendships, while others clustered together at meal-times and lived together in rooming houses. A multiplicity of strengths and weaknesses can be found within the Work-Study Movement.

However, as the numbers of worker-students increased toward the end of 1920, the issues of adaptation to a new world would be overshadowed by the issue of survival as the physical deprivations increased with the student population. The three struggles of 1921 were to provide an unexpected and daunting turn in the road for the Chinese youth in France.

4
A FORK IN THE ROAD

We have now been abandoned! We have been abandoned! Where are
we to find the reasons we have been abandoned? . . . History tells us
a righteous struggle is not immoral. Economics tells us to give is not as
good as to receive. Logic also tells us that those whom good fortune
has forgotten will in the end be sought by good fortune.
—Manifesto of the Creusot Factory Student-Workers (1921)

The Work-Study Movement required a measure of boldness from each participant. At the minimum they had to be willing to leave the familiar environment of China and venture toward new experiences. As the Work-Study Movement gained more adherents, the very success of the program resulted in the beginning of the end of the enterprise. Wave after wave of Work-Study Movement participants arrived in France, and the pressures of survival overshadowed issues of acculturation. Unemployment, the inability to matriculate in educational institutions, and increasing deprivation and physical suffering all pervaded the Work-Study community. Before late 1920 the fundamental problems were intellectual and cultural, but by the end of that year, survival preempted other issues.

The last two chapters have looked at the adventurous reality of the Work-Study Movement from the individual and the group level. This chapter will first survey the organizational transitions within the Work-Study Movement that added to the activist, frenetic atmosphere of the Chinese community within France. Next, the decline of the Work-Study Movement will be discussed. Finally, the three struggles of 1921 will be explored.

Both encomia and eulogies on the Work-Study Movement were delivered before the controversies of 1921 occurred. Few would have predicted the turmoil, the decisive fork in the road, that emerged from the Chinese community's activist responses to their worsening situation and to a national concern. The first struggle, the Twenty-eighth Movement, was an attempt by one segment of the Work-Study students to solicit monetary support from the Chinese government. This movement resulted in defeat and highlighted the disunity of the Chinese community. The second incident, known as the Loan Struggle, concerned a national issue, an attempt by the Chinese government to obtain a loan from France. This incident not only mobilized but also unified the Chinese community in France. The third struggle, the Lyons Incident, resulted from the opening of the Sino-French Institute (SFI) at the University of Lyons, which was viewed by the worker-students as the last hope for the success of their program. Upon learning they would be denied immediate admittance and with the subsequent deportation of over one hundred Work-Study protesters, the Chinese community became dispirited. This disillusionment galvanized a segment of the Work-Study activists into forming the ECCO. Thus, the unfolding of the drama of the three struggles of 1921 catalyzed a number of Work-Study Movement participants to commit to lifetime careers as Communist revolutionaries.

ORGANIZATIONAL TRANSITIONS

Before exploring the decline of the Work-Study Movement and the three struggles of 1921, the shifting organizational context requires our attention. Genuine exploration of new intellectual and cultural interests resulted in changes in existing organizations and the creation of new organizations to meet these fresh challenges and interests.

The Young China Study Association, the New Citizens' Study Society, and the Self-Awakening Society served as moorings in a strange environment for many young Chinese. Yet they were shelters that were rocked by the chaos of Chinese politics and were eventually destroyed by organizational shifts in the dynamic environment of the Chinese community in France. The most stable group was the Young China Study Association, whose members in France, with the important exception of Zhao Shiyan, did not seek the factory experience. However, the French contingent did pursue intensive ideological debates with their comrades in China through association journals and other means, and the Chinese branches of the Young China Study Association suffered the same fissures that developed in most youth groups in China.

The New Citizens' Study Society had the most members committed to the Work-Study Movement ideal. Perhaps it was for this reason that they conducted some of the earliest, and most divisive, political debates, beginning in the summer of 1920, when Cai Hesen proposed the formation of a Marxist party during a three-day meeting in Montargis. As we will see later, alternative organizations developed within the New Citizens' Study Society community, and these eventually served as a springboard for Cai's Marxist proposals.

The Self-Awakening Society membership also split apart. Like the Young China Study Association, its "European" members remained a cohesive group which bound the ECCO together. However, the overall membership divided on the question of Communist commitment. It is significant that Zhang Ruoming and Liu Qingyang later left the ECCO and CCP respectively.

In addition to the conflicts within these youth groups formed in China, the atmosphere was complicated by the proliferation of new organizations within the Chinese community in Europe. For example, in 1923 a unified protest against foreign consolidation of Chinese railways resulted in the formation of an umbrella organization called the United Federation of Chinese Organizations Abroad in France, which consisted of twenty-two separate organizations. Many of these twenty-two organizations had been established before the three struggles of 1921.

Although the SFEA coordinated the travels, work, and education of the worker-students, it was the Chinese Federation (Huaqiao xieshe) that was the center of Chinese activities in Paris. The Chinese Federation was established on 31 August 1919 and was located in a multistoried building across from a park (39 rue de la Pointe, La Garenne-colombes, Seine). It served as a central mailing address for the students in addition to its role as a meeting place. The Chinese Federation was originally set up to unify and assist the Chinese community in France. The services it provided ranged from cheap printing to eventually allowing homeless worker-students to sleep on the floors of the building. The Chinese Federation had a library, sponsored enterprises, and helped its members by setting up a cooperative for daily living expenses to save them money. The fifteen groups that were under this umbrella organization reveal the broad range of the Chinese Federation: for example, the Paris Correspondence Service (Bali tongxin she), the Women's Work-Study Committee (Nüzi qingong jianxuehui), the Chinese Chemistry Study Society (Zhongguo huaxue yanjiuhui), the Far Eastern Biological Study Society (Yuandong shengwu yanjiuhui), the Chinese Labor Union, and the SFEA.[1] An article written in April 1921 by Zhang Ruoming, under the pseudonym Miss V., provides a very useful summary of the various groups, cliques, businesses, and publications of the Chinese community in France. In addition to the Chinese Federation, the SFEA, the Chinese Labor Union, the Frugal-Study Society, and the Work-Study Movement, the article mentions several other groups:

Huagong qingnianhui (YMCA for Chinese Workers)—This organization was for the benefit of workers, and its main purpose was to promote literacy among Chinese laborers. According to Zhang's article, each factory had a branch of this association. The organization was loose-knit in the sense that there were no fixed rules, and members contributed work according to their own wishes. The association published a Chinese vernacular newspaper,

1. See two *Shishi xinbao* articles, 14 November and 22 October 1919, in *FuFa*, 1:161–63.

Xing (*The Awakening*), to better the reading skills of its membership; other activities included movies and speeches.

Xuesheng qingnianhui (YMCA for Students)—This group was not as successful as the workers' YMCA. The difficulty was the deep resentment against religion that had been swelling for many years among the intelligentsia. The Paris branch of the Xuesheng qingnianhui had only about a dozen participants.

Guoji heping cujinhui (Society for the Advancement of International Peace)—This society was originally established during the Versailles Conference to agitate against Chinese approval of the treaty. The society was somewhat dormant after accomplishing its goal, but it did play a role during international conferences and demonstrations.

Bali xuesheng yundongtuan (Students in Paris Exercise Corps)—This group was organized by several students who felt too much attention was being paid to "high culture" and too little to their bodies. The scale of the organization was small, and funding nonexistent. Nevertheless, the corps organized soccer matches and had weekly competitions with French students.

Liu Fa lixueshe (Society for the Encouragement of Study in France)— The purpose of this society was mutual encouragement and cultural interchange. Members would meet before or after classes. The society had its own library, and French scholars were invited to deliver lectures on Sunday evenings.[2]

Among the publications listed, there were two that were labor oriented: the *Huagong zazhi* (*The Chinese Labor Magazine*), published monthly by the Diligent-Work Frugal-Study Association; and the *Huagong xunkan* (*Chinese Labor Weekly*), published by the Chinese Labor Union. Perhaps the most popular publication was the *Lü Ou zhoukan* (*The Travel to Europe Weekly*), which was edited by Zhou Taixuan. These publications contained general news of China, current affairs and world news, commentary, and correspondence.[3]

Miss V. had no scruples about describing all types of Chinese youth, and she was unsparing in her depiction of the student community. She divided students into four groups: (1) the Gongzi pai (the Playboys), who were the government-sponsored students and the sons of the rich (who else could

2. Miss V. [Zhang Ruoming], "Huaren zai Fa jingying zhi ge zhong zuzhi" [The management of each organization of Chinese in France], *Chen bao* (April 1921), in *FuFa*, 1:150–56.

3. Ibid., 153–54. Zhang's article as Miss V. is located in an appendix to *FuFa*, and one can readily understand why. She claims not only that the publications were unsophisticated but that the laborers could not read them anyway.

afford to be corrupted by the materialistic conditions of Paris?); (2) the Liumang pai (the Bullies and Ruffians), who were also corrupted by Western materialism, but instead of succumbing to dissipation, they sunk into a life of crime; (3) the Frugal-Study students; and (4) the Work-Study students. Miss V. saw a difference between the Frugal-Study students and the Work-Study students. Although the former had their misdirected elements, they made the best students, whereas the latter had neither the skill nor the ambition to be successful. In addition, the Work-Study Movement included quite a few troublemakers.[4]

The Chinese business endeavors in France ranged from the silk trade in Lyons, Chinese restaurants in Paris, Chinese cooperatives in Marseilles, to the renowned Paris Doufu Company established by Li Shizeng in 1909. The Paris Doufu Company was an interesting experiment in capitalism, intercultural relations, and the encouragement of Work-Study philosophy. Although Li Shizeng overestimated the potential desire for doufu products among the French, nevertheless the factory expanded from five to over a hundred workers. The success of the Paris Doufu Company spawned the Sino-French Trading Company, which, besides doufu, also delivered other Chinese goods such as tea and books. Li also began a Chinese-language publishing house.[5]

Lyons was an important place for trade between China and France. In an article discussing the 1921 trade fair in Lyons, Tian Yi criticized the lack of foresight by Chinese silk houses in allowing the Japanese to outcompete them in France. He pointed out that in 1909 the amounts of silk traded by China and Japan were equal, but by 1919 Chinese silk exports were only 42 percent of the Japanese level. However, given the then-current economic crisis and the lack of regulation in Chinese silk trading houses, Tian Yi urged the Chinese businessmen to make a greater effort to expand their markets.[6]

As more students arrived, organizational efforts took a more political turn. Two opposing groups, which were to draw together during the events of 1921, were the Society for the World of Work-Study (Gongxue shijie she) and the Work-Study Alliance (Qingong jianxue tongmeng). The former was initially organized in February 1920, under a different name, by several New Citizens' Study Society members, including Li Weihan, Li Fuchun, Zhang Kundi, Luo Xuezan, and He Guo. The original purpose of the

4. Ibid., 155–56.
5. Ibid., 154–55.
6. Tian Yi, "Liang wanguo huayang hui yu Zhong Fa siye" [The Lyons trade fair and the Sino-French silk trade], *Dongfang zazhi* 18 (25 April 1921): 91–92.

Society for the World of Work-Study was mutual help, but the organization's position evolved to a more radical stance, culminating in its Twenty-
eighth Movement decision to refuse to work for the Capitalists.[7]

There was a large current of opinion led by Zhao Shiyan, Wang Ruofei,
Li Lisan, Zhang Bojian, and others that condemned this "lazy" and "non-
productive" attitude. With the view of unifying the Work-Study Movement
into a self-sufficient entity, the Work-Study Alliance was established on 3
March 1921. Over two hundred students joined. On behalf of the Work-
Study Alliance, Zhang Bojian made the following declaration: "We want
to do any kind of productive labor. We want voluntary cooperation. We
want to firmly unite beneath the Work-Study banner."[8] The tensions
within the Work-Study Movement had carved deep cleavages among the
participants.

A group in France that might be classified as both political and religious
was the Young Chinese Catholic Association (Gongjiao qingnianhui), established by the famous Father Lebbe in 1923. This anti-Communist association published a weekly in Chinese and a monthly magazine in French,
Le bulletin de la jeunesse catholique chinoise. Before the organization was officially established, Father Lebbe had been finding homes for needy worker-
students, and his associate, Bernard Liu, had been teaching French to his
compatriots. It is ironic that the paper Zhou Enlai contributed to frequently
while in Europe during his Marxist conversion was Yishi bao (Social Welfare),
which Father Lebbe had established in Tianjin while he was serving in
China. In any case, the association was established to give students a
chance to study by relieving them of financial problems. Over one hundred
students availed themselves of this opportunity.[9]

One can see that the organizational activity in France was quite fruitful.
The foreign environment appeared to encourage the need for group affinity.
The rich diversity of organizational affiliations in France suggests that this
was a time of creativity and exploration for the Chinese youth.

7. Li Weihan, "Huiyi Xinmin xuehui," 35–36, 43–44.
8. Zhang Bojian, "Qingong jianxue bianqian lueshi" [A summary of the changes in the
Work-Study Movement], Shishi xinbao (October 1921), in FuFa, 1:117–21.
9. Jacques Leclerq, Thunder in the Distance: The Life of Père Lebbe, trans. George Lamb
(New York: Sheed and Ward, 1958), 218–41; Wu Qi, "Zhou Enlai tongzhi qingnian shidai
zai Fa De liangguo de geming shenghuo" [The revolutionary life of comrade Zhou Enlai
during his youth in France and Germany], Tianjin wenshi ziliao xuanji 15 (May 1981): 131–
45, see 144; Jiang Zemin, "Canjia liu Fa Bi qingong jianxue de huiyi" [Reminiscences of
participating in the overseas French-Belgium Work-Study Movement], Tianjin wenshi ziliao
xuanji 15 (May 1981): 93–113, see 107; and for a good history of the Yishi bao see Yu
Zhihou, "Tianjin Yishi bao gaishu" [An outline of the Tianjin newspaper Yishi bao], Tianjin
wenshi ziliao xuanji 18 (January 1982): 70–93.

THE DECLINE OF THE WORK-STUDY MOVEMENT

The Work-Study Movement's basic administrative organization, the SFEA, became the focus of increased scrutiny and petitions as the year 1920 drew to a close. The secretary of the association during 1920 was Liu Hou, who had the task of managing educational and factory placement for the increasing number of worker-students. He also shouldered the awesome responsibility of dealing with the economic situation for the Work-Study Movement, from the weekly loans that many sought to the sleeping arrangements in the tents.

Liu was very frustrated and angered by the criticisms that came his way, but he was stirred to his own defense after he was beaten up while consulting with several angry Work-Study participants in the consulate on 10 August 1920. Liu was called upon to hear grievances with the consul, Liao Shisong, who chaired the proceedings, and Yang Taohui, who served as arbitrator. There were about twenty people present, who complained about ill treatment at the hands of the SFEA. When it was suggested to them that this was a government matter and that Yang should meet with Liao and Liu to discuss these issues in detail, an ugly confrontation developed. Liu was surrounded by several of those present and beaten and kicked on the head, back, and legs before his assailants were halted.[10]

Liu Hou wrote several public letters explaining the difficulties of the Work-Study Movement. The problems he identified were several. The preparation for worker-students was inadequate. There was not enough talent or money to manage the movement. The Work-Study Movement had opponents who did not want to see it succeed. Job placement was not easy and the negotiating of matriculation in French schools was often slow and difficult. Finally, the problems were compounded by students who were angry at the SFEA. Liu was not without hope, however. In particular, he still believed that a "change in spirit" might affect the success of the Work-Study Movement. Language skills could be improved, the SFEA was gaining more experience in finding jobs, and people were managing their money more wisely. The students were receiving a warm reception by the French. Significantly, Liu also commented that, according to Xiao Zisheng, the SFI alternative seemed promising.[11]

Liu Hou's point of view was popular with many of the worker-students. "Self-sufficiency" was a watchword for many of them. During this period Wang Ruofei was disparaging those who, "because they had no ambition to

10. Liu Hou, *Shishi xinbao* (October 1920), in *FuFa*, 2:348–64.
11. Ibid., 342–47.

work, complained about those who managed the Sino-French Educational Association."[12]

An appeal made in mid-December by some worker-students also showed that students were not yet alienated from the SFEA or the potentialities of the Work-Study Movement. The appeal called for some amelioration of the wretched conditions endured in France, especially the plight of the tent people, but it also expressed impatience with those who constantly changed jobs, spoiling things for the others. The appeal, which was quite similar in some ways to the one issued at the end of the month by Zhao Shiyan, Chen Gong-pei, and Li Lisan, among others, claimed that its purpose was to increase national strength and ensure the future of succeeding generations. "The students who travel to France and perform hard labor," proclaimed the appeal, "seek knowledge and technical abilities; they want to develop total personalities, to advance the social progress of our nation. *We definitely did not come to France to promote anarchism or build radical parties"* (emphasis mine).[13]

Nonparticipants also offered opinions on the viability of the Work-Study Movement. Zhang Mengjiu, a Young China Study Association member, wrote a critique of overseas study in late 1920. After contrasting various facets of living in the West and the East, Zhang categorized Chinese students in the West as either passive or active. The passive students were "paper chasers," who totally accepted Western schemas or else dismissed every Western theory by claiming they had all appeared earlier in China: they "hear of socialism, it was already discovered by Mozi, hearing of individualism, it was already thought of by Laozi and Zhuangzi." Of the active students there were those who were totally Westernized and desired to be Chinese officials in the West and those who were totally Sinicized and wanted to be officials in China. Those who were well balanced and stood on the middle ground, although they only constituted 1.2 percent of the student population, "were the hope of China's future." With this view of an effective elite, Zhang endorsed an increasingly skeptical view of the viability of the Work-Study Movement:

A year has gone by since the promotion of the Sino-French Educational Association by Messieurs Li Shizeng, Cai Yuanpei, and Wu Zhihui, [and] the internal climate to study in France has risen day by day. But from January of this year [1920] until I have gone abroad, this climate has had a gradual change. A year ago, the whole society of the

12. Wang Ruofei, "Shengxia men qingong riji" [Diary of diligent labor at the Saint Chamond factory], *Shaonian shijie* (1920), in *FuFa*, 2:229.

13. "Liu Fa qingong jianxue sheng zhi huji shu" [The appeal by the travel to France worker-students], *Shishi xinbao* (December 1920), in *FuFa*, 2:365–77.

country, except for a few official types, no matter which circle of age or gender, all approved of study in France. . . . [But now] there are divisions. There are those who approve, those who are opposed, those who are satisfied, and those who are suspicious. Moreover the suspicious clique are the most numerous.[14]

After highlighting the benefits and a few faults of French civilization, Zhang concluded that it was not France but the quality of the Chinese who were studying abroad that was not high.

Li Huang, writing a "Critique of Overseas Study" in the same Young China Study Association issue, echoed the pessimism of Zhang Mengjiu. The promoters of study abroad had been too optimistic and were in for a big disappointment. Although well motivated, the Chinese in France were not well prepared, squandered their resources, and experienced difficulties in adjustment. In an ironic twist to the generational theme, Li did not place his hopes in the government but rather on family influence. He looked to the fathers and older brothers who had previously exercised "no restraint" on the students who went to France.[15] Li Huang, who had served as a voluntary tutor for the tent dwellers and had escorted two groups of Chinese to Paris, was in a better position to objectively critique the students. Yet, it should be remembered that he was not a Work-Study participant himself, because he was entirely supported by his father in Chengdu.

This kind of negative perception of the Work-Study Movement was also shared by some of the more leftist-inclined students. Zhang Ruoming, a Self-Awakening Society member who later joined the ECCO, wrote several scathing critiques of the Work-Study community (both as Miss V. and under her own name). Like Zhang Mengjiu, she was also skeptical of the motivations and abilities of the worker-students.

The mainstays of the SFEA seemed to be disappearing. Li Shizeng left for China in February 1919. The association's secretaries changed several times, confusing the situation because they were unfamiliar with the work of the association. In addition, an atmosphere of distrust and anger lurked just below the surface. The increasingly *rude* manner in which some students made their demands was obvious not only in appeals such as the one mentioned earlier, where the petitioners felt the need to stress their lack of political ambition to form parties, but also in more direct expressions of frustration such as the beating of Liu Hou.

14. Zhang Mengjiu, "Liu Fa liangzhou de ganxiang" [Reflections after two weeks of travel to France], *Shaonian Zhongguo* 2/6 (December 1920): 7–16.
15. Li Huang, "Liuxue pingyi" [A critique of overseas study], *Shaonian Zhongguo* 2/6 (December 1920): 1–7.

The physical attack on Liu Hou presaged the coming violence and polarization in the French scene and the deterioration of traditional modes of discourse begun in the New Culture era. The New Culture ethos involved dialogue, not fisticuffs. Liu Hou, who was a young man himself, invoked the generational theme a little differently from Li Huang. Liu felt that most students perceived the SFEA as a symbol of authority much like the way schools had been viewed in the May Fourth Movement, and the students were acting out their generational desires to "rebel." This was at the very least a provocative insight.

THE TWENTY-EIGHTH MOVEMENT

Cai Yuanpei arrived in Paris on 27 December 1920 with several tasks in mind: to oversee the progress of Lyons University and Charleroi University negotiations, to help with the Institute of Chinese Higher Studies in Paris, and to assist the Work-Study Movement. An overburdened Cai decided that the weight of the last problem was too difficult to shoulder. Indeed, Cai Yuanpei was handling a great deal of responsibility, and his wife in China was very ill during this period.[16] One wonders, however, why he paid so little attention to the worker-students before issuing his two proclamations. According to one account he never read one word of the appeals and met with the student representatives for only two hours at the Chinese consulate in Paris.[17]

Cai's first announcement, published on 12 January 1921, sought to put the Work-Study Movement in perspective by reviewing some organizational history. According to Cai, the Frugal-Study Society, the Diligent-Work Frugal-Study Association, and the SFEA were three separate organizations. Thus, the SFEA was only a part of the Work-Study Movement and should not be burdened with all the responsibility. Since the SFEA never had an independent financial basis and subsisted on contributions, it was unfair of the students to constantly blame the SFEA for their problems or to expect the SFEA to support them. The rest of the document suggested ways in which the students could organize themselves on a regional basis.[18]

Cai's second announcement was released only four days later, on 16 January 1921. The tone was blunter, flatly stating that the SFEA would discontinue loans after February and would refuse to answer any questions about

16. Cai received news of his wife's death during the third week of January (*Lü Ou zhoukan* [January 1921]).
17. "Qingong jianxue de lishi" [The history of the Work-Study Movement] (1921), in Bian Xiaoxuan, "Liu Fa qingong jianxue ziliao," 185.
18. Tian Yi, "Liu Fa qingong jianxue sheng shi guan qingyuan ji," 2–4.

the matter. The SFEA was abrogating all economic responsibility.[19] Zhou Enlai, who wrote an extensive series of articles for the *Yishi bao* on the Twenty-eighth Movement, criticized Cai's actions. He pointed out that the same people were responsible for the organization of all three groups that had created the Work-Study Movement. The SFEA handled all the administrative work for the Work-Study Movement, which was perceived as an enterprise of the SFEA. Zhou felt that since Cai Yuanpei had urged students throughout China to go to France, he could not suddenly revoke his responsibility in an announcement: "Mr. Cai is the president of the Sino-French Educational Association; he has been a promoter of the Work-Study Movement; he cannot but be concerned with the current matters of the Work-Study Movement."[20] Zhou Enlai's point was well taken and exemplified a growing alienation between radical youth and their enlightened elders. A chasm was developing between the Found Generation and the Generation of Lasts and Firsts.

However doubtful the worker-students may have felt about the reasoning behind the announcements, the stark facts remained that in the short term financial aid was required and a long-term strategy of Work-Study in France needed articulation. Several meetings took place without producing any concrete plans.[21] The disparate rationales and motivations for participation in the Work-Study Movement were reflected in the lack of unity during the crisis engendered by Cai Yuanpei's two announcements.

Amidst the feelings of disarray and depression, two factions emerged. One of these was led by Zhao Shiyan, Li Lisan, and Wang Ruofei, who had earlier formed a small labor mutual aid organization advocating the principles of self-sufficiency. Opposing this faction were many members of the New Citizens' Study Society and the Society for the World of Work-Study, commanded by Cai Hesen in Montargis, who advocated a four-year government support plan and who proposed that they proceed en masse to the Chinese legation to present their appeal. By the end of February, both sides had succeeded in consolidating their factions. The Montargis faction[22] applied for a permit to hold a demonstration in front of the Chinese legation, while the Zhao Shiyan clique went on to form the Work-Study Alliance.

19. Ibid., 5–6.
20. Zhou Enlai, "Liu Fa qingong jianxuesheng zhi da bolan," *Yishi bao* (May 1921) (written in February and March), in *FuFa*, 1:12–16.
21. "Qingong jianxue de lishi," 187–88. This source includes an announcement made by student representatives Yin Kuan, Wang Zekai (who later became ECCO founders), and four others revealing the disorganization caused by the January proclamations. At this stage, no organizational scheme to improve the situation was agreed upon.
22. This name was so popular that a history of the city written in 1980 proudly notes

Although they claimed to the community that they were Marxists, the Montargis permit request for a demonstration stated that the intent was to request monetary aid to remain in France and pursue studies. It further promised that there was no intention to create public disorder.[23] The permit was denied, but the Montargis faction still called for a demonstration on 28 February.

Chen Lu, the Chinese minister to France, was warned in advance that a demonstration was in the works. On the morning of 28 February, a crowd of between three and four hundred Chinese gathered outside the legation at 54 rue Babylon, standing in the square de Bon Marché. Chen received eleven representatives inside the legation. Their demands included government support at the rate of four hundred francs each month, per student, for a limit of four years. Chen extended his regrets and offered temporary aid of five francs a person per day for three months and free repatriation and promised an effort by the government to find jobs for the students. The offer was unacceptable to the delegation and to the demonstrators outside, as Chen Lu's subsequent attempt to address the crowd clearly showed. According to a French official report:

> Toward 1:45 the Chinese minister left the legation alone to visit the Bon Marché crowd. When he arrived, the students were grouped around him to hear his explanations. After his talk, the Minister was applauded by a certain number of students, while others were raising protests. At this moment the Minister received some manhandling and could not have disengaged himself without the intervention of the municipal Police.[24]

The police used force to break up the demonstration,[25] but the only arrests were of those members of the delegation inside the legation who refused to leave the premises. However, Chen Lu declined to press charges against those taken into custody. Despite the confusing transliteration of Chinese names in the report, it is clear that among those arrested were Xiang Jingyu and Cai Hesen. Cai was characterized as the leader of the movement and a "dangerous individual" who needed to be watched.[26]

their presence as "le groupe de Montargis," who later went on to become famous leaders of the PRC (Gache, *Les grandes heures de Montargis*, 120).

23. "Les étudiants chinoise en France," 23 February 1921 note, AN, F719200.

24. Note of Monsieur Deveze, 9 March 1921, AOM, SLOTFOM VII, 6. This account agrees in most details with the Chinese account of Tian Yi, "Liu Fa qingong jianxue sheng shi guan qingyuan ji."

25. Tian Yi, "Liu Fa qingong jianxue sheng shi guan qingyuan ji," 6–7.

26. Note of M. Deveze. Out of the eleven delegates, one delegate, "Yu Yu Yu," voluntarily left the legation.

The atmosphere of official disdain for the *rude* Work-Study students increased in the aftermath of the Twenty-eighth Movement. Chen Lu had been aware of the tense situation and before 28 February had sent several telegrams to the Beijing government. In early February he had cabled the government that Cai Yuanpei's announcements had created a potentially violent situation. Students were coming to the legation every day to ask for financial help. If this situation continued, it was bound to shame the country (*dianru guoti*). On 11 February Chen again cabled that the situation was worsening. He hoped that the government had stopped issuing passports. The day before the Twenty-eighth Movement took place, Chen Lu sent a telegram about the impending demonstration and suggested that the idea of sending students home was not only expensive but ineffective as the students wanted aid and would rather die than return to China. Chen Lu's telegram following the Twenty-eighth Movement related the details of what had occurred and then mentioned that it had been a humiliating experience. He had tried to help the students, he said, and did not feel ashamed of his actions. He did not believe he deserved to be placed in the embarrassing situation in which the students had put him. Chen suggested that the government send a special person to deal with these problems, as it was not his job to oversee students. [27]

These telegrams indicate that Chen Lu and the government were changing their attitude toward the Work-Study Movement. Chen Lu was less upset that the students had come for aid than he was about the way they had demonstrated in front of the legation. The fact that Chen Lu went himself to address the students meant that he felt they were still amenable to the older traditions of respect toward authority and customary polite behavior. He found that the old rules did not apply any longer. The younger generation were not operating under the same rules of formality and etiquette. His disillusionment soured him toward the worker-students.

The Twenty-eighth Movement was not only unsuccessful in obtaining its goals but also deepened divisions in the Work-Study Movement. According to Zheng Chaolin these divisions created an environment of acrimony and accusations:

> At that time in the Work-Study Movement there were several good
> leaders of two cliques. One was led by Cai Hesen. He was a Marxist
> from the beginning, and the goals of the movement that he led were

27. Chen Lu, telegrams to the central government (February and March 1921), in *FuFa*, 2:394–96.

spreading propaganda and Marxism. The other clique was headed by Zhao Shiyan, Li Lisan, and Wang Ruofei. This clique opposed Cai Hesen's Montargis faction. I leaned toward the latter group [Zhao Shiyan's], because many of my friends belonged to it. . . . They had been studying Marxism in great detail. . . . but they had not divided society into different parts. . . . they were continuing the May Fourth Movement in France. . . . At this time we heard the criticisms of the Montargis faction against the Zhao faction, saying they were bought out by the Beijing government; their accusations had a seeming basis in fact. At that time the Beijing government sent an official, Zhu Qiqian (he was from Guizhou), and the Zhao clique included Xiong Zinan and Wang Ruofei, who were also from Guizhou. Later it was proved a spurious theory, and it only increased my hostility for the Montargis faction. The leaders [in the Zhao faction] were quite bitter because of this [the rumors]. Xiong Zinan received a real blow to his spirits. Zhao Shiyan even prepared to commit suicide. He wrote a poem; it had several lines; I remember the first few lines: "Close the door, a knife, a rope. . . ."[28]

In his reminiscences of Zhao Shiyan, Li Lisan claimed that the two groups both wanted a Marxist revolution. Before the Twenty-eighth Movement Zhao and Li had organized the Labor Study Society (Laodong xuehui) along with six others, including Liu Bojian and Chen Gongpei. According to Li Lisan, Li and Zhao wanted it to be a Communist organization, but not all were agreed on this point. At the time of the Twenty-eighth Movement, Li personally wanted to participate in the demonstration, but he was too angry at the slanders spread about Zhao. After the Twenty-eighth Movement, Li remarked that it opened up everyone's eyes as to the unreliability of the government in helping the students.[29]

Li Lisan's account is interesting because it tries to establish ex post facto that Li had a Marxist commitment and to suggest that he was sympathetic to the Montargis faction. However, his writings at the time, both before and after the Twenty-eighth Movement, indicate his organizational principles were based on the spirit of self-sufficiency and on the Kropotkin concept of mutual aid, and there was an explicit anti-Montargis sentiment in his activities. For example, two weeks before the Twenty-eighth Movement Li Lisan wrote an article outlining an organizational scheme for self-

28. Zheng Chaolin, "Zheng Chaolin tan Zhao Shiyan he lü Ou zhibu" [Zheng Chaolin discusses Zhao Shiyan and the ECCO] (14 January 1960), Yida qianhou, 2:531–38, the quotation is on 531–32. Xiong Zinan, one of Zhao's closest compatriots, did indeed commit suicide several months later.

29. Li Lisan, "Dui Zhao Shiyan de huiyi" [Remembrances of Zhao Shiyan] (3 September 1960), Yida qianhou, 2:524–25.

sufficient survival. He emphasized organizational unity, free will, the need to increase savings, and mutual aid. One week after the Twenty-eighth Movement Li again published an article affirming his belief in the need for positive organization and self-sufficiency. He chastised the Montargis group for not putting forward positive suggestions but only negative criticisms of the Work-Study Movement.[30]

Zhao Shiyan also wrote several articles setting forth the case for organization and self-sufficiency, although he did not engage in any direct assault on the Montargis faction. Zhao was impatient with the emphasis on money and believed that discussions should center around the concept of "labor," the foundation of the Work-Study Movement.[31]

Given these views of Zhao Shiyan and Li Lisan, the principle of self-sufficiency and nondependence on government became a cornerstone of the Work-Study Alliance, formed in March 1921. The organization urged unity and self-sufficiency, and its members believed in the worth of working in the factories and in mutual aid. More than two hundred worker-students joined the organization, and it dispelled the lingering doubts with regard to the Zhao clique.[32]

Zhang Bojian, whose writings on the Work-Study Alliance were mentioned earlier, also wrote about the Work-Study Movement in general. According to Zhang's characterization, there were three types of worker-students: (1) the real workers (600 people), who were the real leaders of revolution and obtained knowledge via work and often clashed with the intelligentsia, who wanted to replace this worker orientation as the focal point of change; (2) those who did not want to work (200–300 people), probably a dig at the Montargis faction supporters, and who were either preoccupied with waiting for Lyons to open or believed that everyone was the oppressed proletariat; and (3) those who were malingering (100–200 people), probably the group of playboys and bullies that Miss V. mentioned. These people possibly had no intention of working as they were "dissolute, usually rich, rude, played mah-jongg all day, and were lazy."[33]

Other members of the Work-Study Movement community also complained of the Montargis faction. Stigmatizing them as self-serving, the re-

30. Li Lisan [Long Zhi, pseud.], "Wo duiyu zuzhi qingong jianxuehui de yijian" [My opinions concerning organizing the work-study society], *Lü Ou zhoukan* 66 (5 February 1921): 65; Li Lisan [Zuo Fu, pseud.], "Jiaohuan yu huzhu" [Mutual-exchange and mutual-aid], *Lü Ou zhoukan* 69 (5 March 1921): 1–2.

31. Zhao Shiyan, "Huade weilao de qingong jianxuezhe" [The restrictions of the worker-students], *Lü Ou zhoukan* 64 (21 January 1921): 1. Also see his article on 26 February 1921.

32. Li Lisan, "Dui Zhao Shiyan de huiyi," 525–26.

33. Zhang Bojian, "Qingong jianxue bianqian lueshi," 120–21.

spected elder Work-Study participant Xu Teli, who was in his midfifties when he went to France, rather acidly remarked in a two-part article: "The Montargis students have promoted Marxism. However, for their desire of regular yearly aid they are willing to sacrifice their beliefs. . . . I have only heard of sacrificing oneself for one's beliefs. I have never heard of sacrificing a doctrine for one's own interests."[34]

Some of the educated Chinese laborers also were upset by the unwillingness of the Montargis faction to "soil themselves with physical labor." In a riveting, eloquent appeal one laborer wrote how his feelings were hurt because the Montargis faction had "sworn not to be Chinese laborers." He recounted the sufferings of the Chinese Labor Corps, mentioned the long process of consciousness raising among the Chinese laborers, and invited the students to show a spirit of solidarity in their struggles. Echoing the skepticism of Xu Teli on the motives of the Montargis faction, this worker highlighted the perceived ethical inconsistency of government aid: "It is difficult to comprehend [you] labeling us Chinese laborers around the world as perpetual slaves. O Work-Study students! You say that the government is like a pirate. We also see it as a thief. However, if you are seeking government funds, are you not then taking a cut of the pie?"[35]

Although Zheng Chaolin's characterization of the Montargis faction, and specifically of Cai Hesen, as the more developed Marxists is essentially correct, it should be understood that this was a transitional period of radicalization. Cai's initial proposals to establish a Marxist party were vetoed by a majority of the New Citizens' Study Society during the summer of 1920. In a letter written in December 1920, Mao Zedong wrote to his French New Citizens' Study Society cohorts in response to the mid-1920 debates in France that he was more inclined to Cai Hesen's vision of the future rather than that of Bertrand Russell (who had been lecturing during this period at Chinese universities), Li Hesheng,[36] or Xiao Zisheng.[37]

As mentioned previously, the Society for the World of Work-Study had been established in early 1920 as a mutual aid society. It was first named the Society for the Encouragement of Work-Study (Qingong jianxue lijinhui).

34. Xu Teli, "Ou Mengdani tongxue de gongqi" [Criticizing the appeal of the Montargis students], Lü Ou zhoukan 68 and 69 (26 February 1921/5 March 1921): 1, 1.
35. Wuming huagong [Unnamed Worker], "Qingong jianxue gai qiu zizhu ya!" (The Work-Study participants must seek self-help!), Lü Ou zhoukan 70 (12 March 1921): 3–4. In Europe the Chinese laborers participated in the debates concerning the formation of the ECCO and the European Branch of the GMD, in marked contrast to the situation in China during the formation of the CCP.
36. Li Hesheng was an alternative name for Li Weihan, who was one of the founders of the Society for the World of Work-Study.
37. Mao Zedong letter, 1 December 1920, in Yida qianhou, 2:164–72.

Among the founders were Li Fuchun, Zhang Kundi, Ren Li, He Guo, Luo Xuezan, and Li Weihan. The group was formed basically to share new ideas and plan for action and mutual support in the new environment and under adverse conditions. Although Cai Hesen was not a member, the Society for the World of Work-Study often reflected New Citizens' Study Society policy. By the summer of 1920 there were over thirty members.[38]

Luo Xuezan organized the *Gongxue shijie tongxin she* (*Society for the World of Work-Study Newsletter*), which published accounts of the Work-Study Movement in France (especially for distribution in Hunan). The monthly publication included sections on labor conditions, the life of the worker, news of the Chinese laborer, news of the Work-Study Movement, the situation in France in general, random thoughts on traveling to France, and correspondence of the members of the Society for the World of Work-Study. The paper was worker oriented, but it was not a Marxist publication.[39]

It would seem that some Marxist principles were accepted by the Society for the World of Work-Study in varying degrees, but members were not committed to Cai Hesen's vision yet. During most of 1920 the group did not have a Marxist self-identity. For example, Luo Xuezan's letter to Xu Teli in November 1920 was still enthusiastic about the Work-Study Movement principles. Like Wang Ruofei, Luo felt that labor could be enjoyable and that one could study several hours a day while working in a factory. In Luo's view, the work-study scheme had three important advantages: it was useful in solving world problems, it had educational value, and one could learn new ways of living.[40] However, some of Luo's ideas possessed some Marxist inclinations. In a biography of Luo Xuezan the authors cite an early article of his, "The French Laborer" (ca. 1920), that claimed that a solution for economic disparity would encompass a total revision of government organization and a redistribution of wealth. A society based on materialism was empty of spiritual attainment, and Luo felt it was his duty to help achieve the latter for his fellow human beings. Although not committed to Marxism, he had some positive things to say about bolshevism, which Luo perceived as a positive force among French workers.[41] However, under the straitened circumstances of the Work-Study Movement and aided by the

38. Li Weihan, "Huiyi Xinmin xuehui," 35–36.
39. Luo Xuezan letter to Mao Zedong, 25 May 1920, in Hunan sheng zhexue shehui kexue yanjiusuo xiandaishi yanjiushi, *Wusi shiqi Hunan renmin geming douzheng shiliao xuanbian*, 439–40.
40. Luo Xuezan letter to Xu Teli, 12 November 1920, in *FuFa*, 2:291–94.
41. Luo Lizhou and Fan Yinzheng, "Luo Xuezan," in Hu Hua, ed., *Zhonggong dangshi renwu zhuan*, 5:175–203. See 183–93 for Work-Study participation.

dissemination of Marxist literature by Cai Hesen and Xiang Jingyu at Montargis, a major part of the Society for the World of Work-Study got behind Cai by the end of 1920 and supported him in the Twenty-eighth Movement.

The Twenty-eighth Movement outlined several basic areas of conflict and agreement. The Montargis faction and the Zhao clique both thought, from either personal experience or ideological conviction, that there were flaws in the Capitalist system. But the problem was one of method. Should they form a Marxist party? If so, what procedures should they use in forming the party? Should they follow the Russian example? Would working in a factory contribute to capitalism, or would it be an educational tool? The Twenty-eighth Movement did generate some areas of confluence, as most students recognized the need for some sort of organization, agreed that they could not rely on the government, and believed that the failure of the Twenty-eighth Movement was due to the lack of unity among the worker-students. Hoping to answer some of the confusing organizational and ideological questions, Zhao Shiyan began to visit Montargis after the Twenty-eighth Movement in hopes of creating a unified movement.

Zhao and others of his clique, including Wang Ruofei, visited Montargis, attended several meetings of the Society for the World of Work-Study, and discussed the formation of a Communist party. The two groups were approaching a formal agreement at the beginning of the summer.[42] However, events were to overwhelm the student population as news of a three million franc loan negotiation was leaked. This served to shelve the Marxist organizational issue in favor of more immediate community issues, primarily that of urging the exposure and rejection of a Sino-French loan.

THE LOAN STRUGGLE

French businessmen, educators, and government officials who had urged closer Sino-French relations were concerned with the plight of the Work-Study Movement. In May 1921, the Comité franco-chinois de patronage des jeunes chinois en France (CFC) was formed to help the young Chinese currently in France seeking education and employment. A CFC circular invited the Chinese to apply for assistance: "The Comité is at your disposal to help you [and] to facilitate your studies. Student-workers, it will try hard to procure for you employment in industry, commerce, mines, to give you all

42. This is remembered by those on both sides of the Twenty-eighth Movement issue. See Xiao San, *Xiao San wenji* [Collected writings of Xiao San] (Beijing: Xinhua, 1983), 262–63; and Li Lisan, "Dui Zhao Shiyan de huiyi," 526–27.

the possibilities to perfect the French language." Applicants had to agree not to leave the new jobs without the authorization of the CFC, which promised to "examine your case with the greatest attention and the most paternal interest."[43] Less than one year later, the CFC had amassed over 1,200 dossiers, and in less than half a year had distributed over 250,000 francs to educational institutions and students. The numerous cartons containing catalogs and letters of inquiry and recommendation currently deposited at the Archives nationales testify to the industriousness of Eugène Bradier, secretary of the CFC. Although the honorary titles of the CFC went to Painlevé, Senator Hugues Le Roux, Philippe Berthelot, Herriot, Chen Lu, Cai Yuanpei, and others, it was Bradier, on loan from the Ministère des affaires etrangères, who took charge of this immense effort.[44]

Although the benign attitude of the legation and the helpful loans[45] and placement activities of the CFC were bearing fruit, the political tension in the Chinese community in France was intensifying due to two developments during the summer of 1921. The first was the bankruptcy of the Banque industrielle de Chine (BIC), and the second was an attempted loan of three million francs to the Chinese government. Both actions were interconnected and precipitated the second struggle of that year.

Established in 1913, the BIC was promoted by the prestigious Brothers Berthelot, André and Philippe. Both were involved in business and government and enjoyed some renown in cultural circles that included Paul Claudel, Colette, Jean Cocteau, and St.-John Perse.[46] Pursuing a close relation with the Yuan Shikai government and boldly competing with the more conservative Banque de l'Indochine, in less then seven years the BIC acquired 22 agencies, 3,000 clients, and one million francs in deposits. In 1920 the director-general in China, Alexis-Joseph Pernotte, received a 200,000-franc bonus, and the bank distributed 14 percent dividends to investors. However, this bold policy also reflected imprudence and poor in-

43. 1921 Circular of the CFC, AN, 47 AS 8.

44. See particularly Comité franco-chinois de patronage des jeunes chinois en France, Séance du 4 juin 1921, which contains the statutes and names of officials (AAE, série E, Chine, vol. 48).

45. The records of loans by the CFC provide some interesting clues to the whereabouts of many Chinese who later became prominent, as well as some of their earliest signatures: Liou Jeh Kien (Liu Bojian), Lin Wei, Chan Ngai (Chen Yi), Li Ki Ta (Li Jida), Fou Tchong (Fu Zhong), Mou Tsin (Mu Qing), Li Fou Tchuen (Li Fuchun), Tchang Keon Ti (Zhang Kundi), Jen Li (Ren Li), Teng Si Hien (Deng Xixian, Deng Xiaoping), Tsai Lin Pieng (Cai Linbin, Cai Hesen), Siao Tche Fan (Xiao Zhifan, Xiao San), and many others (AN, 47 AS 27).

46. J. N. Jeanneney, "Finances, presse et politique: L'affaire de la Banque industrielle de Chine (1921–1923)," 377–416. There are numerous cartons covering the BIC debacle in the AAE; for the beginnings of the crisis see série E, Chine, vol. 93.

vestment decisions. By 1920, the large dividends could not hide the impending disaster, and frantic efforts by the Banque de Paris et de Pays-Bas and individual entrepreneurs could not save the bank.[47] The crisis was exacerbated by intergovernmental rivalries, and by 30 June 1920, the bank closed its doors, with several consequences. For many Chinese in France it meant the loss of their savings, leaving them stranded and angry. It was a giant blow for the government of Briand, and it enormously damaged French prestige in Asia. The British annual political report for 1921 noted this decline of France in Asia due to the bank failure:

> The blow to French prestige in the Far East can hardly be exaggerated, and it is because the French government realizes this that such desperate efforts are being made to refloat the bank. The latest telegrams from Paris indicate that they have decided to devote a portion of the Boxer indemnity for the purpose. . . . In last year's report it was stated that the French were neither liked or respected by the Chinese. This expedient will hardly increase the Chinese respect for them.[48]

The humiliation of the BIC failure was felt by many concerned with Sino-French relations. In an article on French influence in the Far East, Henri Froidevaux wrote that it was not unlikely that the Chinese would equate the failure of the BIC with the failure of France. Froidevaux urged a strong course of support from the government, not only to promote the material interests of France but also to "recover the face we have lost."[49]

For the Chinese community, losing their savings was the first blow. The second alarm came when the news of a potential French loan to the Chinese government broke in mid-June. Zhu Qiqian was an emissary of the Chinese president, Xu Shichang, and arrived in France ostensibly to receive an honorary degree from the University of Paris, but he was also negotiating a three million franc loan on behalf of the Chinese government. Suspicions seemed confirmed when he was followed to Paris by Wu Dingchang, the famous banker. Thus, not only had many Chinese laborers lost the hard-earned fruits of their labor in the BIC failure, but they had to watch the French government consider a loan to the warlords back in China.

What raised the ire of the Chinese in France was the feeling that the money would just be wasted in the corrupt government's further pursuit of

47. Jeanneney, "Finances, presse et politique," 382, 384–92.
48. B. Alston to Marquess Curzon of Kedleston, "1921 Annual Report—China," PRO, FO 371/8033.
49. Henri Froidevaux, "Pour le maintien de l'influence française en Chine," L'Asie française 198 (January 1922): 6–10.

military consolidation, in addition to refloating the BIC. They viewed Zhu, Wu, and the officials as traitors.[50] Within two weeks the Chinese community in France began to meet and plan unified activity, calling for a general meeting on 30 June. The meeting was attended by between three and four hundred people in the Palais des Sociétés savantes. Five different Chinese organizations sponsored the meeting, and the leaders called for collective action by all classes, workers, businesses, and students. Several speeches were given about the secret loan negotiations, denouncing the government's perfidy. Direct action was called for by the Chinese community. The actions proposed were largely to publicize the situation by sending protest telegrams and letters. Over one thousand letters were sent to French politicians, journalists, and educators.

A resolution passed by the meeting called attention to the unconstitutional nature of the loan negotiation and asserted that it was a pretext for saving the BIC. The resolution sought to alert the French to the immorality of the issue and the lack of guarantees for the future repayment of a loan contracted unconstitutionally.[51]

Chen Lu effectively dispelled suspicions by publicizing two letters to the Chinese community. In the first letter he asserted that the whole situation was fraught with misunderstandings. In the second letter he claimed that Wu had said the bank administrators on the French side did not approve of the loan. Chen stated, "This office can guarantee that this loan negotiation has not become a reality." However, despite Chen Lu's assurances, on 25 July the *Paris Times* revealed that signatures had already been obtained for approval of the loan, which had risen to five million francs.[52]

The Chinese in France were furious with Chen Lu, who was accused of being a traitor. Zhou Enlai expressed the common sentiment when he scolded Chen Lu for his perfidy: "deceiving his compatriots, his heart is full of cruelty, that much is already obvious."[53] Leaders of the angry Chinese community called another meeting on the afternoon of 13 August. It was quite an event, attended by over three hundred people. The agenda had

50. Zhou Enlai, "Lü Fa Huaren jujue jiekuan zhi yundong" [The Chinese in France movement to refuse the loan], *Yishi bao* (written 30 June 1921), in *FuFa*, 2:459–61.

51. "Ordre du jour de la Société générale de la colonie chinoises en France," 30 June 1921, Paris. A copy of this resolution, along with other, more detailed handouts underlining the connection of the loan with the BIC can be found in M. Josselme to Monsieur le Résident Supérieur Guesde, Marseilles, 15 August 1921, dispatch no. 98 (AOM, SLOT-FOM IV, 9).

52. Zhou Enlai, "Zhong Fa da jiekuan jing shixing qianzi yi" [The situation of the signing of the big Sino-French loan], *Yishi bao* (written 30 July 1921), in *FuFa*, 2:472–77.

53. Zhou Enlai, "Zhong Fa da jiekuan an zhi jinxun" [Recent news of the proposals to refuse the Sino-French big loans] *Yishi bao* (written 16 August 1921), in *FuFa*, 2:478–82.

called for speeches followed by discussion and proposals.[54] However, things did not go as planned, as the lively account by Xiao Qing shows:

> Suddenly a car that sounded like the mooing of a cow stopped outside the door. Two rich men entered, each with leather shoes, wearing the newest French clothing, white starched collars, hands jutting crookedly out of their sleeves, a set of "Wilhelm" whiskers, clasping their walking sticks in their hands, a fearless aura about them, surrounded by a worldly manner, still with a slight air of conciliation. They went straight to the chairman's table and talked for a while, until we knew that these men of bravado were sent by the minister [Chen Lu]. One was the first secretary, Wang Zengsi, and the other was the second secretary, Shen Mo. Of the people who attended the meeting, no one liked them . . . but they thought their arrival was a matter of good fortune. Thereupon, Wang Zengsi was invited to report the situation of the loan negotiations.[55]

Apparently Wang's speech was not as slick as his appearance, for he not only alienated the audience but aroused them to such a degree that several members stood up and began beating him. Pandemonium reigned! Wang pleaded to go to the hospital, but the hostile group was not going to let him go without a written guarantee to refuse the loan.[56] The declaration that was signed by Wang, and countersigned by Chen Lu later on, said that the Chinese did not need a secret loan, and if any such loan were arranged, the supervisory committee within the Chinese community would be notified. The last paragraph also stated that Wang wrote the declaration "in total liberty and based on his conscience."[57] The supervisory committee of ten people included a wide range of activists, from Xu Teli and Yuan Zizhen (a labor activist) to Zeng Qi.[58]

The 13 August meeting was seen as a victory, but Chen Lu, who already felt bitter toward the students, was now livid with anger and humiliation. Chen Lu refused to see another worker-student and announced that government aid would cease on 15 September. Zeng Qi, writing under the

54. Dan Lu, "Bali jukuan dahui" [The big meeting in Paris for the loan refusal] *Shishi xinbao* (14 August 1921), in *FuFa*, 2:483.
55. Xiao Qing, "Lü Fa Huaren fandui jiekuan zhi jilie" [The violence of the Chinese in France in their loan opposition], *Chen bao* (14 October 1921), in *FuFa*, 2:490–91.
56. Ibid., 492.
57. "Déclaration écrite de Monsieur Wang Tseng Sze," 13 August 1921, Paris, in "Renseignement provenant de l'agent Jolin," 24 December 1921, Marseilles, dispatch no. 147, AOM, SLOTFOM IV, 9. This dispatch also includes a letter by Chen Lu signed three days later, in addition to a letter and communiqué by the Colonie chinoise.
58. Zhou Enlai, "Zhong Fa da jiekuan an zhi jinxun," 482.

name Yu Gong, claimed that since the students were now living on a bread and water diet, not only would the cessation of aid decrease their chances of fulfilling their mission to work and become educated, but it would endanger their lives and might bring about several suicides. Zeng felt that Chen Lu was "using the most poisonous methods to obtain his revenge."[59]

The CFC was also withdrawing its support, ostensibly because the funding to maintain the Chinese was inadequate. Indeed, funds had been borrowed from and donated by the Chinese legation, the French government, and French banks to the sum of several hundred thousand francs. Writing to the colleges where the CFC had been funding the Chinese, Bradier tendered his regrets that the comité was no longer able to support nine hundred Chinese without resources and would have to suspend the financial obligations on 15 September.[60] However compelling the financial reasons, the timing of the CFC announcement and subsequent reduction of scholarship support indicate some connection with the Loan Struggle. Not only were Philippe Berthelot and his wife prominent supporters of the CFC, but the ill-fated Wang Zengsi also attended most meetings. They were well aware of the increased tension and activism within the Chinese community. For example, on the day of the Lyons Incident, 21 September 1921, Vice-Consul Li Jun reported on the convergence of students at Lyons.[61]

The Chinese community naturally interpreted these withdrawals of support as a gesture of revenge, and yet they were not ready to return home. In response, another mass meeting was held on 6 September, attended by 270 people, to deal with the precarious situation of the Work-Study Movement. The meeting adopted several resolutions that included measures to establish organizations based on home region and profession; to ask for participation from all sectors; to swear not to return to China unless one was very ill; to hold out for places at Lyons University; and to wire all home provinces for monetary aid. Everyone attending the meeting was asked to contribute one franc to the cause. If the home provinces did not respond adequately by 15 September (the cutoff date for aid), then another meeting would be called.[62]

Thus, although the period after the Twenty-eighth Movement saw some recovery due to the efforts of the CFC, the situation in the Chinese com-

59. Yu Gong [Zeng Qi], "Lü Fa Huaren fandui Zhong Fa jiekuan zhi shimo" [The whole account of the movement by Chinese in France against the Sino-French loan], Xinwen bao (August, October 1921), in FuFa, 2:493–504.
60. Bradier letter, 3 September 1921, AN, 47 AS 1 A1/1.
61. See the CFC's 8th Séance minutes, 21 September 1921, AAE, série E, Chine, vol. 48.
62. Yu Gong [Zeng Qi], "Lü Fa Huaren fandui Zhong Fa jiekuan zhi shimo," 503–4.

munity remained volatile due to the failure of the BIC and the loan protest. The subsequent withdrawal of support by the legation and CFC was a devastating blow. Yet a degree of unity developed within the Chinese community as they faced these trials that was to serve them well for the final struggle of 1921, the Lyons Incident.

THE LYONS INCIDENT

The SFI affiliated with the University of Lyons was a concrete attempt to develop intellectual relations between China and France and took several years of effort to establish.[63] When it became known that over one hundred students were being escorted from China to be the first to matriculate at the institute, shock waves rippled throughout the Chinese community. In the past, Work-Study Movement leaders such as Li Shizeng had claimed that positions at the Sino-French Institutes at the University of Lyons and Charleroi University for Workers were intended for the worker-students. Wu Zhihui had said that the SFI was open to all Chinese students in the spirit of the sanctity of labor. Yet not only was Wu Zhihui bringing in new students, but there were also obstacles such as entrance examinations and high tuition fees.[64] As Zeng Qi had pointed out, the students were in dire straits, waiting for jobs, living in miserable hotel rooms or tents, and cut off from their savings. All government aid from China and France was about to be abolished.

The worker-students had nourished strong hopes with respect to the University of Lyons long before problems emerged within the Work-Study Movement. The SFI in Lyons was to be located in facilities that could hold more than two thousand students according to a June 1920 estimate by Xiao Zisheng.[65] Writing a year and a half before the opening of the institute, one unnamed Work-Study Movement student expected that the Lyons enterprise would play a major role in educating the common people and providing on-site factory training, incorporating the principles of student

63. For the development and structure of the Sino-French Institute see Ruth Hayhoe, "A Comparative Approach to the Cultural Dynamics of Sino-Western Educational Cooperation," 12–24, and Chen Sanjing, "Minchu liu Ou jiaoyu de jiannan lishi: Liang Zhong Fa daxue chushen."

64. Zhou Enlai, "Qingong jianxue sheng zai zuihou zhi yunming" [The final fate of the worker-students in France] (December 1921), in FuFa, 1:56; Yu Gong [Zeng Qi], "Qingong jianxue sheng jinzhan Lida zhi qianyin houguo" [The whole story of the occupation of Lyons University by the worker-students], Xinwen bao (November/December 1921), in FuFa, 2:571–82, see esp. 572–74.

65. Xiao Zisheng report of June 1920, in FuFa, 2:591.

autonomy and a labor orientation. He also urged that it open its lectures to all who cared to attend.[66]

The democratic view of education at the SFI was not universally shared. Much of the work involved in setting up the SFI was done by Xin shiji contributor Chu Minyi. He had written enthusiastically to Cai Yuanpei about the institute, which he viewed as an opportunity to provide higher education and develop much-needed talent for China's future. In his letter, Chu definitely disconnected these efforts from the Work-Study Movement.[67]

The official French perspective was congruent with Chu Minyi's. The first sentence of the agreement that established the aims of the SFI proclaimed that the institute was being formed for "d'enseignement supérieur pour les Chinois." The selection process was to include examinations, a test in French proficiency, and submission of secondary school diplomas. The note also mentioned that although the Chinese administrators had the right to select some of the Chinese students already in France who held diplomas, it was doubtful whether this would be "de bonne politique."[68] Maurice Courant, the Asian specialist who was the de facto administrator of the SFI between 1921 and 1926, shared the more limited, elitist vision of the objectives.[69] In preparing for the opening of the SFI, for example, Courant was most concerned with developing a feasible curriculum, keeping in mind the probable need for language development and the need for cultural adaptation.[70]

Wu Zhihui later admitted that he had wanted an open university, but the economic realities were too difficult. It was no coincidence that many of the students he accompanied were from Guangdong, as he had a large donation from that region.[71]

Although news of the entrance exams and tuition and the limited number of students who would be enrolled in the SFI had been circulating since

66. A "Qingong jianxue Student," "Duiyu Liang sheli Zhongguo Daxue zhi xiwang" [Hopes concerning the establishment of the Chinese University at Lyons], Lü Ou zhoukan 13 (7 February 1920): 1.
67. Chu Minyi letter to Cai Yuanpei, 9 April 1920, Beijing daxue rikan, in FuFa, 2:585.
68. "Note relative à L'Insitut franco-chinois," 83–86 (Summer 1921); also see "Régalement de L'Institut franco-chinois de Lyon," 81–82, and "Accord entre L'Université de Lyon et le Comité inter-universitaire chinois," 87–88 (8 July 1921), AAE, série E, Chine, vol. 47.
69. D. Bouchez, "Un défricheur méconnu des études extrême-orientales: Maurice Courant (1865–1935)," Journal asiatique 271 (1983): 43–150.
70. M. Courant to Professor Chabot, 9 September 1921, AAUFC.
71. Zeng Zhongming and Zou Lu, in Faguo Liang Zhong Fa daxue [The Sino-French Institute in France] (Guangdong: Guoli guangdong daxue haiwaibu zhiyi, 1925), discuss aid from Guangdong, which far surpassed that of the Sino-French University at Beijing or French contributions. Also see the Accord mentioned above.

the beginning of the summer, it was several months before unified action emerged.[72] A coalition of Work-Study students was formed and meetings were held throughout September to organize some action to "open" Lyons University (Kaifang Lida). A flyer that announced a mass meeting for 17 September to resolve the Lida question proclaimed, "Our articles of belief are: (1) We swear to struggle to the death for Lida. (2) We will absolutely refuse a partial solution. (3) We refuse to recognize the entrance examinations."[73]

At the meeting three approaches were suggested: (1) a proposal for negotiation by a neutral party; (2) a proposal to wait for more news of the examinations; and (3) a proposal to send a group of students to Lyons to negotiate. The last proposal was the most popular, and it was decided that about a hundred people would go as a "vanguard." Eighteen out of twenty-two Work-Study representatives were included in the vanguard. There were strict injunctions concerning the maintenance of order and delegation of responsibilities. Four representatives were left to mediate in Paris and Lyons.[74]

The peculiar part at this stage was the enthusiasm of Chen Lu. Almost all accounts of the Lyons Incident claim that Chen Lu encouraged the students to go to Lyons. Both French diplomats and the proclamations by the students claimed that Chen Lu had given the students 8,000 francs for train money to reach Lyons.[75] Several reasons can be suggested for Chen Lu's encouragement of the students. First, he was happy to move the center of the storm away from Paris to Lyons. Second, Chen Lu was part of the Anfu clique, and he was politically opposed to Guomindang people such as Wu Zhihui. If Wu, who had been popular with Chinese youth, arrived right in the midst of a political conflict, it would only cause him trouble and, Chen Lu hoped, humiliation. Third, it would appear that Chen Lu wanted to encourage trouble between the Chinese students and the French authorities, thus satisfying his anger toward these students. He seemed to be retaliating for the mortification that the Loan Struggle had created.[76]

---

72. Lü Ou zhoukan 3 (7 May 1921). This raises some important historical questions about the context in which the three struggles of 1921 took place, indicating that it was not a linear series of struggles but that a whole miasma of disorientation existed.

73. Zhou Enlai, "Qingong jianxue sheng zai zuihou zhi yunming," 67.

74. Yu Gong, "Qingong jianxue sheng jinzhan Lida zhi qianyin houguo," 578–79.

75. See A. de Fleuriau to Briand, 19 December 1921, AAE, série E, Chine, vol. 49; Luo Chengding, "Qingong jianxue sheng zhengqu kaifang Lida douzheng de jingguo" [The experiences of the struggle by the worker-students in the protest to open Lyons University], Chen bao (January 1922), in FuFa, 2:553–70, see 553.

76. Yu Gong, "Qingong jianxue sheng jinzhan Lida zhi qianyin houguo," 575–76.

Chen Lu's motivations were certainly not as obscure as the logic of the students in accepting his encouragement and monetary aid. Right to the end they kept appealing to Chen Lu to negotiate, even though Chen had no intention of helping them. Zhao Shiyan and the other leaders of the Lyons Incident really trusted the authorities. This naïveté indicates that traditional values still exerted a strong influence, because in this case neither organization nor ideology was as important as *guanxi* (personal relations) when it came to a basic level of behavioral response in a crisis. The worker-students issued proclamations and held more meetings, including another mass meeting on 20 September, where they again articulated their strategy. Besides sending telegrams to the home government and provinces and conducting propaganda efforts in France, they insisted that the stay at Lyons would be the time to decide all issues, including the question of what should be done with the Boxer Indemnity funds that the French were about to return for distribution. The students were determined to emphasize the life and death nature of their situation.[77] Thus, over one hundred worker-students traveled to Lyons to plead their case with Wu Zhihui, whose imminent arrival had been announced. Once arrived, these worker-students were not allowed to wait in the newly constructed dormitories. They refused to leave the institute and were detained in a military barracks, from which they were deported the following month.

According to the rather extensive coverage in local Lyonnaise newspapers, the over one hundred Chinese *"post-scolaires"* were quite orderly as they converged en masse on Fort Saint-Irénée on 21 September, requesting physical entry to the SFI. They were met by a "surprised" Chu Minyi, who refused to admit them, and a second unsuccessful dialogue was held with Maurice Courant, who had been involved in preliminary preparations for the arrival of the first group of officially accepted students led by Wu Zhihui. In view of the impending arrival of Wu Zhihui's contingent, the persistence of this large crowd of uninvited Chinese was disconcerting. According to a detailed account in the *Lyon républicain*, M. Bressot, the secretary general of the police, and M. Brunaud, the commissaire of the police for St. Just, were called to deal with the students. Both Bressot and the students were calm and polite.

> He [Bressot] approached the group of "insurgents," who nonchalantly waited on the lawn thick with frost, their cigarettes filling the air with blue smoke: " . . . I am treating you as serious men, as students, and I am calling on your better feelings. You cannot stay here any longer;

77. Zhou Enlai, "Qingong jianxue sheng zai zuihou zhi yunming," 69.

yield with good grace and follow me." The young citizens of the Celestial Republic appeared to listen with much attention and interest to this discourse. As one they raised themselves and responded in approximately the following [manner]: "If we are here, it is that we believe we have the right to be here. In founding the Institute, M. Liyuying [Li Shizeng], secretary of the Sino-French Educational Association, had the intention to reserve the places of Chinese students without resources. The presidents, both French and Chinese, of the same society were fully in accord with the demand of the creation of the institute in the goal of aiding the less-fortunate students. Finally, the minister of China in Paris [Chen Lu] agreed with our delegates in an audience and is formally engaged in giving us satisfaction. We therefore have the right to be here and we will stay."[78]

M. Bressot was unwilling to judge the situation, but he calmly and insistently summoned the police to evacuate the students to a nearby military barracks. The large number of students attempting to occupy the dormitories necessitated three bus trips, which were all conducted with cooperation and dignity, except for a slight disturbance caused by the reappearance of Chu Minyi, who became the target of projectiles and verbal abuse.[79]

Calling themselves the "Fédération des comités des étudiants postscolaires sans ressources," the protesting students had prepared handbills, which were reprinted in the local newspaper Le progrès, stating the reasons for their right to be at Lyons in much the same terms as they gave to Bressot.[80] Under the same name, they had also quickly printed a handbill that claimed that the "police of Lyons expelled without any reason the Chinese students, the very intimate friends of France, of the Franco-Chinese Institute of Lyons."[81]

Lyonnaise opinion appeared to be sympathetic to the case of the protesters. A council meeting was held on 24 September to discuss the problem.[82] The citizens of Lyons recognized that raising the resources needed to support the students was beyond their capabilities, and at one point they were alarmed by a report that 500 more protesters were on their way.[83] The "of-

78. "La main vigoureuse de la Police à contraint, hier, les 106 Chinois à évacuer le Fort Saint-Irénée," Lyon républicain, 23 September 1921. The Lyonnaise newspaper accounts were collected and generously given to me by Jean-Louis Boully, at the Bibliothèque municipale de Lyon.
79. Ibid.
80. "Les 'Rebelles' chinois du Fort Saint-Irénée," Le progrès, 23 September 1921.
81. Ibid. These quotations are from the original French written by the Chinese in their handbills.
82. Ibid., 27 September 1921.
83. Ibid., 28 September 1921.

ficial" students and Wu Zhihui were warmly welcomed locally. Headlines in the press proclaimed, "Hoan yin ni! Amis Chinois" (welcome, Chinese friends). Yet, the shadow of the protesters remained and their plight was noted in the "Hoan yin" article, which concluded, "In truth these young men conduct themselves very reasonably."[84] When the protesters were abruptly expelled, the paper claimed, "Everyone is unanimous in regretting that their stay was so brusquely interrupted; they take with them, so they said to us, an excellent memory of Lyons and hope to return."[85]

Dismayed at the inauspicious beginnings for the SFI, the French administrators definitely were not sympathetic to the protesters. In their discussions, correspondence, and articles, they were quite firm in maintaining that the SFI was distinct from the Work-Study Movement. Courant wrote to the Chinese educational inspector, Gao Lu, that "we will never forget the . . . principle of the Institute, which is that it must give a superior education."[86] As Professor Jean Lépine, the president of the institute, remarked in a letter of 30 September 1921 to Chen Lu, the protesters were clearly acting in an illegal manner and had no relation to the institute, which was meant to provide a superior education and was not a "hotel of passage or a refuge for young Chinese without resources."[87]

It would seem that Chen Lu and Li Jun, his secretary, whom he sent to represent him at Lyons, were eager to placate the French scholars and presented a different face to them than to the worker-students. In his letter to Chen Lu, Lépine mentioned that he was reassured by the "regrets" of Chen Lu and that the intellectual relations between the countries would continue to develop.[88] Chen Lu's duplicity is also suggested by the fact that although, according to the protesters, he gave them the funds to travel to Lyons and sanctioned their actions, he then refused to meet with them during the negotiations. According to the French minister to China, Chen Lu and Li Jun worked toward their expulsion from France.[89]

The reaction within the Chinese community displayed continued disorientation and a poor understanding of the situation. Yet it also revealed a growing unity among the numerous Chinese youth organizations. Luo Chengding, who did not participate in the "vanguard" but helped in the negotiations at Lyons, wrote an account of the occupation and the subse-

84. "Hoan yin ni! Amis Chinois," *Le progrès*, 26 September 1921.
85. "Les chinois sont partis," *Le progrès*, 14 October 1921.
86. Courant to Gao Lu, 4 October 1921, AAUFC.
87. Lépine to Chen Lu, 30 September 1921, AAUFC.
88. Ibid.
89. A. de Fleuriau à Briand, 19 December 1921, AAE, série E, Chine, vol. 41. This point was initially raised in an article by Kriegel in her *Communismes au miroir français*, 87.

quent negotiations. According to Luo's information, a Chinese government representative, Li Jun, came to the students on the twenty-third and said not to worry, although the students became concerned because before his arrival there was free access to and from the barracks, but after he left, access was restricted. Wu Zhihui arrived on the scene and visited the encampment on the twenty-fourth and began negotiations.[90]

The negotiations were difficult and unsuccessful for several reasons. The basic problem was that the students had no direct contact with French authorities and had to depend on Chinese officials like Chen Lu and Li Jun, who consistently showed bad faith. For example, a meeting with the French police scheduled for the twenty-eighth did not materialize.[91] Chen Lu was "unavailable" and "had not received any messages," particularly during the day before the students were deported.

Second, although Wu Zhihui's proposals were attractive to some, they did not accord with the student resolve for the opening of Lida and did not offer a more comprehensive solution. The students' relationship with Wu Zhihui was complicated. The students were rapidly coming to regard Wu Zhihui as ineffectual, but yet they remained curiously dependent on him.

Among the various inducements that Wu Zhihui offered were twenty positions for Work-Study students at Lida and 50,000 francs a month for support of seven hundred students. This was not enough for the angry youth, because the money was inadequate (about 70 francs a month for less than half of the students). Wu's most attractive proposal was a program in which some students would be admitted to Lida each year while the others would enter a work-study scheme for two years (four hours of each per day), followed after two years by full-time study. A whole series of proposals and counterproposals was put forth, and there was difficulty in reaching consensus. Consequently, the negotiations dragged on and were overtaken by events.[92] When it came to the crisis point, Wu Zhihui had little influence, as the students finally realized on 13 October, when they discovered that their imprisoned compatriots were about to be shipped home. Wu had shuttled between Lyons and Paris, but when asked by students to intercede to

90. Luo Chengding, "Qingong jianxue sheng zhengqu kaifang Lida douzheng de jingguo," 556–58.
91. Ibid., 560.
92. Kai Sheng, "Wu Zhihui dui qingong jianxue sheng weiyuan hui daibiao zhi hua" [Conversations between Wu Zhihui and the representatives of the committee of the worker-students], *Shen bao* (24 November 1921), in *FuFa*, 2:537–38; Luo Chengding, "Qingong jianxue sheng zhengqu kaifang Lida douzheng de jingguo," 558–70.

prevent expulsion, Wu refused to go to Paris, claiming that in Paris too many people asked him for loans.[93]

Last, having to relay messages back and forth between Lyons and Paris resulted in poor coordination of student actions. The representatives sometimes had different perceptions of their tasks and of the events that were transpiring. While Zhao Shiyan and Wang Zekai were claiming that expulsion was not a possibility and that there was no problem, another representative produced a pamphlet denouncing Chen Lu. Communication between those inside the encampment and those outside became increasingly restricted. When Luo's pass no longer worked, he had to talk to Li Lisan by subterfuge, and finally a guard shouted for him to get away.[94]

Luo Chengding went into the encampment several times to give the imprisoned students news and to ascertain their feelings. They were divided on whether to negotiate only for their release or to use the opportunity to resolve the whole Work-Study Movement issue. Luo recounted talking with Li Lisan, who was very concerned about the possibility of being deported and anxious to be released. Li wanted to know what Wu Zhihui thought about the possibility of deportation. The next day Li's attitude had changed, as he pledged, "Even if they released us from the encampment, we would not go, because this arrest by the French police is to the great shame of us students. We must use Lida to totally resolve the Work-Study Movement problems."[95]

Luo wondered at this change in attitude and soon discovered it had come about because of the Montargis Work-Study representative, Wang Zekai, who likened those arrested at Lyons to one of two legs supporting the Work-Study Movement (the other being the Paris participants). If they left the encampment without achieving a comprehensive solution, then it would be like losing a leg. Wang firmly contended that there was no danger of expulsion. But there were many others who worried about expulsion, and their suspicions were soon to be proved correct.

The expulsion itself was carried out efficiently and on short notice. In the midst of the ongoing negotiations, the detained students were sent under guard to Marseilles, where they immediately set sail for China. The imprisoned students had originally each brought one small piece of luggage with them to Lyons, which they refused to take with them to the barracks during the initial confinement. At the time of expulsion they were not al-

---

93. Luo Chengding, "Qingong jianxue sheng zhengqu kaifang Lida douzheng de jingguo," 569–70.
94. Ibid., 562.
95. Ibid.

lowed to carry the luggage with them; thus personal possessions, including diaries and letters, were lost. Furthermore, they were told that the whole body of worker-students was to be expelled, creating greater feelings of despondency and guilt.[96]

In the past, to be a "returned student" was an honorable position, often leading to a good future, but to be an "expelled returned student" was a humiliating condition, and far more disturbing to those sailing home than their miserable conditions on board the ship. Among the passengers were Cai Hesen, Luo Xuezan, Li Lisan, and Chen Yi. Chen Yi, in particular, took an active role aboard ship in trying to raise the spirits of his compatriots. He was one of four representatives of the expelled students, and after they had reached China, he tried to arrange financial aid and conducted a propaganda campaign on behalf of the expelled students.

Chen Yi's friend Qiu Yang provides us with some very revealing as well as refreshing anecdotal material. Qiu really thought that compared with what many of them had been suffering, the military encampment was not bad at all—they had three meals a day and even meat. The only inconvenience was the insufficiency of beds.[97] Aboard ship, the expelled students tried hard to lift their spirits. According to Qiu, one of the highlights of the voyage was a regional chess competition played on an improvised chessboard. Chen Yi and Li Lisan were each left representing the "honor" of their respective provinces of Sichuan and Hunan. Li Lisan was known for his lack of a sense of humor and could be provoked at the smallest thing. As the pressure of the game mounted, it became obvious that Li was losing:

His [Li Lisan's] face went from white to red to purple; he became angry amidst everyone's amused laughter; he gathered up the chessboard and pieces, ran to the side of the ship, and threw them overboard into the ocean. This chess set was produced by many people picking up small white and black stones in the park while in the military encampment. That Li Lisan threw it away really angered everyone and they wanted to beat him up. But Chen Yi had a smiling expression on his face the whole time; he was very happy to have his victory.[98]

96. "Beipo guiguo liu Fa qingong jianxue sheng tuan xuanyan" [The proclamation of the returned travel to France Work-Study students who were expelled], *Xinwen bao* (28 November 1921), in *FuFa*, 2:611–16.

97. Qiu Yang, "Fu Fa qingong jianxue shiqi de Chen Yi tongzhi" [Comrade Chen Yi during the period of the travel to France Work-Study Movement], *Dagong bao* (Shanghai) (May, June 1949), in *FuFa*, 3:421–34; Qiu Yang is a pen name.

98. Ibid., 431–32.

The students in France were very depressed about the expulsion. Many took it to symbolize the defeat of the Work-Study Movement. One Sichuanese who had been active in the Work-Study Mutual-Aid Corps and had helped with worker publications in France killed himself with a knife on 21 December 1921 while in the hospital.[99] Another student made an attempt in March 1922 to assassinate Chen Lu for his efforts to destroy the Work-Study Movement and his treachery in trying to sell out his country in the loan negotiations. Four shots were fired and although Chen's secretary was wounded, Chen escaped injury. By that time the students were so disillusioned with Chen Lu they sponsored a defense fund for his assailant.[100] The Work-Study Movement was dispirited from this point onward. There were two small groups who returned home soon after the expulsion, but during 1922–23 many more of the worker-students returned home, even though they did receive aid in 1922. Other students, academics, and leaders, such as Cai Yuanpei and Li Shizeng, took an interest in the welfare of the expelled returned students. Tea parties, free room and board at hotels in Shanghai, lectures, meetings, and petitions were organized. The local branches of the SFEA also tried to raise relief money.[101]

In his serialized articles on the Lyons Incident, Zhou Enlai prefaced his reportage with the observation that the expelled students were of high integrity. He also noted that there was no ill feeling toward the matriculating students, who were seen as brothers.[102] This latter opinion changed when in early 1922 Zhou Enlai visited the SFI and found the administrators and student body cold and aloof.[103]

What Zhou Enlai sensed was an attempt by the official Lyons contingent, who were trying to find their own place in the French educational milieu, to disassociate themselves from their expelled peers. While the protesters were fasting on 10 October to observe the anniversary of the 1911 Revolution, the official students attended a banquet and then toured the city and a famous airport.[104] Writing about the institute in *L'Asie française* the next

99. *Chen bao* (6 January 1922), in *FuFa*, 2:679–80.
100. *Chen bao* (16 May 1922), in *FuFa*, 2:711–15. It is an irony that Chen Lu was eventually assassinated. However, it was for his collaboration with the Japanese in 1939.
101. See *FuFa*, 2:603–74, for the relief efforts, proclamations, and petitions.
102. Zhou Enlai, "Qingong jianxue sheng zai zuihou zhi yunming," 52–57.
103. Zhou Enlai, "Jieshao yipian Liang Zhong Fa Daxue haiwaibu zhi canguan ji" [Record of an introduction to the overseas branch of the Sino-French Institute at Lyons University], *Yishi bao* (May 1922), in *Zhou Enlai tongzhi lü Ou wenji* [The collected European writings of Comrade Zhou Enlai] (Tianjin: Wenwu, 1979), 230–31. I would expect that the "overseas branch" refers to Guomindang activities. Zhou Enlai was organizing the European Guomindang during this time.
104. *Le progrès*, 11 October 1921.

spring, Maurice Courant emphasized the developments at the institute and in his conclusion mentioned the Lyons Incident as something that had no connection with the proper activities of the SFI.[105] The impression created by the Lyons Incident was that the official students were *guizu* (sons of nobles), and this was so indelibly marked on the mind of the Chinese public that the students of the SFI issued a proclamation several years later, in 1928, protesting that image.[106]

CONSEQUENCES OF THE THREE STRUGGLES OF 1921

The disarray of the Work-Study Movement after the three struggles of 1921 had several consequences for the worker-students. Some worker-students took advantage of a government offer to return to China, but many refused to leave France and pursued their desire to work and study. Many of them benefited from a return of Boxer Indemnity funds. For others, however, the three struggles of 1921 signified a turning point in their radicalization, leading them away from the route of education to the route of politics. For these more politicized worker-students the three struggles of 1921 signaled several important transformations.

First, the tensions of generational crisis were successfully integrated with the search for a route to national salvation. This road was the turning away from the commitment to change via education to the formula of political party formation. During 1922–23 several Chinese political parties were formed in France, and they recruited hundreds of members. The revolt that had centered on the youth as leaders of youth groups with distinct regional ties now centered on youthful leaders of a national political revolution.

Second, the organizational and ideological polarization that occurred in China after 1920 also took place in France. However, the *impetus* for the political polarization was different for the Chinese in China and those in France. In China, these reorientations came about both through disillusionment with New Culture social experimentation and through provocative ideological debates. Moreover, the founding of the CCP was a divisive factor for the Chinese radical community, creating several organizational schisms. In France, the realignments were in part stimulated by ideological

---

105. Maurice Courant, "L'Institut franco-chinois de Lyon," *L'Asie française* 201 (April 1922): 167–68.

106. Lida Xuesheng Hui [The Lyons University Student Association], "Liang Zhong Fa daxue xuesheng zhi zuiyan" [The crimes of the students at the Sino-French Institute at Lyons University], *Lü Ou zazhi* 1 (September 1928): 33–44. In fact, the Sino-French Institute outlasted the Work-Study Movement. The history and accomplishments of the Sino-French Institute are areas that need further research.

questions, but the personal hardships and gradual disillusionment with the Work-Study Movement were more influential. Also, the "worker-orienta-tion" of the groups formed in France was more pronounced. Most of those who joined the ECCO invested time working in and learning from the factory environment, an experience not commonly shared by the CCP founders, who were involved in educational efforts or local politics.

Third, the networks of personal relations (*guanxi*) and organizational af-filiations began to shift as new radical groups emerged. Old ties were broken and new ties were developed. When the worker-students traveled to France, they depended on their contacts. Many obtained letters of intro-duction from former teachers and officials. Few went without a group of friends or some sort of personal or organizational contact in France. Most worker-students were not used to being away from home, and it gave them a great sense of security to see people from the same region or organization. As the situation in France became more tense, the old affiliations began to lose their value. Many worker-students felt that they had a personal pledge from leaders such as Cai Yuanpei, Li Shizeng, and Wu Zhihui. When the SFEA abrogated all responsibilities, and when it was discovered that Wu Zhihui was bringing other students to matriculate at the SFI, the existing system of personal contacts and organizational affiliations was disrupted. For instance, Li Huang and Xiao Zisheng stood behind the SFEA and the authorities, whereas Wang Ruofei and Zhao Shiyan forfeited their excellent contacts with the authorities and their more conservative friends.

Fourth, the Anarchist alternative was discredited in the view of most of the worker-students in two important ways. The perceived betrayal by important Anarchist leaders such as Wu Zhihui and Li Shizeng led the worker-students to reject the moral leadership of these progressive elders. Moreover, as an organizational formula, anarchism's philosophical rejec-tion of authority had limited appeal at a time when organization was a key point of political commitment.[107] Likewise, during the formation of the CCP, a rejection of anarchism transpired as the social experiments such as the Work-Study Mutual-Aid Corps failed. As Arif Dirlik points out:

> An important precondition for the turn to Communism among these radicals in 1920 was the disillusionment with anarchism that set in as communal experiments foundered upon the realities of power in Chinese society. Faith in anarchism declined; the alternative organi-zation offered by Bolshevism acquired a new credibility. In the mean-

107. For a more detailed exposition of these themes see Marilyn Levine and Geneviève Barman, "The Lyon Incident: Ideology at the Crossroads," paper delivered at the 42d Annual Meeting of the Association for Asian Studies, 5–8 April 1990, Chicago.

time, anarchism had done much to create the organizational units that facilitated the organization of Communism.[108]

However, after 1921, anarchism as an ideological model differed in two significant ways in its impact on the CCP and on the ECCO. The bitterness of betrayal after the deportation that ended the Lyons Incident was a source of deep discord between Wu, Li, and their youthful followers. The polemics and dissection of failure that followed the Work-Study Mutual-Aid Corps could not compare in terms of accusations of personal treachery. As the Creusot manifesto vehemently exclaimed at the beginning of the Lyons Incident, "We have been betrayed!" A second area of significant ideological difference between the Anarchist legacies bestowed upon the CCP and the ECCO is also one of degree, shaped by personal experience. The concepts of mutual aid and the sanctity of labor that were the keystones of the Work-Study Movement still remained influential after the formation of the ECCO. These concepts were part of the living reality of the worker-students, and the influence of these ideas was to remain stronger for them than for many of their CCP cohorts back in China. Zhang Guotao remembered the importance of speaking teams in the process of radicalization during the May Fourth period, but ECCO leaders such as Zhao Shiyan and Li Lisan developed real blisters during their stints of factory work. Thus, in terms of organizational aims, including labor recruitment and strike activities, Anarchist concepts were important molders of radical sensibilities and beliefs, and the three struggles of 1921 did not totally discredit them in the minds of the revolutionaries of the ECCO.

Finally, interregional cooperation was expanded among the Chinese in France during this period. The work in factories, with the exposure to different cultures and races, and the need for organizational action during the political struggles of 1921 induced a greater receptivity to contact with those from other provinces. A good example of this was the friendship that developed between Zhao Shiyan (Sichuan) and Li Lisan (Hunan), who roomed and labored together. Together they organized the Work-Study Alliance and initially fought the Montargis faction during the Twenty-eighth Movement. Another instance of interregional cooperation is evidenced by the backgrounds of the officers of the ECYC: Zhao Shiyan (Sichuan), Zhou Enlai (Jiangsu), and Li Weihan (Hunan).

The shifting of political factions throughout the three struggles of 1921 expressed the ultimate transcendence of regional, ideological, organizational, and personal networks. At the beginning of 1921, the announce-

108. Dirlik, *The Origins of Chinese Communism*, 183.

ments by Cai Yuanpei that abrogated financial responsibility for the Work-Study Movement by the SFEA generated two main responses. Those who rallied around the concepts of mutual aid and self-support, led by Zhao Shiyan, Li Lisan, and Wang Ruofei, were in conflict with those led by Cai Hesen and the Montargis faction, self-proclaimed Marxists, who demonstrated for government support during the Twenty-eighth Movement. These two factions, proceeding through a period of acrimonious debate, began to communicate and were able to unite around the summertime loan crisis, as was the entire Chinese community in France. This cooperation solidified during the Lyons Incident and provided a broad-based cooperative effort in the formation of the ECCO.

Thus, the three struggles of 1921 marked a time of transition. They signified, in an abrupt and lasting manner, a radical change from educational to revolutionary goals. There was a dramatic change from regionally focused youth groups inspired by the New Culture Movement to national political parties moving beyond the boundaries of student protest. The cutting off of financial aid, the betrayal by the progressive elders, and the lack of educational alternatives were all exacerbated by the very real physical miseries the worker-students were undergoing, both in their material life and in their difficult factory labors. Led by the charismatic Zhao Shiyan, some of those remaining in France were soon to transcend intellectual exploration and commit themselves to revolutionary activity. Zhu Yuhe, one of the major historians of the Work-Study Movement, remarked on the linkage between the three struggles and the origins of the ECCO, "It was in the decline of the Work-Study Movement that the success of the ECCO was born."[109]

---

109. Zhu Yuhe–Levine, discussion, 2 November 1985, Shanghai.

5
THE CHOSEN PATH

The ability for common youth to nourish the habit of work-study, . . . if one can recognize it clearly, then one can adventurously experiment, *strengthening the body, supporting artistic habits, speaking the French language,* and in the end be able to . . . overcome everything and effect a new age [of Work-Studyism]. (Emphasis mine)
—Zhou Enlai (spring 1921)

Today, we ought to clearly recognize, that the work of the 1911 Revolution has still not been completed. Moreover, it falls daily and monthly under the pervasive sway of warlords and international imperialism. Because of this, we need a revolution,—we must have an organization, training, discipline, and a unified spirit able to support a long-term people's revolution.
—Zhou Enlai, *Shaonian* manifesto (summer 1923)

The struggles of 1921 made many worker-students angry and bitter. They also made many people determined to express themselves in a more organized and unified manner. Breaking away from their traditional mentors such as Cai Yuanpei, Li Shizeng, and Wu Zhihui, the disaffected youth shed their major emphasis on the revolution of youth[1] and committed themselves to participation in broader ideological political movements, formed political parties, and became the pioneering Found Generation.

The failure of the Work-Study Movement and the subsequent formation of Chinese political parties, such as the ECCO, the European Guomindang (EGMD), and the Chinese Youth Party (CYP), were catalysts to an already energized political environment. This political commitment remained vibrant throughout the decade of the twenties, as exemplified by the organization of Chinese workers in France, mass meetings supported by the PCF during the 1926 anti-imperialism campaign, the formation of United Fronts, and the rancorous disputes. The adherence to Marxism by some of the most prominent Chinese youth activists and the formation of the ECCO were pivotal in this process.

After exploring the ideological conversions of Wang Guangqi, Cai Hesen, Zhao Shiyan, and Zhou Enlai, this chapter will discuss the forma-

---

1. The exception to this trend was the anti-Communist Chinese Youth Party. They kept an emphasis on the role of youth in leading the revolution. In a very real way they froze themselves within the static mold of generational crisis.

tion of the ECCO and its activities. Areas of ECCO activity were broad ranging, from propaganda development and theoretical study to agitation of Chinese workers in Europe. Finally, the involvement of the ECCO with the Communist International will be examined.

THE INTERNAL VOYAGE

The ethos of the New Culture era can be detected in the internal voyage of many of the Chinese searching for a route to national salvation. The worker-students exhibited a sense of inquiry and enthusiasm, as well as a selfless element in their behavior. However, in a direct sense, it was the increasing tempo of radical politics in the Chinese community in France that led a segment of the young Chinese, still seeking to define their identities, to cross the boundary of student struggles and enter the territory of radical politics. Abandoning purely intellectual struggles, they instead took the revolutionary route and adopted a revolutionary ideology. Chalmers Johnson's definition of revolutionary ideology is particularly appropriate to the young Chinese searching in the shadow of the New Culture Movement: "Revolutionary ideologies are thus composed of an analysis of the old order, a transfer culture, and a goal culture, and several ideologies are usually developed in a period of disequilibrium in an effort to overcome the deficiencies of the existing culture."[2] By the mid-1920s there were five Chinese political parties in France.

Chinese intellectuals had long constituted a class that was recruited for government service, providing not only the thinkers but also the "politicians" of China. The Confucian training of these intellectuals, geared to the civil service examination, produced highly cultured, multifaceted individuals whose responsibilities extended beyond administration and education. They were the bulwarks of administration, the protectors of culture and continuity, the "father and mother" of the people, and the conscience of a morality that transcended political ambition.

This cultural perception of the role of the intellectual lent cohesiveness to the Chinese organizational milieu of the twenties. In spite of the constant desire to "merge" with labor and forays into New Learning, *this generation* had experienced childhoods still pervaded with traditional Confucian learning, as well as the inculcation of the idea that this learning was also *career training*. In the fourfold traditional class delineation of scholar, farmer, artisan, and businessman (*shinong gongshang*) there was no delinea

2. Chalmers Johnson, *Revolutionary Change* (Stanford: Stanford University Press, 1982), 87.

tion of the politician as a class. That this traditional ethos still functioned as a deterrent to radicalization was apparent in the debate on how to save the nation—by social reform or by political revolution. Those who advocated social reform opted for the intrinsically Confucian view that one must start with the reformation of the individual. In this way, through example and education, one transformed the masses, leading to a change at the top from the bottom up. This view fitted the traditional leadership role of the intellectual, which was biased toward the pedagogical, rather than the political, role of the intellectual class. The proponents of political revolution were more concerned with alleviating the immediate suffering of the people and believed that reform could take place after power at the top was grasped. They were willing to emphasize the political aspects of the traditional intellectual leadership role. In fact, they discovered that they must define a new role, a new class, a revolutionary class, or, in the words of Yves Chevrier, a difference between the "aristocracy of the mind" and an "aristocracy of the revolution."[3] The potential force intrinsic within this view of a transition from intellectual to revolutionary elite was grasped by Lenin and the Communist International in their Colonial Section (under which the ECCO was officially to operate in Europe). The Comintern questionnaire to identify potential recruits for their section for the "Penetration of Socialist Ideas" began with asking whether there was an *elite* who could serve in the dissemination of revolutionary propaganda (emphasis mine).[4]

Old habits and traditional role models were not easy to dismiss. The Found Generation was still faced with the specter of ancient inhibitions against political involvement, albeit to a lesser extent than Cai Yuanpei, Li Shizeng, Wu Zhihui, and their other mentors. In Mary Rankin's words:

> The picture of 1911 revolutionary organizations that emerges is one of transitional groups part way between traditional Chinese models and twentieth-century revolutionary political organizations in which a disciplined elite seeks mass support to overthrow the government. The very ideas of a revolutionary party and of politics as the proper concern of the whole populace were new and showed the influence of Western ideologies. The difficulties in realizing these ideas were not only the result of the political immaturity of the students, but also of China's

3. Yves Chevrier, Comments presented at the Conference on Democratic Movements in China, "Historical Society for 20th Century China in North America," Columbia University, 22 May 1988.
4. Comité d'études coloniales, "D'élaborer un plan tactique d'action coloniale" (February 1992), AOM, SLOTFOM III, 27.

great size and the unfavorable social and political environments in which the radicals had to operate.[5]

This increasing tension between the role of the intellectual and that of the revolutionary had been submerged in the pervasive ethos of youth revolt and credo of the New Culture and the tight social bonds of youth organizations such as the Young China Study Association and Self-Awakening Society.

In Europe, particularly in France, the more immediate confusion caused by the deteriorating Work-Study Movement and the three struggles of 1921 had overwhelmed and exacerbated these issues of role and identity. The four voyagers Wang Guangqi, Cai Hesen, Zhao Shiyan, and Zhou Enlai exhibited varying degrees of change in their internal voyages toward reform and revolution. Wang Guangqi made a staunch commitment to the role of the intellectual leader, whereas Cai Hesen represented the other extreme of decisive, quick commitment to the role of revolutionary leader. Zhao Shiyan and Zhou Enlai made slower and more painful breaks with their heritage as intellectual leaders.

Wang Guangqi—Walking to the Revolution

Wang Guangqi was one of the most prolific and artful proponents of the social revolution and the more measured tread toward change led by the intellectual. Unlike his Young China Study Association compatriots Zhao Shiyan, who led the ECCO, and Zeng Qi, who led the CYP, Wang Guangqi was never "stigmatized" as a politician.[6]

Writing on the spirit of the Young China Study Association in 1919, Wang Guangqi expressed his lifelong credo that change must involve the whole individual, producing a personal rectification, and then slowly spread throughout society, propagated by concerned intellectuals. He believed this task was encumbered by the growing attention to ideology:

> However, we have a common trend and that is to recognize that con-
> temporary Chinese thought and behavior, no matter under what
> ideology, cannot be successful. If one wants contemporary Chinese to
> have the ability to utilize each kind of ideology, one must first have a
> penetrating reformation of the thought and habits of the Chinese peo-

5. Mary Backus Rankin, *Early Chinese Revolutionaries: Radical Intellectuals in Shanghai and Chekiang, 1902–1911* (Cambridge: Harvard University Press, 1971), 15–16.
6. It is fascinating that in spite of his early death and lack of organizational participation after 1920, Wang Guangqi is a figure highly respected by many Chinese intellectuals. His musical scores, which are heralded as nationalistic, are currently reemerging in China.

ple. One must pass through a period of preparation. This must be the goal of the Young China Study Association, which must energetically pursue this preparatory task.[7]

Wang Guangqi was abandoning neither the prerogatives of the New Culture Movement nor the special responsibility of the intellectual class. Writing that the ideal world would be "classless," with the threefold division of the modern world into the intellectual, laboring, and Capitalist classes having been abolished, Wang also claimed that he was not seeking to lead China into a "utopia" but to enter into a general trend of world reform. In this light, the Chinese intellectuals should be urged to enter the laboring class, and the "most hopeful" (zui you xiwang), in the sense of fulfilling this vision, were those Chinese who went to Europe, both intellectuals and laborers.[8]

Wang Guangqi was clearly affected by his sojourn in Europe, but he had gone to Germany and thus was not directly affected by the three struggles of 1921. Wang became more distanced from his earlier political activities and became absorbed in his vision of internal cultivation as the germination point of societal change. His writings in 1922 show that Wang's perception of the need for social reform and the role of youth and the intellectual class had not changed. Current politics, according to Wang, were bankrupt. With few exceptions the Guomindang members were ruffians (liumang) and did not know the meaning of societal endeavor (shehui shiye). Those involved in politics were tainted by the intrinsic corruption of political change. On the other hand, intellectuals were addressing the real needs of society on a fundamental level: "We have a profession [zhiye]," Wang jibed, "they have none."[9]

Wang's break with many of his compatriots was nowhere better expressed than in his praise of Chinese leaders who were exemplars of the social revolution, such as Liang Qichao, Hu Shi, Li Shizeng, Wu Zhihui, Cai Yuanpei, and Wang Jingwei (although Wang Jingwei had by then switched to advocacy of a political solution). Wang also gave several brief illustrations of foreigners who were to be emulated, including several Japanese and, as a Western example, Leon Trotsky, who symbolized dedication to the princi-

---

7. Wang Guangqi, "Shaonian Zhongguo xuehui zhi jingshen ji jinxing jihua" [The plan of spirit and action of the Young China Study Association] (1919), reprinted in idem, *Shaonian Zhongguo yundong*, 54.

8. Ibid., 71–72.

9. Wang Guangqi, "Shehui de zhengzhi gaige yu shehui de shehui gaige" [The political reform of society and the social reform of society] (1922), reprinted in idem, *Shaonian Zhongguo yundong*, 120–29.

ple of egalitarianism.[10] The European example was particularly important and embodied the necessity for study and preparation in societal change, because Wang believed one needed to understand the spirit of the West on ethical, cultural, social, and technological levels. This understanding must also be integrated with the inculcation of mutual feeling (*ganqing jiaoyu*). To this end, in a more traditional manner than Wang probably realized, Wang believed that the study of ritual and music was important. Wang Guangqi, grandson of a famous Chinese poet, proceeded to obtain his doctorate in music, his way of fulfilling the task of social revolution.

In essence Wang was arguing for an extensive modernist reform, not for revolutionary ideology or organization. Writing in 1927 on the three necessary awakenings in China, Wang pointed to the need to industrialize, to mobilize and unify the people and armies, and to eradicate political factionalism. As much as China could learn from the West, Wang's Sinocentric emphasis never left him: "In the six or seven years I have been in Europe, I have not yet seen a Westerner who was more naturally talented than a Chinese," Wang maintained. The pride in being Chinese came from both the high level and the longevity of Chinese culture. Wang took pains to explain that with the exception of the Jewish people (who had no fixed place of residence or large population), all other cultures of the world had been tainted and mixed, and only the Chinese retained cultural continuity. In the midst of his analysis of China's need to modernize, Wang felt no contradiction in proclaiming, "We know in today's world there is only one ancient civilized people—the Chinese people."[11] Implicit in this viewpoint is the cultural leadership role that was still the responsibility of the Chinese intellectual.

Wang Guangqi never attained the fame of Cai Hesen, Zhao Shiyan, or Zhou Enlai, although they were all mutual acquaintances, and Zhao Shiyan was a protégé. Wang was involved in anti-Japanese work, often contributed articles to journals, composed music, and taught at the University of Bonn from 1932 until his death in 1936. His friends in Europe and China deeply mourned his death and arranged to have his body transported back to China, where several commemoration services were held nationwide. It was not an eventful passing, and his life was not filled with obvious danger, underground activities, turgid policy debates, or violence. Yet Wang Guangqi was the exemplar of a very important pathway for the Found Gen-

---

10. Ibid., 130–50.
11. Wang Guangqi, "Jiaoyu jia duiyu Zhongguo xiankuang yingyou zhi sanda juewu" [The three great awakenings which educators ought to have concerning the current Chinese situation], *Zhongguo jiaoyu jie* 16 (May 1927): 2–13.

eration. It was a road that did not have immediate aims or political goals but emphasized the more comprehensive area of societal transformation from the bottom up led by the egalitarian intellectual, who must have the patience and foresight to lead the social revolution—but not as a revolutionary, who would only become polluted by contact with sordid politics.

Cai Hesen and the First Phase of ECCO Development

Cai Hesen, like Wang Guangqi, had been a popular youth leader. He was active in the New Citizens' Study Society and an ardent advocate of the work-study scheme. But Cai Hesen did not have Wang's commitment to the intellectual class, although like Wang Guangqi, Cai did not work in a factory in France. Perhaps his experience as a business apprentice and late arrival in the educational system or his preoccupation with the more unpretentious Mohist philosophy weakened the bonds with the more traditional Confucian roles. His conversion to Marxism came in early 1920.

By mid-1920 Cai wanted to form a Marxist party among his Hunanese compatriots, and he insisted on convening a five-day meeting, which took place in Montargis in June 1920 at the local college. In the report of Xiao Zisheng, president of the New Citizens' Study Society, it is obvious that Cai succeeded in fracturing the group. The split was between those like Xiao Zisheng, who wanted a moderate reform approach to national problems, and Cai Hesen and his followers, who believed that only a violent revolution led by a Communist party would succeed in national salvation. These were the two extremes. There was a middle group led by Li Weihan and Zhang Kundi, who had formed the Society for the World of Work-Study, a mutual aid organization.[12] This group was not yet convinced by Cai that Marxism was the ideology to follow, and at this time his proposal for the establishment of a Communist party was voted down.[13]

However, the members decided to further explore new ideas together. Cai Hesen had collected over a hundred Western publications, and everyone divided up the work. The five-day meeting also included society business and philosophical discussions. The fifth day included a criticism session and ended with a giant picnic. The criticism session is very revealing of the members' mutual perceptions and attitudes. Cai Hesen was seen as strong but needed to guard against aloofness; Xiao Zisheng was seen as

12. See the section Organizational Transitions at the beginning of chap. 4 and Appendix 2, Organizations.

13. Xiao Zisheng, "Xinmin xuehui fu Fa huiyuan Mengdani huiyi qingkuang" [The membership of the New Citizens' Study Society involved in the travel to France program at the time of the Montargis meeting] (1920), in FuFa, 2:805–9.

very logical but should avoid becoming too narrow-minded.[14] Perhaps Cai Hesen would have had greater success at this point if he had had a less stern and warmer personality, whereas Xiao might have benefited from more personal charm (although he had the greater personal network). Yet many members were interested in Cai's ideas, and eventually eight of the thirteen New Citizens' Study Society members at Montargis joined the ECCO.[15]

The events at Montargis were duly communicated to the New Citizens' Study Society comrades at home, which stimulated them to hold several meetings where the same issues were raised and debated. The correspondence during this period was thoughtful, animated, and profuse. Members would often address their letters to several members at one time to widen the debate. Without a doubt Cai Hesen had a profound impact on his compatriots in China, especially through his urgings to Mao Zedong to start a movement to go to Russia, the leading country in the coming world revolution, to study their example. On the impact of this correspondence, Robert Scalapino commented:

> Mao at this point had unmistakably taken his stand with Marxism, *not* because of any profound understanding of Marxist or Marxist-Leninist theory (except as derived from Cai's descriptions) but because he had been convinced by Cai and possibly others that the Russian route was the only successful road to revolution, and that revolution was necessary for China and the world.[16]

Thus, from the start of his European sojourn Cai Hesen was in many ways an activist. First, his relationship with Xiang Jingyu—their "progressive alliance" (*xiangxiang tongmeng*), an example of free (nonarranged) romance—was famous among contemporary Hunanese as an ideal marriage and was one indication of his dissolving social and political barriers. Second, his early acceptance of Western Marxist theory led him to his attempt in mid-1920 to form a Marxist party out of the New Citizens' Study Society. Third, his leadership throughout 1921 was notable, particularly his insouciant direction of the Twenty-eighth Movement and marked authority during the Lyons Incident.

In addition to his efforts to form a Marxist party, Cai Hesen was most influential as the prototypical Marxist theoretician. Although Cai's understanding of Marxism was not perfect, it was more sophisticated and ad-

14. Ibid., 808.
15. Li Weihan, "Huiyi Xinmin xuehui," 43.
16. Robert A. Scalapino, "The Evolution of a Young Revolutionary—Mao Zedong in 1919–1921," 56.

vanced than that of other Chinese during this period. For example, the first use of the term "Chinese Communist Party" (*Zhongguo gongchandang*) has been attributed to him.[17] Moreover, Cai Hesen may have been central in the theoretical development of Chen Duxiu and fellow New Citizens' Study Society compatriots.[18] As we have seen, Cai wrote many letters and articles and held numerous translation and study sessions in Montargis.

As early as the fall of 1920, Cai Hesen wrote on the central need to choose between reform and revolution. Unlike Wang Guangqi, Cai Hesen perceived both of these options in political modes, not in terms of social reform. Disillusioned by the Versailles Conference, Cai thought that Wilsonian democracy was a bankrupt alternative and only succeeded in exacerbating the current repression in the world. Only the organization of a disciplined Communist party could overcome Capitalist oppression. According to Cai Hesen, Marxist theory revolved around three pivots: the materialist conception of history, the theory of capital in economics, and the theory of class conflict in the realm of politics.[19] Using these three fundamentals one could adopt the "revolutionary Marxist ideology."

Cai Hesen was expelled in the Lyons Incident and upon his return to China was promptly elected to the three-person Central Committee of the CCP in 1922 and given the editorship of the CCP newspaper, *Xiangdao* (*The Guide*). This rapid rise within CCP ranks showed both a real regard for the advanced theoretical sophistication of Cai Hesen and the small number of CCP leaders. Without a doubt his contributions of both theory and strategy in early CCP history were crucial in helping the CCP gain momentum in Chinese mass politics. After the debacle of the Guomindang coup in 1927, Cai Hesen was a key figure in the denunciation of Chen Duxiu, while his own power within the CCP central hierarchy steadily eroded. His capture and death by gruesome torture in 1931[20] were directly attributable to his

17. Xia Honggen, "Dangshi xiaozu ziliao" [Materials on the history of the small Party organizations], *Zhongguo xiandaishi fuyin baokan ziliao* 13 (1982): 100.
18. Cai Bo interview, 4 October 1985 (Beijing). Cai Bo particularly pointed to the correspondence of Cai Hesen with Chen Duxiu before the CCP First Congress, which discussed the theoretical and practical details of Marxism-Leninism. I would like to suggest this as an area of future research. E.g., Arif Dirlik questions where Chen Duxiu learned about Lenin's *Imperialism* before July 1921 (*The Origins of Chinese Communism*, 229–30). It is probable that Cai Hesen had read Lenin during the latter half of 1920. In my discussions with Liu Guisheng, Liu suggested that the Twenty-one Conditions for entering the Communist International were well known to Cai Hesen, who, along with many others, read *L'humanité*, which published these conditions.
19. Cai Hesen, "Makesi xueshuo yu Zhongguo wuchan jieji" [Marxist theory and the Chinese proletariat], *Xin qingnian* 9 (August 1921): 5–10.
20. According to a personal communication (12 December 1985) from CCP historian Shi Guang, Cai Hesen was crucified and disemboweled.

firm discipline in following CCP Central Committee orders to base himself in Hong Kong.

Cai Hesen's impact on the development of the ECCO cannot be under-rated. He was an important stimulus in the formation of the ECCO and was its mentor on theory. Moreover, he quickly became one of the most impor-tant theoreticians for the CCP.

Zhao Shiyan, First General Secretary of the ECCO

Zhao Shiyan was slower to make his commitment to Marxism, but his wider contacts made him the ideal organizer of the ECCO. He not only belonged to the elite Young China Study Association as a precocious younger mem-ber, but he had May Fourth credentials and worked in a French factory attempting to promote a true merging between the intellectual and laboring classes. A born organizer and mediator, Zhao Shiyan had an astute rhetori-cal talent in both his writing and his speech. He was very persuasive.

Zhao Shiyan did not become committed to Marxist politics until the three struggles of 1921, although he had participated in a small Marxist discussion group led by Zhang Shenfu during a period about which Zheng Chaolin remarked, "Everyone was a Marxist of one form or another."[21] Close to the more reform-oriented mentors such as Wang Guangqi and Zeng Qi, Zhao believed in both the revolt of youth and the mutual aid con-cepts espoused by Wang Guangqi during the *Gongdu huzhu* movement. Zhao also subscribed to the sanctity of labor and egalitarian tenets that many young Chinese advocated. Before his embarkation for France, Zhao wrote an article entitled "The Basic Misconceptions of the Work-Study Movement." He claimed that one should not look upon the factory work as a means to an education (*yigong qiuxue*) but as an important tool in itself (*yigong youxue*).[22] Zhao's language abilities and the fact that as a Sichuanese teenager he had adapted well in the north facilitated his quick habituation to the French environment. According to his roommate Fu Zhong, they lived frugally, working different shifts and sharing the same bed and the same winter clothing.[23]

Zhao identified strongly with the Chinese workers under contract from the First World War and worked to free them from their restrictive con-

21. Zheng Chaolin interview, 29 October 1985 (Shanghai).
22. Zhao Shiyan, "Qingong jianxue guannian shang de genben cuowu" [The basic mis-conceptions of the Work-Study Movement], in Zhang Yunhou et al., *Liu Fa qingong jianxue yundong*, 1:389–92.
23. Fu Zhong, "Fu Zhong tan lü Fa qingong jianxue he shehuizhuyi qingniantuan lü Ou zongzhibu" [Fu Zhong discusses the travel to France Work-Study Movement and the ECCP], in *Yida qianhou*, 2:559–63.

tracts. His activities included organizing the Labor Study Society, publishing a paper for Chinese workers, and tutoring them in English.[24]

Zhao's activities during the Twenty-eighth Movement indicate that he was not a Marxist but still believed in the philosophy behind Work-Study. He had signed a petition to the SFEA in December 1920, along with Li Lisan and Chen Gongpei, which specifically eschewed forming a radical party.[25] Zhao and his friends wrote articles decrying the actions and philosophy of the Montargis faction, who were the most visible Marxists. In an article written one month before the Twenty-eighth Movement, Zhao Shiyan claimed that the only "restriction" on the lives of the Work-Study participants was their lack of drive and self-sufficiency. "We do not know our own duties," Zhao protested, as he chided people for being dependent.[26] Zhao's response to the Twenty-eighth Movement was to form the Work-Study Alliance, which was based on the principles of mutual aid and self-sufficiency. Zhao believed so strongly in these principles that when he received some funds from home, he was furious and shared the money with others.[27]

Although Zhao Shiyan typified the philosophy of self-sufficiency, the breaks in the solidarity of the Work-Study Movement troubled him, and he personally sought to repair the rifts by visiting Montargis. As he entered into discussion groups, Zhao began to seriously consider Marxism, especially because he was a worker and had experienced the grueling nature of factory life. After several meetings with the Montargis group, "in the end both sides agreed: Let bygones be bygones; today both sides would unify and mutually study and uphold Marxism."[28]

When the Loan Struggle erupted in the summer of 1921, Zhao Shiyan took an active part and possibly chaired the first meeting on 30 June.[29] During the Lyons Incident, Zhao was a major representative, because he was articulate and known for his ability to be moderate. As a negotiator, he was allowed out of the encampment. He was in Paris when the students were deported, and he saw no need to join them voluntarily. However, his pass-

24. "Zhao Shiyan shengping ziliao," 56–58. This work took place throughout 1920 and 1921.
25. See the petition of 13 December 1920 in FuFa, 2:381–92.
26. Shi Yan, "Huadi weilai de qingong jianxuezhe" [The restricted Work-Study students], Lü Ou zhoukan 64 (29 January 1921): 1.
27. "Zhao Shiyan shengping ziliao," 58.
28. Ibid., 55.
29. According to "Zhao Shiyan shengping ziliao," 59, he led the meeting (zhuchi). In her essay, Peng Chengfu does not mention that he had any official role ("Zhao Shiyan," 11). Zhou Enlai's accounts speak of Mr. Zhao (see FuFa, 2:463). I am hesitant to believe that Zhao led the meeting because of another account at the time which discloses the name of the 30 June meeting chairman as Zhao Zhiyou, which I have not seen as an alternative name for Zhao Shiyan (FuFa, 2:483).

port had been confiscated during his imprisonment at Lyons, and without it he could not accompany Zhang Shenfu, Zhou Enlai, Liu Qingyang, and the others who went to Germany. His tactical mistake of trusting Chen Lu and the loss of his passport made him more suspicious during the rest of his stay in France. His later letters criticize his friends for not being "secretive" enough. After the Lyons Incident, he went to the northern part of France, where the work was more difficult and dangerous, but where he could be more anonymous.[30]

While in the north, Zhao kept up his contacts through extensive letter writing, communicating with those who had gone to Germany, with de-ported Lyons Incident friends, such as Li Lisan and Chen Gongpei, and with people in the Paris region, such as Yuan Qingyun and the Montargis group. According to Zhao's letters, while he was making extensive prepa-rations for setting up the ECYC, he felt oppressed by the "lack of freedom" in France but refused to go home to China although he had been urged to return by several people.[31]

An organizational effort led by Cai Hesen with the support of Zhao Shi-yan, Li Lisan, and recent converts from the moderates such as Li Weihan and Zhang Kundi almost succeeded in forming a Marxist party in the early summer of 1921, before the First Congress of the CCP.[32] The failure to open up the SFI at Lyons, the subsequent expulsions, and the defeat of the Work-Study Movement led in late 1921 and early 1922 to the final resolution by Zhao Shiyan and like-minded Chinese youth to form the ECCO.

Through Zhao's wide range of contacts among Chinese workers, stu-dents, and youth organizations he was able to organize the ECCO in 1922. Within one year he had doubled the size of the ECYC, established an orga-nizational framework, a Party newspaper, extensive cooperation with the Chinese workers, and a pipeline to Moscow for ECCO members who were returning home to China. Zhao Shiyan was in the first group to make use of this Russian route. When he was ordered by the CCP to return, he left France in late March 1923. Zhao spent almost a year in the Soviet Union and returned to China in July 1924, where he worked actively for the Beijing Regional Executive Committee and edited the CCP journal *Zhengzhi shenghuo* (*Political Life*).

Whereas Cai Hesen's letters to Hunan show his preoccupation with the-ory, Zhao's letters show his preoccupation with the necessities of organiza-tion. This pragmatism made him a particularly effective labor organizer,

30. "Zhao Shiyan shengping ziliao," 60–64.
31. *FuFa*, 2:832–39.
32. Cai Bo interview, 4 October 1985 (Beijing).

meeting planner, and cadre trainer. Zhao Shiyan's crowning achievement was guiding the successful occupation of Shanghai in the spring of 1927. He was one of three leaders and the spokesman for the press conference after the uprising. Shortly after the April Twelfth Coup, Zhao Shiyan was captured by the Guomindang and executed on 19 July 1927 at the age of twenty-six.

Zhao Shiyan's commitment to Marxism came from firsthand observation of the egalitarian principles of the May Fourth era put into practice. His factory experience and his growing disenchantment with the viability of the Work-Study Movement shored up his final decision to become a revolutionary. Although he lived a short life, Zhao Shiyan made significant contributions to the ECCO and CCP.

Zhou Enlai and the Fruition of the ECCO

Zhou Enlai's conversion to Marxism was gradual, as revealed by both his own account and his writings while in Europe. In the spring of 1922, Zhou wrote to his old Self-Awakening Society friends about his conversion to Marxism, which took place about one month after the Lyons Incident, while he was in Berlin in late 1921. China scholars tend to ascribe his period in Japan as one of Socialist indoctrination, but in fact Zhou Enlai himself marks his stay in prison in 1920 as his first step and his trip to Europe, with the availability of proper materials, as the second and final step in his commitment to communism.[33] Zhou's view is confirmed by his own writings, which were profuse throughout his entire stay in Europe. Though no documented evidence exists of Zhou Enlai ever working in a French factory, his writings indicate that like Zhao Shiyan he still believed in the value of the Work-Study Movement: "The ability for common youth to nourish the habit of Work-Study, . . . if one can recognize it clearly, then one can adventurously experiment, *strengthening the body, supporting artistic habits, speaking the French language,* and in the end be able to . . . overcome everything and effect a new age [of Work-Studyism]" (emphasis mine).[34] Thus, one can see that in early 1921 Zhou believed that the principles of the Work-Study Movement were still practicable, although he ended his series of articles by claiming that the preeminent condition of success was the factory experience and that formal education was secondary. Still, his emphasis on the necessity for physical fitness, art appreciation, and fluency in French are hardly Marxist prescriptions for revolution.

33. Nankai Daxue Zhou Enlai yanjiushi, *Zhou Enlai qingshaonian shidai jishi,* 75.
34. Zhou Enlai, "Qingong jianxue sheng de da bolan," in *FuFa,* 1:8.

Zhou's characterization of the difference between the Twenty-eighth Movement and the Loan Struggle indicates that like Zhao Shiyan, he was not sympathetic to the most visible of the Marxists: Cai Hesen and the Montargis faction. In comparing the two struggles, Zhou remarked: "Both were connected with government officials, but their characters were very different: one was a question of living; one was a question of nationalism. The former was a spontaneous gathering, for direct action. The second was a meeting, it was open [and] orderly, a gathering under one roof, serving the public interest [congrong yishi ye]."[35]

Strains of incipient disillusionment with the Work-Study philosophy mark the series of articles on the Twenty-eighth Movement. By the time of the Lyons Incident, Zhou's articles were more angry and strident in tone. He himself recognized that this was taking place. At one point he claimed that he held no grudge against the incoming Lyons candidates, they were in truth brothers, but along with Cai Hesen, Chen Yi, and Zhao Shiyan, he felt betrayed.[36]

Like many of his generation, whether Marxist or not, Zhou Enlai used the term "class," and his articles on the English miners' strike in April 1921 were very sympathetic to the labor cause. However, before the end of 1921, Zhou's occasional "class analyses" are not indicative that he identified himself as a Marxist. Many non-Marxists used class analyses during this period. Zhou's writings also reflected concerns that coincided with those of non-Marxists. For example, his view that reparations payments from Germany would inevitably lead to violence echoed the view of some Western attendees of the Versailles Conference, including John Maynard Keynes, who withdrew in protest, and Zhou Enlai's future nemesis, John Foster Dulles, who was a lawyer for the American negotiators.

Finally, although Zhou Enlai wrote about the struggles of 1921 and was probably involved in the Loan Struggle, he was not a key actor until 1922. Li Weihan reinforces this view, commenting that Zhou did not have much of a public profile during the Twenty-eighth Movement or the Lyons Incident.[37] The Lyons Incident was the turning point for Zhou Enlai. He believed that the expulsions and cessation of governmental aid were part of

35. Zhou Enlai, "Lü Fa Huaren jujue jiekuan zhi yundong," in *FuFa*, 2:464. This sentiment indicates the difficulty of understanding exactly what being labeled a "Marxist" meant. As we shall see later in the chapter, Zhou Enlai at this time belonged to a Marxist study group, sanctioned by Chen Duxiu, and yet during the summer of 1921 he still identified the Marxist interests as narrow, whereas a nationalist struggle to prevent loans going to the warlords was more moral.

36. Zhou Enlai, "Qingong jianxue sheng zai Fa zuihou zhi yunming," in *FuFa*, 1:56–57.

37. Li Weihan, "Huiyi Xinmin xuehui," 48.

the revenge for the Loan Struggle: "You destroy their big bowl, they naturally also want to destroy your small bowl."[38] Feeling betrayed and angry,
Zhou left for Berlin shortly after the Lyons Incident and soon officially at-
tested to his belief that Marxism was the only path for national change.

If Zhou's "public profile" was low-key in 1921, the next two years saw an
increasing level of activity that reflected his ideological commitment. Ed
Hammond conveniently divides Zhou's activities into three categories: recruitment, writing, and liaison work.[39] Zhou was a prolific writer even before 1922. According to Wang Yongxiang, he contributed fifty-four essays
to Yishi bao alone.[40] As head of the propaganda section of the ECYC and a
major member of the ECCP, Zhou juggled his various tasks, yet managed to
oversee much of the production of the ECCO propaganda, writing over thirty
essays himself.[41] Zhou's writings often discussed Marxism, appealing to
Chinese workers in France to join the ECCO. In addition to education and
recruitment, other themes were the need for revolution in China and the
upholding of the policy lines of the Comintern, especially anti-imperialist
articles criticizing the Western countries for their exploitation not only of
China but of other countries. ECCO propaganda was also aimed at political
infighting against other contending groups such as the Anarchists and the
Chinese Youth Party.[42]

Zhou spent much of his time shuttling between Paris, Berlin, and Belgium recruiting and indoctrinating members, continually observing and
writing. In late 1922 he recruited Zhu De and Sun Bingwen into the
ECCO.[43] Other famous recruits of Zhou were Ma Zhiyuan, Yuan Zizhen, and
Wu Qi. Zhou Enlai became famous for his ability to communicate with
groups of differing political orientations. The leaders of the Chinese Youth
Party, Zeng Qi and Li Huang, found it hard to resist Zhou's repeated over-
tures of solidarity throughout the Paris years, even though some of the common meetings ended in physical violence.

Elected as the second general secretary of the ECYC, Zhou Enlai was subject to the dictates of the CCP Central Committee in China. He used his

---

38. Zhou Enlai, "Qingong jianxue sheng zai Fa zuihou zhi yunming," in FuFa, 1:61.
39. Ed Hammond, Coming of Grace (Berkeley: Lancaster-Miller, 1980), 18–20.
40. Wang Yongxiang and Liu Pinqing, Weile Zhonghua zhi jueqi, 149.
41. Hou Junchu, "Zhou Enlai tongzhi yu zhonggong lü Ou zhibu" [Zhou Enlai and the
ECCO, Zhongguo xiandaishi fuyin baokan ziliao 4 (1982): 42.
42. See "Zhou Enlai qingshaonian shidai," for an overview of Zhou's writings during this
period. Zhou Enlai, Zhou Enlai tongzhi lü Ou wenji, has photostats of the originals, and the
FuFa collection contains the essays spread throughout four volumes in simplified characters.
43. Beijing shifan daxue [Beijing Normal University], ed., Zhu De tongzhi de qingshaonian
de shidai [Comrade Zhu De during his period of youth] (Nanchang: Jiangxi renmin chubanshe, 1979), 161–70.

talents to carry out their policies, especially in implementing the United Front with the EGMD, which he succeeded in setting up before the United Front was formed in China, and he was able to effect control of the alliance by the ECCO and the left EGMD faction.

Although he had been noted for his organizational abilities in Tianjin during the May Fourth Movement, Zhou's style of leadership became more diversified during this period. One can speculate whether Zhou's increasing sensitivity to the reality of workers and ability to communicate were influenced by the example of his fellow ECCO members, particularly Zhao Shiyan.[44] The French period brought to light the full range of talents that Zhou would display so brilliantly in his later career. He learned to manipulate through propaganda, personal contacts, and personality, and he found a delineated theory and blueprint (Marxism) for national salvation.

Zhou Enlai had a multifaceted political career, which spanned the rise and consolidation of CCP power in China. Upon his return to China he became the political officer at the Huangpu Military Academy in Guangdong and by 1927 was elected to the Central Committee of the CCP. Zhou often served as a political officer and negotiator throughout the next five decades. He was a symbol of moderation during important crises, such as the Long March and the Cultural Revolution. After the CCP's rise to power in 1949, Zhou Enlai became the foreign minister and one of the three leaders to stand on the reviewing stand, alongside Mao Zedong and Zhu De, at the proclamation of the People's Republic of China. For over a quarter of a century Zhou Enlai was one of the most important leaders in the PRC. When he died of cancer on 8 January 1976, the Chinese grieved deeply. Demonstrations commemorating Zhou Enlai grew to such levels that the government used force to put them down.

In sum, the political radicalization of Chinese youth in Europe was not a homogeneous historical occurrence. The choice of reform or revolution, the willingness to join the ranks of politicians as a revolutionary, and the break from traditional Confucian leadership roles and intellectual heritage were all mediated by both personal and general factors, including the impact of the immediate French environment, the three struggles of 1921, the lingering bonds of youth groups, the swelling momentum of new groups that were interregionally oriented, and the theoretical sway of new ideologies ranging from Marxism to fascism. Among the many Chinese youth who undertook this internal journey were those like Wang Guangqi, who main-

44. An interesting project would include analyzing Zhou's writings from 1921 to 1924 with an eye to (1) the changing style from predominantly *wenyan* to *baihua* and (2) changes in rhetorical appeals and audience.

Zhou Enlai in Paris, 1923

Zhou Enlai's apartment in Paris, a meeting place for revolutionary activities

A September 1924 ECYC meeting to wish farewell to Zhou Enlai as he was preparing to return to China. *From left, front row:* no. 1, Nie Rongzhen; no. 4, Zhou Enlai; no. 6, Li Fuchun. *Second row:* no. 1, Liu Puqing; no. 2, Yang Kun; no. 4, Ren Zhuoxuan. *Third row: third from right,* Deng Xiaoping.

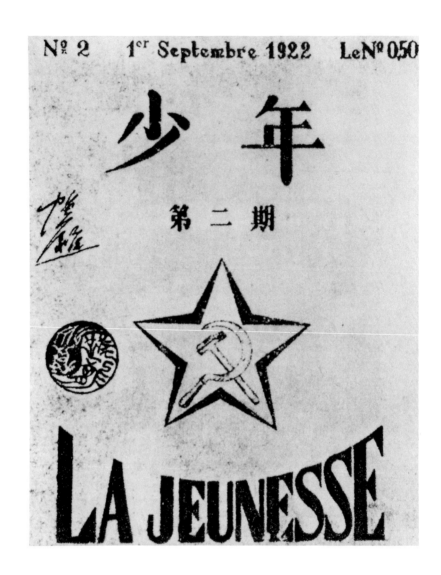

The propaganda organ of the ECCO until 1924: *Shaonian (Youth)*

The propaganda organ of the ECCO after 1924: *Chiguang (Red Light)*

A farewell gathering for Zhou Enlai of the European Branch of the Guomindang. On Zhou Enlai's right is Wang Jingqi, the first general secretary of the EGMD, who was expelled from France the following year and died on board ship. *From right, back row:* no. 2, Yang Kun; no. 3, Ren Zhuoxuan.

A meeting of the European Branch of the Guomindang, which had been officially established in November 1923

Dr. Yang Kun in his nineties. Dr. Yang, who obtained his doctorate from the University of Lyons, has pioneered minority studies in China.

Zheng Chaolin in his nineties. Imprisoned by both the GMD and the CCP, Zheng Chaolin, a prominent Trotskyite, spent a total of thirty-four years in prison. Released in 1979, he has been writing his recollections of the 1920s and 1930s.

tained the banner of social reform, and those like Cai Hesen, Zhao Shiyan, and Zhou Enlai, who opted for a Communist revolution.

THE ORIGIN AND NATURE OF THE ECYC

Although Nie Rongzhen may be correct in his memoirs in saying that the "beginning point of the revolution is forever hard to forget,"[45] the difficulty is that everyone remembers things differently. Observers and historians differ on names, dates, functions, and tasks of the groups. Two key controversies concerning the formation of the ECCO are the origin and nature of the ECYC. Thus, before discussing the ECCO formation, these two issues will be addressed.

The Origin of the ECYC

One version of the origin of the ECYC claims that a small group (*xiaozu*) of Chinese Communists centering around Zhang Shenfu met frequently during the spring and summer of 1921.[46] Zhang Shenfu had come to France to teach at the SFI at Lyons University but resigned after the Lyons Incident. Zhang claimed that he had participated in the organization of the Beijing Branch of the CCP before coming to France. Other members were Chen Gongpei, who had participated in some organizational work for the Shanghai CCP cell; Liu Qingyang, a prominent Self-Awakening Society member, whom Zhang introduced into the Party (and who became his wife within the year); Zhou Enlai, whom Liu introduced to Zhang Shenfu and who purportedly joined the Party in early 1921; and Zhao Shiyan, who supposedly joined the CCP in Shanghai before leaving for France. "This small group decided to lead the preparations for the ECYC."[47]

45. Nie Rongzhen, *Nie Rongzhen huiyilu*, 1:34.
46. Liu Ye, Zhu Yuhe, and Zhao Yuanbi, "Lü Ou Zhongguo dangtuan de jianli jingguo" [The experiences of the establishment of the ECCO, *Dangshi yanjiu* 1 (28 February 1981): 78–79; see also their later article "Shilun lü Ou Zhongguo gongchanzhuyi zuzhi de xingcheng" [A practical discussion of the formation of the ECCO, in Zhu Chenjia, ed., *Zhonggong dangshi yanjiu lun wenxian* [A collection of studies on CCP history] (Hunan: Hunan renmin chubanshe, 1983), 1:170–89; see also Wang Yongxiang, Kong Fanfeng, and Liu Pinqing, *Zhongguo gongchandang lü Ou zhibu shihua*, chap. 3, for this version of ECYC formation.
47. It is unlikely that Zhao Shiyan or Zhou Enlai were stalwart Communists at the beginning of 1921. However, they may have perceived themselves as committed to some form of Marxism. Both certainly had a wide range of contacts. Part of the confusion arises out of the importance later, more politically sensitive interpretations attach to the phenomenon of the *xiaozu* (small group, cell). Did joining a cell mean a total commitment to an ideology or an occasion for intellectual inquiry in an era of changing affiliations? Quotation from Zhang Shenfu, "Zhang Shenfu tan lü Ou dangtuan zuzhi huodong qingkuang" [Zhang Shenfu explains the situation of the ECCO activities], *Tianjin wenshi ziliao xuanji* 15 (May 1981): 87.

Zhang Shenfu is the basic source for this version, saying that "the five of us established a small Communist Party organization. This small organization did not have a name. Everyone clearly understood [we] were Communist Party members, but it was not publicized to the outside."[48] According to Zhang he was the center of the group because he regularly corresponded with Chen Duxiu. The group was fairly autonomous, and Zhang's decisions were usually approved as a matter of course. Zhang remembers both setting up a study society and a paper, *Shaonian (Youth)*.[49] Other memoirs also support the view of a Communist nucleus group. However, according to Zheng Chaolin the small group also included four others: Zhang Bojian, Xie Taokang, Xiao Zizhang, and Xiong Xiong.[50] Additionally, documents confiscated by the French when they arrested Chen Duxiu in Shanghai on 16 August 1922 list European correspondents, among whom are Zhao Shiyan, Zhang Shenfu, and Wu Ming (Chen Gongpei).[51]

An alternative interpretation is that the Paris group led by Zhang Shenfu was not as important as Zhang asserted, nor was it organized as early as Zhang claimed. Discrepancies with other memoirs and original materials have been cited by several historians.[52] For example, a July 1921 letter by Chen Gongpei claimed that a Marxist organization would be formed in the near future, which leads one to conclude that one was not in existence. Wu Shiqi dates the formation of Zhang's group to 1922. His version of the events leading up to the formation of the ECYC suggests a two-phased development. First, Cai Hesen led the earliest attempts to establish a Marxist party, as evidenced by his efforts during the summer of 1920 and the

48. Ibid.
49. Ibid., 87–88.
50. Zheng Chaolin, *Ji Yin Kuan* [Remembering Yin Kuan] (unpublished manuscript, 1983), 43–44.
51. Documents seized in Chen Duxiu's room, Shanghai, 16 August 1922, AAE, série E, Chine, vol. 197. The list also includes Li Cao, Li Ji, Liu Renjing (Berlin), and his son Chen Yannian, among others. Another list of names confiscated during 1922, from a "Bolshevist Reading Room," includes Zhao Shiyan's name as the first on the list of correspondents, followed by Li Fuchun, Luo Chengding, and Chen Yannian, but Zhang Shenfu is not listed (AAE, série E, Chine, vol. 492).
52. For the most lucid presentation of these arguments see Chen Jingtang [Chan Kingtong], "Lun zhonggong lü Ou zong zhibu de faqi zu" [A discussion of the beginning groups of the ECCO, *Zhongguo lishi xuehui shixue jikan* 19 (July 1987): 359–94; Chen particularly contrasts discrepancies within the various testimonies of Zhang Shenfu. Other forceful arguments exist in Ren Wuxiong, "Yida qian liu Fa xuesheng zhong wu gongchandang xiaozu" [The absence of a small Communist group among the travel to France students before the founding of the CCP], *Dangshi yanjiu ziliao* (Sichuan) 2 (September 1981): 65–66; and Wu Shiqi, "Dui youguan lü Ou jiandang jige wenti de tantao" [An examination of several problems in the establishment of the ECCO], *Zhongguo xiandaishi fuyin baokan ziliao* 2 (September 1982): 2–10.

Twenty-eighth Movement. Second, after the Lyons Incident, the various groups were convinced of the need for unification, and their efforts resulted in the actual formation of the ECYC.[53] However, Wu Shiqi's dating of the formation of Zhang's group to 1922 is implausible because Chen Gongpei was expelled in 1921 during the Lyons Incident.

Perhaps the truth lies in recognizing that the organizational importance of the Zhang Shenfu Paris group and Cai Hesen's activities are not mutually exclusive historical phenomena. Leaving aside the discrepancies of various memoirs, one can discern *simultaneous* developments. Zhang Shenfu did receive credentials from Chen Duxiu, giving him a real position of leadership within the small group that met during 1921. The support of the CCP had a very important impact on the development of the ECYC. However, Zhang Shenfu was not as passionately persuasive a Marxist as Cai Hesen, who, as we saw, galvanized the Montargis group of Work-Study participants and pushed toward forming a party from mid-1920 until his expulsion during the Lyons Incident. In terms of theoretical development within the European Chinese Marxist community, Cai Hesen spurred the youthful seekers to a more sophisticated exploration of Marxist theory.[54]

Perhaps more important for the ultimate coordination of the ECCO were the leadership qualities of Zhao Shiyan, the first general secretary of the ECYC. Zhao's contributions were several. Along with his colleagues Li Lisan and Wang Ruofei, he built the important bridges to the Montargis community after the disunity of the Twenty-eighth Movement. Because of his own status as a factory worker, he gained credibility with Chinese factory workers such as Fu Zhong and Ren Zhuoxuan. Zhao's previous participation in the May Fourth Movement, in addition to his affiliation with Li Dazhao and entry into the Young China Study Association, gave him access to older New Culture leaders such as Chen Duxiu. Because he met with Chen in Shanghai, before he left for France, Zhao Shiyan gained entry into Zhang Shenfu's Paris group. It was Zhao who skillfully targeted and recruited the Chen brothers into the ECCO. Finally, without Zhao Shiyan's organizational ability to unify these varying groups, the importance of Chinese Communist cells in Paris, Montargis, and French factories might have been minimal.[55]

53. Wu Shiqi, "Dui youguan lü Ou jiandang jige wenti de tantao," 2–4.

54. I believe this interpretation of ECCO development has been accepted by most ECCO scholars. I particularly valued from a discussion with Zhu Yuhe on 2 November 1985, during which he presented me with the outlines of this paradigm.

55. This does not mean that the roles of other leaders such as Zhang Shenfu and Zhou Enlai or Cai Hesen and Li Weihan were inconsequential. However, it was Zhao Shiyan who had the broad range of personal contacts, which he drew together into a coherent and disciplined whole.

The Nature of the ECYC

What kind of an organization was the ECYC? Although the ECYC was officially a *tuan* (corps, or party members in training), did it function in reality as a *dang* (party)? Liu Ye, Zhu Yuhe, and Zhao Yuanbi assert that "the ECYC was by nature a corps and not a party."[56] Although the name of the ECYC was originally Lü Ou Zhongguo shaonian gongchandang (the European Branch of the Chinese Communist Youth Party), they argue that the founders clearly intended it as a corps, referring to it as a *tuan* in their correspondence. Also, the ECYC never applied for membership to the CCP but to its youth branch. Zhou Enlai officially reported to Shi Cuntong, who headed the CCP Socialist Youth Branch. The group pledged in their regulations to abide by the regulations of the CCP youth branch.[57]

Wu Shiqi disagrees with this interpretation and argues that "except for the differences in ages, in the overall leadership of the struggle, and in the political sophistication of the members, there was absolutely no difference [from a party]."[58] Wu marshals several excerpts from various ECYC memoirs to show that originally the members were participating in a party, but on Chen Duxiu's orders they had to change the name of their group because he did not want two Chinese Communist parties.[59] Wu Shiqi's arguments are persuasive. Western sources on the Communist International also mention the total lack of differentiation between the policies of the Comintern and the Communist Youth International.[60]

However, if the ECYC was a de facto party, the formation of the ECCP in the winter of 1922 indicates that the ECYC was not perceived of as a party and that formally there was a delineation. This was made explicit in letters, articles, and reports. In the official ECCO newspaper, *Shaonian*, an article entitled "Our Organizational Tasks" (1922) expressly claimed that the ECYC was a training ground for the tasks of political coordination with the Communist Party, creating mass organizations, and gaining insight through education. The ECCP was a more comprehensive organization.[61] Reviewing the documentary evidence of the time, *A Historical Narrative of the ECCO* also agrees with this point of view.[62]

56. Liu Ye, Zhu Yuhe, and Zhao Yuanbi, "Lü Ou Zhongguo dangtuan de jianli jingguo," 79.
57. Ibid., 79–80.
58. Wu Shiqi, "Dui youguan lü Ou jiandang jige wenti de tantao," 8.
59. Ibid., 8–9.
60. Witold S. Sworakowski, ed., *World Communism: A Handbook, 1918–1965* (Stanford: Hoover Institution Press, 1973), 92–94.
61. "Women de zhiwu" [Our organizational tasks], *Shaonian* 3 (1922): 2.
62. Wang Yongxiang, Kong Fanfeng, and Liu Pinqing, *Zhongguo gongchandang lü Ou zhibu shihua*, appendix 2.

Thus, in the official sense the ECYC was a "training ground" for the ECCP, and in fact, many members of the ECCP had to be "reintroduced" into the CCP. However, the political tasks converged to a great degree, and thus, the activities largely overlapped. Perhaps Fu Zhong captures the essence of the ECYC organization best when he says, "the ECYC was called a 'youth corps,' . . . in reality the group shouldered very important responsibilities, participating in serious struggles, performing quite a bit of work."[63]

ECCO FORMATION AND ACTIVITIES

The ECYC was formed at the end of June 1922, in a three-day meeting in the Bois de Boulogne. As mentioned above, the major organizational effort must be credited to Zhao Shiyan. Zhao Shiyan wrote to Chen Gongpei about the problems of organizing the ECYC. The biggest impediment was the proposal by Li Weihan and several members of the Society for the World of Work-Study that the society members be allowed to enter en masse into the ECYC. Zhao believed that people should join on an individual basis and that size was not as important as the quality of the organization. He won on this issue but it caused delay. Zhao asked Chen's opinion on a number of organizational questions, particularly what the ECYC's relationship with the CCP would be. The other very interesting request was for Chen to personally write the Chen brothers (Chen Yannian and Chen Qiaonian), who were leaning away from their Anarchist beliefs. Zhao Shiyan himself had no relations with them and hoped Chen Gongpei would check the situation out for him.[64] Later, Zhao lived in the same building as the Chens and was ultimately successful in recruiting them.[65]

Eighteen people attended the first ECYC meeting (June 1922): Zhao Shiyan, Zhou Enlai, Wang Ruofei, Chen Yannian, Chen Qiaonian, Li Weihan, Liu Bojian, She Liya, Yuan Qingyun, Fu Zhong, Wang Linghan, Li Weinong, Xiao Pusheng, Xiao Zizhang, Wang Zekai, Zheng Chaolin, Yin Kuan, and Ren Zhuoxuan.[66] They decided on the name the Chinese Communist Youth Party. The other important decision was to publish a bimonthly newspaper entitled Shaonian. Zhao Shiyan was elected general secretary, Zhou Enlai be-

---

63. Fu Zhong, "Fu Zhong tan lü Fa qingong jianxue he shehuizhuyi qingniantuan lü Ou zongzhibu," in Yida qianhou, 2:563.
64. Zhao Shiyan letter to Chen Gongpei, 26 April 1922, in FuFa, 2:835–37.
65. When Chen Qiaonian was executed in 1928, one year after the deaths of Zhao Shiyan and his brother, Chen Yannian, he yelled out Zhao Shiyan's name as he was killed.
66. Fu Zhong, "Fu Zhong tan lü Fa qingong jianxue he shehuizhuyi qingniantuan lü Ou zongzhibu," 561.

came the propaganda officer, and Li Weihan was in charge of the organization section. The major tasks were recruiting Chinese students and labor in Europe and studying Marxism. Li Weihan left in October 1922 to deliver correspondence to the CCP Central Committee back in China.

Zhao received a letter from Chen Duxiu in November 1922 advising him to start sending groups of Chinese Communists to the Soviet Union to study. In addition Zhao was criticized for concentrating too much on Chinese labor in Europe, when he should be paying more attention to the homeland situation. Chen Duxiu also advised against a newspaper because a Party newspaper and Comintern publications were already in circulation.[67]

Zhao began arrangements for the "Russian pipeline" of Chinese youth and called a meeting for 17–20 February 1923. This meeting was held in a police hall and arranged by Yuan Qingyun as a gathering of Chinese students, the only proviso being that the singing of the "International" was forbidden. Zhao Shiyan chaired the meeting, but because he was leaving for the Soviet Union in March, he did not run for office. This second meeting of the ECYC was attended by forty-two members out of seventy-two (French branch: fifty-eight; German branch: eight; Belgian branch: six).[68] After the meeting Zhou Enlai wrote a detailed report about the proceedings and the rules and regulations. Thus we know that although they pledged absolute loyalty and obedience to the CCP, the ECYC chose to continue with *Shaonian* and chose its own name, retaining the word "Communist" instead of accepting Chen Duxiu's proposed "Socialist," although it replaced "party" with "corps."[69]

The ECYC ratified an organizational structure, and new officers were elected. The Executive Committee was composed of Ren Zhuoxuan, Zhou Enlai, Yin Kuan, Wang Zekai, and Xiao Pusheng (alternates: Liu Bojian, Wang Linghan, and Yuan Zizhen). Zhou Enlai was elected general secretary, Yin Kuan was in charge of the Communist Study Society, Wang Zekai served as head of the Student Movement Committee, Xiao Pusheng chaired

67. Zheng Chaolin, "Zheng Chaolin tan Zhao Shiyan he lü Ou zhibu," 535.

68. Ibid., 535–36.

69. Zhou Enlai, "Lü Ou Zhongguo gongchanzhuyi qingniantuan (Zhongguo shehuizhuyi qingniantuan lü Ou zhibu) baogao di yici" [The first report of the ECYC (Chinese Socialist Youth Corps—European Branch)], in *FuFa*, 2:843–48. This disobedience of CCP Central Committee commands might contain elements of a feeling of greater expertise in revolutionary propaganda-agitation technique, and it may also be evidence of a lingering generational rift. Ironically, Zhou's official report and several Party documents used "Socialist" in the organization's name; but especially after 1923, most articles, handbills, and documents used "Communist" in the name.

the Chinese Labor Movement Committee, and Ren Zhuoxuan took responsibility for the Publications Committee.[70]

Twelve members were picked to attend the Toilers of the East University in the Soviet Union: Zhao Shiyan, Wang Ruofei, Chen Yannian, Chen Qiaonian, She Liya, Gao Feng, Chen Jiuding, Wang Linghan, Zheng Chaolin, Yuan Qingyun, Wang Gui, and Xiong Xiong.[71] This group of Chinese Communists left the next month, passing through Germany. In all, about forty members were to go home by way of the Soviet Union for more political training. One of the travelers to the Soviet Union, Yin Kuan, wrote to the ECCO in 1924 of his impressions of Germany and the Soviet Union. He was impressed by the reality of the revolution and the hoopla of the sixth anniversary celebration, and he ended with a story of a little Russian girl asking him to dance.[72]

Among the highlights of the second meeting was a successful proposal to expel Zhang Shenfu. The report cites Zhang's frequent remarks about quitting the ECYC, but Zheng Chaolin claims that Zhang's expulsion was because he acted very arrogantly and was always giving advice. If no one listened to his advice, he would be "mad as fire." According to Liu Guisheng, who has extensively interviewed Zhang Shenfu, this was indeed a problem. Zhang tended to want to involve himself in the minute details of every activity.[73]

During the debate for expulsion, Zhang's most vehement critics were Chen Yannian and Yin Kuan. Zhou Enlai defended Zhang (who had introduced him and Zhao Shiyan to the Party), and in support of Zhang, Zhao Shiyan stepped down from the chair during the vote. However, in the end, Zhang was officially expelled. As it turned out, both the CCP and the German Branch later repudiated the expulsion, and while in Moscow, Chen Yannian was made to confess the mistake of the expulsion. According to Zheng, the relationship between Zhang Shenfu and Zhao Shiyan deteriorated, even though Zhao had taken Zhang's part, but was mended later in the year in Moscow.[74]

This dispute shows us that the ECCO was no panacea in itself for the generational crisis. In this case Chen Duxiu supported Zhang Shenfu against his son Chen Yannian. Perhaps Chen Yannian's attack in the first place had

---

70. Ibid., 2:846–47.

71. Ibid., 2:847.

72. Shiren [Yin Kuan], "Mosike tongxin" [Moscow correspondence], Chiguang 7 (1 February 1924): 2.

73. Personal communication with Liu Guisheng, 25 October 1985; Zhang Shenfu interview, 25 October 1985 (Beijing).

74. Zheng Chaolin, "Zheng Chaolin tan Zhao Shiyan he lü Ou zhibu," 535–37.

something to do with Zhang's closeness with his father, a mixture of jealousy and rebellion.

The ECCP was formed in secrecy at the end of 1922. Zhang Shenfu was the first ECCP secretary and Zhao Shiyan was the French Branch secretary. Members were recruited from the ECYC and from new CCP members. One CCP member who joined the ECCP was Liao Huanxing, who came to Germany in 1922 and bore letters of introduction to Zhao Shiyan and Zhang Shenfu. Some of the ECCP members joined the European Communist parties, but these parties had little impact. Although the ECYC basically developed and had most of its members in France, Chen Duxiu reported to the Comintern in 1922 that most of the ten "Party members" were in Germany (France: two members; Germany: eight members).[75] Thus by the end of 1922 the ECCO was formed: the ECYC with some public notice and the ECCP in secrecy.

Recruitment and Propaganda-Agitation

The activities of the ECCO were centered on the tasks of propaganda-agitation and recruitment. General propaganda work was accomplished with the publication of Shaonian, which began on 1 August 1922. (Its name was changed to Chiguang [Red Light] in the beginning of 1924.) The newspaper contained articles on relevant news from China and the international scene, translations and interpretations of Communist theory and practice, doctrinal debates with political competitors, organizational news, and correspondence.

The other major task was recruitment among Chinese workers and students in Europe. According to Barman and Dulioust, "[T]he greatest successes of the young communists were actually gained in the field of factory work."[76] Night schools were set up for the workers, and labor-oriented publications were produced.[77] In 1923 Yuan Zizhen, a laborer and an alternate member of the ECYC Central Committee, headed the Huagong zonghui (Chinese Trade Union) under the aegis of the ECCO.[78] Writing in 1923 Yuan Zizhen traced the history of Chinese labor organization in France,

75. Liu Ye, Zhu Yuhe, and Zhao Yuanbi, "Lü Ou Zhongguo dangtuan de jianli jingguo," 80.

76. Geneviève Barman and Nicole Dulioust, "The Communists in the Work and Study Movement in France," Republican China 13 (April 1988): 30.

77. Shi Yisheng, "Huiyi zhonggong lü Ou zhibu de guanghui yeji" [Remembering the glorious achievements of the ECCO in Europe], Tianjin wenshi ziliao xuanji 15 (May 1981): 117–18.

78. Wang Peilian and Zhou Xingwang, "Zhonggong lü Ou zhibu yu Huagong" [The ECCO and Chinese labor], Zhongguo xiandaishi fuyin baokan ziliao 19 (1982): 19.

claiming that the current Chinese Trade Union had learned from past mistakes the need for unity and to prioritize political education over other goals.[79] Wider use of the Chinese workers in France for political purposes was a specifically enunciated goal of the Chinese Trade Union. Zhao Shiyan and Wang Ruofei had prevailed at the founding meeting over the noted Anarchist Li Zhuo, who had argued for keeping the Chinese Trade Union focused solely on labor issues.[80]

ECCO recruitment was quite successful. In 1922 thirty people were members, in 1923 there were seventy-two members, and by 1925 there were between five and six hundred members.[81] Considering that the formal organization of the ECCO occurred one year after that of the CCP and that its pool of potential members was much more limited, the recruitment statistics are impressive. In 1923 total CCP membership was 342; by the time of the May Thirtieth Incident in 1925 the membership was almost a thousand.[82]

In addition to recruitment among Chinese laborers, the ECCO sought to align itself in propaganda-agitation with European Communist parties. As we will see in the following chapter, they were quite successful in gaining support from the French radical community during the anti-imperialist struggles of 1926. The ECCP members in Germany, in general, had closer relations with local Communist parties, with liaison work under way as early as 1922.[83] Xiao Zizhang, whose French was more advanced than that of the others, was assigned the task of establishing contacts with the PCF. Xiao felt very unhappy when they assigned him to the "colonial" section.[84] Several Chinese attended some PCF and youth corps meetings and also participated in some demonstrations. However, it was through Ho Chi Minh (then called Nguyen Ai Quoc) that Xiao, Zhao Shiyan, Wang Ruofei, Chen Yannian, and Chen Qiaonian were formally introduced into the PCF:

> Ho Chi Minh at that time [1922] was an important member of the PCF, and when the PCF was established he made some important contri-

79. Yuan Zizhen, "Lü Fa Huaren gonghui de jingguo" [The experiences of the Chinese Labor Union in France], Gongren xunbao 20/21 (April 1923): 13–18. Yuan asserted that political education was the new phase, which would succeed, whereas the old phase, which had freedom as its goal, was unsuccessful.

80. Wang Yongxiang, Kong Fanfeng, and Liu Pinqing, Zhongguo gongchandang lü Ou zhibu shihua, 184–85.

81. Fu Zhong, "Fu Zhong tan lü Fa qingong jianxue he shehuizhuyi qingniantuan lü Ou zongzhibu," 562. Fu Zhong was the fifth secretary of the ECYC and was in France until the midtwenties, so his estimate should be acceptable.

82. Jacques Guillermaz, A History of the Chinese Communist Party, 1921–1949, trans. Anne Destenay (London: Methuen, 1972), 83.

83. Zhao Shiyan letter to Li Lisan, 25 April 1922, in FuFa, 2:834.

84. Xiao San [Zizhang], "Huiyi fu Fa qingong jianxue he lü Ou zhibu," 2:515.

butions. How did we meet him? . . . in a demonstration, we ran into this Vietnamese, he looked like a Cantonese, so we called out to each other. At that time his spoken Chinese was Cantonese; we did not understand it. But his written characters were pretty good, so we used writing, Cantonese, and French in a mixture to communicate. . . . we became fairly close and he introduced the five of us into the PCF.[85]

In 1925, in support of the May Thirtieth Incident in China, members of the ECYC organized demonstrations throughout Europe. One of their actions was to occupy the legation, again coercing the hapless Chen Lu into signing a telegram supporting their cause. Many of the first leaders had left by this time, but the persecution that took place after this incident involved hundreds of Chinese, and dozens of Chinese were deported. After the arrests and hasty deportations due to the occupation of the legation, the ECYC leadership fell to Deng Xiaoping, then called Deng Xixian.[86] According to the evidence found in the French archives, it would appear that the April Twelfth Coup in 1927 led to several reorganization attempts. By 1928 the ECCO in large part went underground, and the Chinese Communists in France became subsumed under a Chinese-language section of the PCF.[87] The ECCO newspaper Chiguang continued to be published into the thirties. The headquarters of the ECCO seems to have shifted to Germany; the later issues of Chiguang list Berlin as the place of publication. Based on confiscated correspondence and surveillance, the French Sûreté asserted in 1931 that the "Central Committee of the Chinese Communist Party in Europe has its headquarters in Hamburg."[88]

85. Xiao San, "Dui Zhao Shiyan shishu de huiyi" [A few stories in remembrance of Zhao Shiyan], in Yida qianhou, 2:521.
86. Shi Yisheng, "Huiyi zhonggong lü Ou zhibu de guanghui yeji," 123–28. For an in-depth look at the occupation of the Chinese Paris legation see Nora Wang, "Da Chen Lu! Le Mouvement du 30 mai 1925 à Paris," Approches-Asie 7 (1983): 1–33.
87. One leaflet, "Yonghuo Zhongguo linshi suweiai zhongyang zhengfu" (n.d., 1930 or 1931?), is signed by the "Ouzhou gongchandang Zhongguo yuyanbu" (The European Chinese Communist Party, Chinese Language Section). Another ECCO publication, Gongren (The Worker), dated 1932, contained an article whose title included the name "Faguo gongchandang Zhongguo yuyanzu" (The French Communist Party, Chinese Language Organization) (AOM, SLOTFOM V, 48). As Chen Jingtang also points out, according to Liao Huanxing, the ECCO headquarters closed down in 1927 and Chinese-language sections in the various French Communist branches were opened (Chen Jingtang [Chan Kingtong], "Review of Reference Materials on the History of the European Branches of the Chinese Communist Organizations," trans. William L. MacDonald, Republican China 13 [April 1988]: 69–70).
88. Report "A.S. Parti Communiste chinois en Europe," G. Budin, Le Ministre de la Guerre, à M. le Président du Conseil, Ministre de l'Intérieur, 4 December 1931, AOM, SLOTFOM III, 3. This series of reports also includes handwritten reports on various

The post-1927 ECCO publications were not as theoretically advanced as the early writings, but they included in-depth analyses of Communist revolutionary strategy. The perspectives sometimes had an ECCO bias, as evidenced by an article on the Communist bases in 1930 entitled "News of the Zhu-Mao Red Army and the Significance of the Struggle." Zhu De, recruited in Germany, was far more prominent in ECCO eyes than Mao Zedong.

One ECCO member, Xie Weijin (1904–78), who stayed in Europe for almost two decades and was captured fighting for the Communists during the Spanish Civil War, also confirms that ECCO propaganda was linked with that of the European Communist parties and existed into the 1930s. For example, between 1929 and 1933 Xie headed the Chinese Workers-Peasants News Agency (Zhongguo gongnong tongxin).[89] Thus, it would appear that a transfigured ECCO existed after the departure of its most prominent members.

Ideological Training

After the ECYC had formally submitted to the rule of the youth corps back in China, an interesting exchange of advice was published in The Vanguard during the summer of 1923. In an announcement on the ECYC, three objectives were outlined: to coordinate activities with the European Communists and learn their methods, to recruit and support the Chinese workers in Europe, and to support an antireligion campaign.[90] The advice of the ECYC to the Chinese Socialist Youth Corps was quite different in character: to distinguish more clearly the Socialist Youth from the Party and their activities, to pattern their Central Committee representation on the French example, and to strengthen their internal educational work, training, discipline, and service.[91] One might have expected that the home organization would have

---

Chinese Communist radical activities. Interestingly, a report on a German informer, Emil Kroll, written in 1925 also cites the linkage between Hamburg and the CCP (PRO, FO 371/10944).

89. Xie Weijin, "Xie Weijin zizhuan" [The autobiography of Xie Weijin], Dangshi yanjiu ziliao (Sichuan) 4 (October 1983): 58–67 (written in 1953). A 1929 issue of Chiguang, no. 45, lists Y. S. Hsieh, Langenbeckstr. 10, Berlin N.O. 18, on the front cover. Perhaps this is the same Mr. Xie?

90. "Guanyu lü Ou Zhongguo gongchanzhuyi qingniantuan texu zhiwu yian" [A proposal of special tasks for the ECYC], Xianfeng 24 (1 August 1923), in FuFa, 2:854–55. The article cites Father Lebbe, by name, who, as noted above, took steps to combat the Communist trend he perceived among the Chinese youth in Paris.

91. "Lü Ou Zhongguo gongchanzhuyi qingniantuan tixiang guonei dahui de sange jianyian" [Three proposals for the internal assembly by the ECYC], Xianfeng 24 (1 August 1923), in FuFa, 2:856.

enjoined the branch to pay greater attention to theoretical education and Party discipline, rather than the other way around. However, there were several important differences in the situations of the two groups. The ECCO had greater access to a wider range of theoretical works and could directly observe European radical politics in action, which they obviously recommended to the Chinese Socialist Youth Corps for emulation. Moreover, they had greater freedom to meet and discuss as well as to act. Theoretical debates could stretch beyond cities and across countries, through direct discussions and extensive correspondence. The ECCO established a network of study groups all over France, Germany, and Belgium. For example, an article by "Xiong," published in the Collected Correspondence of the Communist Study Society, prefaced an intricate discussion of historical materialism (based on German-language sources) with a reference to a Paris meeting and asked the readers to write responses to the discussion so that the theoretical training could be enhanced.[92]

Meetings often stressed theoretical study, as Wu Qi vividly recalls:

> The Paris Branch would hold a meeting every Sunday morning, . . . the major thing was to study Marxist works, "The Communist Manifesto," etc., discuss the international situation and internal affairs of our country; there were also times when we would hold criticism and self-criticism sessions. These would proceed in this fashion: first one would criticize himself, and then be criticized by his comrades; afterward, one could express various opinions, adding any explanations. In the beginning [this technique] was unfamiliar, but after a time it just became natural.[93]

In comparison, theoretical study in China was often difficult to pursue because of the limited availability of sources. According to Wang Fanxi in his memoir Chinese Revolutionary, during the midtwenties:

> In Peking, or at least in the branches under the district committee for eastern Peking, there were only two books of a theoretical character in circulation at that time. One was the first part of Bukharin's ABC of Communism, and the other was Burkhardt's The Student's "Capi-

---

92. Xiong, "Makesizhuyi de jige zhongyao dian" [Several important points about Marxism], Gongchan zhuyi yanjiuhui tongxin ji 7 (1923), in FuFa, 3:157–68. I think "Xiong" is Xiong Xiong, who was in Germany. It may also be Xiong Rui, but other articles are signed "Rui," so perhaps that is how they distinguished their articles.

93. Wu Qi, "Zhou Enlai tongzhi qingnian shidai zai Fa De liangguo de geming shenghuo," 137.

tal." . . . We were fighting for Communism, but none of us really understood what Communism was.[94]

The theoretical debates within the ECCO were often thoughtful and usually attempted to educate the members in basic Marxist theory. In a public exchange of correspondence, there was a heated response to Zhang Shenfu's assertion that Lenin had departed from Marx in his political and economic administration in the Soviet Union. Fu Zhong claimed in his rejoinder that Marx had never espoused his philosophy as a rigid pattern, but as a living one, to be practically applied, so that the proletariat could establish their control. The "*nouvelle politique économique*" advocated by Lenin was necessitated by the practical circumstances. Quoting Lenin, Fu again used French to clarify: "*Ce n'est pas une évolution, c'est une tactique.*"[95]

Ren Zhuoxuan, one of the leading theoreticians of the ECCO, also responded to this published debate and quoted several authorities on Marxist theory, such as Adoratski, *La dialectique Marxiste dans l'oeuvre de Lénine*, and Dunois, *Karl Marx—farsdativa du Communisme*. Ren also concluded that Zhang Shenfu was mistaken in his views on the difference between Marx and Lenin: "Marx was a person who took Communism from its Utopian aspects and transformed it into its scientific aspects. Lenin is a person who brought Communism [to society] and from its scientific aspects transformed it into its active [*xingdong*] aspect. Naturally, this is incongruent with Comrade Shenfu's view of Leninism as something different from Marxism."[96] This idea of Lenin as revolutionary practitioner was shared by new converts to Communism from other nonindustrialized countries. Georg Lukács, a Hungarian revolutionary, also stressed that "the actuality of the revolution" was the "core of Lenin's thought." Lukács claimed, "For Marx the concrete analysis of the concrete situation is not the opposite of 'pure' theory; on the contrary, it is the culmination of all genuine theory, its consummation, the point where it therefore breaks into practice."[97]

In his numerous articles, Ren Zhuoxuan attempted to identify Party enemies and clarify Marxist-Leninist theories such as class struggle and current ECCO policies such as the United Front with the EGMD. When attacking Party enemies, Ren relied more on invective than argument, but he also

94. Wang Fan-hsi, *Chinese Revolutionary: Memoirs, 1919–1949*, trans. Gregor Benton (Oxford: Oxford University Press, 1980), 30–31.

95. Fu Zhong letter to Shi Fu [Yin Kuan], in *Gongchanzhuyi yanjiuhui tongxinji* [Collected correspondence of the Communist Study Society] 7 (1923), in *FuFa*, 3:188–90.

96. Ren Zhuoxuan letter to Fu Zhong, in ibid., 191.

97. Georg Lukács, *Lenin: A Study on the Unity of Thought*, trans. Nicholas Jacobs (Germany: Jutherhand Verlag, 1967), 11, 43. This book was originally written soon after Lenin's death.

attempted to analyze Marxist theory in its application to the Chinese situation. In an article entitled "The National Revolution and the Class Struggle," Ren begins with a discussion of Marxist concepts such as economic determinism, the means of production, and the theory of surplus value. According to Ren, China had no middle class. There were only two classes: those with property (businessmen and their dependents, the intellectuals) and those without property (laborers and agricultural workers). Although the worldwide revolutionary tide since 1917 had put the proletariat in the ascendant, in colonial and semicolonial countries the natural class struggle was submerged in the struggle against imperialism and remnant feudalistic elements (see the figure). "Therefore," concluded Ren, "the class struggle has caused a complex situation to emerge nationally."[98]

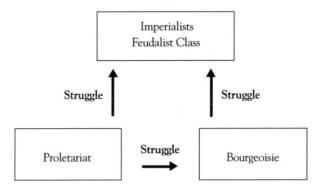

The Situation of the Chinese Class Struggle

The most vibrant political rhetoric often came from the pen of Yin Kuan, who headed the Communist Study Society. He wrote persuasive arguments that showed a knowledge of Marxist theory, but also expressed a sardonic wit that managed not to deteriorate into personal abuse.[99] In his article on the analysis of Marxist ethics, Yin Kuan makes three arguments. The first area of Marxist ethics involved the concept of historical materialism, that

98. Ren Zhuoxuan, "Guomin geming yu jieji douzheng" [The national revolution and the class struggle], *Chiguang* 9 (June 1924): 1–5. The points about the relationship between the weak bourgeoisie and the impact of imperialism had been noted by others in earlier publications; see, e.g., Y. K. [Yin Kuan], "Zai Zhongguo de gongchanzhuyi yundong" [The Communist movement in China], *Shaonian* 9 (May 1923), in *FuFa*, 3:353–56.

99. Yin Kuan was later expelled in the famous 1929 incident, along with Chen Duxiu. He had been involved in propaganda work and, after 1927, was instrumental in editing *Buweiersike*. He was imprisoned several times because he was a Trotskyite.

the superstructure was determined by who controlled the means of production. Yin asserted that the idea of superstructure-determined ethics was not only based on reality but more reliable than individual ethics: "[If] the social environment is reformed, then in an instant the customs, ethics, feelings, etc., will all be reformed."[100] The Marxists did not need to study philosophy, but economics. The second area of Marxist ethics concerned the issue of class struggle. Class struggle was the real force behind society, and so-called traditional ethical values such as freedom and equality were really mobilized for the exploitation of those who labored with their hands for the benefit of the Capitalist exploiters. In scornful and passionate prose Yin contrasted the bourgeoisie and the proletariat: "The bourgeoisie class still has the right of free competition, free exploitation, . . . to freely make war with chemicals and airpower. And the proletariat? Can they freely organize big corporations, open up big factories? *Non.* Do they have the freedom to starve to death? *Bien Sur (Dangran)!*" (French in the original).[101] Yin Kuan's third point was more subtle: when the revolution was successful, if one believed in the ethics of historical materialism and class struggle, there would be no need for the formal ethics of equality or freedom. After the revolution, the abolition of the class system would lead to a situation without oppression, and there would thus be no need for consciousness of freedom or equality, because these concepts would be intrinsic to society: "If there is no demand for equality, then there will be no conceptual ethics of equality."[102]

The polemics on the difference between theory and practice, class struggle and Marxist ethics, all reflect the current Marxist literature in Europe at this time. In July 1920, Lenin published his "Theses on National and Colonial Questions Adopted by the Second Communist International Congress." In this important pamphlet, Lenin wrote that the West had used the idea of equality for exploitation, whereas the Soviet Union wanted to unify the workers of the world. The Soviet Union wished for international resistance to international imperialism and the establishment of truly independent nations. Lenin urged the formation of Communist parties that would take advantage of collaborative efforts. He felt that "only the Soviet system is able to ensure real equality for the nations." Only through a world federation of proletariats could they overcome imperialists.[103]

100. Shi Fu [Yin Kuan], "Makesizhuyi de daodeguan" [The ethical perspectives of Marxism], *Shaonian* 8 (1 April 1923), in *FuFa*, 1:205.
    101. Ibid., 205–6.
    102. Ibid., 207.
    103. Lenin, "Theses on National and Colonial Questions Adopted by the Second Communist International Congress" (28 July 1920), in Jane Degras, ed. and trans., *The Com-*

This pamphlet was quite appealing to colonial and semicolonial peoples and had great success. Ho Chi Minh attributes his conversion to Marxism to reading these "Theses on National and Colonial Questions."[104] Ruth Fischer, who met Ho Chi Minh in the mid-1920s, recalled that "he was temperamentally far more inclined strongly toward action than toward doctrinal debates. He was always an empiricist within the movement."[105] It is not unreasonable to speculate that if Ho Chi Minh was the liaison with the ECCO and the PCF, then he may have influenced several Chinese leaders in this view of the primacy of strategy and praxis. It is notable that after 1925 Ho Chi Minh was to serve as an important aide to Borodin in Canton.

Since translations of articles from *L'humanité*, other European Communist materials, and Russian tracts were commonplace in *Shaonian* and *Chiguang*, perhaps it is not surprising that Trotsky also was translated at some length in the ECCO journals and that several of the most prominent Chinese Trotskyites emerged from the ECCO, such as Yin Kuan, Zheng Chaolin, Wang Zekai, Li Ji, Wu Qi, and Shi Yisheng.[106] As late as the spring of 1929, articles analyzing the Chinese Communist Revolution in Trotskyite terms were published in *Chiguang*.[107]

The numerous public debates and internal discussions among the ECCO cells were extremely important in the development of the leaders and theoreticians of the ECCO. For example, shortly after the formation of the ECCO, Zheng Chaolin recounted organizing a Communist cell with Li Weinong. Meetings were purposefully limited to a few people, and at one such meeting (attended by Li Weihan, Wang Zekai, Qin Shilun, Wang Ruofei, and Yin Kuan) the topic was raised of what attitude should be adopted toward political struggle. Zheng mentions that he argued that three attitudes existed toward the political struggle: standing behind the backward forces, standing for the progressive forces, or standing above the fray:

munist International, 1919–1943: Documents (London: Oxford University Press, 1956), 1:138–44.

104. Ho Chi Minh, "The Path which Led Me to Leninism," in *Selected Writings, 1920–1969* (Hanoi: Foreign Languages Publishing House, 1973), 250. This is, to my knowledge, the only piece of autobiography that Ho Chi Minh wrote.

105. Ruth Fischer, "Ho Chi Minh: Disciplined Communist," *Foreign Affairs* 33 (October 1954): 86–97.

106. E.g., excerpts from Trotsky's "Une école stratégie révolutionnaire" were translated in *Shaonian* 3 (1922): 10–20.

107. "Yifeng gongkai taolun Zhongguo geming wenti de xin" [An open letter to discuss the problems of the Chinese revolution], *Chiguang* 45 (March 1929): 10–15. A response also followed this long letter. By March 1930 the Trotskyites were criticized officially in *Chiguang*.

However, I had not finished speaking when Wang Ruofei interrupted me saying that there only existed two attitudes—there was no third way. I said that a third attitude did exist, for example, [the thought of] Romain Rolland. Thereupon, everyone . . . supported Wang Ruofei and attacked my view. . . . After the meeting dispersed outside it was pouring rain, they wanted to return to the city, I escorted them a bit of the way, but they did not want my escort. . . . [They wanted to discuss his mistake in private.] At the next small organizational meeting they sternly criticized me, remarking that even the masses knew that there was no neutral attitude [toward struggle]. . . . I had previously read Romain Rolland, especially his work opposing the eruption of the First World War, Au-dessus de mêlée, . . . I had adopted this neutral attitude during the factional struggles of 1921 in the Work-Study Movement. . . . [However,] after I entered the factory, my thoughts progressed; I had really wanted to take that opportunity [the meeting] to criticize my own previous thoughts.[108]

In terms of ideological development this inside glimpse reflects several dimensions of ECCO radical activity in Europe: theoretical and policy discussions were easily organized in the relative freedom of the West, the greater access to Western thinkers increased their influence on ECCO members, the reverberations of the three struggles of 1921 were still prevalent in the minds of the Chinese radicals in France, and organizational identification increased after the commitment to Communism had been made.

The organizational meetings to discuss tactics and theory stressed the importance of organizational conformity, in itself a goal. The linkage between ideology and praxis was also a pivotal point of historical progression for both the ECCO and the CCP. Arif Dirlik succinctly summarizes this process:

What made for Marxist identity was not agreement on policy or shared understanding of a theory, but an ideology of action, which rested in the Party's political program. The question of a shared ideology of action was urgent, and this question, rather than the education of members in Marxist theory, in late 1920 occupied the attention of the party leadership. After its initial organizational phase, the party center in Shanghai launched an ideological campaign to ensure that only committed Communists would stay on. While this campaign was mainly directed at socialist competitors, its most important goal was

108. Zheng Chaolin, Ji Yin Kuan, 55–56. Yin Kuan joined the rest in criticizing Zheng during the second meeting, and Zheng intimates that Yin should have recognized the basis of Zheng's discussion of the third attitude, but Yin did not realize the change that factory work had produced.

the streamlining of internal party ideology. With this campaign, the Party would establish ideological criteria for distinguishing proper Communist belief from analogous socialist ideas. The ultimate criterion was "belief in Communism," which meant, in effect, commitment to an organizationally defined interpretation of Marxism. As ambiguities were clarified, Communists were to part ways with other socialists with whom they had continued to cooperate even in the founding of the nuclei. In fall 1920, anarchists left the Party. Over the following year even some of the Marxists in the party would leave, unable to confine their Marxism within the interpretive boundaries imposed by the organizational imperatives of the party they had helped create.[109]

For the ECCO members there was also an increasingly rigid theoretical discipline, an attempt not just to learn about Marxism but to activate organizational discipline as a revolutionary tactic. Internal debate, discipline, purges, polemics with Socialist and other radical competitors, and careful recruitment practices were as important for the ECCO as they were for the CCP in ensuring loyalty.

This pattern of organizational discipline in Communist development, especially after the formation of the Communist International, was operative for Western Communists and Asian Communists. Of the importance of organizational discipline, Karl Radek, an important member of the Communist International who was later purged himself, wrote, "The clarity of thought with which the members of the party understand Communist theory, . . . was quite unimportant when compared to their willingness to reject this or that group of leaders." On this comment, Robert Wohl, who wrote about the founding of the PCF, remarked, "Radek did not go on to explore the implications of his statement further; he did not have to. What he meant was clear enough; discipline and loyalty to the International meant more than any understanding and doctrine."[110]

Similar to other Communist parties, the ECCO later followed the more rigid formulae of propaganda. However, in the beginning stages, the debates on theory were rich in both pedagogical and rhetorical value. Ideological training within the ECCO was a serious undertaking not only for increasing the intellectual sophistication of the Party members but also as a process of reaffirming Marxist beliefs and reinforcing the organizational tactic of discipline and unity.

109. Dirlik, The Origins of Chinese Communism, 216.
110. Wohl, French Communism in the Making, 1914–24, 314.

The Role of the Communist International

One of the major distinctions between the activities of the ECCO and the CCP was the difference in their relationship to the Communist International. The Communist International helped to organize the CCP and had strong representatives such as Voitinsky and Borodin to oversee the development of the Chinese revolutionary scene. In the case of the ECCO, there is no historical evidence that shows the hand of the Communist International in either the formation or the activities of the ECCO.

For many years historians have relied on the memoirs of Li Huang, which make a weak circumstantial case that the Comintern engineered the formation of the ECCO.[111] Due to the paucity of other memoirs and original documents, Li Huang's account of Marxist developments has often been uncritically accepted. Unfortunately, Li's memoir contains numerous errors in both historical fact and interpretation.[112] It is unlikely that contacts with the Comintern and the ECCO were close before 1923. This conclusion is based on the fact that there was no reason for ECCO members not to remark on Comintern connections. In fact, they have dis-

111. Li Huang, "Xuedunshi huiyilu," *Zhuanji wenxue* 16 (June 1970): 4–10, 21. Li Huang's case for Comintern support of the ECCO (as early as 1920) rests on several points. (1) Li argued that the poor and dissatisfied students were easily beguiled into the plots of the Soviet Union because they were angry at the miserable life they had to lead in Paris and because the Comintern gave them money. (2) There were signs of monetary disbursement, such as the lavish apartment of Zhou Enlai, who did not work in a factory, and the fact that in the summer of 1920, ten people who had been living in tents one day suddenly moved to apartments (Li noticed because he had been tutoring students in the tents). Li estimated that the lifestyle would require about 300 francs a month. He also asserted that train money for the Lyons Incident was provided by the Comintern. (3) French Communist workers, teachers, and writers influenced the Chinese youth. Li Huang attended a meeting of Clarté, a group founded by Henri Barbusse, where, according to Li, Communism was clearly propagated. As a tutor, his students were constantly presenting him with Marxist materials in the hopes that Li would translate for them. (4) Last, how could one explain the rapid rise of Zhou Enlai? According to Li, he became so powerful because his English was so good that he became the liaison for the Comintern representative. One's first inclination is to discount many of Li Huang's assertions, such as that concerning the train money (which was more likely given by Chen Lu) and the change in ten students' lifestyle (who could have received funds from home or found jobs). The only real strength of Li Huang's case for direct Comintern involvement is the case of Zhou Enlai, whose English was better than his French. The fact was that Zhou Enlai did indeed shuttle back and forth between Berlin and Paris during his sojourn in Europe, and the Western European Secretariat (an apparatus of the Comintern) functioned in Berlin during this period. Moreover, Zhou did write a series of articles on a coal strike in England during the period when Borodin was imprisoned in Glasgow. Perhaps future research will uncover a Comintern connection with Zhou Enlai.

112. At least two theses reject Li Huang's interpretation. See T'an Hiue-mei, "Le Mouvement étudiant travailleur en France vu Par He Changgong" (Université Paris dissertation, 1979), and Leung, "The Chinese Work-Study Movement."

claimed such connections. The head of the ECCO, Zhang Shenfu, asserted an absence of Comintern contacts.[113] In an interview, Zheng
Chaolin mentioned that the German Branch member, Zhang Bojian,
had a Jewish Comintern connection, but the French Branch had no such
direct connection.[114]

Consideration of documents *from the time* also reinforces the view of minimal Comintern contacts. For example, Zhao Shiyan's letter to Luo Jue
(Luo Yinong) and Peng Shuzhi written a few weeks before he was to leave
for Moscow in 1923 asks them to mediate with the Toilers of the East University and to get in touch with the Soviet representative in Berlin in order
to issue the necessary visas for the students traveling to Russia.[115] This indicates that there may have been some contact, but it was not so productive
or close as Zhao Shiyan would have liked, or else he would have obtained
the visas directly.

Thus, the study period in Russia seems to be the only documentable area
of Comintern-ECCO contact at present. The Comintern funded the Chinese
who traveled to the Soviet Union. According to Liao Huanxing, who was
an important member of the German Branch of the ECCP, the Chinese received Comintern funds from Wilhelm Pieck, who was then a member of
the Prussian Diet. Pieck was one of the few people to survive the purges of
the Comintern, and he later became the president of the German Democratic Republic.[116]

Through the auspices of the Comintern, about forty ECCO members returned home via Moscow and underwent "political training" at Toilers of
the East University.[117] The training usually lasted several months to a year.
The emphasis was on political and social history. Ernestine Evans, a re-
porter for the *Christian Science Monitor,* visited this university in 1922 and
listed the courses: political economy, history of Communism, European
history, social history, biology, geography, history of the cooperative movement, colonial development, nationalism, and arithmetic. "I laughed at

---

113. Zhang Shenfu, "Zhang Shenfu tan lü Ou dangtuan zuzhi huodong qingkuang," 91.
114. Zheng Chaolin interview, 29 October 1985 (Shanghai).
115. Zhao Shiyan letter to Luo Jue [Luo Yinong] and Peng Shuzhi, 14 February 1923,
in *FuFa,* 2:841.
116. Liao Huanxing, "Zhongguo gongchandang lü Ou zongzhibu" [The ECCO], in *Yida
qianhou,* 2:506. Zheng Chaolin also confirmed the Pieck connection (interview, 29 October
1985).
117. For an account of the trip to the Soviet Union and the fate of the first twelve
Chinese to travel this route, see chaps. 3 and 4 of Zheng Chaolin, *Zheng Chaolin huiyilu,
1919–1931* [The memoirs of Zheng Chaolin] (Beijing: Xiandai shiliao biankanshe, 1986)
(originally written in 1945).

the arithmetic, trotting along like a coach dog behind such a magnificent curriculum."[118]

One can see that the Comintern was not a behind-the-scenes puppet master in daily supervision of the ECCO. The evidence is not substantial enough to justify the allegations that the Comintern helped form the ECCO. The only suggestive avenue seems to be some of the circumstances surrounding Zhou Enlai. There is no documentation that Comintern agents attended ECCO meetings, although this was a regular occurrence in China. Most of the evidence reveals that contacts were not close until the spring of 1923. At that point the most material connection was providing funds for study in the Soviet Union. But there are other manners of influence that should be considered. First, the Comintern direction of strategy for the CCP had a direct influence on the ECCO. As a branch of the CCP, the ECCO was obliged to conform to directives from the CCP Central Committee. An example of this was the ECCO-EGMD United Front, which, as we shall see, the ECCO members considered part of both national and international Communist strategy. Other areas of political coordination were the protests of the May Thirtieth Incident (1925) and the Northern Expedition (1926–27).

A second area of Comintern influence that had a vital impact on the ECCO members was their access to Communist propaganda and European Communist Party activities. These linkages with European communism reinforced the attraction of Marxism-Leninism and provided a solid revolutionary model. It is important to note that the propaganda of the Comintern was more broadly disseminated within the ECCO, and concepts such as Party discipline were perhaps more widely exercised in the ECCO, whose members did not quit the Party on the scale of the CCP. It is significant that the ECYC advice to the Chinese Socialist Youth Corps, mentioned above, emphasized the necessity for discipline, theory, and Westernized forms of organization. The broad international underpinning of ECCO theoretical training and the trips by ECCO members to the Soviet Union were important linkages to the Comintern. The ECCO members had seen Marxist-Leninist concepts put into practice by Westerners and non-Westerners. They had experienced the reality of Western imperialism in a manner that was not easily relatable to their comrades back in China. Their greater exposure to propaganda and their greater agitation experience broadened the context of Party organization. This perhaps helps account for the large difference in retention between the ECCO and the CCP, in a rather ironic way. The ECCO members were less likely to revolt against the discipline of Party

118. Ernestine Evans, "Looking East from Moscow," *Asia* 22 (December 1922): 972.

organization because of their fuller theoretical training and exposure, due in part to the efforts of the Comintern in Western Europe.

Third, related to the dimension of Party discipline was the issue of political loyalty to the Communist International.[119] Leaders such as Zhou Enlai, Zhao Shiyan, Wang Ruofei, Chen Yannian, Deng Xiaoping, Liu Bojian, Li Weihan, Li Fuchun, Nie Rongzhen, and Li Lisan were to make significant bows of obedience to Comintern direction throughout important phases of their revolutionary careers, with significant consequences for the Chinese revolution. It should also be noted that many of the most devoted and knowledgeable Trotskyites emerged from the ECCO cohort. During the early 1920s, the writings of Trotsky, who was the expert in French affairs, were often translated in *Chiguang*. Thus, in spite of the defeat of Trotsky by Stalin, it might be contended that loyalty to the Comintern also blossomed among the Trotskyites, who provided the Communist movement with some of its most brilliant theoreticians.

Differences between the CCP and the ECCO are reflected in the areas of propaganda-agitation, Party discipline, and loyalty to the Communist International. In an ironic twist of history, the CCP suffered more direct, often chafing supervision and experienced less internationally oriented theoretical training. In contrast to the ECCO, the CCP contact with the Communist International was indeed more directly concentrated and more extensive on the personal level. However, despite this level of contact, the CCP was not imbued with the sensibility toward concepts such as Party discipline that the ECCO evidently had absorbed through their European experiences.

THE ECCO MATRIX

The formation of the ECCO was stimulated by a unique matrix of events within the Chinese community in Europe. Stirred by the ethos of Chinese

---

119. Further research might be directed toward the interesting comparison of the returnees from Western Europe and those who only went to the Soviet Union. One could argue, with some justification, that those who were directly trained in the Soviet Union had the best understanding of Party discipline and the most loyalty to the Communist International. However, I would make two qualifications. First, the ECCO members had more exposure to theory than the CCP–Soviet Branch members. Conceivably it was not a coincidence that Liu Bojian went from Germany to head the Soviet Branch of the CCP. Second, it is well known that theoretical debate in the Soviet Union was not encouraged on a large scale, especially after the death of Lenin in 1924. Thus, the Soviet-inspired sense of Party discipline for the CCP members in the Soviet Union was more mechanical and more oppressively imposed, in contrast to the relatively freer environment of Western Europe. Perhaps there is a real correlation between the fact that the heyday of ECCO migration to the Soviet Union largely occurred *before* the Bolshevization of Western European Communist parties.

New Culture intellectual inquiry and activism and united by the three struggles of 1921, a section of the worker-students made a dual commitment to communism and revolution. They overcame differences of region and organizational affiliation. They overlooked previous animosities from the three struggles of 1921, in the higher hope of organizational unity and discipline. There were also commonalities: the New Culture legacy, the concern with national salvation and a tacit belief in the efficacy of Western solutions, the physical privations suffered in a foreign country, and the disillusionment with the Work-Study Movement.

The adherence to the Communist Party structure was an important point of stability and optimism. The internal voyage toward Marxism was helped by the egalitarian nature of the ideology. Moreover, after the establishment of the ECCO, ideological theory was scrupulously studied and discussed, along with the strategy of Communist revolution and the Chinese situation. Not only did the ECCO have greater freedom and access to theoretical training in Marxism-Leninism, but their range of political activities was not constrained beneath the shadow of warlord violence. It was in this context that the ECCO became the nucleus of radical politics within the Chinese community in France. Depending on the occasion, the ECCO served as both a target and a promoter of joint activities with other radical political groups such as the Chinese Youth Party, Anarchists, Social Democrats, and the EGMD.

Throughout the decade of the twenties the ECCO was involved in the rich panorama of political action in a foreign arena. This gave them scope and flexibility and forged a generation of sophisticated Chinese revolutionaries.

6
SHIFTING CURRENTS

"The Proletariat and the New Year—A Poem"
And so, Comrades!
Probably it will still take three times!
Perhaps it will take ten times!
But O Comrades, do not despair!
In this three hundred and sixty-five days
We will take this broken room,
And once again make for it a foundation.

. . . .

Comrades, revenge depends on your two hands.
—*Chiguang* (1930)

If we are to restore the people, we have to be determined in our intellectual revolution. If there is another Hongxian emperor [Yuan Shi-
kai], we will still do it that way, no matter how much the political and
social revolutions heat up, we will still do it that way. We will not
change in our resolution, we will not be resigned, we will not be si-
lenced, we will not rest. When we die there will be several tens,
hundreds, thousands, tens of thousands of good people to carry on the
struggle through this black period, and in the end, finally, our hopes
will be realized.
—Li Huang (1921)

In the course of its propaganda and recruitment activities, the ECCO had
both successes and failures. However, the ECCO displayed great flexibility
and was able to cooperate smoothly with initially antagonistic groups when
the situation called for unity. Such occasions included the foreign attempt
to consolidate the Chinese railways and the United Front strategy that the
CCP promulgated. There were other times when political differences could
not be submerged, as typified by the ECCO polemics with the Anarchists
and the CYP. The activist political milieu was one of concordance and
discordance.

This chapter will explore in detail ECCO political activity in France during the twenties. The Railroad Struggle, disputes with the Anarchists, and
ongoing conflicts with the anti-Communist CYP will be examined. Finally,
based on a wide range of archival material, the development of the ECCO-
EGMD United Front will be traced. This alliance both preceded and outlasted the CCP-GMD United Front and was controlled by ECCO and left-
faction EGMD elements.

Before examining ECCO activities in detail, it is important to note that the differences between the ECCO and the CCP in their respective relationships with the Communist International were not the only result of the ECCO's European setting. The openness of the European political climate decreased politically inspired violence, which the Communists in China had to face daily. In 1927, while the Communists in China were trying to evade frightful tortures and murder, the ECCO was sponsoring public forums against the terror in China. In Europe, impassioned debates rather than brute force characterized the disputes between the factions of the United Front. Also, purely European concerns entered into the polemics between competing political groups. In general, the outlook of the European Chinese political groupings was more cosmopolitan than that of their compatriots in China. A final difference was due to the limited pool of Chinese political actors in Europe, which smoothed the path to cooperation between opponents working for a mutual cause. For example, during the spring of 1923, while the ECCO was holding scathing debates with the Anarchists, key ECCO leaders contributed to the May First commemorative issue of *Gongren xunbao*.[1] The issue not only included articles by ECCO writers such as Ren Zhuoxuan and Yuan Zizhen but was edited by Li Shizeng's secretary, Xiao Zisheng, and had poetry by Ou Baisheng. This cooperation may have been a result of lingering personal relations between Xiao and Yuan. However, it also indicated the lack of militancy, which the greater dangers in China increasingly encouraged.

THE ANARCHISTS AND THE RAILROAD STRUGGLE

The activities of the ECCO during 1923 were very successful, whether in debating with rival groups or participating in more general community activities. Two examples of this success were a series of debates with the Anarchists and a movement to protest foreign consolidation of Chinese railways.

By 1923, most Chinese activists were disillusioned with the Anarchist alternative, both for practical reasons of organization and because the Lyons Incident had diminished the moral leadership that Wu Zhihui and Li Shizeng were able to wield. However, anarchism had served as an important ideology of radicalization, and as an ideological alternative it needed to be addressed. The Chinese Anarchists in France had formed an organization

1. This issue was specifically aimed at the Chinese worker in France and underscores that the Anarchist value of the sanctity of labor was still accorded some importance among the members of the ECCO.

in the early twenties and published a newspaper, Gongyu (Surplus Labor), that spoke for their beliefs and against the rising tide of communism. Although a conflict with the Anarchists was not a large item on his agenda, Zhao Shiyan believed that many Anarchists might want to change their allegiance once they realized that the Communist way provided a real solution, not just polemics. He was quite successful in pursuing this low-key strategy, as exemplified by his winning over Chen Yannian and Chen Qiaonian. When Zhao wrote to Chen Gongpei in April 1922, he claimed that he did not want any conflict with the Anarchists, because it would sour the general political consolidation taking place.[2]

In spite of Zhao Shiyan's wishes, the ECCO did have spirited debates with the Anarchists. In a witty and scathing dialogue from March to August 1923, Shaonian published a serialization of Y. K.'s "Conversations between an Anarchist and a Communist."[3] Every Anarchist assertion in the argument is backed up by a reference to the Anarchist newspaper, indicating that they were authentic viewpoints. In discussing the necessity for revolution, the meaning of politics and political solutions, and the definitions of terms such as "nation," "party," and "class struggle," the Communist's views are demonstrated to be more "realistic" than those of the Anarchist.[4] In the end, it was the appeal of concrete, organized activity that prevailed over the Anarchists. As Zarrow suggests, Y. K. "emphasized that the difference between the two doctrines lay more in means than ends."[5] By the end of 1923, the ECCO had gained a clear victory over the Anarchists in Europe. After almost four years of publication, the newspaper Gongyu had to combine with another newspaper, and by 1924 arguments with the Anarchists had lost their importance.[6]

In contrast to the polemical confrontation with the Anarchists, the ECCO made a positive advance on the front of organizational politics in the Railroad Struggle of 1923. The railroad controversy of 1923 began with the Lincheng Incident, when Chinese bandits robbed a train and kidnapped

2. Zhao Shiyan letter to Chen Gongpei, 26 April 1922, in FuFa, 2:837.

3. I think Y. K. was Yin Kuan, who was in charge of the Communist Study Society and whose other articles were written in this light, pithy vein. Yin Kuan also wrote under the name Shi Fu, and it may be of some significance that in the issue of the second installment of the Anarchist debate, he contributed an article on the moral nature of Marxism, discussed in the last chapter.

4. Y. K., "Yige Wuzhengfudang he yige Gongchandang de tanhua" [Conversations between an Anarchist and a Communist], Shaonian (March–August 1923), in FuFa, 3:215–245.

5. Zarrow, Anarchism and Chinese Political Culture, 228.

6. "Gongyu she" [The Surplus Society], in Zhang Yunhou et al., Wusi shiqi de shetuan, 4:209.

twenty-six foreigners, demanding a huge ransom. Foreign opinion was out-raged, and a call arose for foreign administration of Chinese railways.[7] Upon hearing of the proposal for international control of China's railways, the Chinese in France called for a meeting on 3 July 1923.[8] This meeting resulted in protests being directed to various organizations, foreign consu-lates, the French newspapers, and their own consulate. Another meeting was organized for 15 July.

The students had not been as galvanized since the Lyons Incident. In Paris, twenty-two Chinese organizations formed the Zhongguo lü Fa ge tuanti lianhehui (United Federation of Chinese Organizations Abroad in France), and between five and six hundred Chinese attended the meeting on 15 July 1923. He Luzhi, a Young China Study Association member who was closely affiliated with the SFEA, chaired this large gathering. Although the meeting was called to organize a strategy for opposing the consolidation scheme, many used it as a forum to espouse their ideas on national salva-tion. The most radical methods were advocated by Zeng Qi, who gave a militant vision of the political necessities. Zeng proposed to (1) stir up pub-lic opinion; (2) incite mass movements like the May Fourth Movement; (3) overthrow the corrupt government and institute fundamental reforms in order to restore the revolutionary momentum of the 1911 Revolution, which had been halted by corrupt government; and (4) initiate an assassi-nation movement. This last point was, for him, clearly the most important aspect of his plan. This speech is an important link with the radical right platform of the CYP and is not inconsistent with radical right philosophies espoused in Europe at that time.[9]

Zhou Enlai succeeded Zeng Qi on the podium and spoke for over an hour on the struggle against imperialism which the railroad controversy epito-mized. Yuan Zizhen and Liu Qingyang also spoke during the meeting. After only a few speeches it was already after 5:00 p.m., and many in the audience wanted to conclude the meeting. However, the Chinese laborers took of-fense at this because they still had speakers who had not had a chance at the podium. Fistfights broke out and the meeting was adjourned in chaos.

At 8:00 p.m. the same evening, representatives from the twenty-two or-ganizations regrouped and discussed the options, deciding to mount a cam-paign using telegrams, letters, and the press. Their efforts were quite

7. Chan Lau Kit-chang, *The Chinese Youth Party, 1923–1945*, 17. Also see *FuFa*, 2:789–92, for an account in the journal *Dongfang zazhi*.

8. "Lü Fa Huaren fandui liechiang gongguan Zhongguo tielu jishi" [An account of the spirited opposition to the public consolidation of Chinese railroads, by the Chinese in France], *Shaonian Zhongguo* (December 1923), in *FuFa*, 2:759–73.

9. Ibid., 766–67.

successful, especially a "tea party" held at the end of the month for the French press, which about thirty French reporters and ten Chinese representatives attended. The next day several sympathetic editorials appeared.[10] In the end, the foreign consolidation scheme failed to gather momentum.

One of the fascinating aspects of the railroad affair was the ability of the Chinese community in France to cooperate. For example, the committees comprised people from opposite ends of the ideological spectrum: Zeng Qi and Zhou Enlai were both committee secretaries, and the finance committee included He Luzhi and Xu Teli. ECCO members held over one-third of the committee posts.[11] Certainly the ECCO leaders must have been satisfied with the whole affair; not only were their efforts successful but they were emerging as a real voice in the Chinese community in France.

The Railroad Struggle also showed members of the ECCO, who were learning the basics of political agitation, the importance of developing linkages with significant groups in the foreign environment—in this case, with the French journalists. They also learned the importance of accurately targeting a specific audience and choosing an appropriate means of communication. People on the grasslands of China or warlords who could not read would not likely be persuaded by a tea party, but the lesson of communicating on the same level as your potential ally was well learned.

Back in China, the issues of cooperation and radical organizing activity were also prominent in the news during early 1923, when the Chinese railway workers' strike in Beijing-Hankou was ruthlessly suppressed by the warlord Wu Peifu. According to James Harrison, the events of this incident, known as the 7 February Massacre, "showed the skills and limits of Communist agitation and in disconcerting ways foreshadowed the larger disaster of 1927. In both cases, initial gains through cooperation with potential enemies came to little once the stronger partners in the alliance decided they no longer needed the Communists."[12] In 1923–24 in Europe, however, it must have seemed to the ECCO that their party was gaining in ascendancy because they were able to deal deftly with old and new enemies.

The activist milieu that existed in France during the twenties encompassed not only revolutionaries committed to communism but a whole array of activists of other ideologies who also conceived of themselves as revolutionaries. The ECCO established various kinds of relationships with the dif-

10. Ibid., 768–73.
11. Ibid., 771.
12. James Pinckney Harrison, The Long March to Power: A History of the Chinese Communist Party, 1921–72 (New York: Praeger, 1972), 37.

ferent groups. The balance of power within these relationships and the political behavior of the partners differed significantly from case to case. The striking success of the ECCO in 1923 enabled the ECCO to establish a Communist-controlled United Front with the EGMD, but it also spurred the founding of China's most vehement anti-Communist political party, the CYP.

THE ECCO AND THE CHINESE YOUTH PARTY

There was an entire stratum of patriotic Chinese youth who were not participants in the Work-Study scheme. Several of these were members of the Young China Study Association, as was Zhao Shiyan, and most were educated beyond the secondary level. Several of these young people also were familiar with Socialist theories and with the Russian Revolution, but they chose to reject the internationalism of Lenin and instead rallied behind the Western concept of nationalism as a unifying principle of political organization. Some leaders in the Chinese community were convinced that the ECCO was a menace that must be fought.[13]

The moving force behind the CYP was Zeng Qi (1892–1951), who was, as we have seen, a prominent member of the youth revolt. Zeng Qi was born in Luchang, Sichuan, and his early training was Confucian, but with the abolition of the exam system in 1905, he also obtained a Western education. He attended Zhendan University in Shanghai, where he formed attachments with lifelong political compatriots such as Li Huang and Zuo Xunsheng. In 1918, after a period of study in Japan, Zeng returned to China and helped found the Young China Study Association. During his sojourn in Europe (1919–24), Zeng was a prolific journalist and also kept a diary.[14]

Zeng Qi was particularly dismayed at the increasing success of the ECCO and the growing leadership of Zhou Enlai. Writing in his diary Zeng claimed that although Zhou Enlai, who was then the general secretary of the ECYC, used "high-sounding phrases," he nevertheless was full of "a huge amount

---

13. Much of the following section on the CYP was delivered as a paper, "Zeng Qi and the Frozen Revolution," at the Conference on "Roads Not Taken: Oppositional Politics in Twentieth Century China," Washington and Lee University, 20–22 September 1990.

14. Zeng Qi, *Zeng Muhan (Qi) xiansheng yizhu* [The posthumous collection of the writings of Mr. Zeng Qi], in Shen Yunlong, ed., *Jindai Zhongguo shiliao congkan* [Collected materials in modern Chinese history] (Taibei: Wenhai chubanshe, 1954). Zeng Qi's diary, which spans some of his years in Japan and Europe, is published in the same series (Shen Yunlong, ed., *Zeng Muhan xiansheng riji xuan* [Selections from Mr. Zeng Qi's diary] [Taibei: Zhongguo qingniandang dangshi ziliao congwen, 1984]).

of empty talk."[15] By the end of 1923 Zeng and his friends created their own party, the Qingniandang (the CYP).[16] Cleansing the nation of internal factionalism brought on by the warlords and protecting the nation against invasion by outside forces (neiqu guozei, waikang qiangquan) were essential goals of the new party. To accomplish this task the CYP called for a program almost identical with the integral nationalism espoused by Maurice Barrès. The platform of the CYP called for the harmonious unity of all classes in pursuit of economic revitalization and restoration of China's greatness as a civilization. The social reformation would be brought about by an intensive program of national education.[17]

Consciously defining nationalism with European terms, definitions, and examples, the philosopher of the CYP, Li Huang, explained that modern nationalism could emerge only in conflict with foreign powers, citing examples such as the 1870 Franco-Prussian war and the mobilization of nationalist forces brought on by the Dreyfus affair. Much of the essence of nationalism revolved around the territorial imperative, in addition to the nation's soul. Li Huang defined nationalism as

> a specific people occupying a certain piece of land and protecting certain ownership rights [zhuquan]; furthermore, these people, because of the feelings of their own hearts and the conditions of their lives, do not relinquish these proprietorial rights regarding this territory . . . do not allow invaders. The descendants throughout the span of centuries have the responsibility to preserve in memory the hardships that from time to time were overcome by their ancestors; there is a special cultural legacy.[18]

From 1923 until 1929 the CYP was a secret party and officially admitted only to being a youth corps. This subterfuge was deemed necessary for pur-

15. Zeng Qi, Zeng Muhan xiansheng riji xuan, 55 (5 July 1923).

16. For an overall CYP history see Chan Lau Kit-chang, The Chinese Youth Party, 1923–1945. Two useful memoirs by CYP members are Hu Guowei, Bali xinying [Paris impressions], 2d ed. (Taibei: Puti chubanshe, 1970), and Li Huang's writings. For an in-depth discussion of the polemics between the CYP and the ECCO see the thesis of Nicole Dulioust, "Le Parti de la jeunesse chinoise et ses rapports avec le Parti communiste chinois dans les années 1920" (DEA, 1980).

17. For several CYP platforms and memoirs see Zhongguo Qingniandang dangshi ziliao diyi ji [The first collection of Chinese Youth Party materials] (Taibei: Minzhu qiaoshe, 1955). The CYP proposals parallel much of Barrès's final political platform (see Robert Soucy, Fascism in France: The Case of Maurice Barrès [Berkeley and Los Angeles: University of California Press, 1972]).

18. Li Huang, "Shi guojiazhuyi" [An explanation of nationalism] (October 1924), in Shen Yunlong, comp., Guojia zhuyi lunwen ji [Collected writings on nationalism], vol. 971 (Taibei: Wenhai, n.d.): 1–24, quote on 1.

poses of self-preservation and until the situation in China became mature for revolution. However, this did not stop the CYP from aggressively pursuing its political activities.[19] Although Zeng Qi and Li Huang left Paris in September 1924, the political diatribes between the CYP and other groups continued. In addition to attacks and counterattacks in their rival newspapers, several members of the CYP and ECCO also bought handguns, which they brandished at each other, and several instances of violence broke out during assemblies. Numbering over 100 members in their first year, the CYP had some notable successes, especially when the ECCO occupied the Chinese Paris legation in 1925 during the May Thirtieth Incident, and the CYP provided the French police with the names of ECCO members involved in this action to be used in expulsion proceedings.[20] Thus, unlike its negative opinion of the Chinese Communists, the French government had a rather mild view of the CYP. When copies of the CYP propaganda organ *Sine shing* (*Xiansheng*) (*The Pioneer*) were confiscated in Indochina in the late twenties, a French government report claimed that although the CYP started out as revolutionaries, after 1927 they were just *Républicains patriotes*.

In some ways, the French view of the CYP was unjustified, as armed members of the CYP adopted a regimen of target practice for a short period in the midtwenties. Hu Guowei, who was in charge of weapons training for the CYP, asserted that target practice was necessary to deal with Communists and for guerrilla training when they returned to China.[21]

The willingness to use violent means is an important issue during this pre-1927 era, and it is interesting to note from the respective memoirs of the participants that the CYP was more inclined toward violence than was the ECCO. With respect to the occupation of the embassy during the May Thirtieth Incident, Ren Zhuoxuan, writing in 1927, emphasized that it was not an armed invasion and that their only act of destruction was to cut the telephone wire, for which they were charged with the destruction of public property.[22] However, the CYP also surrounded the embassy during the same

19. See the special issue of *Xiansheng*, no. 311 (Paris), "Zhongguo Qingniandang gongkai dangming zhuanhao" [The special issue on the public announcement of the Chinese Youth Party]. In reality this secrecy did not deceive anyone, and although they were often referred to as the Nationalist Clique (or more often by epithets like "running dogs" by their opponents), one finds numerous references to them as the Qingniandang, the Chinese Youth Party.

20. Nora Wang, "Da Chen Lu"; and Wang Yongxiang and Kong Fanfeng, "Zhonggong lü Ou zhibu fandui guojiazhuyi pai de douzheng" [The struggle of the ECCO against the Nationalist Clique], *Zhongguo xiandaishi fuyin baokan ziliao* 3 (March 1982): 11–18.

21. Hu Guowei, *Bali xinying*, 24–25.

22. Ren Zhuoxuan, "Bali zhi beibu xiayu" [My arrest and release from prison in Paris], in idem, *Ren Zhuoxuan pingzhuan* [A critical biography of Ren Zhuoxuan], 2 vols. (Taibei: Bomier shudian, 1965), 1:6–18 (this passage written in August 1927).

period in order to obtain money originally deposited there on behalf of a member who had accidently blown himself up while preparing a bomb. They wanted to return his body to China, but the embassy would not release the funds. In contrast to the ECCO, the CYP members were armed and positioned themselves at the doors and telephones until the funds were delivered. According to Hu Guowei, many CYP members went armed to social functions in case the ECCO provoked trouble.[23]

Very damaging to the CYP quest for political power was the accusation by their opponents that they were "Fascists." This charge was leveled at them as early as 1924, and not just by Communists. The Fascist label in the Chinese context of the early twenties connoted warlord linkages, violent methods, and aspirations to dictatorship. As proof of the CYP's Fascist leanings, the ECCO asserted that the CYP was cooperating with warlords.[24] Epithets such as "running dogs of the warlords" and mention of warlord connections peppered much of the ECCO anti-CYP critiques.[25] As late as 1930, *Chiguang* was still discussing these contacts, accusing the CYP of becoming tools of Wu Peifu.[26]

A more sophisticated critique was offered by the Paris branch of the Chinese Social Democrats, who argued that the ideology of nationalism, especially the territorial nature of the CYP definition (culled from the *Nouvelle Larousse dictionnaire*), was one whose highest development resulted in militarism and imperialism, hence fascism.[27] The Social Democrats also emphasized the warlord connections of the CYP.[28]

Zeng Qi initially provided fuel for this Fascist appellation by praising Mussolini in a poem and declaring his admiration for the way the youth in Italy had recently revived their state.[29] Although Zeng Qi felt personally

23. Hu Guowei, *Bali xinying*, 34–38.
24. For a good overall discussion of this debate see Dulioust, "Le Parti de la jeunesse chinoise et ses rapports avec le Parti communiste chinois dans les années 1920," 9–13.
25. Several of these ECCO articles, including some of the earliest writings of Deng Xiaoping, are published in *FuFa*: e.g., Wu Hao [Zhou Enlai], "Shihua de fangan" [Antitruth], *Chiguang*, May 1924; Xi Xian [Deng Xiaoping], "Qingkan *Xiansheng* zhoubao zhi disi pizaoyao de xinwen" [Please see the fourth bunch of lies in the news in the weekly *Pioneer*], *Chiguang*, January 1925.
26. Zhao Ming, "Guojia zhuyizhe guqin xuejiao 'geming'" [The touted "revolution" of the Nationalist Clique], *Chiguang* 55 (1930): 15–16. It should be noted that from 1924 to 1934 the GMD continued to criticize the CYP for their warlord connections.
27. Bi Yinglin, "'Ou' bian buying zuo er youto neng buzuo de wenzhang" [An essay of "criticism" that should not have to be written but must be written], *Fendou* [*Combat*] 30 (10 April 1926): 8–16.
28. See, e.g., "Guojia zhuyizhe zitao meiqu" [The Nationalist Clique's lack of interest in self-analysis], *Fendou* 37 (25 August 1926), and "Jizhang (!?) sanzhi de shili" [The power of several prose essays (!?)], *Fendou* 30 (10 April 1926): 16.
29. See the original declaration of the CYP; also the declaration in the first issue of the

maligned by these attacks, which he called slander,[30] the example of the efficiency and unity of the Italian Fascist state continued to be cited in CYP propaganda, and a 1930 CYP manifesto proclaimed, "The Young China Party is not ashamed to profess that in the love of their motherland, nationalism and fascism do stand on common ground, but the Nationalist stands for democracy, whereas the Fascist stands for dictatorship."[31] The taint of fascism and the perception of warlord connections were major factors in deterring support for the CYP.

The campaigns against the ECCO by the CYP were perhaps effective in diminishing the positive response to the ECCO among young Chinese intellectuals. They provided a real ideological alternative and an active, feisty political leadership. Their cooperation with French authorities in 1925 certainly helped to facilitate the expulsion of several top ECCO leaders. Yet the CYP was in many ways a feeble shadow in the cataclysmic Chinese political environment. The escalation of violence, foreign invasion, and civil war at home preempted a revolution based on a nationalist ideology that sought to harmonize the classes and promote economic autonomy and national education. The times were not right for an intellectual leadership to prevail. The CYP represented a misplaced modern revolution. The CYP contained some of the most astute and well-informed patriots, but ironically, by aspiring to a cultural restoration, the CYP de facto relegated themselves to a traditional intellectual role and thereby lost any chance to obtain power to implement their modern reformation of the Chinese state. In spite of their political commitment, the CYP leadership were reluctant to be perceived as politicians and conceived of themselves as intellectuals. During a commemoration ceremony for Zeng Qi, held during the mid-1970s, Li Huang characterized his friend as fulfilling his "responsibility as an intellectual." Although they certainly had a political platform, the impression is justified that their identification with the role of the intellectual in a traditional sense was important. Their political platform was not based on a precise political agenda as much as on a cultural ideal—a culture that emphasized education, the best of the traditional Chinese ethos, and a measured but firm entrance into the modern world. Zeng Qi, Li Huang, Zuo Shunsheng,

---

Xingshi zhoubao [The Awakening Lion Weekly] (10 October 1924); and numerous articles by CYP members on nationalism, which also praised the unification of Germany and often linked the Young Italians with the Young Turks.

30. Zeng Qi, "Gongchandang pumie guojiazhuyizhe zhi celue" [The plot by the Chinese Communist Party to destroy the Nationalists] (14 May 1927), in Zeng Qi, Zeng Muhan (Qi) xiansheng yizhu, 90–91.

31. "The Nationalist Movement and the Young China Party" (10 October 1930), pamphlet, in AOM, SLOTFOM V, 43.

and fellow CYP members ostensibly "broke" from tradition, but they could not totally abandon their heritage as intellectuals. At the founding meeting of the ECCO the members debated about loyalty oaths, but the agenda of the CYP called for skits and traditional opera performances by its members. One can in part understand why there is such a mutual bitterness between the Communists and these Nationalist intellectuals. The former resented the latter for their inability to look forward, whereas the latter bitterly regretted losing the past.

THE ECCO UNITED FRONT WITH THE EUROPEAN GUOMINDANG

Although the year 1924 witnessed conflict between the ECCO and the CYP, the ECCO faithfully cooperated with the United Front policy of the CCP and the GMD. In fact, much of the organizational groundwork for the EGMD in France was laid by Zhou Enlai and Li Fuchun. As early as August 1922, Zhou Enlai had met with and aided the GMD representative, Wang Jingqi, with the talk of party organization.[32] Wang Jingqi, who had been expelled in the Lyons Incident, leaned toward the left faction of the GMD. In the summer of 1923 Zhou Enlai wrote to Wang (who had returned for a short time to China) outlining his conception of the CCP-GMD cooperation:

> [In terms of our cooperation], currently in Europe there are the following three tasks: (1) to propagate the necessity for a Democratic revolution in China today and the strategy for accomplishing this; (2) for the Guomindang to incite the Chinese in Europe with real revolutionary spirit; and (3) to industriously undertake the work of organizing and training in the Guomindang.[33]

One of the most significant facts about this cooperation was that the ECCO can take credit for the first United Front with the GMD. The Leninist United Front strategy (the combining of Communist resources with those of advanced political parties) was articulated by ECCO members such as Yin Kuan before the actual merging took place.[34] On 16 June 1923, as ordered by the CCP Central Committee and as negotiated by Zhou Enlai and Wang Jingqi, the ECCO entered en masse into the GMD, although the EGMD was not established until 25 November 1923 in Lyons. By mid-January 1924, Zhou Enlai had organized a Paris section of the EGMD and was asking per-

---

32. "Zhou Enlai qingshaonian shidai jishi," 68.
33. Ibid., 74.
34. Yin Kuan, "Zai Zhongguo de gongchanzhuyi yundong" [The Communist movement in China], *Shaonian* 9 (1 May 1922), in *FuFa*, 3:356.

mission to split the Paris and Lyons correspondence sections because of growth in membership and administrative convenience. In a letter addressed to Peng Sumin at the GMD headquarters in Shanghai, Zhou Enlai summarized the first Plenary Session of the Paris Correspondence Section of the EGMD. It is clear that the Paris section was led by the ECCO. Not only does Zhou Enlai refer to Li Fuchun as the "temporary director" of the Paris section, but he relates that Nie Rongzhen had been elected the new section chief in the January 1924 meeting. Finally, in his conclusion he wrote, "At this point, [Zhou] Enlai has completed the mission given to him by the premier, Mr. [Sun] Zhongshan, and the General Bureau of organizing the Paris Correspondence Section." His salutation praised the Three People's Principles and was signed "Zhou Enlai, Organizer of the Paris Correspondence Section."[35]

Within one year of its establishment the French sections of the EGMD had over 300 members, according to an official 1924 GMD report on overseas branches. Of the 308 members in France, approximately one-third were in Billancourt, a Paris neighborhood where the most radical members of the Chinese community lived, and were most probably Communists.[36] There was also a very active EGMD section in Lyons, whose most prestigious member, Liu Hou, was a former secretary of the SFEA and was the Chinese secretary of the SFI at Lyons.

The ECCO materially helped the EGMD in Europe, but there were EGMD members who distrusted the Communists. In his article "Another Discussion on the Question of Chinese Communists Entering the Guomindang," Zhou Enlai tried to answer United Front critics by saying that the national revolution was the first step for everyone. In other words, the Communists were not abandoning their interests in the class struggle, but the national revolution was emphasized as a first step, in which the proletariat could indeed participate. Zhou asserted that by combining their forces and receiving aid from the Comintern, the alliance was providing a concentration

35. Zhou Enlai to Peng Sumin, "Bali tongxunchu choubeiyuan Zhou Enlai zhi zongwubu changhan" [An extended letter from the Paris correspondent and preparatory official, Zhou Enlai, to the GMD General Affairs Bureau], 18 January 1924, Shanghai Guomindang Archives, Yangmingshan, Taiwan.

36. See the captured "Rapport Kuo-min-tang" (1924), translated into French. This over twenty page report contains specific requests by Wang Jingqi for funds and an analysis of the worker basis of the French GMD branch. The enrollment figures for labor communities of Chinese abroad were quite large: e.g., 1,844 GMD members in Cuba; 1,848 in Mexico; 813 in South Africa; but only 56 GMD members in the United Kingdom and 56 in Japan. France had one of the lower enrollments, although it later was reported in the thousands. See AOM, SLOTFOM VIII, 6, especially pages 4–5, 13, 16, 21.

of revolutionary elements and promoting a quicker overthrow of the warlords.[37]

Although they cooperated with the EGMD, the members of the ECCO felt more comfortable with its left branch and did not hesitate to criticize those on the right. Marxist propaganda did not abate as a result of the cooperation. For example, in his eulogy for Sun Yatsen, Xiao Pusheng was very particular about delineating Sun's last few years, when he led a real national revolution, as those of his greatest contribution. Xiao charted the future course of the Chinese revolution as if it was a foregone historical conclusion; it would have its basis in the masses, and they would unite with the world proletariat.[38]

In general it appears that in contrast with the CCP-GMD alliance in China, the ECCO-EGMD alliance was controlled more by the Communists. This circumstance may have lulled leaders such as Zhou Enlai, Ren Zhuoxuan, Deng Xiaoping, Li Fuchun, Lin Wei, and Nie Rongzhen into a false sense of security during the crucial period before the coup of 1927.[39] It also might have made them less aware of the leadership abilities of Jiang Jieshi (Chiang Kai-Shek) and more confident that the CCP could control the GMD, a view that they still asserted long after the failure of the United Front. For example, writing in 1943, Zhou Enlai criticized Chen Duxiu and other Central Committee members and the Soviet Union for not maneuvering politically for more power to overcome the right faction of the GMD and for not consolidating the CCP members and the leftists to block Jiang Jieshi's seizure of power.[40] Even in his *writings of the time*, Zhou expressed the view that for the revolution to succeed the right faction of the GMD had to be overcome: "In conclusion, we can obviously ascertain from the above political situation in Guangdong that the right faction of the Guomindang will never be revolutionary. [They] are infested with the evil designs of warlordism, and the revolution has only the left faction; it has only the labor-

37. Zhou Enlai, "Zailun Zhongguo gongchanzhuyizhe jiaru guomindang wenti" [Another discussion on the question of Chinese Communists entering the Guomindang], *Chiguang*, 1 June 1924, in *FuFa*, 3:380–84.

38. Xiao Pusheng, "Zhongshan shi yu guomin geming" [Sun Yatsen's death and the national revolution], *Chiguang*, 1 April 1925, in *FuFa*, 3:389–96.

39. By 1927 several of the ECCO returnees were high-level officials occupying over one-third of the CCP Central Committee positions. One can easily see them reinforcing an underestimation of the GMD due to their memories of the weak right faction in Europe.

40. Zhou Enlai, "Guanyu yijiuersi zhi erliunian dang dui Guomindang de guanxi" [Regarding the relationship between the Party and the Guomindang from 1924 to 1926], *Dangshi yanjiu* 2 (1980): 2–9 (written in 1943). It seems as if this was the common perspective of the ECCO members.

ers, peasants, and student masses."[41] Thus, Zhou Enlai had believed that the CCP needed to exert more leadership of the masses *before* April 1927 and openly expressed this sentiment. Perhaps his belief that the right faction could be subordinated was a result of his European experience.

Before the 1927 split, two issues dominated the ECCO-EGMD United Front: the anti-imperialist struggle and the increasing factionalization within ECCO-EGMD politics. We can thank the French police for our knowledge of these matters. The French Sûreté sent "observers" to Chinese meetings and compiled dossiers on Chinese radicals and gathering places such as key restaurants and hotels. They confiscated mail, translated documents, and collected Chinese materials ranging from ballot forms to secret reports. Thus, we have some fascinating evidence of the political activities within the Chinese community from Marseilles to Paris. A typical example is a September 1925 report by the head of the Sûreté in Lyons summarizing the data on seven Chinese who were seen as suspicious (*soupçonneux*) and who had been distributing Communist propaganda.[42]

The fervor of protest that infused the Chinese European community during the May Thirtieth Incident in 1925 lasted beyond the ECCO occupation of the legation in Paris and demonstrations in Brussels. A generalized anti-imperialist movement grew in strength and increasingly worried French security forces. A meeting held on 3 January 1926 at 23 rue Boyer, Paris, was attended by seventy persons to "protest against international imperialism" and was observed and reported in detail by French police. The initial report highlighted speeches by the militant president of the Comité d'action des groupes chinois en France, Teng-Si-Sien (Deng Xixian a.k.a. Deng Xiaoping), and by Fou-Len (Fu Zhong) that called for support for the left-leaning warlord Feng Yüxiang against the Beijing government and cooperation with the Soviet Union against international imperialism.[43] Within a

41. Zhou Enlai, "Zuijin eryue Guangzhou zhengxiang zhi gaiguan" [The political situation of the last two months in Guangzhou] (30 October 1924), in *Zhonggong dangshi jiaoyu cankao ziliao*, 2:47.

42. Confidential note no. 15532 for the police from the Prefecture du Rhône, Agglomération lyonnaise, Service de la Sûreté, 17 September 1925, AN, F7 13438. At least two of the seven people named were Communist representatives in Lyons, Yang Kun and Li Lianggong. This is significant information when combined with other sources; for instance, according to Yang Kun, he was a member of the ECYC. He and Paul Lieu (Liu Puqing) led Communist activities in Lyons. According to Yang Kun, he and Liu are pictured in the second row from the front, farthest left, in the commemorative picture for the farewell party for Zhou Enlai in 1924 (Yang Kun interview, 14 October 1985 [Beijing]).

43. Note of 4 January 1926; these political reports are dated but bear no titles and were probably part of a series sent by the Sûreté Générale to the Préfet de Police (AN, F7 13438); a retyped copy of the 4 January 1926 report is also deposited in AOM, SLOTFOM VIII, 6.

week of this report, supplementary reports appeared with data on the Chinese who spoke at the meeting. For example, the information on Deng Xiaoping included his current address at 3 rue Casteja in Boulogne-Billancourt and noted that "arriving in France in 1920, he first worked in Marseilles, then in Bayeux, Paris, and Lyons. Returning to Paris in 1925, he has been employed in the Renault factory at Billancourt. . . . He is a militant Communist and has made speeches at several different meetings organized by the Chinese Communists, particularly advocating a *rapprochement* with the government of the U.S.S.R."[44] Other Sûreté reports focused on the meeting places favored by the Chinese.[45] The Chinese activists remained unintimidated as propaganda proliferated. A delegation was sent to the League of Nations in Geneva,[46] and regular political meetings were held. On 12 March 1926, forty people attended a commemorative meeting on the death of Sun Yatsen, including representatives from the French and Italian Communist parties and Indochinese and North Africans.[47]

In terms of the internal dynamics of the ECCO-EGMD United Front, the period from 1925 until mid-1927 was one of Communist and left-wing supremacy. Correspondence from Lyons to Wang Jingqi in July 1925 exclaimed "the happy news" that twenty members of the elite SFI had joined the EGMD. These members were "very zealous, very industrious, very confident, and capable of progressing the principles of Sun Yatsen and *the party of the left*" (emphasis mine).[48]

Several factors during 1925 led to serious conflict within the ECCO-EGMD United Front and to the expulsion of the EGMD right faction. The death of Sun Yatsen (and, in France, the illness of Wang Jingqi) led to scrambles for power and influence in France, just as it did in China. Also, some EGMD members, like the Western Hills faction in Canton, continued to be suspicious of Communist intentions. These included some of the highest placed

44. Note of 7 January 1926, AN, F7 13438. Deng had been noticed by the French the previous year when he presided over a meeting of sympathy for the death of Wang Jingqi (report of 16 November 1925, AN, F7 12900).

45. One report of 7 January 1926 concentrated on three addresses in Boulogne-Billancourt: 14 rue Traversière, 3 rue Casteja, and 8 rue Jules Ferry. In early February another report cited more than ten meeting places for the organizations of Chinese "Communists and xenophobes" (report of 4 February 1926, note 952, AN, F7 13438).

46. Several EGMD branches sent delegates in a unified appeal to the League of Nations in September 1926 (*Canton Gazette*, 3 November 1926, in AAE, série E, Chine, vol. 492).

47. Report of 13 March 1926 AAE, série E, Chine, vol. 492, 123–24. According to the report, the "Internationale" was sung.

48. Seized letter to Wang Jingqi, 6 July 1925, AN, F7 12900. Among the four signatures is that of at least one Communist, Liu Puqing, who was later to attend the University of Paris and whose domicile was the headquarters of the radical faction (ECCO) of the EGMD.

officers, such as Xi Wende, Cao Desan, and Zhang Xingdan. The more conservative EGMD elements were seriously alarmed by the ECCO occupation of the Chinese legation and the growing number of high positions in the EGMD occupied by ECCO members.[49]

Violent conflicts arose at several EGMD meetings throughout 1924 and early 1925, including beatings, smashed chairs, and the shooting of handguns.[50] Wang Jingqi was persuaded by Zhou Enlai, Ren Zhuoxuan, Li Fuchun, Gao Yuhan, Liao Huanxing, and other ECCO members to expel leaders of the right faction, including Xi Wende, Cao Desan, and Zhang Xingzhou.[51]

Sensing victory in early 1925, Gao Yuhan wrote to Shanghai of the increasing radicalization of the ECCO-EGMD United Front and exulted, "We have gotten rid of eight-tenths of nine-tenths of these people, and within two or three months the Koumintang [sic] here will become a purely 'Right' [meaning Communist] Koumintang section." The letter went on to criticize the China-based GMD:

> The Overseas Central Committee of the Koumintang Party, very stupidly sent out a telegram instructing the branches in Europe to enlist new members. The telegram contained instructions as to how the enlistment can be encouraged. They are dealing with the Koumintang party almost as if it were the Y.M.C.A. or the Worlds' Students' Feder-

49. Many of the details of the 1925–27 ECCO-EGMD United Front conflicts can be ascertained from original materials, which range from Sûreté analyses and captured correspondence to newspapers, etc. One of the most important documents on the EGMD in France is in the colonial archives. It is a captured report written in March 1929 by the right EGMD branch, which was loyal to Nanjing ("Zhongguo guomindang zhu Fa zongzhibu xiang di Sanci quanguo daibiao dahui baogao Ouzhou dangwu" [Report of the European tasks to the Third National Conference by the General Branch of the Chinese Guomindang in France], AOM, SLOTFOM VIII, 6). This valuable document includes a whole history of the EGMD with charts and a year-by-year analysis of the meetings and membership, listing the members of the various factions. Later memoirs have also been accurate in their assertions; e.g., Shi Yisheng, "Huiyi zhonggong lü Ou zhibu de guanghui yeji," 122–23. Corroborating testimony for Shi's assertion that expulsions took place, as well as for his election, occur in the French colonial archives. Documents captured by the French include translated orders, one of which is signed by "Thi Ich Sanh," which is the Vietnamese transliteration of Shi Yisheng's name (see Circular no. 39, 17 August 1925, AOM, SLOT-FOM VIII, 6). Shi's election at the August 1925 meeting is also verified by the same series of documents.

50. "Rapport fait par un des organes du parti Kouomintang [sic] à Lyon," translated and reprinted from *Minguo ribao* (19, 20 July 1926), AAE, série E, Chine, vol. 492; Wang Yongxiang, Kong Fanfeng, and Liu Pinqing, *Zhongguo gongchandang lü Ou zhibu shihua,* 172–73.

51. "Zhongguo guomindang zhu Fa zongzhibu xiang di Sanci quanguo daibiao dahui baogao Ouzhou dangwu," 2, specifically highlights the role of Li Fuchun, Ren Zhuoxuan, and Liao Huanxing in the manipulation of the expulsions.

ation, or any other association connected with employment or education. Don't you think this is rotten? We have criticized them strongly
in the Guide Weekly and our comrades should propose to the Central
Committee for the withdrawal of these instructions which are suicidal.
We are now co-operating with the Koumintang parties in Europe to
cause these instructions to be withdrawn.[52]

The ECCO members kept up the political pressure against the right faction
of the EGMD. Writing in January 1925 in *Chiguang*, in an article entitled
"The Difference between the Guomindang Left and Right Factions," Ren
Zhuoxuan reiterated the goal of the United Front to rid the country of warlords and foreign imperialism. For Ren it was the contrast between ideology
(*zhuyi*) and proposals and activities (*zhuzhang ji xingdong*) that separated the
right and left.[53] The right faction was hiding behind the abstract notion of
ideology, and by not joining in the fight against internal warlords and external imperialism they were in essence antirevolutionary.[54]

Another round of expulsions was conducted at the Fourth General Assembly of the General Committee of the EGMD, held in Paris in mid-August
1925. Circulars from the meeting show that the meeting went through a
sixteen-item agenda that included two series of expulsions. Fifteen members of the EGMD right faction were expelled as traitors, and the Lyons sub-
committee was charged with illegal activities and was commanded to
reapply for admission into the EGMD. To add insult to injury, newly elected
officials included Communists Deng Xiaoping as president and Liu Puqing
(Paul Lieu) as secretary. Other high offices were held by ECCO members Shi
Yisheng, Gao Yuhan, and Lin Wei.[55]

The right faction of the EGMD had begun a serious reorganization effort,
holding a Third General Assembly in April 1925, establishing a headquarters at 3 rue Thouin, Paris, and printing their own journal, *Sanmin Yuekan*
(*The Three People's Principles Monthly*). In addition to the goal of "expressing
the practice of being loyal disciples of the Three Principles [of Sun Yatsen],"
the right faction conducted serious anti-Communist activities *before* 1927:

52. Yu Hankao letter to Ya Chun, 4 May 1925, PRO, FO 371/10944, 37. I am grateful
to Dilip Basu for giving me a copy of this document.
53. This critique stresses the underlying debate between the concept of politics as anath-
ema to the intellectual and the immediate issue of social justice, which emotionally aided
the transition to self-conscious revolutionary.
54. Hong Tan [Ren Zhuoxuan], "Guomindang zuopai youpai zhi fenhua" [The difference
between the Guomindang left and right factions], *Chiguang* 23 (15 January 1925): 7–9.
55. Meeting Minutes and Circulars 39–42 of the Guomindang European Branch. These
documents were captured in December 1926 and were translated into French by a Sino-
Vietnamese; thus, Lin Wei's name is spelled Lam Uy, and Deng Xiaoping, under the alias
Deng Xixian, is Dang Hy Hien.

[At the Fourth General Assembly in 1926, we decided] . . . we ought to hold the responsibility for the French General Branch of the Guomindang totally in our hands. . . . The Fourth General Assembly formally elected an Executive Committee. Accordingly, we sent Zhang Xingzhou, Xi Wende, and Huang Ying to return to our country and report to the Central Committee [Guomindang]. . . . Comrade Xi in Guangdong went to Lin Zuhan of the Standing Committee to report. Although Lin was a member of the CCP, he felt the strength of our comrade's reasoning and introduced the whole report to the Central Committee of the Party Section. Afterward, Xi Wende further requested to be a representative on the committee, so that he could encourage the rejection of Gao Yuhan's credentials. But this could not be managed. Tan Pingshan, relying on Party regulations, had Huang Ying expelled from the Party registers.[56]

It appears that while the ECCO cooperated with the EGMD, they not only maintained their autonomy but were more successful than their compatriots in the CCP in isolating the right faction of the EGMD. It was no wonder that they believed their political skills were more sophisticated. When they exercised these skills in the European arena, this self-image was not far off the mark, but they still faced formidable opposition from the non-Communist EGMD members.

THE NORTHERN EXPEDITION AND THE APRIL TWELFTH COUP

Although the ECCO was very successful in stifling the right faction of the ECCO-EGMD United Front, their dependence on the left faction placed them in a vulnerable position similar to their CCP compatriots. However, this was not noticeable during the first part of 1927, when huge mass meetings were held throughout France to protest international imperialism.

A mass meeting sponsored by the PCF was held on 18 February 1927 in support of the Chinese Northern Expedition. Presided over by Henri Barbi, over 5,000 people attended, including 250 Chinese and Vietnamese. The celebrated editor of L'humanité, Paul Valliant-Couturier, along with several Asians, spoke at this forum. An EGMD manifesto issued by the leftists urged the French not to intervene against the Northern Expedition and to abolish the unequal treaties. The struggle of the Chinese revolution, it was said, was not only a case of Chinese independence but concerned all oppressed

56. "Zhongguo guomindang zhu Fa zongzhibu xiang di Sanci quanguo daibiao dahui baogao Ouzhou dangwu," 2.

people: "Thus, the Guomindang Party is none other than the leader of a worldwide revolutionary force. Join together, oppressed peoples, in this common struggle against your only oppressor, imperialism." The manifesto ended with the slogans: "Vive le révolution chinoise! Vive l'union du prolétariat et des peuples opprimes! Vive le révolution mondiale!"[57]

On 11 March 1927, another mass meeting in support of the Chinese revolution was held to commemorate Sun Yatsen's death and was attended by 2,500 people, of whom 500–600 were Chinese, Vietnamese, and North Africans. Among the speakers were Marcel Cachin and the head of the PCF, Pierre Semard.[58]

In spite of the successful campaign in support of the Northern Expedition, the underlying tensions and factional propensities within the ECCO-EGMD United Front erupted with the news of the April Twelfth Coup. The coup political scene in France differed from that in China in three significant ways. First, Chinese sympathy was initially against "Tchiang-Kaï-Shek" (Jiang Jieshi); second, the disputes did not produce any of the tremendous bloodletting that occurred in China; and third, although the ECCO-EGMD United Front lasted longer than the CCP-GMD United Front in China, the left faction of the EGMD had split from the ECCO a few months *before* the August debacle in Wuhan, China.

During April 1927, while CCP members in China were desperately attempting to avoid the bloody massacres perpetrated by the GMD, the ECCO-EGMD United Front was able to publish a tract entitled "Manifeste du Parti Kuomintang en Europe contre la trahison de Tchiang Kaï-Shek." Denouncing Jiang for having abandoned the Chinese revolutionary cause, the manifesto claimed that the ECCO-EGMD United Front was responsible only to the Executive Committee in Hankou, which was a disciplined party and "not under the dictatorship of a mediocre personality." The ECCO-EGMD United Front distributed these manifestos to a large assembly of 1,500 people that was held on 27 April at 33 rue de la Grange aux Belles, Paris. The April Twelfth Coup was denounced at the meeting by Europeans and Vietnamese as well as by Chinese. Among the ECCO speakers were a representative from Belgium and Xia Ting. Several anti-Communist Chinese were eventually expelled for disrupting the speakers, and one right-faction EGMD

57. Notes of Agent Désire, 23 February 1927, AOM, SLOTFOM VIII, 6. The Asian speakers were two Vietnamese leaders, an indication that the connections between the CCP and the PCF were weak. It is worth noting that the PCF did not send a representative to the first meeting of the committee against imperialism formed by the Chinese on 3 February 1926. There was communication and support, but it seems to me that the French Communists were more supportive of the Vietnamese and North Africans.

58. Ibid., report of 14 March 1927.

member, Song Guoshu (Son Kono Tchon), briefly seized the podium and defended Jiang's actions as saving the revolution. The meeting ended with a resolution in favor of the Chinese revolution.[59] The right faction of the EGMD also held meetings, including a three-day Congres d'information in late April, where they declared the incompatibility of communism and the principles of Sun Yatsen.[60]

The momentum of the ECCO response within the ECCO-EGMD United Front was disrupted by increasing disunity with the left EGMD. It appears that another round of expulsions took place during May, which resulted in the formation of a separate leftist faction of the EGMD, which made its headquarters at 41 rue des Ecoles.[61] In their history of the EGMD, the right faction stigmatized this group as "opportunists," who "had hopes of becoming officials and accruing wealth."[62] The ECCO faction of the EGMD lost almost two-thirds of its members to this new group, which was headed initially by Yi Guangyi (Yei Kwang Yee), a law student from Fujian.[63] In the 30 June 1927 "Manifeste du Congres de la Confédération du Kuomintang en Europe," Yi Guangyi officially declared the existence of their group as of 22 May 1927. A congress had been held in mid-June, attended by thirty-eight members. Yi made the rather dubious claim of unanimous approval from the GMD Executive Committee in Nanjing. Most of the tract was anti-imperialist and anti-Communist.[64]

59. Ibid., report of 28 April 1927; report entitled "Meeting organise par la délégation en Europe du parti kuo-min-tang chinois sur la nouvelle attitude du General Chang-kai-shek," 28 April 1927, AN, F7 13738.

60. "Note sur la propagande révolutionnaire intéressant les pays d'outre-mer," 31 May 1927, 5–6, AOM, SLOTFOM III, 67.

61. The reason for this split is not very clear, but it might have been based on real ideological differences that arose before the April coup. For example, a Sûreté note from Lyons in 1928 mentioned that Liu Hou had published Guomin (The People) for two issues in March 1926 because of Communist interference (Report from the Sûreté Générale à M. le Ministre du Colonies, 5 March 1928, AOM, SLOTFOM VIII, 6). The pre-August break with the ECCO also may have influenced the Hankou left-GMD government actions against the CCP. Was Wang Jingwei, for example, influenced by events within the ECCO-EGMD United Front? Did he correspond with Liu Hou, Peng Xiang, and others?

62. "Zhongguo guomindang zhu Fa zongzhibu xiang di Sanci quanguo daibiao dahui baogao Ouzhou dangwu," 2.

63. See report by the Sûreté Générale, "A/S de Yei-Kwang-Yee," 24 October 1927, AAE, série E, Chine, vol. 492. Also see the French assessment of the impact of this third group on the colonial cause in "Note sur la propagande révolutionnaire intéressant les pays d'outre-mer," 31 August 1927, 4–7, AOM, SLOTFOM III, 67.

64. "Manifeste du Congres de la Confédération du Kuomintang en Europe," 30 June 1927, AOM, SLOTFOM VIII, 6. Earlier in the year Yi had been quoted in the Communist paper L'humanité as bravely admonishing French Socialists at a meeting to stop the talk and start acting on their sympathies with the Chinese revolution ("Yei Kwang Yee délégué du Kuomintang dénoncé le verbalisme des leaders S.F.I.O.," 4 March 1927).

The remaining, Communist, section of the EGMD, headquartered at 330 rue St. Jacques and led by Liu Puqing and Xia Ting, continued with their own activities, holding an Eighth Congress in mid-July.[65] They engaged in public polemics over the April coup. On 1 June 1927 at the Amphitheatre Descartes of the Sorbonne, *La tribune internationale* held a forum on the evolution of modern China, where a spirited debate took place between the varying EGMD factions. The current split among the revolutionaries was first highlighted by the right-faction organizer, Song Guoshu (Song Kuo Tchou/ Son-Kono-Chou, depending on the French agent), who claimed that the Communists had betrayed the revolution, were tools of the Soviets, and were not believers in the Three Principles of Sun Yatsen. "There is no pretense," Song expostulated, "neither left, neither center, nor right of the Guomindang. In this party, there exist two elements, the Communists and, on the other side, the true members of the Guomindang." From the 330 rue St. Jacques contingent a speech was delivered by Wang Shenghuo(?) (Wang Tri Cheng/Wang Tsi Chin), who countered that Sun Yatsen wanted to redress the workers' plight and that the Hankou government leaders were not Communists. The meeting ended in some disruption as this assertion was challenged. However, the fascinating point is that although there were acrimonious debates and shouting matches, the Chinese community in France was not engulfed in widespread violence. The Chinese in France were well aware that the French government would not tolerate violent or illegal activities. The deportations in 1925 had adequately testified to this limitation on violent activity.

Thus, by mid-1927 the promise of the Northern Expedition had given way to the schisms brought on by the April Twelfth Coup, dividing the ECCO-EGMD United Front into three separate factions: the "extremists" (Communists) at 330 rue St. Jacques, the "rightists" at 3 rue Thouin, and the "leftists" at 41 rue des Ecoles.

THE ECCO-EGMD UNITED FRONT: THREE-WAY SPLIT

The April Twelfth Coup violently shattered the United Front in China and split the ECCO-EGMD United Front into three factions. Although this significantly weakened the revolutionary movement, the factions formed in 1927 survived, undergoing some changes, several years after the coup. The ECCO was the first to form a United Front and the last to dissolve it.

---

65. Le Ministre de l'Intérieur à M. le Ministre des Colonies, "Congres organisé à Paris par la fraction [sic] extrémiste du Kuomintang," no. 5099, AOM, SLOTFOM V, 43.

The Communist "Extremist" Faction: 330 Rue St. Jacques

The ECCO-EGMD United Front had survived the purge of the rightist faction, as witnessed by the flourishing publicity and mass meetings throughout 1926 and early 1927. However, the April Twelfth Coup came as the first in a series of disabling blows. Two other calamities that struck the Communists were the mass expulsions and defections of the left EGMD members and the deportation of Xia Ting, the Communists' most eminent leader.

Only thirty members gave their allegiance to the faction at 330 rue St. Jacques, whereas the leftist EGMD group at 41 rue des Ecoles had more than eighty members.[66] Yi Guangyi, who was now an enemy, had been a talented public speaker for the United Front, and Liu Hou and Peng Xiang had influential connections with the French intellectual world, an important element in the radical milieu of France. Their departure constituted a serious loss for the Communists.

A leadership vacuum resulted when Xia Ting (b. 1903) was deported in September 1927. Xia Ting was a prominent orator in both the Chinese and French communities. Xia had been followed for some time by the French police, who wrote his name as "Sia Ting" in their reports. A February 1927 report mentioned that he had attended the College Jehan Ange in 1925 and was at the Ecole libre des sciences politiques during 1926–27. The police were particularly alarmed at the impassioned rhetoric he used at a meeting organized by the Comité de défense des victimes du fascisme et de la terreur blanche. Giving a GMD salute, Xia Ting went on to speak of the Chinese revolution as part of a worldwide movement and urged others to join him.[67] A later French observer noted the importance of Xia Ting to the "extremist" EGMD:

> The extremist faction is led by a leader of the name *Sia-Ting*, born 17 January 1903 in Anking (China), a student who has had relations with leaders of the French Communist Party and has also published articles in the newspaper *L'humanité* which leave no doubt as to the nature of his opinions. . . . Because of this attitude *Sia-Ting* was expelled by arrest on 9 September 1927. This was certainly reported on 3 January 1928, but SIA-TING left his lodgings at 13 rue Rollin destined for Bel-

66. "Zhongguo guomindang zhu Fa zongzhibu xiang di Sanci quanguo daibiao dahui baogao Ouzhou dangwu," 2. The list of names for both factions roughly corresponds to those in the French police and Sûreté reports.

67. Note A. V. of 1 February 1927, AAE, série E, Chine, vol. 492, 164. Xia Ting also attended an international congress against fascism during March 1927 in Amsterdam.

gium. His current residence is not known. . . . After his departure, the extremist faction was disorganized and dissolved.[68]

The members of the 330 rue St. Jacques faction who were attending the SFI in Lyons were also experiencing difficulties. In the fall of 1927 four students were expelled from the institute because of the influence of Zou Lu, an original member of the Western Hills faction, who as president of the University of Canton controlled the funding from Canton to help support Chinese students at the institute. The expelled students—Long Zhanxing ("Johnson" Long), Xie Qing (Sha Ching), Peng Shiqin (Peng Shih-chin), and Yan Jijin (Yen Chi-chin)—had been important in the reorganization at 330 rue St. Jacques. The letter from Canton (1 July 1927) demanding the expulsion of these students because they were Communists and the subsequent petition by the students for continuing their studies may be found in the dossier of "Johnson" Long. Although he had apparently experienced some trouble while at the Lycée du Parc for throwing a bottle at his neighbor, the report on Long for 1926–27 was that he was an "excellent student" and, with "much application, beginning to write well in French."[69] However, the SFI was threatened from Canton with "suppression of subventions" and denied the petition; the four students were expelled on 1 September 1927.

According to both a French report and the generally accurate rightist EGMD history, the Communists closed down the 330 rue St. Jacques headquarters at the end of 1927 and most of them joined the PCF. A remnant of four or five members, including the expelled Long Zhanxing and Yan Jijin, kept the Communist branch of the EGMD alive at 26 rue des Carmes and continued to publish the newspaper *Guomin*.[70]

There is some intriguing evidence that the Communist movement within the GMD in Europe was not totally moribund by 1928. An edition of *Guomin* with the 330 rue St. Jacques address was printed as late as September 1930. Although the rhetoric is tepid in comparison with previous Communist hyperbole, there is a definite accusation that Jiang Jieshi had created a dictatorship, although the accusation was balanced by the use of his cour-

---

68. Note MP, 7 September 1928, AAE, série E, Chine, vol. 492, 312.
69. Dossier Long, Johnson, no. 180, AAUFC.
70. Note MP, V, September 1928, 312–13; "Zhongguo guomindang zhu Fa zongzhibu xiang di Sanci quanguo daibiao dahui baogao Ouzhou dangwu," 2. This meshes with the assertion that most of the French ECCO members joined the PCF, Chinese Language Section. However, it should not obscure the fact that the ECCO also continued to publish ECCO propaganda such as *Chiguang*.

tesy name, Jiang Zhongzheng, and the testament of Sun Yatsen on the cover.[71]

Suffering expulsions and the loss of political power, it was a tribute to the previous strength of the ECCO-dominated ECCO-EGMD United Front that the Communist faction was muted, not mutilated, by the violence in China during 1927.

The Rightist Faction: 3 Rue Thouin

With the continued publication of their newspaper *Sanmin* and its French version, *Bulletin du Kuomintang en Europe*, the rightist faction of the EGMD was making every effort in the summer of 1927 to become the exclusive representative of the EGMD. Whether through their personal connections or through their long-standing anti-Communist stance, the 3 rue Thouin group was the one officially entrusted by the Nanjing GMD Central Committee to undertake the task of reorganization.

The stated tasks of the 3 rue Thouin group were the defense of the Three Principles of Sun Yatsen and the eradication of Communists, which were seen as interlocked goals:

> The purging of our party is dictated by our preservation instinct and also by our national conscience. . . . The path of our country lies in our party because of the reason for the founding of the Guomindang, the Three Principles of Dr. Sun Yatsen, and it is the sole party in which our people can place their hopes of salvation. . . . Currently our party is recovering its full independence; we must redouble our efforts to defend against all exterior aggression and all interior division. . . . Unissons-nous, camarades![72]

The 3 rue Thouin faction adopted the rationales of the Nanjing government for expelling the Communists, printing the declarations of Nanjing word for word in their *Bulletin*. As part of this strategy they countered accusations about the April coup massacres in a declaration of their own that denounced the Canton Uprising. They claimed the Communists killed

71. This issue of *Guomin* can be found in AOM, SLOTFOM V, 43. Neither the aliases of the authors nor the addresses of the guarantors of the newspaper match those of the leftist EGMD *Guomin* published a year earlier. However, this does not preclude it from being a leftist publication rather than Communist, as factions within the EGMD abounded and the Communists moved away from the 330 rue St. Jacques address. Lastly, the handwriting (all of these papers were handwritten) is very similar to that in the leftist EGMD *Guomin* published in 1929.

72. *Bulletin du Kuomintang en Europe* 2 (September 1927): 2.

thousands of workers, peasants, students, and businessmen, and cost the city one hundred thousand dollars in damages. Emulating the tactical strategy of the Nanjing GMD, the declaration ended:

A bas les communistes chinois—à la solde des Soviets—
A bas l'Impérialisme rouge.
A bas les Impérialismes.
Vive la Révolution Chinoise.[73]

The impression given in the 3 rue Thouin report of 1929 that real opposition did not exist to their control of the EGMD was not entirely consistent with the situation described in their own paper, *Sanmin*, which, for example, in mid-1929 contained an article criticizing Wang Jingwei as an opportunist and another censuring the ubiquitous Johnson Long (Long Zhanxing).[74]

Because of *Sanmin*'s anti-imperialist stance and sympathy for colonized peoples, in 1925 the French government banned it from being distributed in Indochina.[75] However, the articles contained little controversial material other than denunciations of opponents and rather stilted anti-imperialist statements. This may have been due to two reasons. First, the leaders of this EGMD faction were secure in their linkages with the Nanjing government. They were not fighting as those "out of power," because their "revolution" had already obtained control. Second, several leaders were seriously pursuing their education. For example, two members of the Lyons contingent on the Executive Committee, Yang Qian (Yang Chen) and Zhang Wenjia (Cheung Wun Kap), left the institute in February 1927 to undertake more specialized studies, Yang in aviation and Zhang in law.[76] One can assume that the relatively noninflammatory tone of the *Sanmin* articles was a function both of the leaders' energies being directed toward their studies and their fear of jeopardizing their careers.

Because the members of the 3 rue Thouin group were the staunchest anti-Communists, the April coup strengthened their position. Their mem-

73. "Déclaration de la Colonie chinoise en France," 26 December 1927, 3 rue Thouin, Paris, AOM, SLOTFOM V, 43.
74. *Sanmin*, 9 June 1929.
75. Report from Arnoux, file 2526, 19 November 1929, AOM, SLOTFOM V, 43.
76. Dossiers of Yang Chen, no. 44, and Cheung Wun Kap, no. 35, AAUFC; see report of Sûreté Générale à M. Du Courdret, ministre du Colonies, March 1928, AOM, SLOTFOM V, 43.

bership grew throughout Europe, and they were able to sustain their organization beyond the collapse of the United Front.

The Leftist Faction: 41 Rue des Ecoles

After the April Twelfth Coup, the leftist faction of the EGMD was strong in both numbers and talent. Their allegiances were more fluid, and when the initial group underwent a further split in 1928, the leftists were labeled opportunists by their various opponents. However, similar to the Communists, they weathered the political turnabouts after the coup better than their leftist compatriots back in China.

Given the intense political rivalry, the leftist-faction (41 rue des Ecoles) publication *Guomin* was certainly biased, especially against the Western Hills faction and the Communists. Yet the articles have a high level of sophistication. For example, writing in November 1927 on the tenth anniversary of the Russian Revolution, Zhang Junqi discusses some of the achievements of the Soviet Union such as peasant mobilization and the unification of minorities. The revolution was a political success in Russia, but Zhang claimed that the economic policies were only half successful because noncapitalist agriculture could not work. The area of total failure was the international arena, where the Soviets had no success in exporting their revolution.[77] Although containing some degree of rhetorical verbiage, the article also contains a fair amount of objective analysis. Chen Shunong's article in the same issue denounced the Western Hills faction of the GMD. His article, although saturated with disdain, was systematic and logical in its discussion.[78]

An important question concerning the leftist faction is the degree of influence exerted by Wang Jingwei. Wang Jingwei, who as leader of the left GMD faction had temporarily supported the Communists after the April Twelfth Coup, broke with them in August 1927. His uneasy alliance with Jiang Jieshi was eased by his removal to France. Because he symbolized the left faction of the GMD, it is no surprise that Wang had followers in Europe. In July 1928, a self-defense by Wang Jingwei against the aspersions cast on him by Wu Zhihui was published by the Lyons contingent in the *Lü Ou*

77. Zhang Junqi, "Su E Shiyue geming de shizhou jinian" [A commemoration of the tenth anniversary of the Soviet October Revolution], *Guomin* 5 (15 November 1927): 7–9.

78. Chen Shunong, "Dadao fan geming de Xishanpai seban de tebie weiyuanhui" [Overturn the antirevolutionary Western Hills faction's control of the special committee], *Guomin* 5 (15 November 1927): 1–6. A triple issue of *Guomin* published in June 1929 (nos. 4, 5, 6) also exemplified this "objective" and in-depth type of analysis, with a minimal emphasis on diatribe.

tongxin (*Traveling to Europe Correspondence*). In his article "A Fundamental Concept," Wang Jingwei answers Wu's charges and gives his version of the real meaning of the ideology of Sun Yatsen. Wang contended that Sun Yatsen invited the Communists into the Party and that Wu was hypocritical because he did not repudiate them at the time. Perhaps most important, in a passage that raises questions about his own development and later career, Wang Jingwei argues for a greater clarity of ideas in the GMD, claiming that Party discipline without ideology becomes warlordism.[79]

The leftist EGMD underwent a schism in mid-1928, with a division into cliques around two EGMD Party officers, Chen Shunong and Zhang Nan. Chen Shunong (Chen Shu Nun) was enrolled in the SFI at Lyons, but from 1927–29 he was in Paris, studying at the Institute of Psychology at the Sorbonne. Chen had been in a brawl with another fellow EGMD executive officer and Lyons colleague, Peng Xiang (Pon Sian), in June 1927. According to the newspaper *Le petit Parisien*, a political argument led to a fistfight in a Chinese restaurant in the Latin Quarter. The fight resulted in multiple contusions for Peng and a hospital stay with a broken arm for Chen.[80] The incident was reported to China and to the French government.[81] Chen was eventually expelled from the SFI for his failure to go to classes or work on his thesis during 1928–29. It is worth noting that the Chinese secretary of the institute, Liu Hou, was a close friend of Peng Xiang. Peng had joined the Zhang Nan faction in 1928.[82] The Zhang Nan faction, however, also met with some disgrace. According to the 1929 rightist EGMD history, Zhang Nan was arrested by the French police for selling opium, thus giving a black eye to the reputation of the Party in France.[83]

The leftist EGMD faction played an important role in the radical politics within the Chinese community after the dissolution of the ECCO-EGMD

79. Wang Jingwei, "Yige genben guannian" [A fundamental concept], *Lü Ou tongxin* 5 (29 July 1928): 1–9.

80. "La guerre de Chine à Paris," *Le petit Parisien*, 20 June 1927.

81. Dossier of Chen Shunong [Chen Shu Nun], no. 187, AAUFC. See "Secret Report," 28 June 1927, AN, F7 13438.

82. Dossier of Chen Shunong [Chen Shu Nun], no. 187, AAUFC. According to letters written in 1929 that exist in Chen's dossier in Lyons, he claimed that he attended his classes; however, his French professor in Paris repudiated these claims. Letters in Peng Xiang's dossier show quite a different attitude on the part of the French. Peng had returned to China with his wife, but when he wanted to come back and work on his thesis, he received an enthusiastic recommendation letter from Marcel Granet, who cited Peng's contributions to the Chinese community in France (Peng had been an important officer of the SFEA). Once more, this underlines the impact of the relationship between Chinese youth and French intellectuals.

83. "Zhongguo guomindang zhu Fa zongzhibu xiang di Sanci quanguo daibiao dahui baogao Ouzhou dangwu," 2.

United Front. Whereas the ECCO-dominated EGMD (330 rue St. Jacques) were relatively inactive and for the most part merged with the PCF, and the rightist EGMD faction (3 rue Thouin) adopted a complacent stance, the leftist EGMD bequeathed a legacy of sophisticated ideological debate and colorful political antics.

THE STRONG CURRENT

In an atmosphere of intense activism, the paths of political factions within the Chinese community in France converged and parted at various points. This complexity explains in part the development of strong cohorts of leaders not only within the ECCO but also within the CYP and the EGMD. The relative political sophistication that manifested itself in the shifting currents of Chinese political activism was exemplified by the ability of the CYP to actually injure the ECCO; the ability of the ECCO to isolate the right EGMD, and the subsequent creation of the 3 rue Thouin faction as a gesture of independence; and the numerical and ideological force of the left EGMD.

From 1922 until 1927, the ECCO appeared to play a dominant, but by no means exclusive, leadership role in the Chinese activist community. They were able to create a United Front with the EGMD before one was formed by the CCP and actually helped to found the EGMD. They were able to isolate the right faction of the EGMD and elect their own people to high positions. They involved the foreign community and developed effective linkages with the PCF, as demonstrated by the mass meetings in early 1927 in support of the Northern Expedition. Most important, the break with the EGMD did not result in the violent measures that the collapse of the CCP-GMD United Front produced. Furthermore, their previous dominance contributed to the persistence of EGMD activity. Although it appears that by 1928 the ECCO-EGMD United Front was finished, it is possible that several ECCO-EGMD participants were active into the thirties.

The intensity of the political atmosphere in the European environment might also account in part for the relative vitality of the left EGMD within the ECCO-EGMD United Front. The left EGMD was able to cooperate for several years with the ECCO, while maintaining objectivity about the concept of revolution and the needs of China. After the break with the ECCO, which took place *before* that in Wuhan, the left faction emerged as the strongest remaining EGMD faction numerically and ideologically, a phenomenon that did not transpire in China, due to the political supremacy of Jiang Jieshi.[84]

84. Jiang Jieshi's leadership shows very strongly the role of violence in revolutionary ideology. In the short term at least, Jiang's military training and perspective served him

In contrast, although the right GMD faction set up a parallel structure in 1925, their impact within the European Chinese community was definitely less forceful than that of the Western Hills faction in China.

Sophisticated, able leadership and a series of national and international events helped to shape the intensely strong current of political activity within the Chinese community in Europe. Strong leaders within the ECCO such as Zhao Shiyan, Zhou Enlai, Ren Zhuoxuan, Liao Huanxing, and Xia Ting were genuinely able to inspire people, as was Zeng Qi in the CYP and Wang Jingqi in the left EGMD. Chinese political activism was also shaped by the European milieu. The political events transpiring in Europe involved participation: local elections were analyzed, factory strikes were supported, and demonstrations were attended. In addition, the perception of political freedom and the more international perspective fostered by living in Europe influenced the Chinese in Europe. The concept of revolution underwent constant scrutiny by members of all parties, particularly the ECCO between 1922 and 1925 and the left EGMD after 1927. The Chinese activist community had a more "national," less parochial focus on events occurring in China. Thus, they focused their activities on occurrences such as the May Thirtieth Incident but not on localized power plays in China. Furthermore, events in China that affected Europe, such as the Lincheng Incident and the proposed nationalization of Chinese railroads, created special roles for activists on the scene and allowed them to develop connections with Westerners. This process culminated in a tremendous outpouring of French sympathy during the Northern Expedition. It can be contended that the momentum and success of the anti-imperialist movement from 1926 until the April Twelfth Coup helped to maintain the unity of the ECCO-EGMD United Front.

The circulation of leaders, through expulsions and voluntary repatriations, and the loss of ideological vigor within the rhetorical phraseology of an anti-imperialist campaign were underlying weaknesses within the ECCO-EGMD United Front and were revealed by the April coup. There was no substitute for solid leadership or genuine dialogue on revolutionary ideology. Johnson Long could not take the place of a Zhao Shiyan or a Zhou Enlai. The ECCO, with new headquarters in Germany, survived into the late twenties, but in an attenuated form.

The group realignments, the maturation of an astute leadership, the adoption of varying ideological perspectives, and fast-paced events in a foreign country created a dramatic and constant tempo of change within the shifting currents of Chinese politics in Europe.

---

better in assessing the Chinese situation. However, scholars can ill afford to overlook the tacit and expressed radical ideology reflected in his leadership strategies.

CONCLUSION:
THE FOUND GENERATION

One day, when the weather had turned cloudy, Li Weinong whispered to me, "Tomorrow, Sunday afternoon, there will be people sent to speak to you in the park." I agreed. Near the factory there was a small park. I went there and saw Li Weinong, Han Qi, and Qin Shilun. We made arrangements to chat, just Qin Shilun and me. . . . We sat down in the park and Qin Shilun spoke quite a bit. In essence, he said that now was the moment to rise up, to organize a Communist Youth Party, and [I] had been invited to enter the organization. . . . I considered it for a good while before agreeing to participate. . . . It was just like this that the direction of my entire life was decided.
              —Zheng Chaolin, "Remembering Yin Kuan"

The Found Generation, those born between 1895 and 1905, were, in general, an impetuous group. Their rashness, however, was not unprovoked, and the exacerbated generational crisis was fueled by several series of events. The humiliation of the defeat by Japan in the Sino-Japanese War in 1895 colored their earliest childhood memories. The hurried Qing reforms and abolition of the civil service examinations in 1905 disrupted their educational training in Confucian classics. They were the last to memorize the Chinese classics, *as if it counted for a career,* and the first to be educated in the new Western learning, *as if it counted for a career.* Fathers and elder brothers could no longer lead younger sons. In common with Western industrialized nations, the greater ease of travel, the development of mass communications, and other manifestations of modernization also were to divide the Found Generation from their elders. It was no coincidence that these youthful adherents of the New Culture Movement rejected an older generation who could not clearly delineate the future of their own children, much less a path to save the nation. The Found Generation were infused with a sense of having a unique mission: "Only we youth have the purity to save the nation," as Wang Guangqi passionately proclaimed in the middle of the Indian Ocean, "Only we youth. . . . striving forth, striving forth!"

   This study has looked at a portion of the Found Generation, those who went to France under the auspices of the Work-Study Movement. I have argued that these youth overcame organizational and regional differences and were key players in the formation of Chinese political parties in a foreign arena. They graduated from their youth revolt to an adult commitment to ideology and revolution. These visions of ideology and revolution differed from group to group. Some had Communist convictions, others a radical right, anti-Communist stance, and others became Social Democrats or Anarchists. This book has focused on the formation and activities of the European Branches of the Chinese Communist Party and Chinese Communist Youth Corps, the ECCO.

The political leaders that emerged during this period were influenced and motivated by experiences unique to this generation. The nature of their education was one factor. These leaders had all made the transition to studying Western learning for both career and patriotic purposes. The substance of their learning and their differing educational objectives were barriers between the youth and their elders. The level of education pursued or obtained also played a role in the shaping of political sensibility. The Work-Study Movement to France generally selected for those Chinese who had a secondary education. Not surprisingly, those who were able to continue with higher education in France had the more limited political engagement. Perhaps it can be suggested that the revolutionary role was difficult to adopt when higher education was pursued.

The Found Generation leaders came from an environment in which personal values were reflected in organizational affiliation. The leaders were founders or members of youth organizations that provided a forum to explore New Culture values, experiment with new social roles, and mobilize for action. These organizations sponsored a whole series of activities, ranging from speaking teams during the May Fourth Movement to the Work-Study Mutual-Aid Corps. The Work-Study Movement emerged within this New Culture current. The activities of these youth organizations were not just testing grounds for values but also resulted in the formation of long-lasting personal relationships, an important dimension of Chinese political behavior. These relationships were often more important than organizational membership or ideological purity. It also should be emphasized that many of the worker-students in France did not participate in political parties but applied themselves to their ideals of diligent work and frugal study. There were also those who obtained higher educations and returned home to China in triumph. However, the situational determinants in China did not allow for this slower type of social change to prevail and were more responsive to the combination of organization and ideology of the committed revolutionary leaders.

Finally, the element of travel itself had a major effect on the development of China's future leaders. Although feelings of displacement were engendered by traveling to a new world, travel during this period was an important politicizer. New sights and new experiences, particularly for those who traveled to Europe, gave rise to new abilities and new knowledge. In addition, travel reinforced their sense of self-sufficiency and contributed to analytical detachment.

An analysis of the social processes and experiences that shaped the leaders of Chinese organizational activity in Europe directs us to the more general question of the overall, long-term significance of the ECCO. We will look at two areas here. First, what were the significant differences in the developmental paths of the ECCO and the CCP? How did the process of politicization differ in Europe and in China? Second, what impact did the ECCO have on Chinese twentieth-century political history?

The founders of the ECCO shared the same New Culture values and youth group affiliations and had the same goals of national salvation that motivated their CCP compatriots. Yet they were distinguished from the CCP by their experiences. The successes and failures of the Work-Study Movement and the three struggles of 1921 were radicalizing influences experienced directly by the Chinese participants in Europe. As Sheng Cheng said of the unsuccessful bid for education during the Lyons Incident, "We did not get the money, so we became Communists."[1]

The Chinese residing in Europe were also exposed to the Western political scene, unlike their compatriots in China, who were caught up within Chinese internal concerns. The propaganda-agitation skills of the ECCO were sharpened by their participation, for example, in Western factory strikes. They communicated with and sometimes joined the European Communist parties. They learned how to gain the support of Westerners for their political agendas; one example is their success in obtaining European support for the Chinese Northern Expedition in 1926–27.

In a related theme, the process of radicalization for the Chinese in Europe was different because the organizational tasks differed from those of the CCP. In addition to the Work-Study Movement participants, who had a labor orientation, the prime recruits for the ECCO were Chinese laborers, most of whom had worked for the Allies during the First World War. Factory conditions were not only better than in China, but agitation opportunities were far less restrictive. Thus, in several ways the ECCO had an increased understanding of the *proletariat* in the Western meaning. In addition, the ECCO had a less parochial, broader view of the Chinese scene, and this was reflected in their activities. Organizational imperatives included the mass national events in China, such as the May Thirtieth Incident, but did not, for example, include agitating for the autonomy of Hunan or Sichuan. Moreover, although engaged in the same political

1. Sheng Cheng interview, 12 October 1985 (Beijing).

tasks, the ECCO political reality differed from that of the CCP and had consequences for the home organization, as well as for the branch. ECCO campaigns, such as the successful mass meetings against imperialism at the beginning of 1927, and in particular the control by the ECCO of the ECCO-EGMD United Front perhaps gave these ECCO leaders a false sense of security upon their return to China. This may explain the seeming insensibility to danger exhibited by ECCO returnees in the violence of 1927. Confident that they could pit themselves successfully against the GMD they did not fully comprehend the violent potential of their home environment, and thus were decimated. Whether positive or negative, the political lessons learned in Europe had a significant impact on leadership behavior during early CCP development, an influence that has continued throughout the decades.

Explicit in the Work-Study scheme had been the goal of national salvation through adopting Western technology. However, once converted to Marxism-Leninism, the ECCO members gave precedence to the political solution over the technological solution. Those who formed the CCP did not have the understanding of Western technology that the ECCO members had obtained. Perhaps rejection of the Capitalist system entailed a more significant rejection of the technological component for the ECCO participants. With the ECCO returnees such as Deng Xiaoping, Nie Rongzhen, and Li Fuchun playing a pivotal role in the post-1949 modernization of China, this ambivalent view of technology as panacea may be an important explanation for the several instances in which political campaigns took precedence over technological programs. Nie Rongzhen, the important chairman of the Science and Technological Commission, who was responsible for overseeing the atomic program in post-1949 China, had gone to Europe with the "idea of using industrialization to save the country." Yet the disillusionment with the Work-Study Movement and the ideological stimulus he received prompted him to give up his university studies in the pursuit of revolution. As he claimed, "How could [China] industrialize while control was in the hands of imperialists?"[2] Politics took precedence over technology, even in the advanced new world of the West.

Finally, in the process of ideological conversion, just as technological progress became subservient to the class struggle, so Confucian morality became subsumed under Communist morality. Unlike their Western contemporaries, the Chinese in Europe had tightly knit youth organizations to cohere and constrain them in their political quests and behavior. Moreover, unlike their Chinese CCP contemporaries, they were exposed to a broader Marxist theoretical base. Therefore, the rigid Leninist Party structure was

2. Nie Rongzhen, *Nie Rongzhen huiyilu,* 1:9, 26.

not totally unfamiliar and could be viewed with appreciation. Because of the lack of direct Comintern involvement and the more sophisticated ideological training that they received, ECCO members readily absorbed Communist organizational principles such as strict discipline within the Party.[3] The organizational imperative became more important than the Confucian strategy of personal rectification.[4]

The second area of ECCO significance is the ECCO impact on modern Chinese political history. Although the existence of an ECCO cohort within the CCP is difficult to verify from direct evidence, there are suggestive avenues to explore in assessing the impact of the ECCO on the development of the CCP, its revolutionary strategy, and post-1949 political and economic developments. Relationships, ideology, and political behavior were all influenced by life experiences, such as the Long March or the civil war, and it also appears that the ECCO experience had a definite long-term, qualitative impact on the Chinese revolutionary process. For instance, whereas most of the CCP founders had an ephemeral commitment to the CCP, the ECCO members remained CCP members. Far fewer quit or were purged than other Party founders. This area of political loyalty needs more research and analysis. What combination of chance, early training, and later personal encounters led to this kind of commitment? An assessment of ECCO configurations and personal linkages within Chinese politics would be a valuable contribution to historical research. For example, the relationships among Zhou Enlai, Deng Xiaoping, Li Fuchun, and Nie Rongzhen as high Party officials after 1949 reflect earlier leadership linkages within the ECCO and the ECCO-EGMD United Front.

A related area of ECCO long-term significance can be seen in how ECCO members provided sophisticated leadership at both central and regional lev-

---

3. Ironically, if one compares Jiang Jieshi of the GMD and Zeng Qi of the CYP as leaders within the radical right, one can also conclude that from the *ideological* perspective, Zeng had the better understanding of radical right philosophy and organizational principles. Zeng, however, did not have the leadership capabilities of Jiang.

4. As Hue-Tam Ho Tai concludes in her cogent discussion of the Vietnamese radicalization process and the Confucian cultural emphasis on self-rectification: "The introduction of Marxist analytical categories constituted an implicit repudiation of the centrality of the individual, as both target and source of change, which had fed the earlier drive for cultural reform. The idea that class struggle rather than cultural adaptation or personal heroism was the motive force of progress meant that the reformist impulse could be directed outward, at society, the economy, or the political system, instead of inward, at culture, the family, or the self. The place of the individual in society and of his role in history was thus reconceptualized" (*Radicalism and the Origins of the Vietnamese Revolution* [Cambridge: Harvard University Press, 1992], 260). Conversely, it was perhaps the imagery and ethos of the Chinese hero that helped secure the leadership of Mao Zedong, as opposed to the more Westernized ECCO leaders, who had difficulties in breaking away from the organizational imperative and cultivating personality cults.

els during every phase of Chinese revolutionary and post-1949 history. During the twenties, three CCP theoretical journals were edited by ECCO returnees (Cai Hesen, Zhao Shiyan, and Zheng Chaolin). The part that ECCO returnees such as Li Weihan, Chen Yannian, and Mu Qing played in the development of the regional CCP organizations in Hunan, Guangdong/Guangxi, and Sichuan was pivotal. The formation of the CCP Women's Bureau by another European returnee, Xiang Jingyu, was a keystone in obtaining the support of Chinese feminists for the CCP. Li Lisan, Cai Hesen, Zhao Shiyan, Zhou Enlai, Wang Ruofei, and other ECCO returnees were essential agitators in the development of mass movements. The ECCO provided superior military leaders: Zhu De, Chen Yi, Liu Bojian, and Nie Rongzhen, among others. After the formation of the People's Republic of China in 1949, the scope of ECCO leadership can be ascertained by mentioning just a few names: Zhou Enlai, Chen Yi, Li Fuchun, Deng Xiaoping, Nie Rongzhen, and Zhu De.

Although tracing ECCO-CCP leadership networks and actual historical roles would be illuminating, another way to understand the ECCO's impact on Chinese modern history is to characterize the ECCO leadership style. Can understanding the leadership ethos that emerged from the ECCO environment explain later political behavior? As already stated, disillusionment with the Work-Study Movement, the breaking away from older leaders, and the ideological and political-agitation training of this group of leaders had real consequences for Chinese history. But beyond this, we must ask, what elements endured in the political leadership styles of these important Chinese leaders? Drawing together several themes, I propose three areas that typify the ECCO leadership ethos and that merit further attention as an important template of leadership for the CCP in general: the primacy of politics over technological solutions; the Leninist concepts of the Party as vanguard and Party discipline; and long-lasting generational identification.

In terms of post-1949 modernization programs, to understand CCP leadership attitudes toward projects such as the Great Leap Forward, scholars might want to contrast leaders such as Nie Rongzhen and Li Fuchun with Mao Zedong concerning the bases of their ideological commitment and views on technology. Were Nie Rongzhen and Li Fuchun acquiescing in unreasonable project goals only from personal expedience or from their own opinions on the relationship between modernization through technology and the primacy of politics? China scholars may want to reevaluate terms such as "pragmatists" and "ideologues" in ways more congruent with the ideological realities of Chinese twentieth-century politics.

It is notable that over forty ECCO leaders returned through the Soviet Union on their way home to China. More than a dozen of these ECCO members were in Moscow before the death of Lenin in 1924. The commitment to the Party and the sense of discipline that infused the political behavior of ECCO leaders have had important ramifications for Chinese political structure, in particular, the commitment to a single-party system after 1949. For leaders such as Deng Xiaoping who have maintained the rule of the CCP as strongly as Mao Zedong, it is not inconceivable that the Leninist conception of the Party as vanguard has been a lifelong value. Furthermore, this Leninist ideological legacy may help explain the behavior of second-generation political actors such as Li Peng, who upheld the single-party rule of the CCP during the democracy demonstrations in 1989. Is it coincidental that Zhao Shiyan was Li Peng's uncle and that his own father had died young supporting the Communist Revolution?

Finally, a leadership ethos that includes the primacy of politics over technology and stress on Party solidarity has been melded with a strong generational identification. This Found Generation of leaders have held long to the reins of power. They have been reluctant to give way to the "untrustworthy" younger generations, who would tamper with their legacy of revolution. There is a sense of generational uniqueness that stems from having lived in a world where Confucianism was preeminent. There is a sense of generational uniqueness in having created one of the most distinguished contributions to twentieth-century China, the dynamic New Culture Movement, from which modern politics and culture emerged. Last, there is a sense of generational uniqueness that comes from shared sacrifice and suffering. Having believed in the cause of national salvation and revolution, it has been difficult for this generation to see beyond such concepts as political struggle and Party discipline. Perhaps concern for the abandonment of this legacy of revolutionary ethos helps explain why a "hardliner" such as Li Peng has prevailed over a "progressive" politician such as Zhao Ziyang, as survivors of the Found Generation enter their late eighties and early nineties. One might speculate that the moral and political consequences of their actions have been obscured from them by their historical experiences with generational conflict. The sense of betrayal that this generation felt from their older mentors made an indelible impression that has added a rigidity to their sense of generational uniqueness that might otherwise not have existed.

Thus, significantly, the Found Generation were the last to feel the weight of Confucian living in the sense of personal destiny. They had been imbued with the concept of the role of the intellectual, not as a political leader, but as a moral leader. As part of the Found Generation, those who adopted communism retained this moral basis for action but overlaid it with Marxist

BIOGRAPHIES

Borodin, Mikhail
1884–1951.

Born in the Soviet Union, Borodin was one of the most effective foreign agents operating outside the new Soviet regime. Borodin successfully nurtured a Communist movement in Mexico and then spent the early twenties fomenting activities in Europe and Great Britain. Borodin was instrumental in overseeing the United Front progress. He was downgraded but not purged upon his return to the Soviet Union in 1927. However, in 1949 he was arrested while editing the *Moscow Daily News* and sent to a concentration camp. Borodin is perhaps the best known of the Soviet agents in China.

Cai Chang 蔡暢
b. 1900, Xiangxiang, Hunan. Other name: Cai Jianxi (orig.). Positions: CCP Central Committee; Chairperson, National Women's Federation of China.

Cai Chang was a participant in the Work-Study Movement, a New Citizens' Study Society member, and an early supporter of the ECCO. She was the younger sister of Cai Hesen and went to the same school as Xiang Jingyu, her future sister-in-law, while in Hunan. Cai Chang went to France in 1919, together with her brother Hesen, Xiang, and her middle-aged mother. From 1919 to 1924, she worked in several factories, studied in schools, participated with the Montargis faction in the struggles of 1921, and in 1922 married Li Fuchun. Cai and Li were very active in ECCO and EGMD work. Cai Chang was especially involved in the area of worker education. They both went to Moscow to study, Cai returning in 1925. Cai Chang is one of the most important early women Communists and has held a preeminent position in the Party hierarchy since the late twenties.

Cai Hesen 蔡和森
1895–1931, b. Xiangxiang, Hunan. Other names: Linbin, Hexian, Zhihuan, Zeying. Positions: CCP Central Committee, editor of *Xiangdao*, Regional Secretary.

The older brother of Cai Chang, Cai Hesen was one of the most important early Communists. He was an early convert to Marxism, a founder of the New Citizens' Study Society, and an avid proponent of the Work-Study Movement. Cai Hesen was very important in the formation of the ECCO because he stimulated intense debate on ideology (he advocated the adoption of Marxism and the formation of a party) and because of his leadership in the struggles of 1921. He was deported in the Lyons Incident, and upon his return to China entered the top ranks of the CCP, being elected to the CCP Central Committee in 1922. He edited the Party theoretical weekly, *Xiangdao*. Cai Hesen went to Moscow in October 1925 to work for the Communist International. He was very involved in formulating CCP strategy, and after the 1927 violence, Cai was one of those responsible for deposing Chen Duxiu as CCP secretary. Cai became increasingly involved in the factional disputes following the terror of 1927. While doing Party work in Hong Kong, Cai Hesen was captured in 1931 and secretly executed in Guangchou, at the age of thirty-six. Cai was also noted for his "ideal" marriage to Xiang Jingyu, because it was a nonarranged marriage and one based on shared political views. They had two children. In 1926 he and Xiang dissolved their marriage, and he married Li Yichun, who bore him two more children.

Cai Yuanpei 蔡元培

1868–1940, b. Shaoxing, Zhejiang. Other names: He Qing, Jie Min. Positions: Minister of Education (1912–13), Hanlin Academy; Chancellor of Beijing University; President of Board of Universities; Founder and President of Academia Sinica.

Cai Yuanpei is noted for his liberalization of Chinese education. As head of Beijing University he actively promoted academic freedom, the adoption of the vernacular language, the equality of women, and the need for students to take their social and political responsibilities seriously. His role in the May Fourth Movement was well known and widely respected. Cai Yuanpei's role in the Work-Study Movement was also important; he helped set everything in motion, and with his announcements in January 1921, he effectively called things to a halt by relinquishing all formal responsibility for the movement, which sparked political activism throughout 1921. In the midtwenties Cai took a more conservative turn as he involved himself in the GMD. He still participated in academic issues, as president of the Board of Universities and a founder and president of Academia Sinica. Later disillusioned by the GMD government, he worked to protect civil rights, but falling ill he left to settle in Hong Kong in 1937, where he died of illness in 1940. Cai married three times. His second wife died while he was in Europe in 1921.

Chen Duxiu 陳獨秀

1879–1942, b. Huaining, Anhui. Position: First CCP General Secretary.

Chen Duxiu was perhaps the most important instigator of the New Culture Movement and founded the magazine *Xin qingnian* (*New Youth Magazine*) in 1915. Chen taught a younger generation how to question traditional values and advocated the adoption of a scientific, critical, and creative attitude. At first he promoted "Mr. Science" and "Mr. Democracy," but he became a convert to Marxism and helped found the CCP in 1921. Chen was made the scapegoat in 1927 for the failure of the United Front and its bloody repercussions. Deposed as general secretary in 1927, he was expelled from the Party two years later as a Trotskyite. Held in prison by the GMD between 1932 and 1937, Chen spent the last five years of his life, after his release from prison, engaged in scholarly studies.

Chen Gongpei 陳公培

b. Sichuan.

Chen Gongpei was a good friend of Zhao Shiyan and Li Lisan. He was evicted along with the latter in the Lyons Incident. Chen was an early Communist and is often cited as being in the nucleus of people involved in the initial small group of the ECCO. Chen was later involved in the Fujian Incident.

Chen Jiuding 陳九鼎

b. Henan.

Chen was an early member of the ECCO who went to the Soviet Union in 1923. No information is available about him after this.

Chen Lu 陳籙

1876–1939, b. Minhou, Fujian. Other name: Ren Xian. Positions: Diplomat, negotiated the 1915 Treaty of Kiakhta; Chinese High Commissioner to Ulan Bator; 1920–27, Chinese Minister to France; Foreign Minister in Japanese puppet government (Nanjing).

Chen Lu was one of the first of his generation to receive a Western education, studying three years at the Fuzhou Shipyard. Chen studied both English and French, and after his other degrees, in 1907 he obtained a legal degree from the University of Paris. In the same year he began his diplomatic career, attending the Second Peace Conference held at The Hague. Chen Lu remained in diplomatic service after the 1911 Revolution, and before his next sojourn in France, he negotiated the Treaty of Kiakhta, which established the status of Outer Mongolia. Appointed as the Chinese minister to France in 1920, Chen Lu was the major government representative with whom the students contended. During 1921, beginning with a protest in front of the Chinese consulate, relations between Chen Lu and the worker-students deteriorated rapidly. He bitterly resented the "loss of face" that these wild youth were incurring for his country amongst the French by their rude antics. During the 1921 loan negotiations the students coerced him into a position where he could not sign a loan agreement, and it appears that he retaliated by not supporting the students in the Lyons Incident (perhaps even encouraging their more extreme actions), which resulted in deportation for 104 students. Chen Lu's problems were not over; in March 1922 a student tried to assassinate him (wounding someone else), and in June 1925 the Chinese Ministry was physically occupied by students who forced Chen Lu to sign a telegram in support of the May Thirtieth Incident in China. A very early Western biographical account of Chen Lu stated, "Tcheng-loh [Chen Lu] is considered an honest, straight-forward and patriotic official in both Chinese and foreign circles in the Capital" (Cavanaugh, 1:19). However, in 1938 he did collaborate with the Japanese puppet government in Nanjing and was assassinated as a collaborator in 1939 by the Iron and Blood Army.

Chen Pengnian 陳彭年
d. probably ca. 1927.

Chen Pengnian was a laborer who went to France and joined the ECCO. He was killed after his return to China.

Chen Qiaonian 陳喬年
1901–28, b. Huaining, Anhui. Positions: Member of the Hubei Regional CCP Committee, Assistant Head of the Central Committee Organizational Bureau, Jiangsu Organizational Head, Central Committee member (May 1927).

Son of Chen Duxiu and younger brother of Chen Yannian, Chen Qiaonian was a participant in the Work-Study Movement. He and his brother owned a bookshop that distributed political literature. Chen Qiaonian also worked in the French factories. Qiaonian participated in ECCO activities and returned home in 1924. He occupied himself with CCP organizational work until his capture and execution in 1928 in Shanghai, at the age of twenty-seven. Chen Qiaonian married within a couple years of his return to China; they had a child, who died of illness.

Chen Shaoxiu 陳紹休
b. Loyang, Hunan, d. 1921. Other name: Zuanzhou. Position: Instructor at Hunan First Normal School.

Chen was very important in the New Citizens' Study Society hierarchy and very well liked. He participated in the Work-Study Movement, but died of illness shortly after reaching France.

Chen Shengyü 陳聲煜
b. Sichuan, d. 1926.

An early participant in the Work-Study Movement, he joined the ECCO in 1925 and was killed shortly upon his return to China, while working for the Party in Hubei.

Chen Shunong 陳書農
b. 1898, Hunan.

A student at the Sino-French Institute, Chen Shunong was expelled in 1929 for lack of attention to his studies. Chen was heavily involved in the left EGMD, forming his own faction in 1928. The French newspapers carried articles on his fight with Peng Xiang in 1927.

Chen Xiaocen 諶小岑
b. 1897, Tianjin.

One of the founding Self-Awakening Society members, Chen married the activist Li Zhi, and during the early twenties they published a feminist journal and actively helped young women in need. Chen and Li were members of the Socialist Youth but later withdrew into more neutral positions. In his memoir Chen recounts that Zhou Enlai once criticized him as a "vacillator" (yao-bai), and he experienced several years of criticism during the Cultural Revolution.

Chen Weiming 陳微明
b. Haining, Zhejiang, d. 1961. Other name: Sha Kefu.

Chen Weiming was a late arrival on the ECCO scene, arriving in France in 1926. He went to the Soviet Union in 1927 and returned to China in 1931, where he took on educational tasks, including the editorship of Hungse Zhonghua (Red China), and was assistant director of the Educational Bureau of the Jiangsu Worker-Peasant Government. Until 1949, Chen was assistant director of the Lu Xun Arts School, and he held a variety of cultural and educational posts after 1949, until his death from illness in 1961.

Chen Yannian 陳延年
1898–1927, b. Huaining, Anhui. Other name: Lin Mu. Positions: Editor of Shaonian (ECCO), Secretary of Guangzhou and Guangxi Provincial Com-

mittee, Shanghai Standing Committee (after April 1927), Central Committee member (May 1927).

Chen Yannian, son of Chen Duxiu and brother of Chen Qiaonian, is noted as an important inspiration in the ECCO formation. Before the struggles of 1921, he and his brother had been Anarchists. By June 1922 they had changed their positions and attended the first formal meeting of the ECCO. Yannian left France for training in Moscow in 1923 and held responsible CCP positions after his return to China. Unlike his younger brother, Chen Yannian did not marry. While heading the Guangzhou/Guangxi Region, Chen brought a good sense of organization and method to his job, encouraging recruitment and education and increasing the membership. He was called to Shanghai and Wuhan during the troubled times of 1927. His career was on the rise when he was caught and executed in June 1927 at the age of twenty-eight.

Chen Yi 陳毅

1901–72, b. Luozhi, Sichuan. Other name: Zhong Hong. Positions: Commander New Fourth Army; Mayor of Shanghai (1949–57); in 1955 appointed Marshal; Minister of Foreign Affairs, CCP Politburo.

Chen Yi went to France with his older brother Chen Yan. He was very ill on the voyage and on reaching France entered a hospital. However, he soon went to work in a factory and was dismayed by the miserable living conditions he encountered. Chen Yi was one of the non-Hunanese impressed with the arguments of Cai Hesen's Montargis group. He was certainly convinced of the Marxist view of society and economics by the time he was deported in the Lyons Incident. Although he was very depressed personally about his deportation, Chen Yi made efforts to raise the morale of the returned students and sought aid for them once they returned home. Throughout the turbulent pre-1949 period Chen Yi was an effective military leader. According to Boorman's assessment of Chen Yi's post-1949 career, he was one of the few military men who later acquired political power "at the top level of the party" (1:254–59). Certainly a glance at his posts, from mayor to marshal to minister, indicates power and adaptability.

Deng Xiaoping 鄧小平

b. 1904, Guangan, Sichuan. Other name: Deng Xixian. Position: General Secretary, CCP.

Perhaps, next to Zhou Enlai, Deng Xiaoping is the best known name from the ECCO experience, due to attaining the highest post possible in the CCP hierarchy. Deng was only sixteen when he went to France and spent most of his time working in a Renault factory. Deng was, however, politically oriented and helped with the printing of the ECCO publications. By 1924, after Zhou Enlai and others had left, Deng began to rise to one of the top leadership positions in the ECCO. By 1925 he also held important posts in the EGMD. He was one of those responsible for the occupation of the Chinese consulate in the summer of 1925, and left soon after for the Soviet Union. Upon his return to China, Deng became a political officer for the army. After the establishment of the PRC his star began to rise, and he obtained high positions within the CCP. He fell out of favor several times, most notably during the Cultural Revolution, but he made a comeback and steadily consolidated his power as the most important post-Mao leader in the 1980s.

Deng Yingchao 鄧穎超

b. 1903, Xinyang, Henan. Other name: Deng Shuwen. Positions: Vice-Chairperson, National Women's Federation of China; CCP Central Committee.

At the age of sixteen Deng Yingchao was giving speeches on street corners during the May Fourth Movement. She was a founding member of the Self-Awakening Society. Although she did not go to France, Deng was involved in many political activities, especially feminist issues. Soon after Zhou Enlai returned to China, they were married and were mutually supportive in their distinguished careers within the CCP.

Fan Yi 范一

b. Fuxun, Sichuan, d. 1927.

Fan Yi was an early Work-Study Movement participant. He joined the CCP in 1924 and was killed in the violence of 1927.

Fu Zhong 傅鐘

b. 1897, Sichuan. Positions: Fifth Secretary of the ECYC, Central Committee CCP.

Fu Zhong left for France in 1919. He worked in a factory and roomed with Zhao Shiyan. Fu attended the first meeting of the ECCO and served as the fifth secretary. Fu left France in 1925, after helping to organize the occupation of Chen Lu's office. Fu Zhong went to the Soviet Union before returning to China. During the period between August 1927 and June 1928, Fu was on the Military Standing Committee and served on the Central Committee in 1928. Fu participated in military affairs, propaganda, and political work. He sided with Zhang Guotao in the midthirties, but later obtained the trust of Mao Zedong. Even during the Cultural Revolution, Fu retained various positions.

Gao Feng 高風

b. Huarong, Hunan, d. 1926. Positions: Baoding Provincial CCP Committee, Secretary of the Hebei Regional Committee.

Gao Feng was an early Work-Study Movement participant. In 1922 Gao joined the ECCO and in 1923 went to study in the Soviet Union. Returning home Gao worked in Baoding and Hebei, and was killed by the warlords in 1926.

Ge Jianhao 葛建豪

1865–1943, b. Xiangxiang, Hunan.

Ge Jianhao was the mother of Cai Hesen and Cai Chang and accompanied her children to France at the age of fifty-five. She was a model of the emerging modern woman of China; she rebelled against her husband several times, refusing to bind her daughters' feet and supporting her son's decision not to become a shop apprentice. At the age of forty-five Ge Jianhao graduated from a school in Hunan that taught female educators and proceeded to open a weaving school for young girls. It was in her home that the New Citizens' Study Society met, eating dumplings and discussing politics. Ge Jianhao bore six children; two of her sons died as members of the CCP (and also her daughter-in-law Xiang Jingyu, killed in 1928). After she returned to China, Ge was uprooted several times because of the danger to her due to her childrens' political activities, finally settling in Yongfeng in 1928. Apparently the death of Cai Hesen was kept hidden from her. Her husband died in 1932. She died in 1943 at the age of seventy-eight.

Guo Chuntao 郭春濤

b. Hunan, d. 1950. Other name: Ming Zhong.

Guo participated in the Work-Study Movement and was deported as a result of the Lyons Incident. At first Guo participated in the Socialist Youth, but afterward he joined the GMD. Later, in the period of resistance against the Japanese, Guo joined the Third Force groups. After 1949 he held a government post for a brief time but died in 1950.

Guo Fangrui 郭方瑞

b. Hunan. Other name: Guobin.

A Work-Study Movement participant from Changsha, Guo arrived in France in 1919 and studied at Montargis. In 1922 Guo went to mining school in Belgium, graduated in 1925, and worked in a factory until 1927, when he returned home to participate in the Northern Expedition.

Guo Longzhen 郭隆眞

1894–1931, b. Daming, Hebei. Other names: Linyi, Nanchen. Positions: Hebei Provincial Committee, Secretary of Manchurian Provincial Labor Organization Committee.

Guo Longzhen, who was a Muslim, was a founder of the Self-Awakening Society and a leader of the May Fourth Movement. She went with Zhou Enlai, Liu Qingyang, and Zhang Ruoming to Paris in 1920, where she ended up eventually at Montargis. Joining the ECCO in 1923, one of her activities was writing articles. In 1924 Guo went to the Soviet Union for half a year. Upon her return she not only carried on with feminist work (especially contributing articles to feminist papers) but had Party and labor organizational responsibilities. She was particularly skilled at propaganda work and recruitment. Guo Longzhen was imprisoned in 1930 and executed on 5 April 1931 in Jinan, one week before her thirty-eighth birthday. (According to Dr. Yang Kun she was killed one year earlier.) Although not as well known as other early CCP feminists like Xiang Jingyu or Yang Zhihua, Guo made important contributions to CCP organizational efforts. Her personal integrity and revolutionary zeal are remembered by her colleagues.

He Changgong 何長工

1900–87, b. Huarong, Hunan. Position: Vice-Minister of Geology.

Although He Changgong was not one of the most crucial ECCO members, he is one of the best known because of the memoir he published. He spent most of his time studying and learning French, with minimal involvement in the struggles of 1921. He attended Charleroi University for Workers and became an engineer. He was a Communist and after returning to China was involved in labor organizational and military activities. After 1949, He's technical expertise was tapped, and he occupied various posts, working for the Ministry of Heavy Industry, Aeronautical Industry Bureau, and the Ministry of Geology. In recent years, He Changgong helped to recollect the past and was president of the Committee to Study Chinese Communist Party Officials.

He Guo 賀果

b. Yuqing, Hunan. Other names: Peizhen, Peiqin.

He Guo, a New Citizens' Study Society member and Work-Study Movement participant, is an interesting case of a person who left the CCP but obtained high positions after 1949. He Guo was expelled by the French in the Lyons Incident, and he joined the CCP in 1922, participating in military affairs. He also involved himself in labor organization after 1927. He Guo left the CCP in 1930. After 1949 he was elected to the National Peoples'

Congress and worked as an official for Guiyang. Recently, He Guo has published his diary of his French experience.

He Luzhi 何魯之

1891–1978, b. Huayang, Sichuan. Positions: A founder of the Chinese Youth Party, Professor of Mathematics.

He Luzhi was active in the Young China Study Association, enrolled in the University of Paris, and headed the effort to resist foreign consolidation of Chinese railways in 1923. He was a secretary of the SFEA and a founder of the Chinese Youth Party. He returned to China in 1926, where he became a professor of mathematics. He Luzhi retained his anti-Communist convictions and remained a firm supporter of the Chinese Youth Party.

Herriot, Edouard
1872–1957.

Herriot was one of the most prominent Frenchmen participating in the Sino-French Educational Association. He served not only as the mayor of Lyons but as the leader of the Radical Party and was heavily involved in national politics, serving as foreign minister, prime minister, vice-premier, and senator of the Rhône District. During Herriot's first term as prime minister (1924–25), he supervised France's recognition of the Soviet Union. However, Herriot did not support the Chinese students in the Lyons Incident, nor did he support the French Communist Party, although he formed leftist coalitions during his political life.

Ho Chi Minh 胡志明

1890–1969, b. Nghe-Tinh, Viet Nam. Other names: Nguyen Sinh Cong, Nguyen Tat Thanh, Nguyen Ai Quoc, Comrade Vuong. Positions: Founder of the Indochinese Communist Party, Chairman (Chu Tich) of the Democratic Republic of Viet Nam.

Ho Chi Minh is one of the most famous revolutionaries of the twentieth century. He attended a Western school in Viet Nam, left the country in 1911, and did not return for thirty years. However, he spent his time abroad organizing and agitating for the overthrow of French colonialism and a Marxist revolution in Viet Nam. Ho Chi Minh was in France from 1917 until 1924, when he attended the Fifth Congress of the Communist International in Moscow. Among Ho's more important achievements are the founding of the Indochinese Communist Party (1930) and leading the resistance to the Japanese during the Second World War and the August 1945 revolution that officially overthrew the French and established the Democratic Republic of Viet Nam. He successfully vanquished the French, after several years of guerrilla warfare and set the pattern for the defeat of American forces in Viet Nam. Ho Chi Minh died of cancer at the age of seventy-nine. After his death, the Vietnamese leadership were unable to achieve a balance between the Soviet Union and the PRC, who were undergoing the Sino-Soviet split. Ho Chi Minh was respected as a leader even by many of his adversaries.

Hou Changguo 侯昌國

b. Hunan.

Hou was the roommate of Cai Hesen during his secondary education in Hunan. Hou was involved in the Twenty-eighth Movement and later joined the GMD. An engineer, Hou worked for the Shanghai Water and Electric Company. After 1949 he remained in China working as an engineer.

Hu Guowei 胡國偉

b. Guangdong.

A founder and author of a lively memoir of the Chinese Youth Party, Hu Guowei, unfortunately, does not give much personal information. After 1949 Hu settled in Taiwan.

Huang Jian 黃堅

Position: General Secretary, EGMD.

A notable organizer of the right-faction EGMD, Huang Jian was often cited by the French Sûreté. Huang studied law in France.

Huang Qisheng 黃齊生

1878–1946, b. Anxuan, Guizhou.

One of the older Work-Study Movement participants, Huang Qisheng was also the uncle of Wang Ruofei. Huang served as a role model of patriotic devotion in the Work-Study Movement. He also tried to arbitrate during the struggles of 1921. Huang went to Yanan during the war, and he died in 1946 in the same airplane crash as Wang Ruofei.

Huang Shitao 黃士韜

b. Hexian, Guangxi, d. 1927. Position: Head of the Guangxi Special Organization Bureau (1926).

Huang was an early Work-Study Movement participant who entered the German section of the ECCO in 1925. Afterward he went to the Soviet Union to study and returned to China in 1926, where he worked in his native Guangxi. He was killed in 1927.

Jiang Jieshi 蔣介石

1887–1975, b. Zhejiang. Other name: Jiang Zhongzheng. Positions: President of the Republic of China, head of the Guomindang.

Jiang Jieshi is more commonly known in the West as Chiang Kai-shek, head of the Kuo-min-tang government. The romanization Jiang Jieshi reflects the true pronunciation of his name and is slowly gaining in usage. Jiang Jieshi was the leader of the GMD after consolidating power in 1927. He terminated the CCP-GMD United Front in a bloody counterrevolution in April 1927, after the major victories of the Northern Expedition to oust the warlords. Jiang was the leader of the Republic of China from 1927 until his death in 1975. From 1949 onward, the Republic of China has been located on the island of Taiwan. Jiang Jieshi is remarkably underresearched in comparison with the Communist leaders, especially given the variety and extent of his activities. Jiang married twice, and his eldest son, Jiang Jingguo, headed the government of the Republic of China until his death in 1988.

Jiang Zemin 江澤民

1903–89, b. Jiangjin, Sichuan. Other name: Hong Gong. Positions: Belgian Bureau of Student-Workers (1924), technical posts.

Jiang Zemin went to France in 1920 and worked in factories until 1922, when he went to Charleroi University for Workers on the advice of Nie Rongzhen. Jiang graduated in 1926 as an engineer. He was politically active, heading the Belgian Bureau of Student-Workers in 1924 and joining the Communist Party. In 1926, Jiang went to the Soviet Union to study at Sun Yatsen University. Jiang is listed as holding technical posts in Bartke's *Who's Who* (1981).

Lao Junzhan 勞君展

b. Changsha, Hunan, d. 1976. Other name: Qi Rong.

Lao Junzhan went to France in 1920 and studied nuclear physics. Lao had been politically involved during the May Fourth Movement and had joined the New Citizens' Study Society. After returning to China in 1927 she taught in Wuhan, Shanghai, and Beijing. She became politically involved again in 1935, agitating for resistance against the Japanese. After 1949 she still taught and held a post at the Educational Ministry. Lao married one of the most famous May Fourth Movement leaders, Xu Deheng, who was also in France during the early twenties.

Li Dazhao 李大釗

1888–1927, b. Luoting, Hebei. Other name: Shou Chang. Positions: A founder of the Young China Study Association, a founder of the CCP, member of the Central Committee.

Li Dazhao, along with Chen Duxiu, was one of the initiators of the CCP. He had been a strong influence for the New Culture Movement, and as the head librarian at Beijing University had been in the forefront of the latest intellectual and political activity of the period. Li is generally noted as the first confirmed Bolshevik in China. Whereas Chen Duxiu had a more aloof personality, Li mingled with his protégés. Although Li Dazhao had been one of the most fervent supporters of the United Front with the GMD, he has not been held in contempt, because he died a martyr's death in 1927.

Li Fuchun 李富春

1899–1975, b. Changsha, Hunan. Positions: Assistant Secretary for the Jiangxi Provincial Committee; CCP Central Committee; Chairman, State Planning Commission.

Li Fuchun, a New Citizens' Study Society member, was not a founding member of the ECYC, but he did join by 1923 and was very important in performing United Front work in France. He worked in factories the few years he was in Europe. Li went to the Soviet Union for some training before he returned home, either in 1925 or 1926. He became assistant secretary for the Jiangxi Provincial Committee in 1926. Li Fuchun's rise in the CCP was not as swift as that of others in the beginning; he was elected to the Central Committee for the first time in 1934. Li and his wife, Cai Chang, both participated in the Long March (1935) and other important CCP events. After 1949 Li acquired more prominent positions, notably the chairmanship of the State Planning Commission, making him responsible for formulating economic policy. He was also involved in overseeing heavy industries. Both Li Fuchun and Cai Chang were purged during the Cultural Revolution.

Li Huang 李璜

1895–1991, b. Chengdu, Sichuan. Other names: You Chun, Xue Dun. Positions: Founder of the Chinese Youth Party; Central Committee, Chinese Democratic League; attended the founding meeting of the United Nations.

Li Huang is an important symbol of the "third force" in China. A Young China Study Association member, he went to France in early 1919 and studied sociology and literature, eventually obtaining a master's degree. Li's father was a well-to-do merchant in Chengdu, so Li did not have to work in a factory. However, he spent much time tutoring the Work-Study students in French, which he had studied assiduously in China. Li became alarmed by the rising trend of Marxism among his fellow youth, and in December 1923, with his friend Zeng Qi and ten others, he founded the Chinese Youth Party, a vehemently anti-Communist organization. The Chinese Youth Party also made a stand against the GMD, in particular when Jiang Jieshi took command. This opposition by an important segment of Chinese intellectuals (Zuo Shunsheng, Zeng Qi, He Luzhi, Hu Guowei, etc.) lasted until the war against Japan, when the Chinese Youth Party formally agreed to cooperate in the government. Li Huang was one of those who refused to cooperate with the government after 1947. He moved to Hong Kong, where he lived for over twenty years, until he decided to move to Taiwan.

Li Huang wrote several books on French literature and has spent most of his life as an educator, teaching at universities throughout China. He was important in organizing against the Communists when they passed through Sichuan during the Long March. Li Huang also participated in the Central Committee of the Chinese Democratic League in the early forties, and he attended the founding conference for the United Nations in 1946.

Li Ji 李季

Li Ji went to Frankfurt, Germany in 1921, where he became a prominent ECCO member. He was a noted Trotskyite. After 1949, he pursued his career in literature.

Li Jida 李季達
b. Sichuan, d. 1926.

Li Jida went to France early and became a member of the ECYC in 1922. Li joined the CCP the next year. He died in Tianjin in 1926.

Li Lisan 李立三
b. 1899, Liling, Hunan. Other names: Long Zhi, Zuo Fu. Positions: Propaganda Chief, CCP Central Committee.

Li Lisan was an early participant in the Work-Study Movement. He sided with Zhao Shiyan in the Twenty-eighth Movement, but became a firm Marxist later that year. He was expelled in the Lyons Incident, immediately involving himself with Communist activities when he returned to China. Li was particularly effective in labor agitation work at the Anyuan mines and during the May Thirtieth Incident. According to the Klein and Clark biographical dictionary Li Lisan was one of the better speakers of the CCP and a very good organizer. After the debacles of 1927 and the failed uprisings of Qu Qiubai, Li Lisan became the propaganda chief of the CCP. Along with the Comintern, Li Lisan formulated the policy of urban uprisings in

1930, which failed. Li was taken to task for this failure and spent the next fifteen years exiled in the Soviet Union. He returned during the ending of the war and helped with the situation in Manchuria. After 1949 Li Lisan held minor posts in the government. He was one of the targets of the Cultural Revolution, and it is rumored that he committed suicide in the latter part of the sixties.

Li Lin 李林
b. Hunan, d. 1925?

Li Lin joined the ECCO and upon his return to China served in the north in labor union organizing. He was killed in the land reform movement.

Li Shizeng 李石曾
1881–1973, b. Beijing. Other name: Li Yuying. Position: A founder of the Work-Study Movement.

Son of a famous Qing official, Li Shizeng found it easy to be assigned as an attaché in Paris. Li studied biology at the Pasteur Institute and was politically involved as an editor of the Anarchist journal *Xin shiji*. Among his other activities Li founded a soybean products factory and a publishing enterprise. Li Shizeng numbered among his close friends Cai Yuanpei and Wu Zhihui, who formed several organizations devoted to frugal work-study abroad for Chinese students. The last of these, the Sino-French Educational Association, succeeded in bringing over 1,600 students to France. However, none of the leaders could efficiently organize enough accommodations, educational positions, or jobs for the youth, thus creating a tense situation. Li Shizeng, who optimistically returned to China in 1919, tried to obtain aid and worked on the agreement with the French to open the Sino-French Institute at Lyons University. Unfortunately, the educational positions were not given to the destitute Chinese youth who were already in France, and the Lyons Incident ensued. By and large an educator, Li was also involved with GMD politics. Li became more conservative during the early 1920s. After 1949 Li had residences in Uruguay and Taiwan.

Li Weihan 李維漢
1897–1983, b. Liling, Hunan. Other names: Li Hesheng, Luo Mai. Positions: First Organizational Secretary of the ECYC; Hunan Provincial Committee Secretary (1922–27); CCP Central Committee, Chairman, Nationalities Affairs Commission.

Li Weihan's career in the Work-Study Movement and the CCP is very interesting. A member of the New Citizens' Study Society, he was not in the Mao-Cai clique and held more moderate views than they did. Li went to France in October 1919 and had to live in a tent until he obtained a job in the spring of 1920. During the summer of 1920 in the crucial debates at Montargis, Li Weihan came out against forming a Marxist party. However, due to the struggles of 1921, Li was eventually a founding member of the ECYC and its first organizational secretary. Li was chosen by the other members to hand-deliver a message to the CCP Central Committee in the fall of 1922, so he returned to China. There he was the secretary of the Hunan Provincial Committee for five years. With the exception of Cai Hesen and possibly Xiang Jingyu, Li Weihan was the only ECCO returnee who was elected to the CCP Central Committee before 1927 (in 1925). After the violence of 1927, Li Weihan's career did not regain its momentum, and he lost his former prominence. Li held responsible positions both before and after 1949, particularly in the areas of minorities and United Front work, but he did not achieve the eminence his early career indicated he might.

Li Weinong 李慰農

b. Anhui. Position: Shandong Provincial Committee Secretary.

Li Weinong was a founding member of the ECYC. When he returned to China, he participated in labor organization in the north and was later assigned as Secretary of the Shandong Provincial Committee. Li Weinong was killed by the warlords in Qingdao (midtwenties?).

Liao Huanxing 廖煥星

Position: A leader of the German Branch of the ECCP.

Liao Huanxing carried some important messages in 1922 from the CCP Central Committee to Zhao Shiyan in Paris and to Zhang Shenfu in Berlin. Liao worked and studied in Berlin and proved himself a capable organizer for the German section of the ECCP in 1923. Liao was later imprisoned in Siberia by Stalin, until the latter's death in 1953.

Lin Xiujie 林修杰

1900–28, b. Nanchong, Sichuan. Positions: Jiangxi Provincial Committee Organizational Secretary (1926), Yangxian Regional Committee Secretary, Jiujiang Regional Secretary.

Lin went to France in 1920 and joined the Party in 1925. He went to the Soviet Union in 1925 and returned to China in 1926. He was betrayed and killed in 1928.

Lin Wei 林蔚

1901–28, b. Xiangtan, Hunan. Other name: Qiao Sheng.

Lin Wei joined the ECCO in France, where he helped form the United Front, rising high in the EGMD hierarchy. Lin was important in expelling right-faction EGMD members. He left to study military tactics in the Soviet Union in 1925. Lin returned in 1926 and worked on organizational committees in Hunan (perhaps holding a regional secretary position). He became the secretary of the Tilu region and was killed by the GMD in 1928 at the age of twenty-seven.

Liu Bojian 劉伯堅

1895–1935, b. Pingchan, Sichuan. Other names: Liu Yongfu, Liu Yonggu, Da Zhi. Positions: Head of the Soviet Branch of the CCP (1923–26), Political Officer of the Red Army.

Liu Bojian was a Work-Study participant who went to Belgium instead of settling in France. He studied at Charleroi University for Workers and became very involved in the ECCO. He attended the founding meeting and was in one of the first groups to go to the Soviet Union. His stay in the Soviet Union was not only for study but because of his organizational capabilities. He was the head of the Soviet Branch of the CCP for three years, overseeing more than 200 CCP members studying in the Soviet Union. In 1926 Liu returned home to perform political work in Feng Yüxiang's army until the violence of 1927 and the loss of Feng's patronage. For the next eight years Liu was involved in political mobilization in the army and labor agitation. He wrote articles, delivered speeches, and taught military tactics. One of Liu's greatest achievements was the co-opting of the GMD's 26th Route Army. Married in 1927, he and his wife had three sons. In 1935 Liu Bojian stayed behind with some others to delay the GMD troops and give those who left on the Long March a chance to escape. Liu was captured and executed on 21 March 1935. He wrote several letters from prison, admonishing his sons to study, perform factory labor after the age of eighteen, marry late, and carry on the revolution.

Liu Mingyan 劉明儼

b. 1900, Anhua, Hunan.

Liu Mingyan was a participant in the Lyons Incident and was expelled along with 103 others. It appears that he returned to France and was involved in the United Front, possibly the ECCO, and attended the Sino-French Institute at Lyons (1925–26). After 1949 he performed cultural work in Hunan.

Liu Puqing 柳圃青

b. 1905? Other name: Paul Lieu.

Liu Puqing was an important ECCO member in the mid-1920s and was important in the United Front, serving in 1925 as an alternate executive delegate. His name is often cited in the reports of the French Sûreté.

Liu Qingyang 劉清揚

1902–77, b. Tianjin, Hebei. Position: Deputy Director, All China Federation of Democratic Women.

Liu Qingyang, a Muslim from Tianjin, was an important student activist during the May Fourth Movement, uniting the actions of Tianjin with the rest of the country. Liu went to France in 1920 with other Self-Awakening Society members. According to most sources Liu Qingyang was important in setting up a Communist Party nucleus before the ECCO was formed. She married Zhang Shenfu, a prominent disciple of Chen Duxiu, in the spring of 1921. Liu and Zhang moved to Berlin after the Lyons Incident. They helped found the ECCO although Zhang was rather controversial. Liu gave Zhou Enlai his initial introduction to Zhang Shenfu and Communist politics. However, after 1927, Liu broke with the Party, two years after her husband. Although Liu broke with the CCP, she still worked on feminist issues and involved herself in the Third Force Democratic movements. Before the 1949 victory she went over to the Communist-held liberated zone. She held prominent positions in many organizations after 1949, most notably as deputy director of the All China Federation of Democratic Women. She died in 1977 and received an official commemoration celebration two years later.

Long Zhanxing 龍詹興

b. 1902, Canton. Other name: Johnson Long.

A student at the Sino-French Institute, Long Zhanxing was a member of the extremist (ECCO) faction of the United Front. In September 1927 he was expelled from the institute for his Communist beliefs along with Xie Qing (Sha Ching), Peng Shiqin (Peng Shih-chin), and Yan Jijin (Yen Chi-chin). Long and his compatriots kept the radical faction alive after 1927 at 26 rue des Carmes.

Lozeray, Henri

1898–1952.

Henri Lozeray was one of the national secretaries of the French Federation of Young Communists. He also had close ties with the secret apparatus of the French Communist Party and Comintern. He participated in colonial work. It is possible that Lozeray may have been a contact for the Chinese Communists in France, who were officially a youth corps, and for Ho Chi Minh, who was the preeminent colonialist agitator.

Luo Xuezan 羅學贊

1893–1930, b. Xiangtan, Hunan. Other name: Rong Xi. Positions: Ti Yu Regional Director, Head of the Organizational Bureau of the Hunan Provincial Committee.

Luo Xuezan was the most prolific correspondent in the New Citizens' Study Society. Supported in his schooling by his grandfather until he reached eighteen, Luo went to work to earn his school fees at Hunan's First Normal Middle School, where he was in the same class as Mao Zedong. Luo was a firm believer in an organized and arduous schedule of study and exercise. Luo went to France in 1919, worked in a factory, and helped to form the Society for the World of Work-Study. He changed many of his more moderate views during 1921, and after he was expelled during the Lyons Incident, he joined the CCP upon his return to China. Luo involved himself in labor organizing and was particularly successful in forming a rickshaw union in Changsha. Luo also contributed to various propaganda organs and was involved in educational work. After 1925 Luo worked in the peasant movement in Hunan and headed the Organizational Bureau of the Hunan Provincial Committee. The GMD captured and executed him in 1930. Luo Xuezan was noted for his optimistic and jovial personality.

Luo Yinong 羅亦農

1902–28, b. Xiangtan, Hunan. Other name: Luo Jue. Positions: Jiangsu-Zhejiang Regional Secretary, CCP Central Committee.

Luo Yinong was one of the first Communists to learn Russian, attending the Russian school in Shanghai and receiving instruction in the Soviet Union beginning in 1921. Luo stayed in the Soviet Union until 1925. He worked in Guangdong and then headed the Jiangsu-Zhejiang region and was one of the leaders of the Three Violent Uprisings in Shanghai. Luo Yinong was elected to the Central Committee in 1927 and was executed the next year while carrying on activities in Shanghai.

Ma Zhiyuan 馬志遠

1893–1939, b. Gaoyang, Hebei.

Ma Zhiyuan joined the ECCO and also studied in the Soviet Union. His entry in the ECCO was notable because he was a worker, not a student. He returned to China in 1925, performing Party work in Tianjin, Beijing, and

Shenyang. Ma was active in military resistance to the Japanese and was killed in 1939.

Mu Qing 穆青

1898–1930, b. Hejiang, Sichuan. Other name: Shu Shan. Positions: Guangdong Organizational Head, Sichuan Organizational Head.

Mu Qing went to France in 1920 and joined the ECCO during 1922. In 1924 he went to the Soviet Union and stayed for two years, returning in 1926 to head the Organizational Bureau of the Guangdong Provincial Committee. He was later appointed organizational head of the Sichuan Provincial Committee and possibly of the Hubei Provincial Committee (1928). Mu was a very responsible leader, and during the Canton Uprising went to great risks to ascertain the condition of his colleagues. He was arrested and tortured several times in those four years. Once, his wife, Wang Linruo, obtained his release with a daring subterfuge. However, he was positively identified in 1930 and executed.

Nie Rongzhen 聶榮臻

1899–1992, b. Jiangjin, Sichuan. Other name: Xiang Shang. Positions: Marshal, Vice-Premier, CCP Central Committee; Chairman, Scientific and Technological Commission.

Nie Rongzhen went to France in 1919 and studied there for one year before he went to Belgium and the Charleroi University for Workers. Although Nie was active politically, joining the ECYC in 1922 and the ECCP in 1923, he concentrated on his studies more than many other youth. According to his own memoir, however, he abandoned his studies for political activities. In September 1924 he left for the Soviet Union, where he studied for two years. Nie returned to China to teach at the Huangpu Military Academy. Nie was involved in many of the pivotal Communist moments— particularly, the Nanchang Uprising, the Canton Uprising, and the Long March. During the War of Resistance against Japan and the civil war he performed considerable military feats. After the establishment of the PRC in 1949, Nie frequently served in high office, not only because of his military experience but also for his technical expertise. Nie Rongzhen was an important shaper of Chinese scientific and technological progress, particularly in the development of the atomic bomb.

Peng Xiang 彭襄

1897–, b. Hunan.

An early secretary of the Sino-French Educational Association, Peng Xiang was a graduate student at the Sino-French Institute. Peng was a notable member of the left EGMD and joined the Zhang Nan faction in 1928, earlier having a notorious fistfight with Chen Shunong. Peng was very close to Liu Hou and several prominent French intellectuals. After returning to China with his wife, Fan Xinqun, Peng came back to France in the early thirties to work on his thesis on marriage in China.

Pieck, Wilhelm
1876–1960.

Pieck was a prominent member of the German Communist Party from its inception until his death, surviving all purges and changes of leadership. He was a member of the Prussian Diet (1921–28) and a deputy to the Reichstag until Hitler's ascension to power. Pieck was also a high official in the Comintern apparatus. In 1949 he became the president of the German Democratic Republic, a position he held until his death. We know from Liao Huanxing's memoir that Pieck was the one who disbursed the money for the Chinese Communists who traveled from Europe to the Soviet Union in the early twenties.

Ran Jun 冉鈞
b. Jiangjin, Sichuan, d. 1927. Position: Organizational Secretary, Sichuan Provincial Committee.

Ran Jun was an early Work-Study Movement participant and joined the ECCP in 1923. Ran worked in Sichuan doing organizational work and was killed in Chongqing during the violence of 1927.

Ren Zhuoxuan 任卓宣
1895–1990, b. Nanchong, Sichuan. Other names: Ye Qing, Ji Qing, Ti Xian. Positions: Executive Committee, ECYC; Publications Committee Head, ECYC.

Ren Zhuoxuan was one of the most influential founding members of the ECCO. He wrote numerous articles for *Chiguang* on Marxist theory and ECCO politics. Ren became the leader of the ECYC and was imprisoned for his role in the occupation of the Chinese legation during the May Thirtieth protest. Expelled by the French, he returned to China through Moscow. He performed CCP work in Guangdong and Hunan. Ren Zhuoxuan was captured twice by the GMD after 1927, and in 1928 renounced his membership in the CCP. According to CCP historians he betrayed his former comrades after his defection. After 1928 Ren Zhuoxuan opened a bookstore and wrote prolifically on anti-Communist themes. In 1949 he went to Taiwan, where he was editor of *The Political Review* (*Zhengzhi pinglun*).

She Liya 佘立亞

b. Changsha, Hunan, d. 1927. Other name: Wang Yanxia. Positions: CCP Wusong, Shanghai Municipal Secretary, Huxi Regional Secretary.

She Liya was an early Work-Study Movement participant and was a founding member of the ECYC. He went to the Soviet Union in 1923 and returned to participate in labor organization in China, basically working in the Shanghai area. She Liya was killed in the violence of 1927.

Sheng Cheng 盛成

b. 1899, Jiangsu. Positions: A founder of the French Communist Party, Chairman of the Labor Federation in France.

While Sheng Cheng was a Work-Study participant, he did not overtly involve himself in ECCO politics. He attended the Congress of Tours in 1920 and for over forty years was an underground agent of the Communist International. Sheng was the first Chinese to attend college in Montpellier, and he later wrote an autobiography in French, *Ma mère,* that included an introduction by the famous poet Paul Valéry. Sheng was involved in political agitation, attending international conferences and working for the rights of Chinese workers in France. Upon his return to China in 1930, Sheng pursued an academic career and settled in Taiwan before 1947, where he stayed until the midsixties. He returned to the PRC in the late seventies and is pursuing philological research. President Mitterand awarded Sheng Cheng the Legion of Honor medal, and his book is being reissued in France.

Shi Limu 師立木

b. Jiangjin, Sichuan.

Shi Limu was a Work-Study Movement participant. He joined the ECCP in 1924 and returned to China to assume the position of Secretary of the Sichuan Provincial Military Committee. He was killed in Jiangjin (n.d.).

Shi Yi 史逸

1901–27, b. Anhui.

Shi Yi went to Germany in 1922 and joined the ECCP in 1923. He went to the Soviet Union for further study and returned to China in 1926, where he became involved in military work. He taught at Wuchang University until August of 1927, when he went to Guangzhou and was killed in the ensuing violence.

Shi Yisheng 施益生

1902–, b. Guiping, Guangxi.

Shi Yisheng, a Work-Study Movement participant, went to Berlin in 1922 and to France in 1924. In 1924 he was introduced by Zhou Enlai into the ECCP. Shi occupied high positions in the ECCO-EGMD United Front. After the occupation of Minister Chen Lu's office in 1925, Shi decided to go home via Moscow. He was imprisoned by Stalin in Siberia, and after his release in 1953, he returned to China.

Souvarine, Boris

1895–1968.

One of the most fervent early supporters of the Third International, Souvarine's career as a mainstream Communist was always controversial and quickly ended by 1926. Cai Hesen's articles mention Souvarine several times, and it is possible that Souvarine may have met with some Chinese radicals.

Sun Bingwen 孫炳文

b. Nanji, Sichuan, d. 1927.

Sun Bingwen participated in the Wuchang Uprising in 1911. In 1922 he went to Germany and joined the ECCP. He also studied in the Soviet Union, returning to China in 1925. Sun worked at the Huangpu Military Academy and was an important person in the United Front. He was killed by the GMD in the April massacre of 1927.

Thorez, Maurice

1900–64.

Maurice Thorez was a long-time survivor of the French Communist Party and Comintern. He headed the French Communist Party from 1930 onward. After the Second World War, Thorez joined the national government until the Communists were removed in 1947. Although it is doubtful that Thorez had contact with the ECCO in the early twenties, it is likely that he did have a personal relationship with Ho Chi Minh through the years. When he was a minister in 1946, he did not use his influence during the fateful Fontainebleau Conference to persuade the government to release their colonial claims on Viet Nam.

Wang Guangqi 王光祈

1892–1936, b. Chengdu, Sichuan. Other name: Ruo Yu. Positions: A founder of the Young China Study Association and the Work-Study Mutual-Aid Corps.

A prominent May Fourth activist, Wang Guangqi helped initiate student activism by helping found the Young China Study Association and the Work-Study Mutual-Aid Corps. Wang went to Europe in 1920 and studied music in Berlin, where he obtained his doctorate. He taught at the University of Bonn. Although he contributed to educational magazines and wrote books on music, Wang Guangqi had been disillusioned by his early organizing efforts and did not involve himself directly in politics in any formidable manner after 1920. He was, however, an important symbol of the Young China Study Association ethos. After his death in Germany, his friends made sure his body was transported back to China for burial.

Wang Gui 王圭

Wang Gui was an early member of the German Branch of the ECCO. He went in the first group of Chinese to the Soviet Union in 1923. Zheng Chaolin mentions that he saw Wang Gui during the Northern Expedition, but not later. No further information about him is available.

Wang Jingqi 王京岐

d. 1925. Position: Chairman and founder of the European Guomindang.

Wang Jingqi was expelled in the Lyons Incident, returned to China, and under orders from Sun Yatsen returned to France and collaborated with Zhou Enlai to form the EGMD in France. A leftist, Wang agreed to Communist proposals during 1925 to expel several right-faction members. Expelled a second time by the French, Wang Jingqi died aboard ship in 1925.

Wang Jingwei 汪精衞

1883–1944, b. Guangdong. Other name: Wang Zhaoming.

Wang Jingwei was a leader of many movements. He began his career with an assassination attempt and ended it as head of the Japanese puppet government during the Second World War. Wang was a promoter of the Work-Study Movement, having spent time in Japan and Europe. He rose within the GMD and was one of three leaders after the death of Sun Yatsen. Wang Jingwei led the leftist faction of the GMD and for a short time headed a rival government in Wuhan after Jiang Jieshi's coup of 1927. However, Wang Jingwei abandoned the Wuhan effort, although he was still a rival to Jiang. In 1940 Wang accepted the post of head of state for the Japanese puppet government. Wang's life ended in an ironical twist as he saw his friends assassinated for their collaboration with the Japanese, and he himself was injured. Wang died in 1944, before the end of the conflict.

Wang Linghan 王凌漢

Position: Secretary, Wu Xi Region.

Wang Linghan was one of those who attended the first meeting of the ECYC. He was also one of the first group of Chinese who went to the Soviet Union in 1923. Upon his return, he became Secretary of the Wu Xi region. No further information about him is available.

Wang Renda 王人達

1900–57, b. Liuyang, Hunan.

An early Work-Study Movement participant, Wang joined the ECYC in 1922 and the ECCP in 1924. He spent over two decades in the Soviet Union, returning in 1957, and died the same year in Beijing.

Wang Ruofei 王若飛

1896–1946, b. Anxun, Guizhou. Other name: Lei Yin. Positions: Henan-Shenxi Regional Committee Secretary, CCP Central Committee Secretary, member of CCP Central Committee.

Wang Ruofei went to France in 1919 with his uncle Huang Qisheng. He worked for three years in the factories. Although coming from a moderate position, he was angered by the struggles of 1921 and participated in the founding of the ECYC. Wang went to the Soviet Union and returned to China in 1925. He worked in several posts before being elected to the Central Committee in 1927. Wang attended the Sixth Congress of the CCP in Moscow, where he was not reelected to the Central Committee. In 1931 he returned to China after spending three years in the Soviet Union and was arrested. Wang Ruofei spent over five years in prison. After he was released during the Second United Front he participated in diverse activities for the CCP. Helping with negotiations in 1946, Wang was killed in an airplane accident.

Wang Zekai 汪澤楷

Other name: Ke Ti. Positions: ECCO Executive Committee (1923), Anyuan Provincial Committee Head (1923–24), Jiangxi Provincial Committee Head (1926–28).

An important student representative during the Lyons Incident, Wang Zekai was a founding member of the ECYC. He was elected in January 1923 to head the Student Movement Committee. When Wang returned to China, he was sent to Anyuan. Later, he was the head of the Jiangxi Provincial Committee for three years. Wang was expelled from the CCP in 1929 with other Trotskyites. He was arrested in the forties. In the late fifties he was in Guilin.

Wei Bi 魏璧

b. Changsha, Hunan, d. 1969.

Wei Bi was a New Citizens' Study Society member. She was one of the first of the group to go to France and graduated from Lyons University in 1927. She returned to China and taught at Sun Yatsen University. After 1949 she continued with her educational vocation at Zhongguo Renmin University. She died of illness in 1969. Wei Bi was a close friend of Lao Junzhan.

Wu Qi 吳琪

b. 1898, Jiangsu.

Wu Qi went to France in 1919 and was a negotiator during the Lyons Incident. Later he was arrested by the French police and went to Germany. He was an active participant in the ECCO. He returned to China in 1926 and went to work in Canton. Wu Qi later faced long imprisonment as a Trotskyite. After his release he worked at the Shanghai Revolution Museum until his death.

Wu Yuzhang 吳玉章

1878–1966, b. Rongxian, Sichuan. Other name: Yong Shan. Position: President, Institute of Socialism.

Wu was an active member of the Tongmenghui and the early GMD. He spent over thirty years of his life in foreign countries, particularly Japan and France. Wu Yuzhang was an important educator and promoter of the Work-Study Movement. He was introduced into the CCP by his student Zhao Shiyan in 1925. Wu joined the Communists in Yanan. His later activities centered on the reform of the Chinese language, and he was an important sponsor of simplified characters.

Wu Zhihui 吳稚輝

1864–1953, b. Jiangsu. Other name: Jing Heng.

Along with Li Shizeng, Wu Zhihui was one of the more dynamic personalities in modern Chinese history. Involved in the Tongmenghui, Wu Zhihui traveled to many countries in Europe and to Japan. He studied in Scotland and lived in England for several years. Wu edited Xin shiji with Li Shizeng, and he also helped found the various organizations of the Work-Study Movement. Wu became more conservative in the early twenties and was part of the Western Hills faction of the GMD, which wanted the expulsion of the Communists from the United Front. After 1949 Wu·lived in Taiwan.

Xia Ting 夏霆

b. 1903, Anjing.

Xia Ting was the leader of the extremist EGMD faction during the split following the April coup in 1927. He had close linkages with the French Communist Party. He was known for his oratory and highly visible presence at international meetings. Xia was expelled by the French in September 1927.

Xiang Jingyu 向警予

1894–1928, b. Xupu, Hunan. Other name: Zheng Yu. Positions: First Head of the Women's Bureau of the CCP, CCP Central Committee(?).

Xiang Jingyu is often cited as one of the most important early feminists in the Communist movement. She was a brilliant student and an active member of the New Citizens' Study Society. Xiang helped organize women who wanted to participate in the Work-Study Movement. She left for France in 1920 and went to work and study at Montargis. She married Cai Hesen the same year. Xiang had previously felt that education was the route for national salvation, but during 1919–20 she became a staunch Marxist. After Cai Hesen was expelled, Xiang followed him in 1922. She joined the CCP and was given important responsibilities. Xiang Jingyu was a very persuasive organizer and, like her husband, worked long hours. They had two children, who stayed with Ge Jianhao. In 1925 Xiang went to the Soviet Union. It was during this time that her marriage with Cai developed problems and they permanently separated in 1926. In 1927 Xiang organized factory labor in Guangzhou and then went to Wuhan, where she was captured in March. She was executed on 1 May 1928 at the age of thirty-four.

Xiao Pusheng 蕭樸生

d. 1926. Other name: Jue Nu.

Xiao was a founder of the ECYC. He was an alternate to the Executive Committee. After he returned to China, he performed CCP work in Jinan, where he died of illness in 1926.

Xiao Zisheng 蕭子升

b. 1893, Xiangxiang, Hunan. Other names: Xiao Xudong, Xiao Yu. Position: First President, New Citizens' Study Society.

Xiao Zisheng is an interesting case of an active and brilliant personality committed to moderate means for national salvation. Xiao worked for the Sino-French Educational Association and believed in education as the best means of national reform. As first president of the New Citizens' Study Society and secretary to Li Shizeng, Xiao had a profound influence on his fellow Hunanese youth. He defeated Cai Hesen's proposal to form a Marxist party in the summer of 1920. After his return to China, Xiao worked for the GMD government in the Ministry of Education. After 1949 Xiao lived in Europe for several years and then moved to Uruguay, where he oversaw the Chinese library collection that had been assembled by his mentor, Li Shizeng.

Xiao Zizhang 蕭子暲

1897–1983, b. Xiangxiang, Hunan. Other names: Xiao San, Zhi Fan, Tian Guang. Positions: Head of the Zhangjiakou Regional Committee, Communist Youth League.

Xiao Zizhang, the younger brother of Xiao Zisheng, wrote prolifically about the Work-Study Movement in the early twenties. He was a New Citizens' Study Society member and a founder of the ECYC. Because of his good French, Xiao Zizhang was the liaison between the ECCO and the French Communist Party. Later Xiao went to the Soviet Union. He returned to China and participated in CCP activities, holding various posts, mostly in the Communist Youth League. Xiao's interests were in cultural spheres; he wrote books and promoted better intercultural relations. He spent many years as the cultural ambassador to the Soviet Union. During the Cultural Revolution, Xiao was imprisoned for several years.

Xie Weijin 謝唯進

d. 1978.

Xie was an early participant in the ECCO. He stayed in Europe performing Comintern propaganda and organizational work for many years. After 1949 Xie worked for the air force in China.

Xiong Jing 熊靜

b. 1904, Hunan.

Xiong Jing was a charity student of Xu Teli's at Chuyi Elementary School. He left with Xu to go to Europe but could not endure the miserable conditions. Xiong accepted aid from Father Lebbe's organization and went to study in Belgium, where he graduated in 1925 in engineering. He worked as an airplane inspector in Belgium and was persuaded by Shen Yijia to return to China in the early thirties. Xiong stayed after 1949, and in 1956 joined the CCP.

Xiong Rui 熊銳

b. Guangdong, d. 1927.

After a short time in France, Xiong Rui went to Germany and helped with the German Branch of the ECCP. When he returned to China he taught at the Huangpu Military Academy. He was killed in the violence of 1927.

Xiong Xiong 熊雄

1892–1927, b. Yifeng, Jiangxi.

Xiong Xiong was involved in the revolutionary politics of 1916 on behalf of Sun Yatsen. In 1920 he went to France and then to Germany and participated in the formation of the ECCO. In 1923 he left for the Soviet Union. In 1925 he returned to China and assumed a position at the Huangpu Military Academy. Xiong Xiong was killed in the violence of 1927.

Xu Deheng 許德珩

b. 1895, Jiujiang, Jiangxi. Position: Minister of Aquatic Products.

Xu Deheng was one of the most famous May Fourth Movement activists. In 1920 he went to France, studying until 1927, when he returned to China. While he was in France, Xu was involved in the struggles of 1921, severing his relations with Wu Zhihui over the Lyons Incident. Xu was also elected as a secretary in the organizational efforts to oppose foreign consolidation of Chinese railways in 1923. Xu Deheng was an important member of the third force in China, participating in the December Ninth Movement in 1935 and organizing the Democracy and Science Discussion Group. Xu and his wife, Lao Junzhan, stayed in China after 1949 and held various posts. In 1956 Xu was appointed Minister of Aquatic Products.

Xu Teli 徐特立

1877–1968, b. Changsha, Hunan. Other name: Xu Zhouxun. Positions: Central People's Government Council, China Peace Committee, All-China Educational Workers' Trade Union, China Geographic Society.

Xu Teli is usually cited as one of the most revered elders of the Communist revolution, along with Wu Yuzhang. Xu was also important to the Work-Study Movement as an example of an older participant (he was in his forties). Xu was an important educationalist in Hunan, working at several schools in the Changsha area. Xu studied and worked in France, and in 1923 he returned to China. In 1927 he joined the CCP and went to the Soviet Union for several years of study. After 1949, Xu participated in governmental activities at high levels.

Yan Changyi 顏昌頤

d. 1929. Position: CCP Military Affairs Committee (1927–28).

Yan Changyi was one of the students expelled in the Lyons Incident. Yan joined the CCP and participated in military affairs, joining the Northern Expedition and the Nanchang Uprising in 1927. Yan was betrayed in 1929 and executed along with Peng Pai.

Yang Kun 楊堃

b. 1900, Hebei.

One of the original students at the Sino-French Institute, Yang Kun was also a member of the ECCO until 1927. He obtained his doctorate in sociology in 1930 and promoted minority studies and Western social science in China, heading the History Department at Yunnan University for over thirty years in the post-1949 period. Yang is currently at Beijing Normal University. He is the widower of Zhang Ruoming.

Yang Qian 楊潛

b. 1901, Canton. Position: Executive Committee of the European Guomindang.

A student at the Sino-French Institute, Yang Qian left the institute for Paris in 1927 to study aviation. Yang was a high-ranking member of the right-faction EGMD from 1926 to 1927.

Yi Guangyi 伊光彝

b. 1899. Other name: Yee Kwang Yee.

While studying law in Paris, Yi Guangyi headed the first reorganization of the left-faction EGMD in the spring of 1927, before the split of the CCP and the Wuhan government. Yi was a notable orator, and articles appeared about him in L'humanité.

Yin Kuan 尹寬

d. 1952. Positions: ECYC Executive Committee; Zhejiang Provincial Committee Head (1925), Anhui Provincial Committee Head (1927).

Yin Kuan was an initial founder of the ECYC and served on the Executive Committee and as head of the Communist Study Society. After his return to China he worked in both Zhejiang and Anhui. Yin was expelled in 1929 as a Trotskyite and later imprisoned.

Yuan Qingyun 袁慶雲

b. Sichuan.

Yuan Qingyun was a founder of the ECYC and a good friend of Zhao Shiyan. While Zhao did not have his passport, all his mail went through Yuan Qingyun in Paris. Yuan was one of the first ECCO members to go to the Soviet Union. Nothing further is known about his activities.

Yuan Zizhen 袁子貞

b. Hebei, d. 1927. Position: Secretary of the Shijiazhuang Region.

Yuan Zizhen was an example of a politicized laborer. He was a founding member of the ECYC. Yuan was an alternate to the Executive Committee of the ECYC. He often helped with labor issues and publications. He returned in 1923 to China and became secretary of the Shijiazhuang region. Yuan became involved in the organization of railroad workers. He was killed in Tianjin in 1927.

Zeng Qi 曾琦

1892–1951, b. Luchang, Sichuan. Other names: Mu Han, Yu Gong. Position: A founder and Chairman of the Chinese Youth Party.

Zeng Qi was a lifelong anti-Communist and an important opponent of the ECCO in Europe, fostering opposition to the Communists and their United Front policy with the EGMD. In December 1923, Zeng Qi along with eleven others formed the Chinese Youth Party. He served as the chairman of this organization through the Second World War. Zeng Qi had also been instrumental in the Young China Study Association and was one of the students who returned from Japan in 1918, one year before the May Fourth Movement. Zeng Qi is important because he illustrates that non-Communists were not necessarily less "radical." Zeng constantly published antitraditionalist tracts, involved himself in the new journalism, and advocated assassination as an important tactic to overthrow the corrupt warlords. After the Communist victory, Zeng moved to the United States, where he died in 1951.

Zhang Bojian 張伯簡

b. Yunnan, d. 1925. Positions: A founder of the Work-Study Alliance, Guangdong-Guangxi Military Affairs Committee Secretary.

Zhang Bojian was a founder of the Work-Study Alliance, and after the Lyons Incident he went to Germany, where he helped found the German Branch of the ECYC. Among the tasks Zhang performed for the CCP when he returned to China were railroad labor organization in Shanghai, publishing responsibilities, and secretary of the Guangdong-Guangxi Military Affairs Committee. Zhang died of illness in 1925. Zhang was noted for his Comintern connections.

Zhang Guotao 張國燾

b. 1897, Jishui, Jiangxi. Other name: Te Li. Position: CCP Central Committee.

Zhang Guotao was a protégé of Chen Duxiu. During the twenties Zhang was involved in policy-making and labor organization efforts. Zhang spent the thirties in the Henan-Anhui Soviet and met Mao Zedong and Zhu De in the Long March, while he and two other groups were attempting (unsuccessful) treks of their own. Later, power struggles ensued, and Zhang left the CCP in 1938, eventually settling in Hong Kong. In recent years Zhang has published his memoirs, which have sparked much controversy and response from other early CCP members.

Zhang Kundi 張昆弟

1894–1930, b. Yiyang, Hunan. Other name: Zhi Fu. Positions: Shandong Provincial Committee Secretary (1927), Northern Bureau (1928).

Zhang was a popular member of the New Citizens' Study Society, known for his ruggedness and inquisitive nature. Zhang went to France in 1919 but was expelled in the Lyons Incident. On his return to China, Zhang mostly worked in the north in Shandong and in the Northern Bureau. Zhang was killed in 1930 at the age of thirty-six.

Zhang Ruoming 張若名

1902–58, b. Baoding, Zhili. Position: ECCO Executive Committee (1924).

Zhang Ruoming was a graduate of the Tianjin Zhili First Normal Female School and a founder of the Self-Awakening Society. She was a prominent participant in Tianjin May Fourth student politics and was imprisoned with Zhou Enlai and Guo Longzhen for half a year in 1920. A Frugal-Study student, Zhang joined the ECCO but quit in 1924. Pursuing studies at the Sino-French Institute, Zhang wrote an eloquent thesis on André Gide, which was read and personally praised by Gide. Zhang returned to China with her husband, Yang Kun, in 1931 and entered academic life. She had some minimal participation in third policy politics. In 1958, afflicted with cancer, and depressed by the anti-intellectual campaign, Zhang Ruoming committed suicide.

Zhang Shenfu 張申府

1893–1986. Other names: Zhang Songnian, "R." Position: Liaison between ECCO and Chen Duxiu.

Zhang Shenfu, a disciple of Chen Duxiu, had been an Anarchist when he first went to France in 1920. Zhang had been a member of the Young China Study Association but publicly severed his ties with this group. According to his own account, Zhang led four others (Liu Qingyang, Zhou Enlai, Zhao Shiyan, and Chen Gongpei) in forming a nucleus for the ECCO. Zhang had been hired as an instructor at the Sino-French Institute but resigned after the Lyons Incident and moved to Germany with Liu and Zhou. The ECYC expelled him during their second meeting in February 1923. Neither the German Branch of the ECYC nor the Comintern accepted the expulsion, and Zhang was reinstated. Zhang went to the Soviet Union in 1923 and upon his return to China was at first unsuccessful in obtaining academic employment. He quit the CCP in 1925.

Zhang Wenjia 張文甲

b. 1901, Canton. Position: Executive Committee, Guomindang.

A member of the right faction of the Guomindang, Zhang Wenjia left the Sino-French Institute in 1927 to pursue legal studies.

Zhao Shiyan 趙世炎

1901–27, b. Youyang, Sichuan. Other names: Qin Sun, Guo Fu, Dong Sheng, Shi Ying. Positions: First General Secretary of the ECYC, Head of the French Branch of the ECCP, CCP Central Committee, Propaganda Chief of the Northern Bureau, Organizational Head of the Zhejiang Provincial Committee, Secretary of the Shanghai Confederation of Labor Unions, Secretary of Shanghai Municipality.

Zhao Shiyan was the key member of the ECCO who did the necessary work to unify the various Marxist factions. He had led a group in opposition to Cai Hesen's at the beginning of 1921, but the groups cooperated during the Lyons Incident. Zhao organized the first and second meetings of the ECYC and in 1923 went to the Soviet Union. He returned to China in 1924, where he assumed a variety of tasks. Among his greatest contributions were his theoretical writings in the Party newspaper *Xiangdao* and his own journal, *Zhengzhi shenghuo* (*Political Life*), which he edited. Zhao was elected to the CCP Central Committee in 1927. He was a popular speaker and a superlative organizer. In 1925 Zhao married Xia Zhixu, who was also a CCP member. Zhao Shiyan was executed in the violence of 1927 at the age of twenty-six. Before his capture he quickly ensured the safety of other CCP members by giving his wife a message for Wang Ruofei. The village of Youyang has a commemorative museum for Zhao Shiyan.

Zheng Chaolin 鄭超麟

b. 1901, Fujian. Position: An editor of *Buweiersike*.

Zheng Chaolin was a founder of the ECYC. He was a member of the Zhao Shiyan clique during the Twenty-eighth Movement. Zheng went to the Soviet Union in 1923. When he returned to China he was mostly involved in propaganda with the paper *Xiangdao* and the Publishing Bureau (1927–28). In the chaos of the April Twelfth Coup, Zheng became an editor of *Buweiersike* (*The Bolshevik*). Zheng was labeled a Trostskyite and expelled from the CCP. He was imprisoned by the GMD during the forties and by the Communists from 1952 until 1979. Zheng is one of the ECCO members who in recent years has written useful memoirs of other members of that period.

Zhou Enlai 周恩來

1898–1976, b. Huaian, Jiangsu. Other names: Wu Hao, Fei Fei. Positions: CCP Central Committee, Premier, Vice-Chairman.

Next to Mao Zedong, Zhou Enlai has been the most researched Chinese Communist. Zhou Enlai was known for his diplomatic abilities in smoothing over rough situations. Zhou Enlai was the second secretary of the ECYC and coordinated the CCP policy of the United Front with the GMD by setting up their European office. From 1922 to 1924, Zhou shuttled back and forth between Berlin and Paris. Upon his return to China in 1924, Zhou Enlai occupied the important position of political officer at Huangpu Military Academy. His stature and position were strong during the next fifty years. Although Zhou served on the pre-1927 Military Committee, his real abilities were as a politician. After 1949, Zhou Enlai made a very effective foreign minister, scoring international successes at the Geneva Conference of 1954 and the Bandung Conference of 1955. When he passed away in 1976, China lost one of its most important leaders.

Zhou Taixuan 周太玄

b. Sichuan.

Zhou Taixuan was a founder of the Young China Study Association and a prominent example of self-sufficiency. Zhou was a prolific writer on educational topics and also a journalist. Zhou's activism was similar to Wang Guangqi's: he did not participate in the militant conservatism of the Chinese Youth Party, and yet he did not adhere to the Communist vision of immediate revolution. After 1949, Zhou Taixuan apparently remained in China, where he wrote some memoir pieces. Zhou died in the midsixties during the Cultural Revolution.

Zhu De 朱德

1886–1976, b. Yihong, Sichuan. Other name: Yu Jie. Positions: CCP Politburo, founder of the Red Army.

Zhu De was introduced into the ECCP by Zhou Enlai in 1922. He was an older man and some were mistrustful of him because of his earlier connections with warlords and his opium habit, but Zhou Enlai saw his potential. Zhu returned to China and a very successful military career, leading the Communists to victory against the Japanese and the GMD. At the ceremony declaring the People's Republic of China, Zhu De stood with Mao Zedong and Zhou Enlai on the rostrum. After 1949 he continued to hold high posts and positions.

Zhu Xi 朱洗

b. 1899, Zhejiang.

Zhu Xi was one of the first Chinese to study at Montpellier and later entered the Sino-French Institute. He wrote about the factory side of the Work-Study Movement and later was important in the effort for the return of the Boxer Indemnity. Zhu Xi became a prominent scientist.

Zuo Shunsheng 左舜生

b. 1898, Changsha, Hunan. Positions: Editor-in-Chief of China Commercial Press, Minister of Agriculture and Forestry, Executive Yuan.

Zuo Shunsheng was an active leader in both the Young China Study Association and the Chinese Youth Party. Zuo was a latecomer to the French scene, living there from 1926 until 1928, but his contacts with Li Huang and Zeng Qi were important for all parties concerned. An educator and a prolific writer, Zuo was editor-in-chief at the China Commercial Press for over ten years. He was an anti-Communist, and as a Chinese Youth Party member also anti-GMD. However, in 1938, the Chinese Youth Party changed its position and Zuo was appointed the Minister of Agriculture and Forestry, and he also was a part of the Executive Yuan. After 1949, Zuo settled in Hong Kong, but he also spent time in Taiwan.

Appendix 2
ORGANIZATIONS

Comité franco-chinois de patronage des jeunes chinois en France

The Comité franco-chinois de patronage des jeunes chinois en France (Faguo jianhu Zhongguo liu Fa qingnian weiyuanhui) was formed during the spring of 1921, in response to the economic woes of the poor Chinese students in France. It not only saw to some repatriations and raised 250,000 francs on behalf of the Chinese but also sponsored intercultural exchanges, in short, replacing the role of the Sino-French Educational Association. After the Loan Struggle in 1921, because of the economic infeasibility of supporting several hundred students each month, the financial aid was cut back.

ECCO (European Branches of the Chinese Communist Organizations)

See Lü Ou Zhongguo shaonian gongchandang *and* Zhongguo gongchandang lü Ou zhibu.

Gongchandang (The Chinese Communist Party—CCP) 共產黨

The CCP was formed in July 1921 in China. In 1924 the CCP, under orders from the Comintern, entered en masse into the Guomindang in the First United Front, which lasted until the successes of the Northern Expedition of 1927 and Jiang Jieshi's coup. At this time a mass slaughter of CCP members occurred, including some of the most prominent returned ECCO members, such as Zhao Shiyan and Chen Yannian. During the War of Resistance against Japan, the CCP and the GMD formed one more United Front, which lasted until the confrontation in 1949, when the CCP came to power.

Gongdu huzhu tuan (Work-Study Mutual-Aid Corps)
工讀互助團

Promoted by the famous student activist Wang Guangqi, the Work-Study Mutual-Aid Corps began in Beijing, in early 1920. Inspired by the New Culture Movement, the aims of the corps included working four hours a day, studying four hours a day, and contributing to the costs of mutual living. Branches of the corps spread to major cities throughout China. However, the effort was short-lived and failed for a variety of reasons: lack of capital, lack of financial expertise, and the demanding agenda.

Gongxue shijie she (Society for the World of Work-Study)

工學世界社

Originally called the Qingong jianxue lijin hui (The Society for the Encouragement of Work-Study), the group was formed in February 1920 by Hunanese Li Weihan, Li Fuchun, Luo Xuezan, Ren Li, Zhang Kundi, He Guo, Li Lin, and others. The purpose of the group was to provide comfort and mutual encouragement in a foreign land, as well as a network of material support. More radical members of the New Citizens' Study Society like Cai Hesen tried to get the organization to adopt a Marxist platform. While progressive, the Society for the World of Work-Study did not adopt any radical policies until the Twenty-eighth Movement, and by the time of the formation of the ECCO most members were committed Marxists. The membership of the society grew to over forty and included Xiao Zizhang, Bo Lie, Wang Renda, Hou Changguo, Guo Chuntao, Ou Yangtai, Liu Mingyan, Jiang Zekai, and Xiao Ba.

Gongyushe (The Surplus Society) 工餘社

This Anarchist organization was established at the beginning of 1922. One of the most famous students, Hua Lin, was the leading Anarchist, but the group originally counted on the support of Chen Yannian and Chen Qiaonian, who joined the ECCO in the summer of 1922. The society published a newspaper, which lasted until mid-1925, and held lively debates with the ECCO. The focus of the Gongyushe critique of communism was the totalitarian nature of the Soviet Union's regime and more philosophical issues.

Guomindang (The Chinese Nationalist Party) 國民黨

Founded by Sun Yatsen, the Guomindang was the modernized version of the revolutionary organization Tongmenghui. Sun Yatsen, unable to control the Chinese national apparatus after the Revolution of 1911, made his base in the south and eventually consented to aid from Bolshevik Russia and a United Front with the CCP. After Sun Yatsen's death in 1925, Jiang Jieshi successfully pursued the Eastern and Northern Expeditions, took control of the GMD, and purged the Communists in 1927. The thirties were the decade of the GMD, but they lost the civil war with the CCP and since 1949 have maintained their government in retreat on the island of Taiwan.

Hua Fa jiaoyuhui (The Sino-French Educational Association)

華法教育會

Founded in March 1916 in Paris by Cai Yuanpei and other educators such as Li Shizeng, Wu Yuzhang, and Wu Zhihui, the Sino-French Educational Association's goals included the interchange of students and culture. After the First World War the need for more labor in France led to a mass promotion of a Work-Study program in China. Over 1,600 youth, most of them processed by the Sino-French Educational Association, went to France between 1919 and 1921. But the Sino-French Educational Association did not anticipate the logistical problems of placing so many students and ensuring that they had an adequate level of French or factory skills. In January 1921, the Sino-French Educational Association abrogated financial responsibility for the Work-Study Movement, and the political struggles of 1921 ensued. Although the Sino-French Educational Association still functioned, and in 1922 helped to distribute aid to the remaining worker-students, its heyday was over.

Huagong hui (The Chinese Labor Union) 華工會

Formed in January 1920, the Huagong hui was one of several Chinese labor organizations whose main goal was to protect the interests of Chinese laborers left in France after the First World War. With over 6,000 members, the Huagong hui also set up schools for laborers and published newspapers. The organization also tried to encourage its members not to gamble or otherwise waste their money. Later, the ECCO would take over the leadership and recruit from the union. In the early twenties, the organization's name was changed to Huagong zonghui (Chinese Trade Union).

Huaqiao xieshe (The Chinese Federation) 華僑協社

The Huaqiao xieshe was an umbrella organization that provided many groups with a central place to gather and hold activities. Formed in August 1919, the Huaqiao xieshe sponsored all kinds of organizations, from a Chemistry club, the Paris Correspondence Service, to the Chinese Labor Union. Finally, when the Work-Study Movement was at its lowest point, the floors of the Huaqiao xieshe were covered with the sleeping bodies of Work-Study students.

Jianxuehui (The Frugal-Study Society) 儉學會

The Frugal-Study Society was established in February 1912 by Cai Yuanpei, Li Shizeng, Wu Yuzhang, and Wu Zhihui. It promoted study and frugal living in the West, and at least three groups of students went under the Frugal-Study Society auspices to France. The society was often called the

Liu Fa jianxuehui, but there were also societies set up for England and the United States. The First World War interrupted the flow of Frugal-Study Society members to the West. Although the society was defunct as an organization after the First World War, many students designated themselves Jianxue students, most often to emphasize the fact that they would live frugally but were not about to become laborers. However, in the end, most students had no choice in the matter.

Juewushe (The Self-Awakening Society) 覺悟社

Although the Young China Study Association and the New Citizens' Study Society had met before the May Fourth Movement, the Self-Awakening Society was formed in September 1919. The society, composed of twenty members in Tianjin, sought to develop through debate and activities a new political consciousness among its members. The most prominent members of the Self-Awakening Society were Zhou Enlai, Liu Qingyang, Ma Jun, Guo Longzhen, and Zhang Ruoming. Zhou, Liu, Guo, and Zhang all went to France by the end of 1920. The Self-Awakening Society never developed to the degree of the New Citizens' Study Society or the Young China Study Association, but it followed the same pattern of dissension and disintegration.

Lü Ou Zhongguo shaonian gongchandang (The European Branch of the Chinese Communist Youth Party)
旅歐中國少年共產黨

With a beginning membership of over forty, the youth party was founded in June 1922, led by Zhao Shiyan, Zhou Enlai, and Li Weihan. Officially sanctioned by the CCP, it strove to inculcate its members with Marxist theories and recruit new members. Its propaganda organ was *Shaonian* (*Youth*) and later *Chiguang* (*Red Light*). In early 1923, on orders of the CCP, the youth party changed its name to the Zhongguo shehui zhuyi qingniantuan lü Ou zhibu (the European Branch of the Chinese Socialist Youth Corps) but often retained the word "Communist" in their title, in spite of these orders. By 1925 its membership had reached 500–600 people.

Lü Ou zhonggong zong zhibu 旅歐中共總支部

See Zhongguo gongchandang lü Ou zhibu.

Qingong jianxuehui (The Diligent-Work Frugal-Study Association)
勤工儉學會

The Work-Study Movement was predicated on the principles of this society, which were diligent labor and thrifty study. The society was formed

in March 1915 in Paris to encourage and promote the Work-Study principles. Cai Yuanpei cited the practical responsibilities of the Qingong jianxuehui toward the worker-students in his announcements of 1921, but the
statutes of the society specifically stated that the nature of the organization
was not material but spiritual.

Qingong jianxue tongmeng (The Work-Study Alliance)
勤工儉學同盟

The Work-Study Alliance was formed by Zhao Shiyan, Wang Ruofei, Li
Lisan, Zhang Bojian, and several others in response to the early crises of
1921. The philosophy of the Work-Study Alliance was one of self-
sufficiency and mutual aid. The students did not want the support of a corrupt warlord government, in direct opposition to the Montargis faction and
the Twenty-eighth Movement. Within several weeks there were over 200
student-laborers who joined the Work-Study Alliance. Disturbed by the
disunity in the student movement, Zhao Shiyan, who headed the Work-
Study Alliance, eventually reached an accord with the Montargis faction.

Qingniandang (The Chinese Youth Party)   青年黨

The Chinese Youth Party was formed by Zeng Qi, Li Huang, Hu Guowei,
and nine others in December 1923. Zeng Qi, the leader of the party, had
wanted to form such a group since the beginning of 1923. The Chinese
Youth Party was adamantly opposed to the ECCO reliance on the Russian
model of revolution and was especially antipathetic to Russian aid. Referred
to as the Nationalist Clique, the Chinese Youth Party wanted slower, but
progressive, change in the Chinese social and political system. They emphasized change through education and the cultivation of public opinion.
The Chinese Youth Party was a true third alternative but also suffered under
a label of being associated with warlords and espousing an ideology similar
to fascism. Although its members were willing to use violence, their influence in China, even when the leadership went home in 1924, while not
negligible, was never extensive.

Shaonian Zhongguo xuehui (The Young China Study Association)
少年中國學會

Formally established in the summer of 1919, the Young China Study Association had actually existed the year before. It was an association of youth
who were interested in leading China into a new age. Many of the most
prominent and thoughtful students led the progressive organization, such as
Wang Guangqi, Zeng Qi, Zhou Taixuan, and Li Dazhao. Incorporating the

values of the New Culture era, the Young China Study Association's motto was "Our Association dedicates itself to Social Services under the guidance of the Scientific Spirit, in order to realize our ideal of creating a young China." By 1922 the association was split over the question of whether to study and provide a basis for discussion of varying solutions to China's problems or to foster social movements. The question was never decisively answered, and by 1925 the group was essentially dissolved.

Xinmin xuehui (New Citizens' Study Society) 新民學會

The New Citizens' Study Society was a group of patriotic youth formed in Hunan. Like the Self-Awakening Society and the Young China Study Association, it served as a forum of intellectual debate. It was formed in April 1918, and the first president of the group was Xiao Zisheng, who influenced the group by becoming active in the Work-Study Movement. By 1919 there were over sixty members, of whom almost a third eventually went to France. Both the French section and the Hunan section were wracked by the same questions that assailed the other groups—over what role they should play and what route they should choose for national salvation. Half the members became Marxists, and the other half had other affiliations by 1921–22.

Zhongguo gongchandang lü Ou zhibu (The European Branch of the Chinese Communist Party—ECCP)
中國共產黨旅歐支部

Originally formed in the winter of 1922, the ECCP apparently used the ECYC as a recruiting ground. Since both organizations had the same goals and tactics, as well as overlapping membership, I refer to them collectively as the ECCO (European Branches of the Chinese Communist Organizations). The ECCO was involved in recruitment, ideological training, and propaganda-agitation activities. During the first phase of ECCO activities (1922–25) the ECCO recruited 500 members. During this period the ECCO sent several groups back home through the Soviet Union. Another major activity involved the domination, along with the leftists, of the European GMD until the coup of 1927. During the May Thirtieth Incident of 1925, the ECCO occupied the Chinese Ministry in Paris, and several leaders were expelled from France. After the violence of 1927, the ECCO was largely incorporated into a Chinese-language branch of the French Communist Party. However, the ECCO organ Chiguang was published into the thirties. It appears that the headquarters shifted in the late twenties from Paris, France, to Hamburg, Germany.

Zhongguo lü Fa ge tuanti lianhehui (The United Federation of Chinese Organizations Abroad in France)

中國旅法各團體聯合會

The federation was formed during the Railroad Struggle (1923) and comprised twenty-two different organizations. The federation survived the Railroad Struggle and reflected the more conservative stance of the Chinese Youth Party, as it was headed by Chinese Youth Party faithfuls such as He Luzhi. By 1925 over thirty-three organizations had joined.

Zhongguo shehui minzhudang (The Chinese Social Democratic Party)

中國社會民主黨

Although the Zhongguo shehui minzhudang is not a well-known organization, it had over 500 members in the French community between 1924 and 1929. Formed in the winter of 1922, the party published a paper, *Fendou* (*Combat*), which lasted for more than 100 issues. The organization had some lively internal political divisions.

BIBLIOGRAPHY

ARCHIVAL MATERIALS

Archives de l'Association universitaire franco-chinoise (AAUFC), Lyons
Archives du Ministère des affaires étrangères (AAE), Paris
Archives nationales (AN), Paris
Archives nationales, Section d'outre-mer (AOM), Aix-en-Provence
Centre de recherches et de documentation sur la Chine contemporaine, Ecole des
   hautes études en sciences sociales, Paris
Chinese Communist Party History Archives, Qinghua University, Beijing
Guomindang Shanghai Archives, Yangmingshan
Public Record Office (PRO), London

WESTERN LANGUAGE SOURCES

Bailey, Paul. "The Chinese Work-Study Movement in France." *China Quarterly* 115
   (September 1988): 441–61.
Bailey, Thomas A. *Woodrow Wilson and the Lost Peace*. Chicago: Quadrangle Books,
   1963.
Barman, Geneviève, and Nicole Dulioust. *Etudiants-ouvriers chinois en France:
   1920–1940*. Paris: Editions de l'Ecole des Hautes Etudes en Sciences Sociales,
   1981.
———. "Un groupe oublie: Les étudiantes-ouvrieres chinoises en France." *Etudes
   chinoises* 6, no. 2 (1987): 9–46.
———. "La France au miroir chinois." *Les temps modernes* 498 (January 1988):
   32–67.
———. "The Communists in the Work and Study Movement in France." *Republi-
   can China* 13 (April 1988): 24–39.
Bartke, Wolfgang. *Who's Who in the People's Republic of China*. New York: M. E.
   Sharpe, 1981.
Becker, Jean-Jacques. *The Great War and the French People*. Translated by Arnold
   Pomerans. New York: St. Martin's Press, 1986.
Blick, Judith. "The Chinese Labor Corps in World War I." East Asian Research
   Center Papers on China, no. 9:111–45. Cambridge: Harvard University Press,
   1955.
Bloch, Marc. *Strange Defeat: A Statement of Evidence Written in 1940*. Translated by
   Gerard Hopkins. London: Oxford University Press, 1949.
Boorman, Howard L., and Richard C. Howard, eds. *Biographical Dictionary of Re-
   publican China*. 5 vols. New York: Columbia University Press, 1967.
Bouchez, D. "Un défricheur méconnu des études extrême-orientales: Maurice
   Courant (1865–1935)." *Journal asiatique* 271 (1983): 43–150.

Brandt, Conrad. *Stalin's Failure in China, 1924–1927.* New York: W. W. Norton, 1958.

————. "The French-Returned Elite in the Chinese Communist Party." Institute of International Studies, Berkeley Reprint no. 13. Hong Kong: Hong Kong University Press, 1961.

Burns, James MacGregor. *Leadership.* New York: Harper Colophon, 1978.

Cavanaugh, James. *Who's Who in China.* 6 vols. Hong Kong: Chinese Materials Center, 1982.

Chan, Gilbert F., and Thomas H. Etzold, eds. *China in the 1920s: Nationalism and Revolution.* New York: New Viewpoints, 1976.

Chan King-tong. "Review of Reference Materials on the History of the European Branches of the Chinese Communist Organizations." Translated by William L. MacDonald. *Republican China* 13 (April 1988): 59–86.

Chan Lau Kit-chang. *The Chinese Youth Party, 1923–1945.* Centre of Asian Studies Occasional Papers and Monographs, no. 9. Hong Kong: University of Hong Kong, 1972.

Chang, Howard S. "Chinese Students in Japan." *Chinese Students' Monthly* 13 (April 1918): 322–25.

Chang Kuo-t'ao. *The Rise of the Chinese Communist Party: 1921–1938.* 2 vols. Lawrence: University Press of Kansas, 1971.

Chevrier, Yves. "Utopian Marxism: 'Populist Strains' and Conceptual Growth Pains in Early Chinese Communism, 1920–1922." In Yu-ming Shaw, ed., *Reform and Revolution in Twentieth Century China.* Taibei: Institute of International Relations, 1987.

Chi Hsin. *Teng Hsiao-ping: A Political Biography.* Hong Kong: Cosmos Books, 1981.

Chow Tse-tsung. *The May Fourth Movement: Intellectual Revolution in Modern China.* Cambridge: Harvard University Press, 1960.

Cowley, Malcolm. *Exile's Return: A Literary Odyssey of the 1920s.* Rev. ed. New York: Viking Press, 1956.

Degras, Jane., ed. and trans. *The Communist International, 1919–1943: Documents.* 3 vols. London: Oxford University Press, 1956.

De Tarr, Francis. *The French Radical Party: From Herriot to Mendes-France.* London: Oxford University Press, 1961.

Dirlik, Arif. "The New Culture Movement Revisited: Anarchism and the Idea of Social Revolution in New Culture Thinking." *Modern China* 11 (July 1985): 251–300.

————. *The Origins of Chinese Communism.* New York: Oxford University Press, 1989.

Dirlik, Arif, and Edward S. Krebs. "Socialism and Anarchism in Early Republican China." *Modern China* 7 (April 1981): 117–51.

Drachkovitch, Milorad M., ed. *Marxist Ideology in the Contemporary World: Its Appeals and Paradoxes.* New York: Books for Libraries Press, 1973.

Dumas, Georges. "Les étudiants japonais et les étudiants chinois en France." *Annales de l'Université de Paris* 7 (January/February 1932): 26–48.

Evans, Ernestine. "Looking East from Moscow." *Asia* 22 (December 1922): 972–76.

Fergani, François. "Etudiants-ouvriers chinois à Montargis." *Les amis du vieux Montargis* 1 (n.d.): 3.

Fischer, Ruth. "Ho Chi Minh: Disciplined Communist." *Foreign Affairs* 33 (October 1954): 86–97.

Fitch, Noel Riley. *Sylvia Beach and the Lost Generation: A History of Literary Paris in the Twenties and Thirties.* New York: W. W. Norton, 1983.

Fitzgerald, F. Scott. *This Side of Paradise.* New York: Charles Scribner's Sons, 1920.

Forrest, David V. "Vietnamese Maturation: The Lost Land of Bliss." *Psychiatry* 34 (May 1971): 111–39.

Franz, Uli. *Deng Xiaoping.* Translated by Tom Artin. New York: Harcourt Brace Jovanovich, 1988.

Froidevaux, Henri. "Pour le maintien de l'influence française en Chine." *L'Asie française* 198 (January 1922): 6–10.

Furnivall, J. S. "Capitalism and Communism in Burma and the Tropical Far East." *Historical Studies (Australia and New Zealand)* 4 (May 1951): 299–314.

Gache, Paul. *Les grandes heures de Montargis.* Roanne: Editions Horvath, 1980.

Gide, André. *The Counterfeiters.* Translated by Dorothy Bussy. New York: Vintage Books, 1951.

Gluck, Mary. *Georg Lukács and His Generation, 1900–1918.* Cambridge: Harvard University Press, 1985.

Guillermaz, Jacques. *A History of the Chinese Communist Party, 1921–1949.* Translated by Anne Destenay. London: Methuen, 1972.

Hammond, Ed. *Coming of Grace.* Berkeley: Lancaster-Miller, 1980.

Harrison, James Pinckney. *The Long March to Power: A History of the Chinese Communist Party, 1921–72.* New York: Praeger, 1972.

Hayhoe, Ruth. "Towards the Forging of a Chinese University Ethos: Zhendan and Fudan, 1903–1919." *China Quarterly* 94 (June 1983): 323–41.

———. "A Comparative Approach to the Cultural Dynamics of Sino-Western Educational Cooperation." *China Quarterly* 104 (December 1985): 12–24.

Hemingway, Ernest. *A Moveable Feast: Sketches of the Author's Life in Paris in the Twenties.* New York: Charles Scribner's Sons, 1964.

Herriot, Edouard. "In the Far East." *Pamphlets on the Sino-Japanese Question,* no. 5 (1933). U.S. Library of Congress.

Holubnychy, Lydia. *Michael Borodin and the Chinese Revolution, 1923–1925.* Ann Arbor: Michigan University Microforms International, 1979.

Hsu Kai-yu. *Chou En-lai: China's Gray Eminence.* New York: Doubleday, 1968.

Hsueh Chun-tu, ed. *Revolutionary Leaders of Modern China.* London: Oxford University Press, 1971.

Hue-Tam Ho Tai. *Radicalism and the Origins of the Vietnamese Revolution.* Cambridge: Harvard University Press, 1992.

Hulse, James W. *The Forming of the Communist International.* Stanford: Stanford University Press, 1964.

Isaacs, Harold. *The Tragedy of the Chinese Revolution.* Stanford: Stanford University Press, 1951.

Jacobs, Daniel. *Borodin: Stalin's Man in China.* Cambridge: Harvard University Press, 1981.

Jeanneney, J. N. "Finances, presse et politique: L'affaire de la Banque industrielle de Chine (1921–1923)." *Revue historique* 514 (April–June 1975): 377–416.

Johnson, Chalmers. *Revolutionary Change.* Stanford: Stanford University Press, 1982.

Klein, Donald W., and Anne B. Clark. *Biographic Dictionary of Chinese Communism.* 2 vols. Cambridge: Harvard University Press, 1971.

Kriegel, Annie. *Communismes au miroir français.* Paris: Gallimard, 1974.

———. "Generational Difference: The History of an Idea." *Daedalus* 107 (Fall 1978): 23–38.

Lazitch, Branko, and Milorad M. Drachkovitch. *Lenin and the Comintern.* Stanford: Hoover Institution Press, 1972.

———, eds. *Biographical Dictionary of the Comintern.* Stanford: Hoover Institution Press, 1973.

Leclerq, Jacques. *Thunder in the Distance: The Life of Père Lebbe.* Translated by George Lamb. New York: Sheed and Ward, 1958.

Leung, John Kong-Cheong. "The Chinese Work-Study Movement: The Social and Political Experience of Chinese Students and Student-Workers in France." Ph.D. dissertation, Brown University, 1982.

Levine, Marilyn. "The Found Generation: Chinese Communism in Europe, 1919–1925." Ph.D. dissertation, University of Chicago, 1985.

———. "The Diligent-Work Frugal-Study Movement and the New Culture Movement." *Republican China* 12 (November 1986): 72–74.

———. "ECCO Studies: Overview of an Emerging Field." *Republican China* 13 (April 1988): 4–23.

———. "Barrières abolies: Zhang Ruoming et André Gide." *Etudes chinoises* 7 (Autumn 1988): 37–57.

Li Tien-min. *Chou En-lai.* Taibei: Institute of International Relations, 1970.

Li Yu-ning. *The Introduction of Socialism into China.* New York: Columbia University Press, 1971.

Liang Ch'i Ch'ao. "Causes of China's Defeat at the Peace Conference." *Millard's Review* 9 (19 July 1919): 262–68.

Lin Yusheng. *The Crisis of Chinese Consciousness: Radical Anti-traditionalism in the May Fourth Era.* Madison: University of Wisconsin Press, 1979.

Loewenberg, Peter. *Decoding the Past: The Psychohistorical Approach.* New York: Alfred A. Knopf, 1983.

Marr, David. *Vietnamese Anticolonialism.* Berkeley and Los Angeles: University of California Press, 1971.

Meisner, Maurice. *Li Ta-chao and the Origins of Chinese Marxism.* New York: Atheneum, 1977.

Meral, Jean. *Paris in American Literature*. Translated by Laurette Long. Chapel Hill: University of North Carolina Press, 1989.

Miller, Martin A. *The Russian Revolutionary Emigres*. Baltimore: Johns Hopkins University Press, 1986.

Nguyen Khac Vien. *Tradition and Revolution in Vietnam*. Berkeley: Indochina Resource Center, 1974.

Paige, Glenn D., ed. *Political Leadership: Readings for an Emerging Field*. New York: Free Press, 1972.

———. *The Scientific Study of Political Leadership*. New York: Free Press, 1977.

Picciola, André. "Barbusse et la question coloniale." *Europe revue littéraire mensuelle* 52 (September 1974): 190–201.

Pollard, Robert T. *China's Foreign Relations: 1917–1931*. New York: Macmillan, 1933.

Prost, Antoine. *Petite histoire de la France au XXᵉ siècle*. Paris: Librairie Armand Colin, 1979.

Rankin, Mary Backus. *Early Chinese Revolutionaries: Radical Intellectuals in Shanghai and Chekiang, 1902–1911*. Cambridge: Harvard University Press, 1971.

Robrieux, Philippe. *Histoire intérieure du Parti communiste*. Vol. 4. Paris: Fayard, 1984.

Roots, John McCook. *Chou: An Informal Biography of China's Legendary Chou En-lai*. New York: Doubleday, 1978.

Saich, Tony. *The Origins of the First United Front in China: The Role of Sneevliet (Alias Maring)*. 2 vols. Leiden and New York: E. J. Brill, 1991.

Scalapino, Robert A. "The Evolution of a Young Revolutionary—Mao Zedong in 1919–1921." *Journal of Asian Studies* 1 (November 1982): 29–61.

Scalapino, Robert A., and George T. Yu. *The Chinese Anarchist Movement*. Westport, Conn.: Greenwood Press, 1961.

———. *Modern China and Its Revolutionary Process*. Berkeley and Los Angeles: University of California Press, 1985.

Schorske, Carl E. "Generational Tension and Cultural Change: Reflections on the Case of Vienna." *Daedalus* 107 (Fall 1978): 111–22.

Schwarcz, Vera. "Out of Historical Amnesia: An Eclectic and Nearly Forgotten Chinese Communist in Europe." *Modern China* 13 (April 1987): 177–225.

Scott, Peter T. "Chinese in the Trenches." *War Monthly* 8, no. 76 (May 1980): 8–13.

Sheng Cheng. "Lettre d'un comrade chinois." *Bulletin communiste* 54 (8 December 1921).

Sheridan, James E. *China in Disintegration: The Republican Era in Chinese History, 1912–1949*. New York: Free Press, 1975.

Shiu Wentang. "Les organisations politiques des étudiants chinois en France dans l'entre-deux guerres." Doctoral dissertation, Université de Paris VII, 1990.

Siao Yu [Xiao Zisheng]. *Mao Tse-tung and I Were Beggars*. New York: Syracuse University Press, 1959.

Snow, Edgar. *Red Star over China*. Rev. ed. New York: Random House, 1968.

Solomon, Richard H. *Mao's Revolution and the Chinese Political Culture.* Berkeley and Los Angeles: University of California Press, 1971.

Sung, K. H. "China's Call to Her Returning Students." *Chinese Students' Monthly* 18 (November 1922): 44–46.

Sworakowski, Witold S., ed. *World Communism: A Handbook, 1918–1965.* Stanford: Hoover Institution Press, 1973.

Ta Chen. *Chinese Migrations, with Special Reference to Labor Conditions.* U.S. Department of Labor, Bureau of Labor Statistics. Washington: Government Printing Office, 1923.

Tsu, Y. Y. "Chinese Students in Europe." *Chinese Students' Monthly* 19 (November 1923): 31–32.

Tuchman, Barbara W. *The Proud Tower: A Portrait of the World before the War, 1890–1914.* New York: Bantam Books, 1966.

Van de Ven, Hans J. *From Friend to Comrade: The Founding of the Chinese Communist Party, 1920–1927.* Berkeley and Los Angeles: University of California Press, 1991.

Wang, C. T. *The Youth Movement in China.* New York: New Republic, 1927.

Wang Fan-hsi. *Chinese Revolutionary: Memoirs, 1919–1949.* Translated by Gregor Benton. Oxford: Oxford University Press, 1980.

Wang, Nora. "Deng Xiaoping: The Years in France." *China Quarterly* 92 (December 1982): 698–705.

———. "Da Chen Lu! Le Mouvement du 30 mai 1925 à Paris." *Approches-Asie* 7 (1983): 1–33.

———. "Paris/Shanghai, débats d'idées et pratique sociale, les intellectuels progressistes chinois, 1920–1925." 3 vols. Thèses d'état, Université de Paris, 1986.

Wang, Y. C. *Chinese Intellectuals and the West: 1872–1949.* Chapel Hill: University of North Carolina Press, 1966.

Weidenbaum, Rhoda Sussman. "Chou En-lai, Creative Revolutionary." Ph.D dissertation, University of Connecticut, 1981.

Whitson, William W. "The Concept of Military Generation: The Chinese Communist Case." *Asian Survey* 13 (November 1968): 921–47.

Wilson, Dick. *Zhou Enlai: A Biography.* New York: Viking, 1984.

Wohl, Robert. *French Communism in the Making, 1914–1924.* Stanford: Stanford University Press, 1966.

———. *The Generation of 1914.* Cambridge: Harvard University Press, 1979.

Wright, Mary C., ed. *China in Revolution: The First Phase, 1900–1913.* New Haven: Yale University Press, 1968.

Yen Ching-Hwang. *Coolies and Mandarins: China's Protection of Overseas Chinese during the Late Ch'ing Period, 1851–1911.* Singapore: University of Singapore Press, 1985.

Yuan Tung-li. *A Guide to Doctoral Dissertations by Chinese Students in Continental Europe, 1907–1962. Chinese Culture Quarterly* reprint (1963).

Zarrow, Peter. *Anarchism and Chinese Political Culture.* New York: Columbia University Press, 1990.

EASTERN LANGUAGE SOURCES

"Bali Huagong hui" [The Parisian Chinese Labor Union]. *Xin qingnian* 7 (1 May 1920): 1–7.

"Bali zhi shenghuo" [Life in Paris]. *Dongfang zazhi* 17 (May 1920): 40–41.

Beijing shifan daxue [Beijing Normal University], ed. *Zhu De tongzhi de qingshaonian de shidai* [Comrade Zhu De during his period of youth]. Nanchang: Jiangxi renmin chubanshe, 1979.

Bian Xiaoxuan. "Liu Fa qingong jianxue ziliao" [Travel to France Work-Study Movement materials]. *Jindaishi ziliao* 2 (1955): 174–208.

Cai Hesen. *Cai Hesen wenji* [The collected works of Cai Hesen]. Beijing: Renmin chubanshe, 1980.

———. "Xiang Jingyu tongzhi" [Comrade Xiang Jingyu]. *Jindaishi yanjiu* 4 (1982): 1–3 (written in 1927).

"Canjia Guangzhou qiyi de Yuenan tongzhi de huiyi" [Remembrances of Vietnamese comrades who participated in the Canton Uprising]. *Guangdong wenshi ziliao* 27 (1980): 302–3.

Chen Duxiu. "Falanxi ren yu jinshi wenming" [The French and contemporary civilization]. *Xin qingnian* 1 (September 1915): 1–4.

———. "Liu xuesheng" [Overseas students]. *Xin qingnian* 7 (December 1919): 118–19.

Chen Jingtang [Chan King-tong]. "Zhonggong lü Ou zong zhibu zhi chengli" [The establishment of the ECCO]. *Dongya jikan* 15 (July 1984): 33–56.

———. "Lun zhonggong lü Ou zong zhibu de faqi zu" [A discussion of the beginning groups of the ECCO]. *Zhongguo lishi xuehui shixue jikan* 19 (July 1987): 359–94.

———. "Jinzhan lida shijian yu zhonggong lü Ou zong zhibu chengli" [The occupation at Lyons and the establishment of the ECCO]. *Zhuhai xuebao* 14 (n.d.): 263–82.

Chen Sanjing. *Qingong jianxue yundong* [The Work-Study Movement]. Taibei: Zhengzhong shuju, 1981.

———. "Minchu liu Ou jiaoyu de jiannan lishi: Liang Zhong Fa daxue chushen" [The difficult beginnings of study abroad in Europe: A preliminary examination of the Sino-French Institute at Lyons University]. In *Zhongyang yanjiuyuan jindaishisuo minchu lishi yantaohui lunwenji*, 991–1007. Taibei: Academia Sinica, 1984.

———. *Huagong yu Ouzhan* [The Chinese Labor Corps in the First World War]. Taibei: Academia Sinica, 1986.

Chen Shunong. "Dadao fan geming de Xishanpai seban de tebie weiyuanhui" [Overturn the antirevolutionary Western Hills faction's control of the special committee]. *Guomin* 5 (15 November 1927): 1–6.

Chen Xiaocen. "Juewushe ji qi chengyuan" [The Self-Awakening Society and its founders]. *Tianjin wenshi ziliao xuanji* 15 (May 1981): 156–94.

Dai Xugong. *Xiang Jingyu zhuan* [A biography of Xiang Jingyu]. Beijing: Renmin chubanshe, 1981.

Deng Ye. "Wusi shiqi de gongdu huzhu zhuyi ji qi shijian" [The ideology and practice of mutual aid during the May Fourth period]. *Zhongguo xiandaishi fuyin baokan ziliao* 23 (1982): 9–15.

Deng Yingchao. "Wusi yundong de huiyi" [Reminiscences of the May Fourth Movement]. In *Zhou Enlai de sheng ziliao xuanji,* 20–27.

"Di Sanci Guoji Gongchandang dahui zhi jingguo jige guo laodong yundong zhi xianzai diwei" [The experiences of the Communist Third International and the current position of labor movements in several countries]. *Dongfang zazhi* 18 (November 1921): 61–66.

Dou Aizhi. "Cai Hesen yu *Xiangdao* zhoubao" [Cai Hesen and the weekly *Xiangdao*]. *Zhongguo xiandaishi fuyin baokan ziliao* 1 (January 1982): 61–66.

"Duiyu liang sheli Zhongguo daxue zhi xiwang" [Hopes concerning the establishment of the Chinese University at Lyons]. *Lü Ou zhoukan* 13 (7 February 1920): 1.

"Faguo shehuidang taidu zhi biangeng" [The transformation in attitude of the French Socialist Party]. *Dongfang zazhi* 17 (June 1920): 35–38.

Fu Zhong. "Fu Zhong tan lü Fa qingong jianxue he shehuizhuyi qingniantuan lü Ou zongzhibu" [Fu Zhong discusses the travel to France Work-Study Movement and the ECCP]. In *Yida qianhou,* 2:559–63.

Guo Fangrui. "Liu Fa qingong jianxue zayi" [Random memories of the travel to France Work-Study Movement]. *Hunan wenshi ziliao xuanji* 11 (1979): 73–81 (written in February 1963).

Guo Sheng. *Wusi shiqi de gongdu yundong he gongdu sichao* [The Work-Study Movement and work-study thought tide of the May Fourth period]. Beijing: Jiaoyu kexue chubanshe, 1986.

Guo Zhengzhao. "Wang Guangqi yu Shaonian Zhongguo" [Wang Guangqi and the Young China Study Association]. In *Zhongguo jindai xiandaishi lunji* [Collected essays on modern and contemporary Chinese history], 301–70. Taibei: Academia Sinica, 1986.

He Changgong. *Qingong jianxue shenghuo huiyi* [Reminiscences of the Work-Study Movement]. Beijing: Renmin chubanshe, 1958.

He Luzhi. *He Luzhi zhi xiansheng wencun* [The written traces of Mr. He Luzhi]. Taibei, Chingcheng, 1978.

Hou Junchu. "Zhou Enlai tongzhi yu zhonggong lü Ou zhibu" [Zhou Enlai and the ECCO]. *Zhongguo xiandaishi fuyin baokan ziliao* 4 (1982): 39–44.

Hu Guowei. *Bali xinying* [Paris impressions]. 2d ed. Taibei: Puti chubanshe, 1970.

Hu Hua, ed. *Zhonggong dangshi renwu zhuan* [Biographies of personalities in Chinese Communist Party history]. 30 vols. Shaanxi: Shaanxi renmin chubanshe, 1980–89.

Hu Shi. "Gongdu zhuyi shixing de guancha" [An examination of the practice of Work-Study]. *Xin qingnian* 7 (April 1920): 1–4.

Hu Zhu. "Wo zhude pension" [The pension where I live]. *Shaonian Zhongguo,* "Falanxi hao" [The French number], 2/4 (15 October 1920): 79–85.

Hua Lin. "Yu quanguo gexian choupai gongfei liu Fa gaoque shu" [A high-level discussion regarding the public aid of the whole country and every district to be sent to the students studying in France]. *Dongfang zazhi* 14 (1917): 183–84.

Hua Yingshen, ed. *Zhongguo gongchandang lieshi zhuan* [Biographies of Chinese Communist martyrs]. Beijing: Qingnian, 1951.

Huang Chenxia. *Zhonggong junren zhi* [Chinese Communist military personages]. Hong Kong: Contemporary Research Institute, 1986.

Huang Liqun. *Liu Fa qingong jianxue jianshi* [A concise history of the travel to France Work-Study Movement]. Beijing: Jiaoyu kexue chubanshe, 1982.

Huiyi Cai Hesen [Remembrances of Cai Hesen]. Beijing: Renmin chubanshe, 1980.

Hunan geming lieshi zhuan [Biographies of Hunan martyrs]. Changsha: Ousu duwu, 1952.

Hunan sheng zhexue shehui kexue yanjiusuo xiandaishi yanjiushi [Hunan Provincial Center for Philosophy and Social Sciences—the Modern History Research Unit]. *Wusi shiqi Hunan renmin geming douzheng shiliao xuanbian* [Selected materials on the May Fourth period and the revolutionary struggles of the Hunanese]. Changsha: Hunan renmin chubanshe, 1979.

Jiang Fuwei. "Liu Fa qingong jianxue xiaoshi" [Small events of the travel to France Work-Study Movement]. *Wenshi ziliao* 34 (1980): 30–40.

Jiang Zemin. "Canjia liu Fa Bi qingong jianxue de huiyi" [Reminiscences of participating in the overseas French-Belgium Work-Study Movement]. *Tianjin wenshi ziliao xuanji* 15 (May 1981): 93–113.

Jinian Xiang Jingyu tongzhi yingyong jiuyi wushi zhounian [Remembering Comrade Xiang Jingyu on the occasion of the fiftieth anniversary of her fearless martyrdom]. Beijing: Renmin chubanshe, 1978.

Lai Jinghu. "Minchu shidai de Hunan qingnian" [The youth of Hunan during the beginning of the Republic]. *Zhuanji wenxue* 14 (March 1970): 37–41.

Li Chen Sheng, Danielle. "Liang Zhong Fa daxue haiwaibu tongxuelu" [Records of the students at Lyons University, Sino-French Institute]. *Ou Hua xuebao* 1 (May 1983): 127–50.

Li Dazhao. "Qingnian yu laoren" [Youth and elders]. *Xin qingnian* 3 (April 1917): 1–3.

———. "Shaonian Zhongguo de 'shaonian yundong'" [The youth movements of the Young China Study Association]. *Shaonian Zhongguo*, no. 3 (September 1919): 1–3.

Li Huang. "Liuxue pingyi" [A critique of overseas study]. *Shaonian Zhongguo*, no. 2 (December 1920): 1–7.

———. "Puohuai yu jianshe ji qi yubei gongfu" [The tasks of destruction and construction]. *Shaonian Zhongguo* 3 (March 1922): 30–36 (written in October 1921).

———. "Zaitan duiyu Shaonian Zhongguo de yubei gongfu" [Another discussion of preparatory tasks for the Young China Study Association]. *Shaonian Zhongguo*, no. 3 (March 1922): 36–42 (written in December 1921).

———. "Shehui zhuyi yu shehui" [Socialism and society]. *Shaonian Zhongguo*, no. 3 (June 1922): 1–5.

————. "Xuedunshi huiyilu" [Memoirs from the *Xue Dun* study]. 7 parts. *Zhuanji wenxue* 16 and 17 (Summer/Fall 1970): 6–15, 6–16, 15–21, 21–30, 4–10, 19–23, 19–24.

————. "Zeng Muhan xiong yi jindao zhishi fenzi de shidai zeren" [Brother Zeng Muhan has totally fulfilled the responsibility of his generation of intellectuals]. *Zhuanji wenxue* 92 (July 1976): 14–16.

Li Lisan [Long Zhi, pseud.]. "Wo duiyu zuzhi qingong jianxuehui de yijian" [My opinions concerning organizing the work-study society]. *Lü Ou zhoukan* 66 (5 February 1921): 1.

———— [Zuo Fu, pseud.]. "Jiaohuan yu huzhu" [Mutual-exchange and mutual-aid]. *Lü Ou zhoukan* 69 (5 March 1921): 1–2.

————. "Dui Zhao Shiyan de huiyi" [Remembrances of Zhao Shiyan]. In *Yida qianhou*, 2:524–25 (written in September 1960).

Li Ming. "Jinian Cai Hesen tongzhi" [In remembrance of Comrade Cai Hesen]. In *Hunan geming lieshi zhuan*, 15–17.

Li Qin. "Cai Hesen dui jiandang de zhongda gongxian" [The enormous contributions of Cai Hesen in building the Party]. *Zhongguo xiandaishi fuyin baokan ziliao* 7 (July 1982): 11–15.

Li Weihan. "Huiyi Xinmin xuehui" [Memoirs of the New Citizens' Study Society]. In Xu Rihui, ed., *Wusi yundong zai Hunan huiyilu*, 17–58.

————. *Huiyi yu yanjiu* [Remembrances and studies]. 2 vols. Beijing: Zhonggong dangshi ziliao chubanshe, 1986.

Li Wen and Bi Xing, eds. *Wang Guangqi nianpu* [A chronology of Wang Guangqi]. Beijing: Renmin yinyue chubanshe, 1987.

Li Wen, Bi Xing, and Zhu Zhou, eds. *Wang Guangqi yanjiu lunwenji* [Collected essays of studies on Wang Guangqi]. Chengdu: Wang Guangqi yanjiu xueshu taolunhui, 1985.

Li Yipin. "Wang Guangqi." In Zong Zhiwen and Zhu Xinxian, eds., *Minguo renwu zhuan* [Biographies of the Republican period], vol. 3. Beijing: Zhonghua shuju, 1981.

Liao Huanxing. "Zhongguo gongchandang lü Ou zongzhibu" [The ECCO]. In *Yida qianhou*, 2:502–10.

Lida xuesheng hui (Lyons University Student Association). "Liang Zhong Fa daxue xuesheng zhi zuiyan" [The crimes of the students at the Sino-French Institute at Lyons University]. *Lü Ou zazhi* 1 (September 1928): 33–44.

Lin Yuxun. *Zhongguo liuxue jiaoyu shi* [Materials concerning overseas Chinese education]. Taibei: Hua Gang, 1980.

"Liu Fa jianxuehui jiangyanhui zhi yanshuo" [The speeches presented at the travel to France Frugal-Study Association meeting]. *Dongfang zazhi* 14 (September 1917): 177–83.

Liu Shuya. "Lü Ou zhanzheng yu qingnian zhi juewu" [The war in Europe and the awakening of youth]. *Xin qingnian* 2 (October 1916): 1–8.

Liu Ye, Zhu Yuhe, and Zhao Yuanbi. "Lü Ou Zhongguo dangtuan de jianli jingguo" [The experiences of the establishment of the ECCO]. *Dangshi yanjiu* 1 (28 February 1981): 75–80.

———. "Shilun lü Ou Zhongguo gongchanzhuyi zuzhi de xingcheng" [A practical discussion of the formation of the ECCO]. In Zhu Chenjia, ed., *Zhonggong dangshi yanjiu lun wenxian* [A collection of studies on CCP history], 1:170–89. Hunan: Hunan renmin chubanshe, 1983.

"Lü Fa Huagong gonghui jianzhang" [Guidelines for the travel to France Chinese Labor Union]. *Xin qingnian* 7 (1 May 1920): 1–7.

Lu Han. "Wode liu Fa qingong jianxue shenghuo de yiduan" [A glimpse at my life as a worker-student]. *Geming* 68–87 (1928–29).

Luo Luo. "Falanxi wenhua zhi weiji" [The dangerous situation of French civilization]. *Dongfang zazhi* 17 (November 1920): 4–6.

Luo Shaozhi. "Caimu Ge Jianhao" [Mother Cai, Ge Jianhao]. In Hu Hua, ed., *Zhonggong dangshi renwu zhuan*, 6:47–57.

Luo Shaozhi, Liu Peicheng, He Guozhi, and Yu Danyang. "Cai Hesen." In Hu Hua, ed., *Zhonggong dangshi renwu zhuan*, 6:1–46.

Luo Zhanglong. "Huiyi Xinmin xuehui: You Hunan dao Beijing" [Reminiscences of the New Citizens' Study Society: From Hunan to Beijing]. In *Yida qianhou*, 2:256–79.

Ma Huiqing. "Wusi yundong zai Tianjin" [The May Fourth Movement in Tianjin]. *Jindaishi ziliao* 2 (April 1958): 78–111.

Nankai daxue Zhou Enlai yanjiushi [Nankai University Zhou Enlai Research Institute]. "Zhou Enlai qingshaonian shidai jishi" [A chronicle of Zhou Enlai's youth]. *Tianjin wenshi ziliao xuanji* 15 (May 1981): 1–85.

Nie Rongzhen. *Nie Rongzhen huiyilu* [The memoirs of Nie Rongzhen]. 3 vols. Beijing: Zhanshi chubanshe, 1983–85.

Peng Chengfu. "Zhao Shiyan." In Hu Hua, ed., *Zhonggong dangshi renwu zhuan*, 7:1–48.

———. *Zhao Shiyan*. Chongqing: Chongqing chubanshe, 1983.

Peng Shuzhi. *Ping Zhang Guotao de wode huiyi* [Criticism of Zhang Guotao's personal memoirs]. Hong Kong: Qianwei, 1975.

Qin Xianci. "Zeng Qi xiansheng yu Shaonian Zhongguo xuehui" [Mr. Zeng Qi and the Young China Study Association]. *Zhuanji wenxue* 2 (July 1976): 33–36.

Qinghua University Faculty Research Unit on the History of the Communist Party, comp. *FuFa qingong jianxue yundong shiliao* [Documents on the travel to France Work-Study Movement]. 3 vols. Beijing: Beijing chubanshe, 1979–80.

"Qingnianhui yu liuxuesheng zhi guanxi: Lü qingnian *jinbu zazhi*" [The relationship between the youth organizations and the study abroad students: Excerpts from *Progressive Youth Magazine*]. *Dongfang zazhi* 14 (September 1917): 196–98.

Qiu Shi. "Liu Fa qingong jianxue yundong de lishi zuoyong" [The historical uses of the Work-Study Movement]. *Zhongguo xiandaishi fuyin baokan ziliao* 9 (March 1983): 6–10.

Ren Wuxiong. "Yida qian liu Fa xuesheng zhong wu gongchandang xiaozu" [The absence of a small Communist group among the travel to France students before the founding of the ccp]. *Dangshi yanjiu ziliao* (Sichuan) 2 (September 1981): 65–66.

Ren Zhuoxuan. "Wuyi de lishi yu yiyi" [The history and significance of May first]. *Gongren xunbao* 20/21 (23 April 1923): 4–12.

———. "Guomin geming yu jieji douzheng" [The national revolution and the class struggle]. *Chiguang* 9 (June 1924): 1–5.

——— [Hong Tan, pseud.]. "Guomindang zuopai youpai zhi fenhua" [The difference between the Guomindang left and right factions]. *Chiguang* 23 (15 January 1925): 7–9.

———. *Ren Zhuoxuan pingzhuan* [A critical biography of Ren Zhuoxuan]. 2 vols. Taibei: Bomier shudian, 1965.

Renmin de zhongcheng zhanshi: Mianhuai Chen Yi tongzhi [The people's loyal warrior: Our beloved comrade Chen Yi]. Shanghai: Renmin chubanshe, 1979.

Rong Ci. "Xiang Jingyu." In Hu Hua, ed., *Zhonggong dangshi renwu zhuan*, 6:58–91.

Sheng Cheng. *Bali yiyu* [Memories of Paris]. Hong Kong: Yazhou, 1957.

Shi Yisheng. "Huiyi zhonggong lü Ou zhibu de guanghui yeji" [Remembering the glorious achievements of the ecco in Europe]. *Tianjin wenshi ziliao xuanji* 15 (May 1981): 114–30.

Shu Xincheng. *Jindai Zhongguo liuxue shi* [Modern Chinese overseas studies]. Shanghai: Zhonghua shuju, 1927.

———, comp. *Zhongguo jindai jiaoyushi ziliao* [Chinese modern educational materials]. 3 vols. Beijing: Renmin jiaoyu chubanshe, 1961 (originally compiled in 1927).

———. "Huiyi Wusi fandi douzheng de yimu" [Reminiscences of a chapter in the May Fourth anti-imperialist struggle]. In Xu Rihui, ed., *Wusi yundong zai Hunan huiyilu*, 155–60.

Tan Guoying. "Zhou Enlai yu zhonggong zhengquan zhi jianli" [Zhou Enlai and the establishment of power by the Communists]. Master's thesis, National Zhengzhi University, 1978.

Tao Ligong. "Lü Ou zhi ganxiang" [Thoughts while abroad in Europe]. *Xin qingnian* 7 (1919): 49–55.

Tao Yongshu and Liu Bingqiu. "Cai Hesen guanyu wuzhuang douzheng de lilun" [Cai Hesen's theories concerning violent struggle]. *Zhongguo xiandaishi fuyin baokan ziliao* 4 (April 1982): 18–24.

Tian Yi. "Liang wanguo huayang hui yu Zhong Fa siye" [The Lyons trade fair and the Sino-French silk trade]. *Dongfang zazhi* 18 (25 April 1921): 91–92.

———. "Liu Fa qingong jianxue sheng shi guan qingyuan ji" [An account of the official petitions of the travel to France worker-students]. *Jiaoyu zazhi* 13 (20 July 1921): 1–7.

Truong Chinh. "Ho chu tich da tiep chu nghia Lenin va truyen ba vao Viet Nam nhu the nao?" [How did Chairman Ho receive Leninism and distribute it into Viet Nam?]. *Nghien Cuu Lich Su* 132 (May/June 1970): 248–55.

Wang Guangqi. "Shaonian Zhongguo zhi chuangzao" [The creation of a young China]. *Shaonian Zhongguo* 2 (19 August 1919): 1–7.

———. "Wei shenma bu neng shixing gongdu huzhu zhuyi" [Why the doctrine of work-study mutual aid was not able to be practiced]. *Xin qingnian* 7 (April 1920): 13–15.

———. "Deyizhi qingnian yundong" [The German youth group movement]. *Shaonian Zhongguo* 4 (July 1923): 1–25.

———. *Shaonian Zhongguo yundong* [The Chinese youth movement]. Shanghai: Zhonghua shuju, 1924.

———. "Jiaoyu jia dui yu Zhongguo xiankuang yingyou zhi sanda juewu" [The three great awakenings which educators ought to have concerning the current Chinese situation]. *Zhonghua jiaoyu jie* 16 (May 1927): 2–13.

Wang Guangqi xiansheng jinian ce [A commemoration of Mr. Wang Guangqi]. In Shen Yunlong, ed., *Jindai Zhongguo shiliao congkan*, vol. 188. Taibei: Wenhai, 1936.

Wang Jianying. "Kangri zhanzheng yiqian Zhongguo gongchandang lingdao jiegou de bianhua qingkuang" [The changing situation of the leadership structure of the CCP before the War of Resistance with Japan]. *Jindaishi yanjiu* 1 (1983): 121–48.

Wang Jingwei. "Yige genben guannian" [A fundamental concept]. *Lü Ou tongxin* (Lyons) 5 (31 July 1928): 1–9.

Wang Peilian and Zhou Xingwang. "Zhonggong lü Ou zhibu yu Huagong" [The ECCO and Chinese labor]. *Zhongguo xiandaishi fuyin baokan ziliao* 19 (1982): 17–24.

Wang Yizhi. "Huiyi Zhang Tailei" [Remembering Zhang Tailei]. *Jindaishi yanjiu* 2 (1983): 1–31.

Wang Yongxiang and Kong Fanfeng. "Zhonggong lü Ou zhibu fandui Guojiazhuyi pai de douzheng" [The struggle of the ECCO against the Nationalist Clique]. *Zhongguo xiandaishi fuyin baokan ziliao* 3 (March 1982): 11–18.

Wang Yongxiang, Kong Fanfeng, and Liu Pinqing. *Zhongguo gongchandang lü Ou zhibu shihua* [The history of the ECCO]. Beijing: Zhongguo qingnian chubanshe, 1985.

Wang Yongxiang and Liu Pinqing. *Weile Zhonghua zhi jueqi: Zhou Enlai qingnian shiqi de shenghuo yu douzheng* [Rising up for China: The early period of the life and struggles of Zhou Enlai]. Tianjin: Tianjin chubanshe, 1980.

Wang Yunwu. "Cai Jiemin xiansheng de gongxian" [The contributions of Mr. Cai Jiemin]. *Dongfang zazhi* 37 (16 April 1940): 1–4.

Wei Hongyun. *Zhongguo xiandaishi ziliao xuanbian* [Selections of modern Chinese materials]. 3 vols. Heilongjiang: Heilongjiang renmin chubanshe, 1981.

Wu Qi. "Zhou Enlai tongzhi qingnian shidai zai Fa De liangguo de geming shenghuo" [The revolutionary life of Comrade Zhou Enlai during his youth in France and Germany]. *Tianjin wenshi ziliao xuanji* 15 (May 1981): 131–45.

Wu Shiqi. "Dui youguan lü Ou jiandang jige wenti de tantao" [An examination of several problems in the establishment of the ECCO]. *Zhongguo xiandaishi fuyin baokan ziliao* 2 (September 1982): 2–10.

Wu Yuzhang. *Wu Yuzhang huiyilu* [The memoirs of Wu Yuzhang]. Beijing: Renmin chubanshe, 1978.

Wu Zhihui [Wu Jingheng, pseud.]. "Lun Ou jianxue zhi qingxing ji yijia jiuxue zhi shenghuo" [A discussion of living thriftily in Europe and the life of the overseas student]. *Xin qingnian* 4 (February 1919): 150–72.

Xiang Xianyi and Xiang Xianbei. "Xiang Jingyu nianpu jianpian de buyi" [An addendum to the chronology of Xiang Jingyu]. *Zhongguo xiandaishi fuyin baokan ziliao* 1 (January 1982): 58–60.

Xiao San [Xiao Zizhang]. "Huiyi fu Fa qingong jianxue he lü Ou zhibu" [Remembering the travel to France Work-Study Movement and the ECCO]. In *Yida qianhou*, 2:511–16.

———. "Dui Zhao Shiyan shishu de huiyi" [A few stories in remembrance of Zhao Shiyan]. In *Yida qianhou*, 2:519–23.

———. *Xiao San wenji* [Collected writings of Xiao San]. Beijing: Xinhua, 1983.

Xiao Yu [Xiao Zisheng]. *Huiyi wode xiaoshi liaoliao* [Memories of my youth]. Taiwan: Yiwen, 1969.

Xie Hong. "Faguo qingniantuan" [The youth groups of France]. *Xin qingnian* 2 (October 1916): 1–3.

Xie Weijin. "Xie Weijin zizhuan" [The autobiography of Xie Weijin]. *Dangshi yanjiu ziliao* (Sichuan) 4 (October 1983): 58–67 (written in 1953).

Xin Zhongguo dangzhengjun renwu zhi [Biographies of the new China's political military officials]. 2 vols. Hong Kong: Hai Tian, 1977.

Xu Deheng. "Wusi yundong liushi zhounian" [The sixtieth anniversary of the May Fourth Movement]. *Wenshi ziliao xuanji* 61 (1979): 4–36.

Xu Jianyuan. "Cai Hesen tongzhi zai jiandang chuqi de jiechu gongxian" [The brilliant contributions of Comrade Cai Hesen in establishing the Party]. *Zhongguo xiandaishi fuyin baokan ziliao* 4 (April 1982): 13–17.

Xu Rihui, ed. *Wusi yundong zai Hunan huiyilu* [Reminiscences of the May Fourth Movement in Hunan]. Hunan: Hunan renmin chubanshe, 1979.

Xu Teli. "Ou Mengdani tongxue de gongqi" [Criticizing the appeal of the Montargis students]. *Lü Ou zhoukan* 68 and 69 (26 February 1921/5 March 1921): 1, 1.

Xun Yu. "Liu Fa wenti" [Problems of studying in France]. *Jiaoyu zazhi* 21 (October 1929): 107–8.

Yida qianhou. See Zhongguo shehui kexueyuan xiandaishi yanjiushi.

Yin Kuan. "Yin Kuan tan Zhao Shiyan he lü Ou zhibu" [Yin Kuan discusses Zhao Shiyan and the ECCO]. In *Yida qianhou*, 2:539–44 (written in 1960).

Yu Zhihou. "Tianjin *Yishi bao* gaishu" [An outline of the Tianjin newspaper *Yishi bao*]. *Tianjin wenshi ziliao xuanji* 18 (January 1982): 70–93.

Yuan Zizhen. "Lü Fa Huaren gonghui de jingguo" [The experiences of the Chinese Labor Union in France]. *Gongren xunbao* 20/21 (April 1923): 13–18.

Zeng Qi. "Xuehui wenti zatan" [An informal discussion of the Study Society's problems]. *Shaonian Zhongguo* 3 (March 1922): 76–80.

———. *Zeng Muhan (Qi) xiansheng yizhu* [The posthumous collection of the writings of Mr. Zeng Qi]. In Shen Yunlong, ed., *Jindai Zhongguo shiliao congkan* [Collected materials in modern Chinese history]. Taibei: Wenhai chubanshe, 1954.

Zeng Zhongming and Zou Lu. *Faguo Liang Zhong Fa daxue* [The Sino-French Institute in Lyons, France]. Guangdong: Guoli Guangdong Daxue haiwaibu zhiyi, 1925.

Zhang Mengjiu. "Liu Fa liangzhou de ganxiang" [Reflections after two weeks of travel to France]. *Shaonian Zhongguo* 2 (6 December 1920): 7–16.

———. "Zhuyi wenti yu huodong wenti" [Problems of ideology and action]. *Shaonian Zhongguo* 3 (8 March 1922): 57–76.

Zhang Shenfu. "Ying Fa gongchandang—Zhongguo gaizao" [Communist parties of England and France—Chinese reforms]. *Xin qingnian* 9 (1 July 1921): 1–3.

———. "Zhongguo gongchandang jianli qianhou qingkuang de huiyi" [Some remembrances of the situation before and after the establishment of the CCP]. In *Yida qianhou*, 2:548–54.

———. "Zhang Shenfu tan lü Ou dangtuan zuzhi huodong qingkuang" [Zhang Shenfu explains the situation of the ECCO activities]. *Tianjin wenshi ziliao xuanji* 15 (May 1981): 86–92.

Zhang Yunhou, Yan Xuyi, Hong Qingxiang, and Wang Yunkai, comps. *Wusi shiqi de shetuan* [The organizations of the May Fourth period]. 4 vols. Beijing: Sanlian, 1979.

Zhang Yunhou, Yan Xuyi, and Li Junchen, comps. *Liu Fa qingong jianxue yundong* [The travel to France Work-Study Movement]. 2 vols. Shanghai: Shanghai renmin chubanshe, 1980, 1986.

Zhao Shiyan. "Qingong jianxue guannian shang de genben cuowu" [The basic misconceptions of the Work-Study Movement]. In Zhang Yunhou et al., *Liu Fa qingong jianxue yundong*, 1:389–92 (written in 1920).

———. "Huade weilao de qingong jianxuezhe" [The restrictions of the worker-students]. *Lü Ou zhoukan* 64 (21 January 1921): 1.

———. *Zhao Shiyan xuanji* [Selected writings of Zhao Shiyan]. Chengdu: Sichuan renmin chubanshe, 1984.

"Zhao Shiyan shengping shiliao" [Materials on the life of Zhao Shiyan]. *Wenshi ziliao xuanji* (Beijing) 58 (1979): 36–163.

Zheng Chaolin. "Zheng Chaolin tan Zhao Shiyan he lü Ou zhibu" [Zheng Chaolin discusses Zhao Shiyan and the ECCO]. In *Yida qianhou*, 2:531–38 (written in January 1960).

———. *Ji Yin Kuan* [Remembering Yin Kuan]. Unpublished manuscript, 1983.

———. "Huiyi Chen Yannian xiongdi" [Remembering Brother Chen Yannian]. *Zhong bao* (Hong Kong) (December 1983): 54–56.

———. *Zheng Chaolin huiyilu, 1919–1931* [The memoirs of Zheng Chaolin, 1919–1931]. Beijing: Xiandai shiliao biankanshe, 1986 (originally written in 1945).

Zhonggong dangshi jiaoyu cankao ziliao [Educational materials concerning the CCP]. 2 vols. Beijing: Renmin chubanshe, 1978.

Zhonggong shi cankao ziliao [Primary materials of CCP history]. 2 vols. Beijing: Renmin chubanshe, 1979.

Zhongguo geming bowuguan dangshi chenlie yanjiubu [Research Section of the Museum of the Chinese Revolution and Party Exhibits]. *Zhongguo dangshi zhuyao shijian jianshi* [A summary of important Chinese Party affairs]. Chengdu: Sichuan renmin chubanshe, 1982.

Zhongguo qingniandang dangshi ziliao diyi ji [The first collection of Chinese Youth Party materials]. Taibei: Minzhu qiaoshe, 1955.

Zhongguo shehui kexueyuan xiandaishi yanjiushi [Research Unit on Contemporary History of the Chinese Academy of Social Sciences], eds. *Yida qianhou* [Before and after the founding of the CCP]. 2 vols. Renmin chubanshe, 1980.

Zhonghua Minguo dangdai mingrenlu [Who's who in the Republic of China]. Taibei: Zhonghua shuju, 1978.

Zhonghua quanguo fulian hehui funü yundong lishi yanjiu shi [Chinese National United Women's Movement Research Unit]. *Zhonghua nüyinglie* [Brave female martyrs of China]. Beijing: Renmin chubanshe, 1981.

Zhou Enlai. *Zhou Enlai tongzhi lü Ou wenji* [The collected European writings of Comrade Zhou Enlai]. Tianjin: Wenwu, 1979.

———. "Guanyu yijiuersi zhi erliunian dang dui Guomindang de guanxi" [Regarding the relationship between the Party and the Guomindang from 1924 to 1926]. *Dangshi yanjiu* 2 (1980): 2–9 (written in 1943).

Zhou Enlai de sheng ziliao xuanji [Selected materials on the life of Zhou Enlai]. Hong Kong: Xin zhong tu hua, 1977.

Zhou Shizhao. *Women de shibiao: Xu Teli* [Our model teacher: Xu Teli]. Beijing: Beijing chubanshe, 1958.

Zhou Taixuan. "Faguo jiaoyu zhi gaige" [The reform of French education]. *Jiaoyu zazhi* 11 (February 1919): 7–11.

———. "Liuxue wenti de ge mianguan" [Several aspects of the overseas educational problems]. *Zhonghua jiaoyu jie* 16 (August 1926): 1–13.

Zhou zongli de qingshaonian shidai [The young period of Premier Zhou]. Chengdu: Sichuan chubanshe, 1979.

Zhu De tongzhi de qingshaonian de shidai [The young period of Comrade Zhu De]. Nanchang: Jiangxi renmin chubanshe, 1979.

Zhuang Qi. "Liu Fa qingong jianxue" [The travel to France Work-Study Movement]. *Jiaoyu zazhi* 12 (June 1920): 1–9.

Zong Zhiwen and Zhu Weixian, eds. *Minguo renwu zhuan* [Biographies of the Republican period]. 3 vols. Beijing: Zhonghua shuju, 1981.

Zuo Shunsheng. "Wang Guangqi xiansheng shilue" [A narrative of Mr. Wang Guangqi]. In Shen Yunlong, ed., *Wang Guangqi xiansheng jinian ce* [A commemoration of Mr. Wang Guangqi], vol. 188. Shanghai: Wenhai, 1936.

Zuo Xunsheng. *Zuo Xunsheng zi xuanji* [The writings of Zuo Xunsheng]. In Shen Yunlong, ed., *Jindai Zhongguo shiliao congkan*. 2 vols. Taibei: Wenhai, n.d.

PERIODICALS AND NEWSPAPERS

French

Approches Asie
L'Asie française
Bulletin de l'Association amicale franco-chinoise
Bulletin du Kuomintang en Europe
Le Chesnoysien, Montargis
Etudes chinoises
Gatinais, Montargis
Lyon républicain, Lyons
Le progrès, Lyons
Revue historique

Asian

Buweiersike
Chiguang, Paris and Berlin
Dangshi yanjiu
Dangshi yanjiu ziliao, Sichuan
Dongfang zazhi
Fendou (Le Combat), Paris
Geming lieshi zhuanji ziliao
Gongchandang
Gongren, Paris
Gongren xunbao, Paris
Guomin, Paris
Guomin, Lyons
Huagong zazhi, Paris
Hunan wenshi ziliao xuanji
Jiaoyu zazhi
Jindaishi yanjiu
Jindaishi ziliao
Lü Ou zazhi, Paris
Lü Ou zhoukan
Nghien cuu lich su, Hanoi
Sanmin, Paris
Shaonian
Shaonian Zhongguo
Tianjin wenshi ziliao xuanji
Wenshi ziliao
Wenshi ziliao xuanji

Xiangdao
Xiansheng (Sinesheng), Paris
Xin qingnian
Zhong Fa jiaoyu jie (L'Education franco-chinoise), Lyons
Zhongguo xiandaishi fuyin baokan ziliao
Zhonghua jiaoyu jie
Zhuanji wenxue

INTERVIEWS

Cai Bo, 4 October 1985 (Beijing)
Guo Sheng, 6 December 1985 (Beijing)
Hou Junchu, 15 November, 14 December 1985 (Beijing)
Hu Hua, 5 December 1985 (Beijing)
Jiang Zemin, * 25 October 1985 (Beijing)
Li Xin, 19, 21 October 1985 (Beijing)
Liao Yongwu, 26 November 1985 (Tianjin)
Sheng Cheng, * 12, 18 October; 23 November 1985 (Beijing)
Wang Yongxiang, 26 November 1985 (Tianjin)
Wu Shiqi, 13, 15 December 1985 (Beijing)
Dr. Yang Kun, * 14 October 1985 (Beijing)
Zhang Hongxiang, 26 November 1985 (Tianjin)
Zhang Shenfu, * 25 October 1985 (Beijing)
Zheng Chaolin, * 29 October 1985 (Shanghai)
Zhong Shaohua, 8 December 1985 (Beijing)

* ECCO participant.

INDEX

Northern Expedition: and Communist International, 171; ECCO support of, 191–92, 194, 201, 205; mentioned, 218, 222, 234, 240, 246, 247

Opium, 200
Organizations (youth groups). *See* New Citizens' Study Society; Self-Awakening Society; Work-Study Movement; Work-Study Mutual-Aid Corps; Young China Study Association
Ou Baisheng, 175

Painlevé, Paul (aviator, educator, CFC), 93–94, 116
Paris: as political environment, 3, 11, 177, 187, 190, 200; as destination, 19, 106, 107, 117, 188; as post–World War I cultural center, 20, 64, 89–90; and Chinese Anarchists, 24, 29, 30; and SFEA, 26, 36; Chinese embassy in, 38, 107, 181, 187; as locus of Work-Study experience, 84, 86, 100, 123, 127–28; ECCO activities in, 145, 146, 149, 162, 184–85, 190; and Zhang Shenfu group, 151–53
Paris Correspondence Service, 100
Paris Doufu Factory. *See* Li Shizeng; Work-Study Movement
Paris Times, 118
PCF. *See* French Communist Party
Peng Huang, 52n38
Peng Shiqin, 196, 228
Peng Shuzhi, 170
Peng Sumin, 185
Peng Xiang, 193n61, 195, 200, 200n82, 215, 230–31
Pernotte, Alexis-Joseph, 116
Perse, St.-John (Aléxis Léger, poet), 116
Personal relations (*guanxi*): and political behavior, 7, 41, 43, 96, 124, 132, 175, 207; French relations influenced by, 24, 24n32, 26, 93, 200, 200n82, 225, 233; and organizational affiliations, 42, 62, 132, 204; in marriage, 44n6, 53–54, 142, 211–12, 219, 222, 223, 228, 230, 237; of siblings, 50n28, 51n36, 55, 56, 61, 61n70. *See also* Factional groupings; Feminism; Regionalism
Petit Parisien, 200
Pieck, Wilhelm, 170, 231
Political factions. *See* Factional groupings
Political parties. *See* Anarchism; Chinese Communist Party; Chinese Youth Party; ECCO; European Branch of the Guomindang; French Communist Party; Guomindang; Socialists; Trotskyites
Politicians: career status of, 136–37, 139
Preparatory schools. *See* Work-Study Movement
Le progrès, 125
Propaganda (Chinese newspapers and journals, 1920s). *See* Chiguang; Gongxue shijie tongxin she; Gongyu; Guomin; Huagong zazhi; Lü Ou jiaoyu yundong; Lü Ou tongxin; Lü Ou zhoukan; Sanmin Yuekan; Shaonian; Shaonian Zhongguo; Xiangdao; Xiansheng; Xin qingnian; Yishibao; Zhengzhi shenghuo

Qin Shilun, 166, 203
Qingniandang. *See* Chinese Youth Party
Qingong jianxue yundong (Diligent-Work Frugal-Study Movement). *See* Work-Study Movement
Qingong jianxuehui. *See* Diligent-Work Frugal-Study Association
Qiu Yang, 129

Racism, 71–72, 81, 95–96
Radek, Karl, 168
Railroad Struggle of 1923, 176–79, 202, 252
Ran Jun, 231
Regionalism: as dimension of leadership, 4, 42, 146, 207–8; and Work-Study Movement, 34, 35, 37, 74–75, 96, 129; and youth groups, 43; growth of interregionalism, 43, 62, 73–74, 131, 132, 133–34, 150, 203; and same province (*tongxiang*) organization, 73–74; suggested as solution to economic difficulties, 107–8, 120; mentioned, 211–12, 214, 218, 226, 227, 229, 232, 235, 238; *See also* Li Lisan; Liu Qingyang; Zeng Qi; Zhao Shiyan
Religion (Western): and antireligion campaigns, 46, 161; and Zhou Enlai, 60; and anticlericalism in France, 87–88; and organizations, 100–101, 103. *See also* Lebbe, Father; YMCA
Remarque, Erich Maria, 116
Ren Li, 114, 116n45, 247
Ren Zhuoxuan: post-ECCO leadership of, 4n3, 5; as factory worker, 153; and the ECCO, 155, 156–57, 175, 181, 186, 189, 189n51, 202; on class struggle, 163–64; on the United Front and ideology, 190; description of, 231. *See also* Deng Xiaoping; ECCO; European Branch of the Guomindang; Zhao Shiyan